P9-AGE-083

PEARSON CUSTOM LIBRARY

PEARSON

Cover Art: Courtesy of Michael R. Martin, Darryl Johnson, Photodisk, DK Images, Photodisc/Getty Images, and Prentice-Hall, Inc. "TEM of Gardnerella vaginalis bacteria" courtesy of Alloy Photography/Veer; "Bacterium background" Courtesy of Fedorov Oleksiy/Shutterstock; "Silhouette of a lizard on a leaf back lit by sunlight" courtesy of Santhosh Kumar/Veer; "Frog on leaf" courtesy of Kerstin Klaassen/iStockphoto; "Baby feet" courtesy of igabriela/Veer; "Mother Giraffe and Youngster" courtesy of Peter Malsbury/iStockphoto. "Red blood cells, 3d illustration" courtesy of nobeastsofierce/Fotolia. "cancer cell" courtesy of vitanovski/Fotolia.

Copyright © 2015 by Pearson Learning Solutions
All rights reserved.

Permission in writing must be obtained from the publisher before any part of this work may be reproduced or transmitted in any form or by any means, electronic or mechanical, including photocopying and recording, or by any information storage or retrieval system.

Additional copyright information is included, where applicable, as a footnote at the beginning of each chapter.

Pyrex, pHydrion, Chem3D Plus, Apple, Macintosh, Chemdraw, Hypercard, graphTool, Corning, Teflon, Mel-Temp, Rotaflow, Tygon, Spec20, and LambdaII UV/Vis are registered trademarks.

Chem3D Plus is a registered trademark of the Cambridge Soft Corp.

The information, illustrations, and/or software contained in this book, and regarding the above mentioned programs, are provided "as is," without warranty of any kind, express or implied, including without limitation any warranty concerning the accuracy, adequacy, or completeness of such information. Neither the publisher, the authors, nor the copyright holders shall be responsible for any claims attributable to errors, omissions, or other inaccuracies contained in this book. Nor shall they be liable for direct, indirect, special, incidental, or consequential damages arising out of the use of such information or material.

The authors and publisher believe that the lab experiments described in this publication, when conducted in conformity with the safety precautions described herein and according to the school's laboratory safety procedures, are reasonably safe for the students for whom this manual is directed. Nonetheless, many of the described experiments are accompanied by some degree of risk, including human error, the failure or misuse of laboratory or electrical equipment, mismeasurement, spills of chemicals, and exposure to sharp objects, heat, body fluids, blood or other biologics. The authors and publisher disclaim any liability arising from such risks in connections with any of the experiments contained in this manual. If students have questions or problems with materials, procedures, or instructions on any experiment, they should always ask their instructor for help before proceeding.

Attention bookstores: For permission to return unused stock, contact us at *pe-uscustomreturns@pearson.com*.

Pearson Learning Solutions, 501 Boylston Street, Suite 900, Boston, MA 02116
A Pearson Education Company
www.pearsoned.com

Printed in the United States of America.

V092

ISBN 10: 1-269-79024-2
ISBN 13: 978-1-269-79024-6

Laboratory Safety: General Guidelines

1. Notify your instructor immediately if you are pregnant, color blind, allergic to any insects or chemicals, taking immunosuppressive drugs, or have any other medical condition (such as diabetes, immunologic defect) that may require special precautionary measures in the laboratory.

2. Upon entering the laboratory, place all books, coats, purses, backpacks, etc. in designated areas, not on the bench tops.

3. Locate and, when appropriate, learn to use exits, fire extinguisher, fire blanket, chemical shower, eyewash, first aid kit, broken glass container, and cleanup materials for spills.

4. In case of fire, evacuate the room and assemble outside the building.

5. Do not eat, drink, smoke, or apply cosmetics in the laboratory.

6. Confine long hair, loose clothing, and dangling jewelry.

7. Wear shoes at all times in the laboratory.

8. Cover any cuts or scrapes with a sterile, waterproof bandage before attending lab.

9. Wear eye protection when working with chemicals.

10. Never pipet by mouth. Use mechanical pipeting devices.

11. Wash skin immediately and thoroughly if contaminated by chemicals or microorganisms.

12. Do not perform unauthorized experiments.

13. Do not use equipment without instruction.

14. Report all spills and accidents to your instructor immediately.

15. Never leave heat sources unattended.

16. When using hot plates, note that there is no visible sign that they are hot (such as a red glow). Always assume that hot plates are hot.

17. Use an appropriate apparatus when handling hot glassware.

18. Keep chemicals away from direct heat or sunlight.

19. Keep containers of alcohol, acetone, and other flammable liquids away from flames.

20. Do not allow any liquid to come into contact with electrical cords. Handle electrical connectors with dry hands. Do not attempt to disconnect electrical equipment that crackles, snaps, or smokes.

21. Upon completion of laboratory exercises, place all materials in the disposal areas designated by your instructor.

22. Do not pick up broken glassware with your hands. Use a broom and dustpan and discard the glass in designated glass waste containers; never discard with paper waste.

23. Wear disposable gloves when working with blood, other body fluids, or mucous membranes. Change gloves after possible contamination and wash hands immediately after gloves are removed.

24. The disposal symbol indicates that items that may have come in contact with body fluids should be placed in your lab's designated container. It also refers to liquid wastes that should not be poured down the drain into the sewage system.

25. Leave the laboratory clean and organized for the next student.

26. Wash your hands with liquid or powdered soap prior to leaving the laboratory.

27. The biohazard symbol indicates procedures that may pose health concerns.

The caution symbol points out instruments, substances, and procedures that require special attention to safety. These symbols appear throughout this manual.

Measurement Conversions

Metric to American Standard	American Standard to Metric
Length	
1 mm = 0.039 inches	1 inch = 2.54 cm
1 cm = 0.394 inches	1 foot = 0.305 m
1 m = 3.28 feet	1 yard = 0.914 m
1 m = 1.09 yards	1 mile = 1.61 km
Volume	
1 mL = 0.0338 fluid ounces	1 fluid ounce = 29.6 mL
1 L = 4.23 cups	1 cup = 237 mL
1 L = 2.11 pints	1 pint = 0.474 L
1 L = 1.06 quarts	1 quart = 0.947 L
1 L = 0.264 gallons	1 gallon = 3.79 L
Mass	
1 mg = 0.0000353 ounces	1 ounce = 28.3 g
1 g = 0.0353 ounces	1 pound = 0.454 kg
1 kg = 2.21 pounds	

Temperature

To convert temperature:

$$^{\circ}C = \frac{5}{9}(F - 32) \qquad\qquad ^{\circ}F = \frac{9}{5} + 32$$

Table of Contents

■

The Protozoans

Over 60,000 species of flagellates, amebas (or amoebas), opalinids, spore formers, and ciliates, often called collectively the protozoa, represent some of the most fascinating organisms to both novice and experienced microscopists. The tremendous number of individuals found in one drop of water can be overwhelming. Until recently, these mostly microscopic and primarily unicellular organisms were grouped in a single Phylum Protozoa [PRO-to-ZO-ah; G., *proto*, first + G., *zoon*, animal]. Most protozoologists now agree that this grouping constituted a heterogenous assemblage of distantly related forms. Many biologists place the protozoans within the Subkingdom Protozoa (Kingdom **Animalia**) containing at least six, probably polyphyletic phyla (Levine et al. 1980). Others prefer the term *protists* instead of *protozoa* and follow Whittaker (1969) in grouping the subkingdom under the Kingdom **Protista**. However, it is generally recognized that protozoans are not invertebrates. Nevertheless protozoans play important roles in the web of life and are fascinating and challenging organisms to study. For these reasons, and because they have traditionally been studied in invertebrate zoology courses, we cover them here.

Few places on the earth are devoid of protozoans. Free-living forms occur in aquatic habitats, moist soils, and decaying organic matter. Many protozoans are important parasites of plants, animals, and humans. Nearly one-half of the 60,000 protozoan species are fossils; some have been in existence at least since the **Precambrian** (Fig. 1).

The basic body plan is the single eukaryotic cell representing a functionally complete organism that performs all physiological processes found in multicellular animals or the **Metazoa** (G., *meta*, after or between + G., *zoa*, animal). Some biologists prefer to call protozoans acellular [G., *a*, without] organisms instead of unicellular, to emphasize the complete, functional organismal viewpoint.

Protozoan organelles tend to be more specialized than those found in the typical cell of metazoans. Some of the common organelles (together with their functions) are as follows: **food vacuole** or **phagosome** (digestion), **contractile vacuole** or water expulsion vesicle (water regulation), **myoneme** (contractile), **paraflagellar swelling** and **stigma** (sensory), **extrusome** (food getting and defense), and **pseudopodium, flagellum**, and **cilium** (food getting and locomotion). The traditional designation of protozoans as amebas, flagellates, spore formers, and ciliates was based primarily on their locomotory organelles.

Some species are colonial and can be seen with the unaided eye. However, there are no tissues, organs, or germ layers. Digestion is intracellular, occurring within food vacuoles. Respiration and excretion are accomplished by diffusion across the cell membrane. Reproduction is by **budding, fission, conjugation,** or **syngamy.** The motile form is often called a **trophozoite** (trophont), whereas the nonmotile form is called a **cyst.**

Selected representatives of the major phyla will be studied in the following exercises. Your instructor may provide additional examples for study.

From *Invertebrate Zoology*, Sixth Edition, Robert L. Wallace and Walter K. Taylor. Copyright © 2002 by Pearson Education, Inc.
Published by Prentice-Hall, Inc. All rights reserved

The Protozoans

TIME (IN MILLIONS OF YEARS)

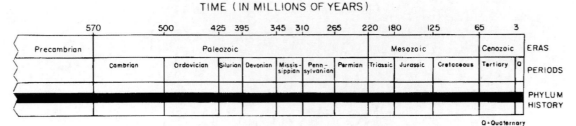

Figure 1. Geologic history of the Subkingdom Protozoa. Based on geological and biochemical evidence we know that the origin of protist, dates to at least 2.7 billion years ago.

Classification

The higher classification of protozoans has undergone many changes in the past decade. Authors of textbooks of Invertebrate Zoology, General Zoology, and General Biology do not always agree what higher taxa (e.g., phyla, subphyla, class, and order) should be used for a particular group. In this edition of our manual we present a classification that reflects the opinions of many authors; however, we fully realize that some instructors will not agree totally with the system given below. The major changes in this edition from the 5th edition occur in separating the flagellates, amebas, and opalinids into separate phyla, instead of the single Phylum Sarcomastigophora. Also, the Phylum Ciliophora has undergone some substantial modifications.

a. Flagellated Protozoans. Main organelle for movement is the flagellum. Nucleus monomorphic.

(a.) **Plantlike Flagellates (Phytoflagellates)**

The bodies of these protozoans or protists typically possess chloroplasts (organelles with chlorophyll) and eyespots. Botanists regard these flagellates to be algae.

1. **Phylum Dinophyta (Dinoflagellata).** Dinoflagellates. Body with a transverse groove and a ventral groove, each containing a flagellum. Cell body naked or covered with cellulose plates. Colorless or with yellow or brown chromoplasts. Marine and freshwater. Examples: *Glenodinium*, *Gymnodinium*, *Gonyaulax*, and *Ceratium.*

2. **Phylum Euglenophyta.** Euglenid Flagellates. Cells with one or two flagella that arise anteriorly within the reservoir. Both chloroplast-containing and colorless forms present. Stigma present in colored forms. Most are freshwater. Examples: *Euglena* and *Peranema.*

3. **Phylum Chlorophyta.** Volvocid Flagellates. Cells usually with two flagella, one chloroplast, and two contractile vacuoles. Protists with chlorophyll *a* and *b*. Solitary or colonial forms are known. Examples: *Chlamydomonas, Gonium, Eudorina,* and *Volvox.*

(b.) **Animal-like Flagellates (Zooflagellates)**

These organisms typically lack chloroplasts and eyespots.

4. **Phylum Choanoflagellida.** Choanoflagellates. Flagellates with a single anterior flagellum encircled by a funnel-shaped collar of microvilli. Both solitary and colonial forms are known. Choanoflagellates are similar to choanocytes (collar cells) of sponges (Phylum Porifera). Marine or freshwater. Examples: *Monosiga, Codosiga,* and *Proterospongia.*

5. **Phylum Metamonada.** (Order Diplomonadida). Bilateral symmetrical flagellates parasitic primarily in alimentary canal of host. Trophozoites with one or two karomastigonts (e.g., complex of flagellum, nucleus, and associated organelles), each with one to four flagella. Examples: *Giardia* and *Hexamita.*

6. **Phylum Parabasalia.** (Order Hypermastigida). Gut inhabitants of termites, cockroaches, and woodroaches, possessing many flagella. The motile cell usually is uninucleate. Example: *Trichonympha.*

7. **Phylum Kinetoplastida.** Parasitic, endocommensal, and free-living protozoans with cells possessing one to two flagella. The kinetoplast is the largest extranuclear repository of DNA for any cell type. Life cycle involves vertebrate and invertebrate hosts. Examples: *Leishmania, Bodo,* and *Trypanosoma.*

b. Opalinid Protozoans. Ovoid protozoans with numerous cilia in oblique rows covering the entire body. Cytosome and cytopharynx are absent.

8. **Phylum Opalinata.** Opalinids. Two or many monomorphic nuclei. Reproduction is usually asexual, longitudinal binary fission. Most are gut commensals of frogs and toads. Example: *Opalina.*

c. Ameboid Protozoans. Primary means of locomotion is ameboid movement involving pseudopodia typically on the trophozoite. Cell body is naked, with a test, or with an internal skeleton. Reproduction is primarily by binary fission.

9. **Phylum Rhizopoda (Rhizopodea).** Sarcodines that use lobopodia, filopodia, or reticulopodia.

(1.) **Class Lobosea.** Sarcodines with pseudopodia lobose to filiform in shape. Cells are usually uninucleate. Cell body either naked or in a test. Both free-living and parasitic forms are known. Examples: *Amoeba proteus, Chaos carolinense (=Pelomyxa carolinensis), Entamoeba histolytica, Arcella,* and *Difflugia.*

(2.) **Class Filosea.** Filiform pseudopodia that often branch and sometimes anastomose. No flagellate stage known. Cell body is naked or in a test. Examples: *Lecythium* and *Euglypha.*

(3.) **Class Granuloreticulosea.** (Order Foraminiferida). Foraminiferidans (forams). Amebas primarily with delicate granular reticulopodia and a test of one to many chambers. Tests usually calcareous. Most are marine. Examples: *Globigerina, Elphidium,* and *Allogromia.*

10. **Phylum Actinopoda.** Radiolarians. Mostly planktonic amebas with actinopods (axopods) and delicate filopods radiating from a spherical body. Capsular membrane between ectoplasm and endoplasm present in most forms.

(1.) **Class Acantharea.** Radiolarians. Skeleton of strontium sulfate with centrally joined radial spines. Mostly planktonic; all marine. Examples: *Acanthometra* and *Collosphaera.*

(2.) **Class Polycystinea.** Radiolarians. Planktonic marine radiolarians with skeleton of silica and a perforated capsular membrane. Example: *Thalassicolla.*

(3.) **Class Phaeodarea.** Radiolarians. Planktonic marine radiolarians with skeletons, when present, of silica and organic matter. Capsular membrane with three large pores. Spines of skeleton hollow. Examples: *Aulacantha* and *Circoporus.*

(4.) **Class Heliozoea.** Sun Animalcules. Primarily freshwater amebas with a skeleton, when present, of siliceous or chitinoid scales and spines. Central capsule with membrane absent. Examples: *Actinosphaerium* and *Actinophrys.*

d. Spore-forming Protozoans. Parasitic protozoans with apical complex at some stage in the life cycle.

11. **Phylum Sporozoa (Apicomplexa).** Entirely parasitic forms lacking cilia or flagella (except for flagellated microgametes). Nucleus is vesicular. Both asexual and sexual phases present in the life cycle. Spores lacking polar filaments.

(1.) **Class Gregarinea.** Gregarines. Mature trophozoites large. Parasites in guts and body cavities of annelids and arthropods. Examples: *Gregarina* and *Monocystis.*

(2.) **Class Coccidea (Sporozoea).** Coccidian Sporozoans. Mature trophozoites are small and intracellular. Examples: *Eimeria, Plasmodium,* and *Toxoplasma.*

(3.) **Class Piroplasmea.** Parasites of red blood cells of vertebrates. Transmitted by ticks. Spores lacking. Example: *Babesia.*

12. **Phylum Microspora.** Intracellular parasites mainly of insects. Spores with a polar filament. Example: *Nosema.*

13. **Phylum Myxozoa (Myxosporidia).** Obligate, extracellular parasites of annelids and poikilothermic vertebrates (mainly fish). Spores with polar filament and encased in several valves. Usually two polar capsules present. (Recent analyses suggest that these organisms may be degenerate metazoans.) Example: *Myxosoma.*

e. Ciliate Protozoans. Protozoans with cilia.

14. **Phylum Ciliophora.** Ciliate Protozoans. Cells typically with cilia and dimorphic nuclei: macronucleus and micronucleus. Reproduction is primarily by asexual transverse binary fission (homothetogenic) and sexual conjugation.

(1.) Class Kinetofragminophora. Oral region of body bearing cilia, but lacking compound ciliary organelles.

(a) Subclass Gymnostomata. Cell mouth at or near body surface and located anterior or laterally. Body ciliation mostly uniform. Examples: *Coleps, Didinium, Dileptus,* and *Lacrymaria.*

(b) Subclass Vestibulifera. Cell mouth within a vestibule and bearing distinct ciliation. Examples: *Balantidium* and *Colpoda.*

(c) Subclass Suctoria. Suctorians. Sessile and generally stalked protozoans. Tentacles at the distal end. Adults lack cilia which are present in the free-swimming larva. Mostly ectosymbionts on aquatic invertebrates. Examples: *Acineta, Ephelota,* and *Podophrya.*

(2.) Class Oligohymenophora. Compound ciliary organelles associated with an oral apparatus.

(a) Subclass Hymenostomata. Body ciliation uniform. Oral structures not conspicuous. Examples: *Colpidium, Paramecium, Pleuronema,* and *Tetrahymena.*

(b) Subclass Peritricha. Oral ciliary band usually conspicuous. Most are sessile with reduced body ciliation. Example: *Vorticella.*

(3.) Class Polyhymenophora. Buccal membranelles at oral region. Body ciliation uniform; some with compound organelles (e.g., cirri).

(a) Subclass Spirotricha. Characteristics of the class. Examples: *Blepharisma, Bursaria, Spirostomum, Stentor, Euplotes,* and *Stylonychia.*

A. Flagellated Protozoans

The flagellum is the primary locomotory organelle of this large and diverse group. Flagellates are mostly free-living; however, there are a number of parasitic forms that cause sickness, and even death, to man and other animals. This diverse group of protozoans are often divided into plantlike (Phytoflagellates) and animal-like (Zooflagellates) forms.

These plantlike flagellates have a cell wall of cellulose, chloroplasts, and stigma. The usual type of nutrition is holophytic (autotrophic). Representatives of the following three orders will be emphasized: Order Dinoflagellida (*Ceratium, Glenodinium,* and *Gymnodimium*), Order Euglenida (*Euglena and Peranema*), and Order Volvocida (*Chlamydomonas and Volvox*).

Order Dinophyta (Dinoflagellida). Dinoflagellates are widely distributed in marine, brackish, and freshwater habitats. Most are free living. Dinoflagellates have an unequal pair of flagella. One is ribbon-like and typically lies in a transverse surface furrow called the **cingulum** or **girdle** (Fig. 2). The second flagellum is directed posteriorly and usually in a longitudinal furrow, the **sulcus**. Reproduction is by binary fission and syngamy.

The region above the cingulum in armored forms is the **epitheca** (epicone in unarmored ones); below the cingulum is the **hypotheca** (hypocone in unarmored ones). Unarmored or naked species (e.g., *Gymnodinium*) have a cell covering of membranes, whereas thecal plates of cellulose or other polysaccharides occur on armored species (e.g., *Ceratium* and *Glenodinium*). Many dinoflagellates (e.g., *Noctiluca, Gonyaulax,* and *Pyrocystis*) are bioluminescent and their bluish-green glow can be seen for some distance in the oceans. Certain genera, such as *Gonyaulax* and *Gymnodinium,* may occur in hugh numbers; these blooms are often called **red tides**. Millions of cells per liter of water may be produced. Blooms of *Gymnodinium breve* produce toxins that directly kill fish and some invertebrates. The toxins of other species may be concentrated in the bodies of clams, oysters, and scallops, rendering these organisms unsafe for human consumption. Deaths of manatees in coastal waters of Florida have been blamed on dinoflagellate toxins.

■ Observational Procedure: Order Dinoflagellida

1. Make a small ring, using a thick suspension of methyl cellulose, on a glass slide. Add a drop of the culture in the center of the ring, cover with a coverslip, and observe under low power of a compound microscope. After the organism is located, change to high magnification.

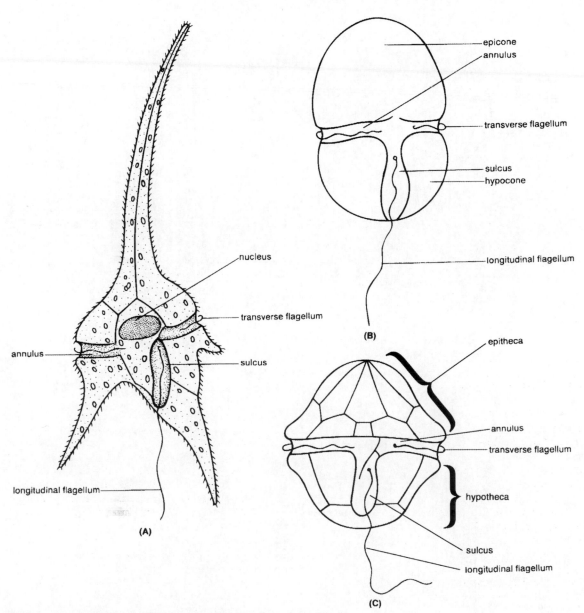

Figure 2. Dinoflagellates: (A) Ceratium. (B) Gymnodinium. (C) Glenodinium.

2. Describe the locomotion of these protozoans. Attempt to locate the cingulum and sulcus in a stationary individual. Can you see flagella beating? What variations in the body shape, size, and structure do you see, especially in *Ceratium*, which has hornlike extensions (Fig. 2A)? What might cause these variations?

3. Examine prepared slides of several species of dinoflagellates (e.g., *Ceratium, Glenodinium,* and *Gymnodinium)*. Note the nature of the body covering. *Ceratium*

has one apical horn and one to three antapical horns. The nucleus should be evident. Locate the cingulum and the sulcus. ∎

Phylum Euglenophyta. Euglenoid flagellates are primarily freshwater organisms. Over 800 species in at least 37 genera have been described. Most species are bilaterally symmetrical with bodies elongated, ovoid, spherical, or leaflike. Both chloroplast-containing and

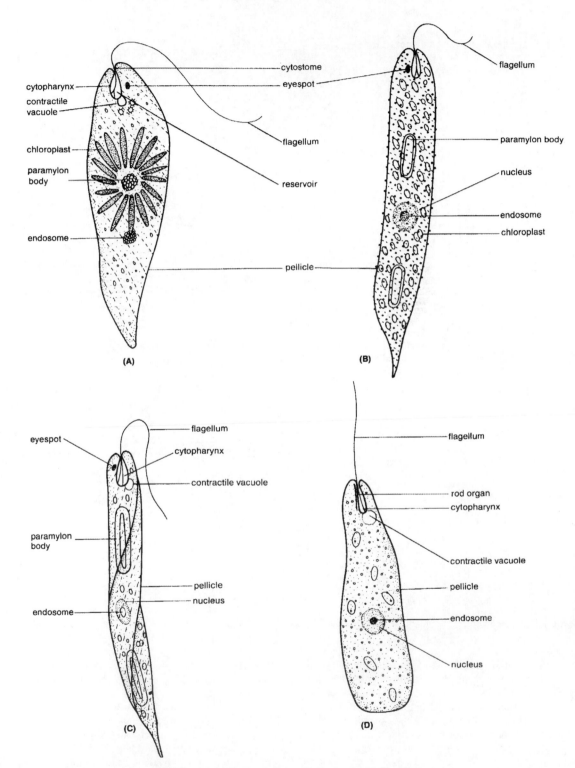

Figure 3. Selected protozoans. (A) *Euglena viridis*. (B) *E. spirogyra*. (C) *E. oxyuris*. (D) *Peranema*.

colorless forms are common. Chloroplasts vary in number and shape according to the species.

The anterior end of the cell is invaginated forming a flask-shaped **reservoir** (Fig. 3A). The narrow part of the reservoir is sometimes called the **cytopharnyx** and its opening the **cytostome** (cell mouth). Most euglenoid flagellates have two flagella (generally unequal in length) and a contractile vacuole near the reservoir. All species with an **eyespot** (stigma) have the photoreceptor or **paraflagellar swelling** near the base of the longer, emergent flagellum and opposite to the eyespot. Surrounding the cell is a **pellicle**, consisting of interlocking proteinaceous strips and microtubules beneath the cell membrane. Rapid changes of body shape, called euglenoid movement, are seen in many euglenoids. A single nucleus with **endosome** (nucleolus) is present. Reproduction is primarily by longitudinal fission.

■ Observational Procedure: Order Euglenida

1. Add a drop of the *Euglena* culture in the center of a ring of methyl cellulose and cover with a coverslip.

2. Examine under low power of a compound microscope to locate the organism and then change to high power (Fig. 3). Describe *Euglena's* movement and body shape. Does the cell rotate, creep, or glide? Do all individuals move in the same direction? Are any of the individuals showing **euglenoid movement?** Euglenoid movement in *E. viridis* is somewhat jerky. *Euglena gracilis* exhibits pronounced euglenoid movement, but not all *Euglena* species perform this movement.

3. The outer covering of the organism is the pellicle. The forward end is generally less pointed than the trailing end. Carefully focus on the forward end with the fine adjustment to see movement of the whiplike flagellum. You might want to make another wet mount and add a drop of Lugol's iodine solution before applying the coverslip. The solution will stain the flagellum, but will kill the organism. Near the reservoir is a contractile vacuole and a reddish eyespot (stigma). The eyespot is more easily seen in strains lacking pigment. The paraflagellar swelling at the base of the long flagellum will not be observed.

4. Much of the organism's cytoplasm contains chlorophyll-containing chloroplasts. Is your specimen greenish in color? The shape and position of the chloroplasts vary with the species. What shape are the chloroplasts in your species? In *E. viridis* the chloroplasts radiate from a common **paramylon body** (carbohydrate storage area). In the chloroplasts, there may be **pyrenolds**, proteinaceous bodies containing starch reserves. Although chlorophyll allows *Euglena* to manufacture its own food, this organism also has saprozoic nutrition; that is, it absorbs nutrients across the body surface in the absence of light. Holozoic nutrition, the ingesting of whole organisms, has never been demonstrated in *Euglena*; however, it does occur in *Peranema*, a relative of *Euglena*.

5. Attempt to locate the ovoid nucleus of the organism. This organelle is often obscured by chloroplasts and is best observed in colorless phytoflagellates. If a drop of acidified methyl-green stain is added to the culture, the nucleus will stain bright green. The nucleus can be observed in the prepared slide.

6. Examine a prepared slide of *Euglena* under high power of a compound microscope. Note the body shape. Locate the nucleus. Can you see the nucleolus (endosome) within the nucleus? Are chloroplasts evident? Carefully focus on the anterior end of a specimen. Attempt to see the flagellum, reservoir, eyespot, cytostome, and cytopharynx. These are more easily seen in the larger species of *Euglena*. *Euglena* reproduces by longitudinal binary fission. Are any individuals undergoing division? ■

Peranema. This freshwater, euglenoid phytoflagellate is similar to *Euglena,* but is colorless, lacks the eyespot, has a long trailing flagellum. Nutrition, is holozoic. The two rodlike structures (**rod organ**) near the reservoir are for food-catching (Fig. 3).

■ Observational Procedure: *Peranema*

Mount a drop of the culture on a slide as before. Observe the shape and movement of *Peranema*. Can you see striations in the pellicle? *Peranema* undergoes pronounced euglenoid movement. Observe a prepared slide of *Peranema* and compare the organism with *Euglena*. ■

Figure 4. *Chlamydomonas*, a unicellular volvocida flagellate.

The Protozoans

Phylum Chlorophyta. Most species occur in still fresh-water ponds and ditches. The organisms usually have two flagella of equal length directed anteriorly, two contractile vacuoles, one large chloroplast, a red eyespot, and a centrally located nucleus (Figs. 4 and 5). The chloroplast is cup-shaped, usually grass green, and contains chlorophylls *a* and *b* and other pigments. Associated with the chloroplast is a single basal pyrenoid body with stored starch. Asexual and sexual means of reproduction are present.

Figure 5. Volvox. (A) One zooid (cell). (B) Surface view of coenobium showing position of zooids in relation to cytoplasmic bonds. (C) Daughter colony formation, gametogenesis, and zygospore formation (diagrammatic). Lower case letters indicate sequence of development for three different processes: clockwise—daughter colony formation, female gamete and zygospore formation, and male gamete formation.

Chlamydomonas. *Chlamydomonas* is a small (9–16 μm), solitary volvocid. Over 500 species, mostly freshwater, belong to this genus (Fig. 4).

■ Observational Procedure: *Chlamydomonas*

Prepare a wet mount of *Chlamydomonas* as before. Note the ellipsoid shape and bilateral symmetry. Examine a stained slide of *Chlamydomonas*. Not all structures in Fig. 4 will be observed. Near each flagellum is a contractile vacuole. Observe the single, large chloroplast and nucleus. Attempt to see the eyespot in the anterior half of the chloroplast. The single pyrenoid body probably will not be seen. ■

Volvox. *Volvox* is a green, spherical or ellipsoidal colony (**coenobium**) surrounded by a cellulose cell wall. The colony may reach 1.5 mm in diameter. The phytoflagellate is common in ponds, ditches, and pools. Colony formation in *Volvox* is similar to embryonic development in some metazoans.

The organism consists of many cells or **zooids** (500–60,000) embedded in a single surface layer in a gelatinous matrix (Fig. 5). The colony consists of mainly somatic (vegetative) and some reproductive zooids. Each somatic zooid is chlamydomonas-like with two flagella directed outward; the zooids are often attached laterally by protoplasmic connections. The few fertile zooids (**gonidia**) are somewhat larger than the somatic ones. Vegetative reproduction results in a hollow sphere, the **daughter colony**, formed by repeated mitotic division of a gonidium that has lost the flagella. When the parent dies, the daughter colony is released in the water where it forms a new colony. Colonies of *Volvox* are monoecious or dioecious. Sexual maturation involves formation of female and male gonidia. One egg (**macrogamete**) develops from the female gonidia. Those of the male result in sperm packets (**plakeas**) of 16 to 512 biflagellate **microgametes**. One sperm cell penetrates the colony and fertilizes the egg. A thick, protective wall surrounds the zygote, forming a **zygospore**. When the parent colony disintegrates, the zygospore is released. Inside the zygospore repeated division occurs and during the spring a new colony is formed.

■ Observational Procedure: *Volvox*

Prepare a wet mount of the *Volvox* culture using methyl cellulose. Raise the coverslip with clay or other supports. Study the organism under low power and then change to high power of a compound microscope. Describe movement of the colony. Observe the daughter colonies if present. How many are there? Do they move about inside the colony or remain stationary? Can you tell if the colony possesses sexual stages? The zooids are very small and details of structure will not be observed. Examine a prepared slide of *Volvox*. Observe the general anatomy of the colony and compare it with the living organism. ■

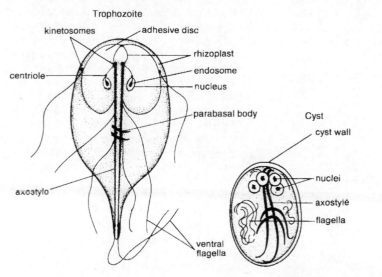

Figure 6. *Giardia intestinalis*, trophozoite and cyst.

Figure 7. Two flagellated protozoans. (A) *Trichonympha* (After Cable). (B) Trypanosome.

In contrast to the Phytoflagellates, the Zooflagellates lack chromoplasts, eyespots, cellulose coverings, and other plant features. Nutrition is primarily heterotrophic. Representatives of three phyla will be emphasized: Metamonada, Order Diplomonadida *(Giardia)*; Parabasalia, Order Hypermastigida *(Trichonympha)*; and Kinetoplastida *(Leishmania* and *Trypanosoma)*.

Phylum Metamonda. (Order Diplomonadida) These zooflagellates generally are found in the digestive system of their hosts. The best known species is *Giardia intestinalis (= lamblia)* from the human small intestine (Fig. 1.6). Heavy infections cause severe diarrhea. Transmission is by cysts passed in the feces.

■ Observational Procedure: Phylum Metamonda (Order Diplomonadida)

Examine a prepared slide of *Giardia intestinalis* under oil immersion of a compound microscope (Fig. 6). The trophozoite is pear-shaped, with two parallel rods (**axostyles**) running longitudinally in the middle of the or-

ganism. Note the two large, ovoid nuclei with endosomes and eight flagella. *Giardia* has a large ventral **adhesive disc** for attachment to the host's intestinal mucosa. Are cysts present? They have distinct cell walls, usually four nuclei (two in young cysts), axostyles, and flagella.

Most students will not have an opportunity to observe live *Giardia*, but if you live in a region where this protozoan is endemic and if the local hospital is cooperative, you may be able to work with live samples. *Take great care to follow the instructions of your laboratory instructor.*

To observe the living organism, collect a very small amount of fresh feces on an applicator stick. Transfer the feces onto a glass slide. Add a drop of normal saline solution and Lugol's iodine solution to the sample. The iodine solution should be diluted 1:5 with distilled water. Mix well, spread out the sample, and cover with a coverslip. Locate the organism under low and then high magnification. Do not use oil immersion unless directed by the instructor. Compare the fresh trophozoite and cyst with those observed in the prepared slide. ■

Phylum Parabasalia. (Order Hypermastigida) These zooflagellates live in the intestines of termites, cockroaches, and wood-roaches. The motile cell has one nucleus, many flagella, and multiple parabasal bodies (Fig. 7A).

■ Observational Procedure: Phylum Parabasalia. (Order Hypermastigida)

Obtain a slide of *Trichonympha*. Note the body shape, position of nucleus, and arrangement of flagella (Fig. 7A). Living specimens may be seen by examining the gut contents of a termite. Place the termite on a glass slide. Hold the anterior end of the termite's body with forceps. Pull the remaining body posteriorly with another pair of forceps until the gut contents emerge onto the slide. Spread the contents thinly, add a small drop of diluted methyl cellulose, and examine under low and high powers with the compound microscope. There may be several species and genera represented. Note the shape of the body and arrangement of the flagella. *Calonympha* (Order Trichomonadida) may be in the gut contents; it has an axostyle and several anterior nuclei which are lacking in *Trichonympha*. ■

Phylum Kinetoplastida. Parasites of blood and tissue parasites of vertebrates as well as free-living forms are in this phylum. Several species of *Trypanosoma* and *Leishmania* are dreaded human pathogens in tropical regions, causing **sleeping sickness, Chagas' disease,** and

Kala azar. The motile cells have one or two flagella. A key feature of these organisms, for which the group is named, is the **kinetoplast** (Fig. 7B). This is a large, stainable mass of mitochondral DNA located near the base of the locomotory apparatus. The kinetoplast is usually larger than the kinetosome.

■ Observational Procedure: Phylum Kinetoplastida

Observe prepared slides of *Trypanosoma* and *Leishmania* under oil immersion. Note the body shape and single locomotory flagellum that is either free or attached to the undulating membrane, depending upon the species and the stage of the life cycle (Fig. 7B). Study the locational relationship of the nucleus, basal body, and kinetoplast in each genus.

Living *Trypanosoma lewisi* may be obtained from an infected rat by examining its blood. Put a drop of blood on a glass slide and quickly cover with a coverslip. Observe under low power of a compound microscope and search for movement. A moving trypanosome causes the red blood cells to move. Examine the parasite under high power. Do you see the undulating membrane moving? ■

B. Opalinid Protozoans

The precise taxonomic position of these protozoans has been, and continues to be, uncertain. Because they have cilia opalinids have been grouped with the ciliates, yet the type of ciliature possessed by the typical cilates differs from the ciliature of opalinids. Opalinids have been considered to be related to flagellates and to amebas. In this edition we have put the opalinids in a phylum of their own, Phylum Opalinata.

Members of Phylum Opalinata [O-pa-LIN-a-tah; N.F., opaline, like an opal in appearance] are found primarily in the intestines of amphibians; a few species occur in fish. Their flattened leaf-shaped bodies are covered with numerous cilia (Fig. 8). There are at least two monomorphic nuclei. A cytostome and cytopharynx are lacking; ingestion is by pinocytosis and egestion is by exocytosis.

■ Observational Procedure: *Opalina*

Examine a prepared slide of *Opalina*. Note the body shape, body ciliation, and nuclei (Fig. 8). ■

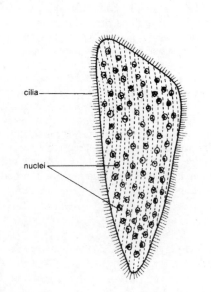

cilia

nuclei

Figure 8. *Opalina* (After Cable).

C. Amoeboid Protozoans

The presence of pseudopodia, cytoplasmic extensions of the motile cell, is the major feature of amebas. The pseudopodia, of various types, are involved in both feeding and locomotion. The body is naked (e.g., *Amoeba proteus*) or provided with a test or outer covering (e.g., *Difflugia*). Most species are free-living. Reproduction by binary fission is common. Two diverse phyla will be studied: Rhizopoda and Actinopoda.

Phylum Rhizopoda. This large group of amebas includes five classes differentiated primarily on the type of pseudopodia present. Included in the Phylum Rhizopoda [ri-ZOP-o-de-ah; G., *rhiz*, root + G., *podos*, foot] are slime molds (Class Mycetozoea), that have both animal and plant features. Slime molds will not be studied.

Class Lobosea

The Lobosea [LO-bo-SE-ah; G., *lobos*, lobe] includes amebas that produce lobose to filiform pseudopods. Their bodies are naked or housed in a secreted proteinaceous covering (test). Habitats are varied: in fresh and salt waters, in moist soils, on plants, in manure, in sewage waters, and in guts of plants and animals. Some are parasitic (e.g., *Entamoeba histolytica*).

■ Observational Procedure: *Amoeba proteus* or *Choas* (= *Pelomyxa*) *carolinense*

1. To prevent crushing the ameba, small pieces of a broken coverslip or bits of clay can be used to raise the coverslip used to cover the sample being examined. Place a drop of the ameba culture, taken from the bottom of the jar; on a glass slide and cover with a coverslip. Locate the organism under low power of a compound microscope and then change to high magnification.

2. Body size ranges from 100–500 μm, depending on whether the organism has assumed a round or extended shape. Describe the symmetry of your specimen. Observe movement of the organism. *Amoeba proteus* (Fig. 9) has large, conspicuous pseudopodia called lobopodia used in food-capture and locomotion. The body area opposite the advancing pseudopodia is the **uroid end**. Note the streaming of the cytoplasm within the body and as a pseudopodium is formed.

3. The cytoplasm consists of an outer, clear, firmer region (**gel** or ectoplasm) and an inner, granular, more liquid region (**sol** or endoplasm). The sol contains the organelles. These areas represent different colloidal states and have been used to explain in part amoeboid movement. Observe an extending pseudopodium. Note the large clear area of ectoplasm, the **hyaline cap**, at the end of the pseudopodium. This is the region of sol-to-gel conversion. Do other pseudopodia have the cap?

4. Do you see a large, clear spherical area in the endoplasm? This is the contractile vacuole, a water-regulatory organelle. The vacuole forms near the advancing end, but discharges its contents at the uroid end. At the time of expulsion, the vacuole is about 30 μm. Make an effort to see the vacuole discharge.

5. Scattered throughout the endoplasm are food vacuoles (5–20 μm) where intracellular digestion occurs. A food vacuole consists of food material and fluid surrounded by a membrane.

6. Examine a prepared slide showing whole mounts of the organism. Compare the shape and size of the stained amebas to that of the living organism. The nucleus should be evident. Are food vacuoles present? Can you identify any of the food items within the food vacuoles?

7. *Amoeba proteus* reproduces by binary fission. Observe prepared slides showing fission in *A. proteus*. Is the division equal?

8. *Chaos carolinense* is a large ameba (over 300 μm) that can be seen with the unaided eye, especially against a dark background. The ameba is found in swampy freshwaters where it feeds on protozoans and small invertebrates. Examine the living ameba first with

Figure 9. *Amoeba proteus.*

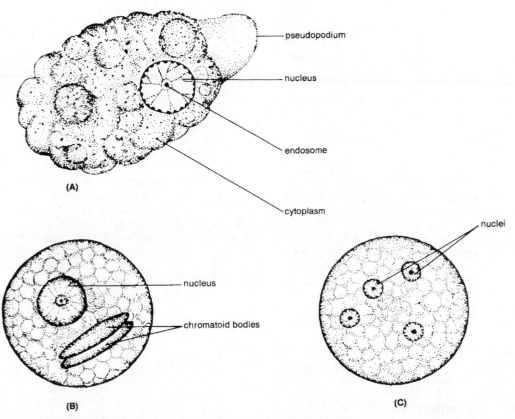

Figure 10. Entamoeba histolytica. (A) Trophozoite. (B) Immature cyst. (C) Mature cyst.

the low power and then under high power of a compound microscope. Compare its size and shape to that of *A. proteus*. Describe the shape of the pseudopodia. Are hyaline caps present? Unlike *A. proteus*, *Chaos* has 1,000 or more nuclei and several contractile vacuoles that range in size from 30–40 μm.

9. Examine a prepared slide and observe the pseudopodia, ectoplasm, and endoplasm. Look for food vacuoles, contractile vacuoles, and nuclei. ■

Entamoeba histolytica. This widely distributed intestinal parasite of man, apes, monkeys, dogs, rats, cats, and other animals causes **amebic dysentery** or **amebiasis**. The parasite produces large abscesses in the intestinal lining. Sometimes the ameba causes death in its host when it penetrates the gut, enters the bloodstream, and invades vital organs such as the brain, liver, and spleen. Other *Entamoeba* species in humans are *E. gingivalis*, a commensal in the mouth where it feeds on leucocytes, and *Entamoeba coli*, a commensal in the colon. Fecal contamination via cysts (except *E. gingivalis*, which lacks cyst and is transmitted by kissing) is the mode of transmission and infection.

■ Observational Procedure: *Entamoeba histolytica*

1. Examine prepared slides of *E. histolytica* containing trophozoites and cysts (Fig. 10). Locate the organism under high power and then under oil immersion of a compound microscope. The ameboid trophozoite is 15–40 μm long, depending on whether it is in the round or extended state. The ectoplasm is clear and the endoplasm is granular. There are usually four nuclei in the mature ameba. The structure of the nucleus is important in identifying *E. histolytica*. A nucleus stained with hematoxylin has fine, beadlike peripheral chromatin and a small (less than 1.0 μm) centrally placed endosome. In *E. coli* the trophozoite usually has eight nuclei, each with a large eccentric endosome and coarse peripheral chromatin. Both species lack contractile vacuoles. Food vacuoles are small (2–3 μm).

2. Examine the slide carefully for cysts. The mature cyst (10–20 μm) is round, smooth, and has four nuclei (3.5–6 μm). Eight amebas develop from a single cyst. In hematoxylin-stained specimens, dark-staining bar-like rods may be seen. These are **chromatoid bodies** which represent an accumulated mass of RNA. The number varies from one to four. As the cyst ages, these bodies disappear. In contrast, *E. coli* has more chromatoid bodies that resemble a bundle of splinters. Reproduction is by binary fission.

3. To study the living organism, prepare a fecal sample as was done for the *Giardia*. _Be careful not to contaminate anything that may later come into contact with your hands or clothing; wash your hands thoroughly after completing this exercise._

4. First locate the trophozoite or cyst with low power and then change to high power of a compound microscope. Do not use oil immersion unless directed by the instructor. Does the trophozoite move quickly? Describe the appearance of the nucleus. How does it differ from that observed in the stained slide? The chromatoid bodies appear as whitish refractile bodies instead of dark-stained structures observed in the prepared slide. Does your *E. histolytica* contain erythrocytes as a result from having recently fed on the intestinal mucosa? ■

Arcella vulgaris. *Arcella* is a beautiful testate ameba often found on aquatic plants (Fig. 11A,B). The rigid, chitinoid test is variable in shape and size depending upon the species studied. The opening (**pseudostome**) into the test is on the ventral side and is rounded in shape.

■ Observational Procedure: *Arcella vulgaris*

Examine living specimens of *Arcella*. The organism is 100–150 µm in the round shape and 50–80 µm high. Describe the color of the test. *Arcella* is binucleate; each nucleus has an endosome (Fig. 11A, B). Can you see the lobose pseudopodia projecting through the pseudostome as the organism moves and feeds? Examine a prepared slide of *Arcella*. Locate the pseudopodia, nuclei, and pseudostome. ■

Difflugia. *Difflugia* is covered by a protective test (Fig. 11E). Members of the genus are beautiful organisms and are widely distributed on freshwater plants.

■ Observational Procedure: *Difflugia*

Prepare a sample from the culture as you did for *A. proteus*. Examine closely the ovoid test (Fig. 11E). Note its color and shape; attempt to determine of what materials the test is composed. Can you see through the test? Is the pseudostome circular? Locate the pseudopodia as they extend and retract. Is the ameba moving and feeding? Examine a prepared slide and compare it with the living organism. ■

Class Filosea

Most amebas in this class are herbivorous or bactivorous and have bodies protected in a test. The tests are often formed of siliceous scales with attached spines and other assorted debris. Scales may be lacking, but spines and other particles are attached to the test. Many species occur in freshwater, often with lobose amebas. A distinguishing feature of these amebas, from which the class name is derived, is the presence of a filopodium. This long pseudopodium is filamentous, generally without anastomoses and a central axial rod. It is used in food capture and locomotion.

Lecythium. This herbivorous ameba is found in freshwater. Individuals typically occur in clusters or groups.

■ Observational Procedure: *Lecythium*

Locate living specimens of *Lecythium* with the low power of a compound microscope and then change to high power. The organism is 30–40 µm in diameter and lives within a clear, ovoid test that has a round pseudostome (Fig. 11C). There is a single spherical nucleus. Note the clear filopodia, some of which are branched. Compare stained slide preparations with the living material. ■

Euglypha. Species in this large genus are often found living on freshwater plants. The test is covered with internally secreted scales that are transported to the outer surface of the ameba (Fig. 11D). The scales are in definite patterns and may or may not have spines.

■ Observational Procedure: *Euglypha*

Examine living *Euglypha* with a compound microscope. Note the shape and pattern of the scales forming the test (Fig. 11D). How would you describe their shapes? Observe the filopodia. ■

Class Granuloreticulosea

This large class typically contains amebas that have filamentous pseudopodia with branching anastomosing networks of protoplasm. This type of pseudopodium is a **reticulopodium** (granuloreticulopodium or rhizopodium). Most species have a single-chambered (**unilocular**) or multichambered (**multilocular**) test (Fig. 12). The first-formed chamber is the **proloculum**. Multichambered **foraminiferidans** are single individuals and not colonies. Perforate shells have many pores,

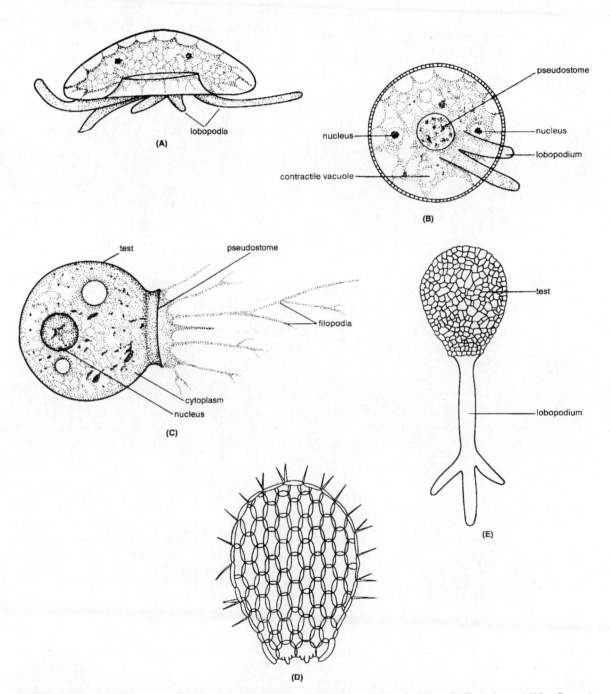

Figure 11. Testate ameba. (A) *Arcella*, side view. (B) Apical view (After Barnes). (C) *Lecythium*. (D) *Euglypha* test (After Barnes). (E) *Difflugia*.

whereas imperforate shells generally have one (e.g., the oral aperture) pore.

Order Foraminiferidia. There are more described species of foraminiferidans (34,000) than any protozoan group. *Globigerina* is a predominate genus; much of the ocean's ooze consists of large deposits of the shells of *Globigerina* species. Foraminiferidans (forams) are ancient, primarily marine amebas. Forams are large in size (0.5 mm–1 cm), but larger ones (12 cm) are known from the fossil record. The composition, mostly of calcium carbonate, arrangement of chambers, and openings of the test vary. The test is covered by a portion of the cytoplasm (Fig. 12). In multilocular forams the cytoplasm and rhizopodia extend through surface pores as well as the oral aperture. In unilocular species, the pseudopodia extend from the oral opening of the shell. Multilocular species add chambers in definite patterns as they grow. The test is absent in a few species.

Figure 13. A radiolarian, *Podocytris*.

The complex life cycle involves multiple division and alternation of haploid and diploid generations.

■ Observational Procedure: Foraminiferidans

Obtain prepared slides and/or unmounted specimens of several species of forams. Examine the organisms with the compound and dissection microscopes. Note the shapes of the specimens and how chamber formation has taken place. Are the surfaces of the tests adorned with ribs, keels, spines, or other structures? Are the tests of some of the forams perforated with holes? Is the perforate or imperforate test the more abundant? You might want to examine bulk specimens against a black background. Do any of these specimens coil? If so, determine the direction of coiling.

Return your microscope to low power and obtain a pair of polarizing filters. Notice how these filters stop all transmitted light when they are rotated 90° out of phase from one another. Orient the filters so that light passes through them and place one filter above the foram preparation (**analyzer**) and another on top of the light source of the microscope (**polarizer**). You will probably have to refocus the microscope to bring the specimen into focus. While observing the forams, rotate the polarizer until it is out of phase with the analyzer. The background will be dark due to the exclusion of light by the crossed filters; however, the forams will appear to be bright. This phenomenon, called **birefringence**, occurs because the $CaCO_3$ of the test has two or more

(A)

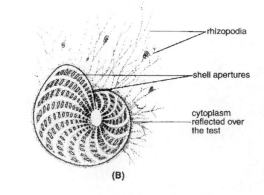

(B)

Figure 12. Two foraminiferidans. (A) *Allogromia* with unilocular shell (After Schulze). (B) *Elphidium* with multilocular shell (After Jahn).

The Protozoans

principal refractive indices (is highly ordered) and will rotate light themselves, thus permitting light to pass through the second filter. ■

Phylum Actinopoda

Four classes are recognized currently in the superclass Actinopodea [AK-tin-OP-o-de-ah; G., *aktinos* + G., *podos*, foot]. Members of the three marine classes (e.g., Acan-

tharea, Polycystinea, and Phaeodorea) are commonly called **radiolarians**. The fourth class, Heliozoea, is primarily freshwater; they are commonly called the **sun animalcules**.

Members of all classes have a type of pseudopodium called an **axopodium** (actinopodium). This straight, slender pseudopodium possesses an axial rod (**axoneme**) composed of microtubules. Axopodia are radially arranged and used primarily in feeding rather than in locomotion. Most of these amebas have tests of silica.

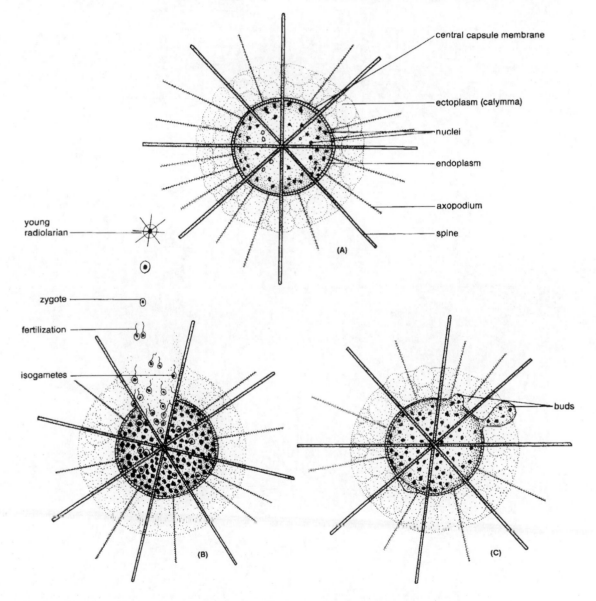

Figure 14. Radiolaria. (A) Mature individual. (B) Gametogenesis and syngamy. (C) Budding.

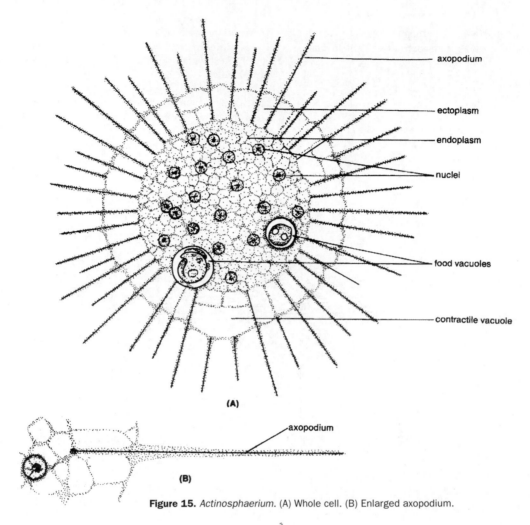

(A)

(B)

Figure 15. *Actinosphaerium.* (A) Whole cell. (B) Enlarged axopodium.

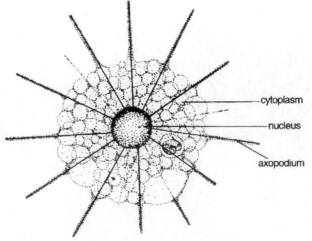

Figure 16. *Actinophrys.*

Radiolarians

Radiolarians are among the oldest protozoans. All are marine and currently assigned to three classes. Most radiolarians are planktonic and pelagic. Their beautiful skeletons are composed primarily of silica and strontium sulfate or calcium aluminum silicate, with radially arranged spines that extend outward from the center of the body (Figs. 13 and 14). A central capsule, a double or single pseudochitinous or mucinoid membrane, divides the body into an inner, granular endoplasm and an outer, frothy mass of ectoplasm (**calymma**). The central capsule has pores (**fusules**) that allow outward passage of the axial rods of the axopodia. One or more nuclei occur in the endoplasm. Axopodia arise from the capsule membrane and extend through the ectoplasm. They are sticky and capture prey that is carried by the streaming cytoplasm to the central capsule where digestion occurs within a food vacuole. The ectoplasm on one side of the axopodium moves toward its tip, while the other side moves toward the test. Binary fission, budding, and sporogenesis have been observed.

■ Observational Procedure: Radiolarians

Study prepared slides of radiolarian skeletons from several genera and species. Note the sizes and shapes of the skeletons as well as the varied ornamentations such as spines, thorns, and hooks. How do these organisms resemble the architectural structure known as a geo-desic dome? How do they resemble the carbon form known as fullerene? Are the skeletal elements of any of the radiolarians specimens birefringent? ■

Class Heliozoea

Heliozoans [G., *helios*, sun + G., *zoon*, animal] are among the most beautiful protozoans. Most species are freshwater and generally benthic or attached to substrates such as rocks and plants. Heliozoans are spherical in shape and lack the central capsule of radiolarians, but have long, slender, granule-studded axopodia (Figs. 15 and 16).

■ Observational Procedure: Heliozoans

Examine living specimens of *Actinosphaerium* and *Actinophrys* in depression slides under low and high powers of the compound microscope (Figs. 15 and 16). Note their spherical shape, the lack of skeletal spicules, and the radiating axopodia. Observe the streaming ectoplasm as it moves over the axopods. Which of the two organisms is the largest? Note that the ectoplasm of *Actinosphaerium* is highly vacuolated with a frothy appearance, whereas the endoplasm is a dense, granular central mass. The multinucleated endoplasm has many axial rods originating from its outer portion. The endoplasm of *Actinophrys* is uninucleate and the axial rods attach to the nuclear membrane. Are contractile vacuoles present? ■

D. Spore-forming Protozoans

There are over 4,000 species of many genera in this group. All are endoparasites, living in both invertebrate and vertebrate hosts. All lack cilia, flagella, or pseudopodia. The life cycles are complex and involve the production of sporelike stages. Some of the most devesting diseases of man have their origin from these spore-formers. Two phyla, Sporozoa or Apicomplexa (*Gregarina, Monocystis, and Plasmodium*) and Myxozoa or Myxosporidia (*Myxosoma*) will be studied.

Phylum Sporozoa (Apicomplexa). Members of Sporozoa [SPOR-o-ZO-ah; G., *sporos*, seed + *zoon*, animal] or Apicomplexa [A-pi-com-PLEX-ah; L., *apex*, tip + L., *complex*, twisted around] have a distinctive suite of structures called the **apical complex**. The structures are distinguishable only with the electron microscope. The somewhat simple-structured cells always have a

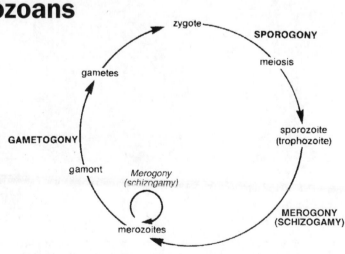

Figure 17. Generalized life cycle of Apicomplexa.

The Protozoans

vesicular nucleus. Cilia or flagella are lacking, except in flagellated microgametes of some groups. All members are parasitic and both asexual and sexual phases are present in the life cycle. Spores lack polar filaments. Representatives of two of the three classes will be studied in this exercise: Gregarinea (gregarines) and Coccidea (coccidians).

Generalized Life Cycle

The life cycle is complex, usually involving multiple fission, gamete production, and one or more hosts (Fig.

17). All stages in the life cycle, except the 2n zygote, are haploid.

Gregarines. There are two types of gregarines. (1) **Aseptate** (acephaline) forms lack septa dividing the body into segments (Fig. 18). These gregarines are found especially in the coeloms of polychaetes, oligochaetes, sipunculids, nemerteans, and mollusks. (2) **Septate** (cephaline) gregarines have septa dividing the body (Fig. 19). The anteriormost segment, a modified holdfast organelle called an **epimerite**, usually

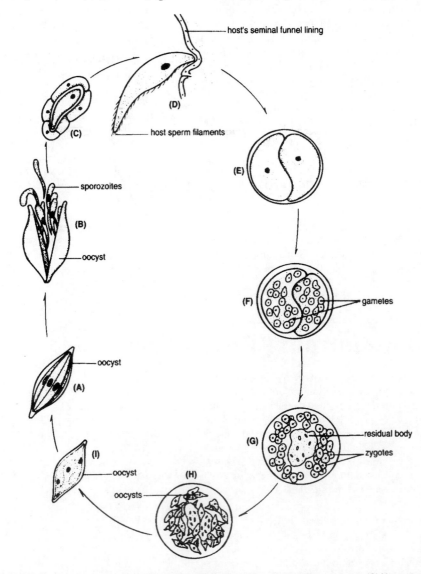

Figure 18. *Monocystis* life cycle. (A) Oocyst containing sporozoites. (B) Sporozoites released from oocyst. (C) Young trophozoite. (D) Mature trophozoite with sperm tails clustered about the outer surface. (E) Pair of encysted trophozoites. (F) Production of isogametes. (G) Zygotes within a gametocyst. (H) Oocysts developing. (I) One oocyst.

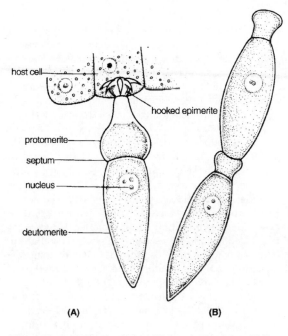

host cell

hooked epimerite

protomerite

septum

nucleus

deutomerite

(A)   (B)

Figure 19. Cephaline gregarine. (A) Attached to host. (B) Two gregarines in syzygy. Note the lack of the epimerite.

breaks off when the trophozoite detaches from the host. The middle segment is the **protomerite** and the posterior **deutomerite** contains the nucleus. Septate gregarines are common in the guts of insects, millipedes, and crustaceans.

Monocystis: An Aseptate Gregarine. Monocystis is a large genus with about 72 species. The trophozoites (100–240 μm long) of most species live in the seminal vesicles of earthworms where they feed on developing earthworm sperm cells (Fig. 18). Tiny filaments, seen on the surface of the trophozoite, are the tails of disintegrated spermatozoa. The life cycle of *Monocystis* is similar to that of most gregarines (Fig. 18). The trophozoites pair off and unite together in a process called **syzygy** [siz-i-GE; G., *zygon,* yoke]. A cyst wall forms around the trophozoites. Each trophozoite, now a **gamont**, undergoes multiple fission producing isogametes that undergo syngamy with isogametes from the other gamont, so forming zygotes within a gametocyte. Each zygote is surrounded by its own wall and develops into a biconical **oocyst (sporocyst)**. Each oocyst (17–25 by 8–10 μm) forms eight **sporozoites** by meiosis and mitosis (sporogony). Oocysts are released when the earthworm dies and decays or perhaps via feces of the earthworm. Eight sporozoites are released in the next earthworm's gut after the oocyst is ingested. The sporozoites traverse the gut and enter the seminal vesicles where they mature into trophozoites.

■ Observational Procedure: *Monocystis*

Examine prepared slides (section and smear) of *Monocystis agilis* showing developmental stages in the seminal vesicle of earthworms. Identify as many stages as possible, using Fig. 18 as a guide. Is any one stage more abundant than the rest?

To obtain living *Monocystis*, put an earthworm in 7% alcohol for about 30 minutes. When the worm is fully anesthetized, take sharp-pointed scissors or scalpel and make a shallow, dorsal cut in the body wall from segments 10–15. Extend two cuts each through both sides of the body wall. The cream-colored **seminal vesicles** should be evident. Excise a small part of the vesicle and place it on a clean slide. Add a drop of water to the piece of vesicle and tease apart with dissection needles to make a very thin smear. Cover with a coverslip and examine under low and high magnifications of the compound microscope. Do the stages differ from those observed in the prepared slides? ■

Gregarina: A Septate Gregarine. Gregarina is the largest genus of septate gregarines. The mature trophozoite (350–500 by 185–200 μm) parasitizes the guts of insects (Fig. 19). With maturity, the epimerite detaches from the body and two trophozoites unite a head-to-tail in syzygy. A wall forms about the two, but each trophozoite maintains its individuality. Each trophozoite develops into a spherical gamont within its own cyst wall. Multiple fission occurs inside each gametocyte, resulting in many gametes; the gametes are released with breakdown of the gametocyte wall. Syngamy results in zygotes that develop into oocysts. Infection to a new host is by ingestion of oocysts. Meiosis inside the oocyst results in eight sporozoites. The sporozoites emerge in the host after the oocyst is ingested and soon develop into trophozoites.

■ Observational Procedure: *Gregarina*

Obtain a live insect such as a grasshopper or cockroach and cut off the head. Open the body with sharp-pointed scissors or scalpel. Locate the tube-shaped intestine in the ventral area of the body and remove carefully with forceps. Place the intestine on a glass slide, tease it open, and add a drop of water. Cover the gut contents with a coverslip and examine with low power of a compound microscope. Change to high magnification once the organism has been located. Locate the immature trophozoites. Can you distinguish the epimerite, protomerite, and deutomerite? Based upon your study of

Monocystis, can you identify other stages of the life cycle of *Gregarina*? Study prepared slides and compare with the living organism. ∎

Class Coccidea

Sporozoea. The mature trophozoites of members of this class are small and intracellular. Coccidians are perhaps the most important infectious disease-causing parasites of humans because the parasite, *Plasmodium*, that causes malaria belongs to this class. Over 3.5 million humans die annually from malaria; some biologists believe that malaria is responsible for over one-half of all human deaths worldwide. The vector of *Plasmodium* in humans is the female *Anopheles* mosquito. Four species of *Plasmodium* cause malaria in humans (*P. falciparum, P. malariae, P. ovale,* and *P. vivax)* and these species differ in details related to frequency of multiple fission, morphology of schizonts (merozoites), and gametocytes (gamonts). A brief study of *P. vivax* will be made (Fig. 20).

Plasmodium vivax. Of the four malarial diseases in humans, the type caused by *Plasmodium vivax* is the most common and widespread, but not the most severe. When an infected female *Anopheles* mosquito takes a blood meal (only females bite), the spindle-shaped sporozoites leave her salivary glands and enter a victim's bloodstream. Within a few minutes, the sporozoites enter primarily liver cells. Here they grow and multiply by several schizogonous divisions, producing **merozoites**. These merozoites are sometimes called metacryptozoites; however, they are morphologically similar to other merozoites. The merozoites enter the bloodstream, invade the erythrocytes, and transform into **trophozoites**. In a stained slide the young trophozoite inside an erythrocyte resembles a signet ring: the single nucleus is ruby red and is perched on one side of a blue ring of cytoplasm. This is often called the **ring stage**. Inside the erythrocytes, the ring-shaped trophozoites grow and undergo several nuclear divisions. The erythrocytes increase in size to accommodate the growing trophozoites. The cytoplasm of an infected erythrocyte contains fine spots called **Schuffner's dots**. In older trophozoites a brownish iron-containing residue from metabolized hemoglobin may be observed. The multinucleated trophozoite is an immature **schizont** (merozoite) distinguished by having many nuclei throughout a continuous cytoplasm. With maturity, the cytoplasm of the schizont divides into distinct smaller bodies each with a nucleus. This mature schizont is called a **segmenter**. When the erythrocyte ruptures the small nucleated merozoites are released into the bloodstream. Chills and fevers, so characteristic of malaria,

occur when toxic wastes are released in the bloodstream with rupture of erythrocytes. The released merozoites invade other erythrocytes. Some merozoites develop into male and female **gametocytes** (gamonts). The male **microgamete** (microgamont) has a pale cytoplasm and a large nucleus with irregular granules. The female **macrogamete** (macrogamont) has a dense cytoplasm, a small compact nucleus, and a dark red nucleolus. A mature gametocyte nearly fills the erythrocyte. The gametocytes circulate in the blood and further development ceases until a mosquito takes a blood meal which includes the gametocytes.

Upon entering the mosquito's stomach, each gametocyte undergoes gametogenesis. One microgametocyte undergoes three nuclear divisions to produce eight flagellated microgametes, the process of **exflagellation**. In the stomach of the mosquito, each microgamete fertilizes a female macrogamete. The resulting motile zygote is called an **ookinete** that lodges on the wall of the mosquito's stomach. Here the ookinete develops into an **oocyst**. Growth of the oocyst occurs and inside it, numerous **sporoblasts** (future sporozoites) form by meiosis and multiple fission. With rupture of a mature oocyst, 10,000 or more sporozoites are released and migrate to and enter the salivary gland. When the mosquito takes a blood meal, the infective sporozoites enter the host and the cycle repeats.

∎ Observational Procedure: *Plasmodium vivax*

Microscope slides with sections of infected human liver, human blood smears, and preparations showing mosquito salivary glands and stomach are necessary to study developmental stages in the life cycle of *Plasmodium vivax*. Some of the stages may be set up as special demonstrations. Additional preparations representing other *Plasmodium* species may be provided. Do not expect to find all stages on one slide preparation. Examine the slides under high power of the compound microscope and then under oil immersion. Extreme care must be exercised when using oil immersion to prevent breaking the slide and causing damage to the lens. Refer to Fig. 20 as you make your observations.

Liver Section. Find the large schizonts among the liver cells. Note the size of the parasite with that of a liver cell.

Blood Smear. Find a ring stage of a young trophozoite.
1. Note the single ruby red nucleus perched on a bluish ring of cytoplasm.
2. Find trophozoites in various stages of growth. Observe Schuffner's dots in the cells cytoplasm. Distinguish the parasite's nuclei from the brownish, iron-containing residue from metabolized hemoglobin.

The Protozoans

Figure 20. Life cycle of *Plasmodium*. (A) Infective stage (sporozoites) enter human, invade liver cells, undergo multiple fission (merogony), and become merozoites. (B) Some merozoites instead of reinvading liver cells, enter erythrocytes. These merozoites increase in numbers by multiple fission. (C) Some merozoites become microgametocytes (potential male gametes) and macrogametocytes (potential female gametes). (D) Gametocytes enter mosquito with a blood meal and become gametes. (E) Fertilization of macrogamete and microgamete results in a motile zygote (ookinete). The ookinete encysts on the mosquito's stomach wall and becomes an oocyst. Inside the oocyst the sporozoites develop. (F) With rupture of the oocyst, the released sporozoites enter the salivary glands of the mosquito and remain there until a blood meal is taken.

3. Locate a schizont with many nuclei in a uniform cytoplasm and segmenters with merozoites. The merozoites may not be as distinct as they appear in drawings. Attempt to locate the free spindle-shaped merozoites in the blood. These minute bodies are often difficult to find in most smears.

4. Look for microgametocytes and macrogametocytes. You may experience difficulty differentiating between the two. The microgametocyte has a large nucleus with irregularly distributed granules and a pale blue cytoplasm. The blue cytoplasm of the macrogametocyte appears dense and the smaller compact nucleus may show a dark red nucleolus.

Mosquito Sections. Observe a preparation showing exflagellation of the microgametocyte.
1. How many tail-like structures are present?
2. Examine a stomach preparation of the mosquito showing oocysts. How many oocysts are present?
3. Observe a preparation showing sporozoites. Describe their shape. ∎

Phylum Myxosporidia (Myxospora). These are obligate, extracellular parasites in body cavities, in gills, and various tissues of poikilothermic vertebrates (especially fish) and annelids. Entire fish populations may be destroyed by the parasite. Unlike the Sporozoa and microsporans (Phylum Microspora), a spore with one to two ameboid **sporoplasms** and one to six (usually two) **polar capsules** and **coiled filaments** are present (Fig. 21). The polar filaments are holdfast structures. Each uninucleate ameboid sporoplasm enters the host when a spore is ingested and grows into a multinucleate trophozoite. The trophozoite feeds on the host's tissues

and undergoes multiple fission (schizogony), thereby increasing the infection. Eventually sporogony occurs and one or more spores are produced.

Research indicates that these organisms may be members of the metazoan lineage. We continue myxozoan coverage here because their study is a nice complement to the sporozoan parasites and as a matter of tradition. Consult the following reference for more information on this topic.

Smothers, J.F., C.D. von Dohlen, L.H. Smith, Jr., and R.S. Spall. 1994. Molecular evidence that the Myxozoan Protists are Metazoans. *Science* 265: 1719-1721.

■ Observational Procedure: *Myxosoma*

Examine prepared slides of *Myxosoma* or other myxozoans. Specimens can often be found in the gills of certain fish. Note the shape and size of the parasite (Fig. 21). If spores are available, locate the polar filaments, polar capsules, sporoplasm, and nuclei. ■

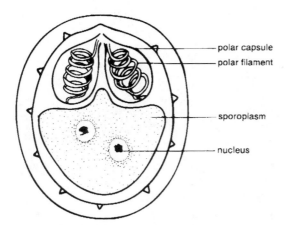

polar capsule
polar filament

sporoplasm

nucleus

Figure 21. Myxosoma.

E. Ciliate Protozoans

Phylum Ciliophora. Ciliated protozoans represent the largest in size and the most homogenous group of protozoans. The available evidence indicates that these animals share a common ancestry. At some time in their life cycle, cilia or compound ciliary structures (e.g. cirri) are present for food-acquiring or locomotion.

The approximate 8,000 species of Ciliophora [SIL-e-OF-or-ah; G., *cilium*, eyelash + G., *phora*, to bear] occur in all major ecological habitats. Most are free living and phagotrophic. Ciliates are the most structurally complex group of protozoans. Unique features include cilia, **dikaryotic nuclei**, complex cortex and associated organelles, and modes of reproduction. Most ciliates have a cytostome and cytopharynx for ingestion of food, at least one fixed contractile vacuole to regulate cytoplasmic water content and ion concentration, and a **cytoproct (cytopyge)** for egestion of digested food from food vacuoles. A variety of organelles collectively called **extrusomes** release materials from the cell. These include **mucocysts** that coat the body and help form cysts, **toxicysts** that eject toxins to capture prey, **haptocysts** for

prey-capture, and **trichocysts** that are nontoxic explosive organelles whose exact function is unknown.

The dikaryotic nuclei distinguish ciliates from other protozoans. The small, compact **micronucleus** is primarily involved in genetic and sexual recombination, undergoing mitosis and meiosis. The larger, polyploid **macronucleus** regulates the metabolic processes of the cell. The macronucleus develops from the micronucleus, but can usually replicate once formed.

Certain ciliates have **membranelles** and **cirri**, specialized ciliary organelles, used in locomotion and food getting (Fig. 26). Membranelles, composed of 2 or 3 rows of short cilia, appear as a thin membrane, whereas cirri are ciliary tufts that function as a unit. Cilia usually cover most of the cell. The outer portion of the ciliate body is called the **cortex**. This includes the outer plasma membrane and the membrane-lined alveoli (together called the **pellicle**) and the **infraciliature** (Fig. 22). The latter is a complex network consisting of **kinetosomes** and associated microtubules and fine, striated kinetodesmal fibrils. The kinetosomes plus

Figure 22. Structure of cortex and associated infraciliature of a ciliate (After Peck 1977).

associated fibrils form kinetids, which may be arranged in a row called a **kinety**. Kinetids may have one (monokinetid), two (dikinetid), or more (polykinetid) kinetosomes. Kinetid distribution and specializations over the ciliate body are used in taxonomy.

Reproduction is primarily by transverse binary fission; the plane of division is across the long axis of the body (homothetogenic fission). This is unlike symmetrogenic fission of flagellates, where the longitudinal furrow forms between rows of kinetosomes, if present. Budding occurs in some ciliates. Free gametes are not formed during the sexual process, rather, micronuclei are exchanged between two sexually compatible individuals in a process called conjugation.

Representatives from three classes of the Phylum Ciliophora will be studied: Kinetofragminophora (*Didinium*, *Balantidium*, and *Ephelota*), Oligohymenophora (*Paramecium* and *Vorticella*), and Polyhymenophora (*Bursaria*, *Spirostomum*, *Stentor*, *Euplotes*, and *Stylonychia*).

Class Kinetofragminophora. Oral region of body bearing cilia, but lacking compound ciliary organelles.

Subclass Gymnostomata. Cell mouth at or near body surface and located anterior or laterally. Body ciliation mostly uniform.

Didinium nasutum. This species (125 μm long) is a freshwater, raptorial ciliate feeding almost exclusively on *Paramecium*. Several didiniums may attack and kill one paramecium with discharged toxic trichocysts.

■ Observational Procedure: *Didinium nasutum*

Place together on a depression slide a small drop each from cultures of *Didinium* and *Paramecium*. Cover with a coverslip and observe under low and high powers of the compound microscope. Note the barrel-shaped body with the posterior end round and the cone-shaped anterior end (Fig. 23A). The cytostome, located at the tip of the proboscis, can be greatly expanded to swallow a paramecium. Describe the feeding process if *Didinium* is seen taking a paramecium. Is a contractile vacuole evident? Note the girdle of cilia around the middle of the body and another circle around the anterior end. These cilia can be seen in a prepared slide along with the macronucleus and contractile vacuole. Describe the shape of the macronucleus. ■

Subclass Vestibulifera. The cell mouth is associated with a densely ciliated depressum called the **vestibulum**, it bears a distinct ciliation.

25

The Protozoans

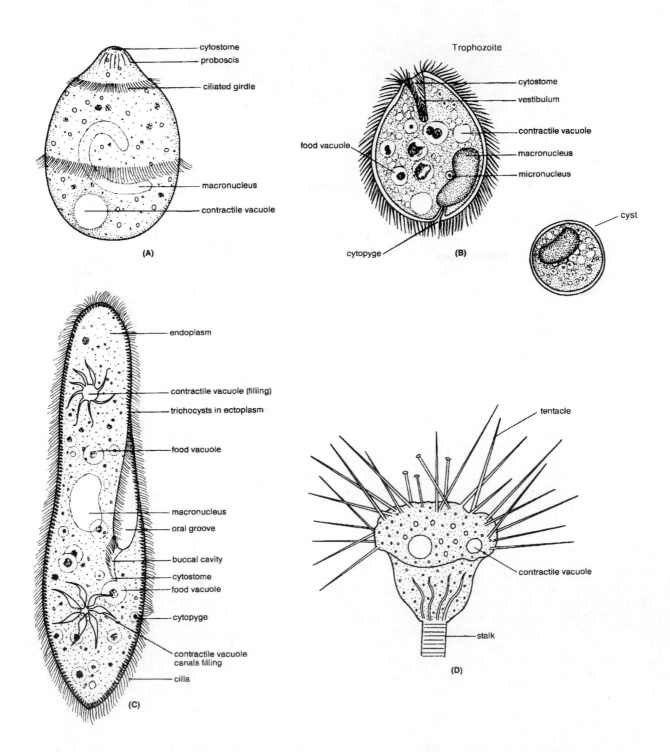

Figure 23. Ciliates and suctoria. (A) *Didinium nasutum.* (B) *Balantidium coli,* trophozoite and cyst (After Kudo). (C) *Paramecium caudatum.* (D) *Ephelota.*

Balantidium coli. This medium-sized ciliate (50–100 µm long) is a common commensal in the cecum and large intestine of pigs. In humans, *Balantidium coli* is a pathogenic parasite that invades the intestinal mucosa.

■ Observational Procedure: *Balantidium coli*

Obtain a prepared slide of *Balantidium coli* and locate the ovoid trophozoite under low and then high power (Fig. 23B). The anterior end is more pointed than the posterior end. Body cilia occur in oblique, longitudinal rows. Attempt to locate the cytopyge (cell anus) at the posterior end and the cytostome and long vestibulum in an apicoventral position near the anterior end. Note the large, sausage-shaped macronucleus and two contractile vacuoles, one at the posterior and one at the anterior end. The vesicular micronucleus may not be evident.

Balantidium coli is transmitted via contaminated food or water containing the ovoid cysts (40–60 µm in diameter) passed in the host's feces. Cysts often stain poorly and the large macronucleus and one contractile vacuole are the most conspicuous organelles observed. Look for cysts in a prepared slide. Note the size, shape, and structure of the cyst wall. Locate the large macronucleus and contractile vacuole. The micronucleus will probably not be observed. Are food vacuoles evident? ■

Subclass Suctoria. Suctorians are carnivorous ciliates found in both marine and freshwater habitats. Suctorians get their name from the way they obtain their food. Mature suctorians are usually sessile, stalked, lack cilia, and have one or more tentacles. Immatures are ciliated and lack the stalk and tentacles.

Ephelota. *Ephelota* (250 by 220 µm, with a stalk of up to 1.5 mm) is a marine suctorian and is often found attached to the marine hydroid *Obelia*.

■ Observational Procedure: *Ephelota*

Examine living specimens or prepared slides with a compound microscope. Note the short, thick, flat-tipped tentacles and their arrangement (Fig. 23D). The stalk enlarges distally. Do the tentacles and stalk extend or contract in the living organism? Do you see myonemes or striations in the stalk? Suctorians have **haptocysts** at the tip of the tentacles used in feeding. Can you see a contractile vacuole? Examine a prepared slide and locate the curved, elongated macronucleus. ■

Class Oligohymenophora. Compound ciliary organelles associated with an oral apparatus.

Subclass Hymenostomata. These ciliates have an oral cavity that is either shallow or deep. The body ciliation is typically uniform. Some members have trichocysts.

Paramecium caudatum. This is the most widely distributed species of paramecium. It is 150–300 µm long, has a single large macronucleus, and has one compact micronucleus (Fig. 23C). The species occurs in freshwater streams and ponds containing plants and decaying organic matter. *Paramecium caudatum* is holozoic, living on bacteria, algae, and small animals.

Paramecium aurelia with two micronuclei and *P. multimicronucleatum* with four or more micronuclei and three to seven contractile vacuoles are similar species to *P. caudatum*. *Paramecium busaria*, unlike the abovementioned species, has unicellular **zoochlorellae** as symbionts in its body.

■ Observational Procedure: *Paramecium caudatum*

1. Place a drop of the paramecium culture on a glass slide containing a ring of methyl cellulose. Cover with a coverslip and locate an individual under low power of the compound microscope.

2. Observe locomotion in the paramecium. Note the organism's forward spiral movement as it slowly rotates on its long axis. Does the organism change its direction of movement by reversing the beat of its cilia? Can the organism bend its body?

3. Locate an individual that has ceased moving rapidly and observe under high power. The anterior end is narrower and more blunt than the broad, pointed posterior end (Fig. 23C). Can you see beating of the cilia?

4. Locate the oblique depression on the right side of the body. This is the **oral groove**; it gives the organism an asymmetrical shape. The oral groove leads to a buccal cavity (oral cavity).

5. Note the longitudinally arranged cilia covering the entire body and lining the oral groove. The buccal cavity has on its inner surface numerous cilia arranged in two major bands. These cannot be observed with the light microscope. Food trapped in the oral groove travels through the buccal cavity, then through the cytostome, where a food vacuole is formed. Formation and circulation of food vacuoles can be observed by dusting a few grains of powdered carmine on the under surface of a coverslip before it is placed over the culture sample. ■

6. The outermost membrane layers of the body are called the pellicle. If a fresh drop of culture is allowed to dry on the slide uncovered, a hexagonal pattern on the pellicular surface can be seen with the compound microscope.

7. In the ectoplasm are numerous rodlike trichocysts that alternate with the bases of the cilia. Each trichocyst is discharged through a pellicular pore and is not reused once discharged. Trichocysts are quickly regenerated. An electron micrograph of a discharged trichocyst resembles a golfer's tee attached to a long, striated shaft. If a small drop of acetic acid, methylene blue, or Dahlia stain is added to a paramecium sample, the organisms should discharge numerous trichocysts.

8. Behind the posterior end of the oral groove is a small permanent opening through which solid wastes are voided. This is the cytoproct (cytopyge); it is difficult to observe in the living organism.

9. A contractile vacuole with radiating canals occurs at each end of the paramecium. These are in fixed positions and open to the outside via a pellicular pore. If an-

Figure 25. Bursaria.

other preparation is made and some of the water removed by placing a blotter or piece of filter paper near the edge of the coverslip, the vacuoles can be observed.

10. The macronucleus and micronucleus are located near the center of the paramecium. Observe these in a prepared stained slide since they are difficult to see in the living organism. The larger macronucleus is kidney-shaped and the smaller micronucleus lies in a depression of the macronucleus.

11. *Paramecium* reproduces asexually by transverse binary fission (across the kineties) while sex occurs by conjugation. Examine prepared slides showing fission and conjugation in *Paramecium*.

12. If live cultures of two different mating types of *Paramecium* are available, prepare a slide using a small drop from each culture. Gently mix this preparation, cover with a coverslip, and observe under low power of a compound microscope. Does each encounter between individuals result in conjugation? What does that indicate? How long after an encounter does it take before conjugation begins? How long does it last? Examine any mating pairs that you may find under high power. How are the two individuals connected? What do all of these observations tell you about the process of conjugation in *Paramecium*? ■

Subclass Peritrichia. The oral apparatus, when present, is distinct. The oral structures are located in a ventral oral cavity or deeper infundibulum. The oral region can be contracted. Sessile forms are usually stalked and with reduced body ciliation.

Vorticella. Vorticella is a solitary, but often gregarious ciliate with a long stalk (up to 4.2 mm long). The stalk can retract and extend because of a large fiber called a

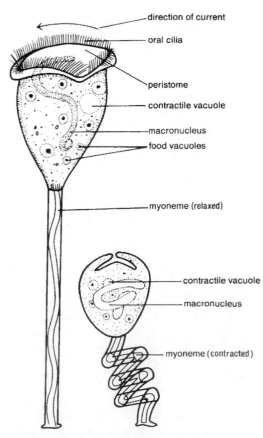

Figure 24. Vorticella (expanded and contracted).

myoneme (spasmoneme). Members of the genus occur in both fresh and marine waters. *Vorticella* is a suspension feeder on bacteria.

■ Observational Procedure: *Vorticella*

Place a drop of culture containing *Vorticella* in a ring of methyl cellulose. Cover with a coverslip and observe under low power of a compound microscope. Note the inverted bell shaped body and stalk (Fig. 24). The stalk can appear like a coiled spring as it retracts and extends. Do you see popping movements of the individuals? Observe beating of the membranelles that lie in a peristomal groove around the bell. There is one inner set of cilia and one row that projects outward like a shelf. Do all rows beat in the same direction? What function might this movement serve? Are food and contractile vacuoles evident? Look for the elongate sausage- or horseshoe-shaped macronucleus. It can be observed in a prepared slide. ■

Class Polyhymenophora. Buccal membranelles at oral region. Body ciliation uniform; some with compound organelles (e.g., cirri).

Subclass Spirotricha. Characteristics same as given for the class.

Bursaria truncatella. This large (500–1,000 μm long), broad, carnivorous ciliate has uniform body ciliation. The species is found in freshwater. There is an apical mouth and a large, funnel shaped buccal (oral) cavity with membranelles on its left and right walls.

■ Observational Procedure: *Bursaria truncatella*

Make a wet mount from the *Bursaria* culture and observe under low and then with high power of a compound microscope. Describe the organism's movement. *Bursaria* is ovoid with the anterior end truncate and the posterior end round (Fig. 25). The ventral surface is flat, but the dorsal surface is convex. Note the funnel-shaped buccal cavity beginning at the anterior end and extending to the end of the body where it gives rise to the cytostome. A lengthwise fold divides the peristome into two chambers. Along the lateral and posterior edges of the body are many contractile vacuoles. Attempt to see the long, band-shaped macronucleus. *Bursaria* has several micronuclei. Compare what you see in the living organism with that in a prepared slide. ■

Spirostomum ambiguum. This freshwater ciliate is slender, somewhat flattened, and very elongated. It may reach a length of 3.5 mm. Body ciliation is short and arranged in longitudinal rows.

■ Observational Procedure: *Spirostomum ambiguum*

Examine living specimens under low and high magnifications of a compound microscope and note their size and shape (Fig. 26B). Observe beating of the cilia. Do cilia cover the entire body? Note that the posterior end is more blunt than the anterior end. Which end usually moves forward? Like *Stentor*, *Spirostomum* contracts its body with myonemes. Can these be seen? Attempt to see at the posterior end the large contractile vacuole with a long dorsal canal. The peristome, bordered by short adoral membranelles, occupies an area about two-thirds of the body length. Study a prepared slide and observe the dark-stained macronucleus. Describe its shape. Is the micronucleus evident? ■

Stentor coeruleus. *Stentor coeruleus* is a large (1–2 mm long), freshwater ciliate with a conspicuous adoral zone of membranelles around the ciliated peristome. The contractile body is vase or trumpet in shape. Body ciliation is uniform and there are well-defined myonemes possessed by the organism.

■ Observational Procedure: *Stentor coeruleus*

Place a drop of the *Stentor* culture in a ring of methyl cellulose and cover with a coverslip. Observe with both low and high magnifications of the compound microscope. Note the size and shape of this protozoan (Fig. 26A). The bluish color is derived from a cytoplasmic pigment called **stentorin**. Which end moves forward in a swimming specimen? Locate an individual that has become attached to a surface. Observe the active-moving adoral membranelles around the peristome. In what direction do these fused rows of cilia beat? *Stentor* is a suspension feeder. Identify the area where the membranelles lead to a spiral-shaped buccal cavity (oral cavity). Your specimen should extend and contract its body. Longitudinal contractile filaments called **myonemes** shorten the body; microtubular arrays lengthen the body by sliding. Myonemes lie in the pellicle and may be observed in stained preparations. Locate the contractile vacuole with its long collecting canal. Is its position constant or variable? Attempt to see the moniliform-shaped (beadlike) macronucleus. The macronucleus and other structures can be seen in the prepared slide. ■

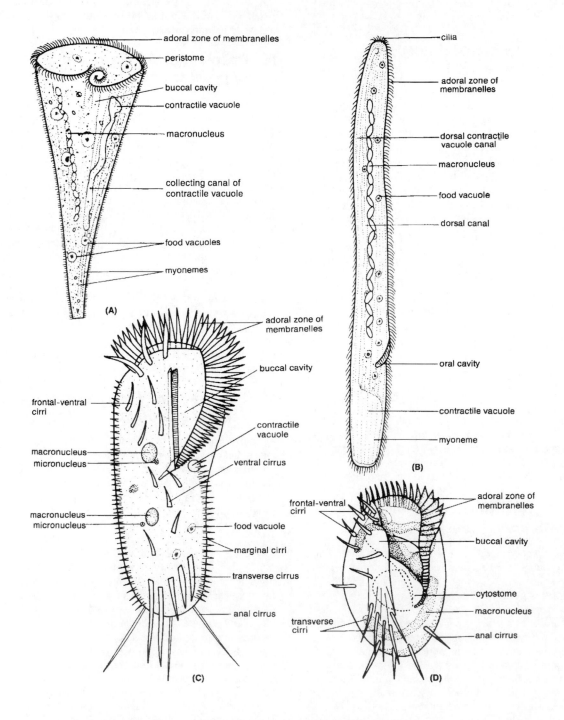

Figure 26. Selected ciliates. (A) *Stentor*. (B) *Spirostomum ambiguum*. (C) *Stylonychia*. (D) *Euplotes*.

Euplotes. *Euplotes* (100–195 μm) occur in fresh and brackish waters. Symbiotic zoochlorellae are sometimes present in their bodies. The ovoid body is more or less dorsoventrally flattened. Somatic or body ciliation is reduced; cirri and oral ciliature are usually conspicuous.

■ Observational Procedure: *Euplotes*

Observe living *Euplotes;* note its size, body shape, and way of movement (Fig. 26D). Does the organism creep, crawl, or dart about? Observe the 9 or 10 frontal-ventral cirri, the five transverse cirri, the four anal (caudal) cirri, and adoral zone of membranelles. Are these involved in locomotion? Examine a stained slide and locate the large C-shaped macronucleus as well as the membranelles and cirri. The buccal cavity is broadly triangular in shape. Is a posterior contractile vacuole present? ■

Stylonychia. *Stylonychia* is a common freshwater genus, but does occur in marine waters. The body shape of these ciliates is usually ovate and dorsoventrally flattened. Oral membranelles for food capture and cirri for locomotion are characteristic.

■ Observational Procedure: *Stylonychia*

Examine living specimens under low and high magnifications of a compound microscope. Describe its size and shape. Observe how the specimen darts about. Locate the three anal (caudal) cirri, eight frontal-ventral cirri, five ventral cirri, five transverse cirri, and several marginal cirri on the ventral surface of the body (Fig. 26C). These fused tufts of cilia serve as leglike structures. Can you see membranelles around the wide buccal (oral) cavity? Attempt to see the contractile vacuole near the membranelles. *Stylonychia* has two macronuclei and two micronuclei. Observe these, along with the structures described above, in the prepared slide. ■

The Protozoans

Protozoa   **Worksheet 1**

Name: _____   Date:_____

Course #:_____ / Section #: _____   Grade: _____

1. Identify the species of protozoans and a general geographic location that are associated with the following.

    a. giardiasis   _____ | _____

    b. coccidiosis   _____ | _____

    c. red tide   _____ | _____

    d. amebiasis   _____ | _____

    e. Chagas' disease   _____ | _____

    f. human malaria   _____ | _____

    g. sleeping sickness   _____ | _____

    h. kala azar   _____ | _____

2. Give one or more genera of protozoans that possess the following structures.

    a. cytostome _____   i. polar filament _____

    b. eyespot (stigma) _____   j. haptocyst _____

    c. pseudostome _____   k. epimerite _____

    d. anal cirri _____   l. axopodium _____

    e. plakeas _____   m. calymma _____

    f. vestibulum _____   n. rod organ _____

    g. myoneme _____   o. theca _____

    h. cytopyge _____   p. ectoplasm_____

3. Why do marine protozoans tend to have fewer contractile vacuoles and contractile vacuoles which funtion less frequently than freshwater forms? Discuss.

The Protozoans

4. How might the hornlike extensions in the dinoflagellate Genus *Ceratium* function?

5. Given what you know about the natural habitat of the protozoan *Giardia* and the amount of oxygen present there, consider the kind of metabolic byproducts of its metabolism. Why might you expect this organism to cause severe diarrhea ?

6. Calculate the rate of movement across the slide of two or more of the protozoans studied in this exercise and compare their relative rate of movement to your rate of movement during your day. Do this on a per body length basis.

   Your speed   Protozoan 1 _____   Protozoan 2 _____

7. Discuss how an undulating membrane is a modification of a standard cilium.

THE METAZOA

Metazoans, unlike protozoans, are composed of numerous, specialized cells arranged in layers. In primitive metazoans the outer layer serves for protection and for sensory response, while the inner layer functions in digestion. Cells between these layers function in support, conduction of nutrients, reproduction, and muscular contraction. In the least complex metazoans, cells having similar functions form aggregations known as tissues (tissue grade). In more advanced metazoans, two or more tissues combine to form organs (organ grade). In the most advanced forms, combinations of specific organs form specialized organ systems (system grade). Although these grades do not have taxonomic status, they may be thought of as a logical way of organizing the metazoan phyla.

Branch Parazoa [G., *para*, beside + G., *zoon*, animal] includes two phyla, **Porifera** and **Placozoa**. Both phyla have a cellular or poorly defined tissue grade of construction. In the Porifera the body has numerous pores, canals, and chambers lined with specialized, flagellated feeding cells. The Phylum Placozoa contains one species, *Trichoplax adhaerens*. This enigmatic organism resembles a microscopic pancake and is composed of a loose mesenchyme surrounded by layers of epithelial cells on the upper and lower sides (Pearse 1989; Pearse et al. 1994).

Branch Mesozoa [G., *meso*, middle] contains a single phylum of the same name. This enigmatic phylum contains minute parasitic and commensal marine animals composed of a single, outer cell layer and an inner, reproductive layer of one or more cells. Mesozoa has been thought of as a link between protozoans and metazoans, but some workers believe that their primitive characteristics are secondary, resulting from a long evolution as obligate parasites (Hochberg 1982; Lapan and Morowitz 1972).

Branch Eumetazoa [G., *eu*, good] includes the remainder of the metazoan phyla. These $\approx$ 30 phyla are of the tissue, organ, or system grade of construction. Recently several research groups have attempted to build a phylogeny of the Metazoa. Some of those studies are based on morphology alone while others have emphasized molecular data such as the sequence of the 18S ribosomal subunit.

Aguinaldo, A.M.A., J.M. Turbeville, L.S. Linford, M.C. Rivera, J.R. Garey, R.A. Raff, and J.A. Lake. 1997. Evidence for a clade of nematodes, arthropods and other moulting animals. *Nature* 387: 489-492.

Clark, R.B. 1964. *Dynamics in Metazoan Evolution: the Origin of the Coelom and Segments.* Clarendon Press, Oxford.

Fernholm, B., K. Bremer, and H. Jörnall, (eds.). 1989. *The Hierarchy of Life.* Elsevier Science Publishers, Amsterdam: 471-488.

Field, K.G., G.J. Olsen, D.J. Lane, S.J. Giovannoni, M.T. Ghislin, E.C. Raff, N.R. Pace, and R.A. Raff. 1988. Molecular phylogeny of the Animal Kingdom. *Science* 239: 748-753.

Funch, P. and R.M. Kristensen. 1995. Cycliophora is a new phylum with affinities to Entoprocta and Ectoprocta. *Nature* 378: 711-714.

Garey, J.R., M. Krotec, D.R. Nelson, and J. Brooks. 1996. Molecular analysis supports a tardigrade-arthropod association. *Invertebr. Bio.* 115: 79-88.

Hillis, D.M. 1987. Molecular versus morphological approaches to systematics. *Ann. Rev. Ecol. Syst.* 18: 23-42.

Hochberg, F.G. 1982. The "kidneys" of cephalopods: a unique habitat for parasites. *Malacologia.* 23: 121-134.

Lake, J.A. 1990. Origin of the Metazoa. *Proc. Natl. Acad. Sci. USA* 87: 763-766.

Lapan, E.A., and H. Morowitz. 1972. The Mesozoa. *Sci. Am.* 227: 94-101.

Meglitsch, P.A. and F.R. Schram. 1991. *Invertebrate Zoology.* Oxford University Press, New York, NY.

Minelli, A. and F.R. Schram. 1994. Owen revisited: a reappraisal of morphology in evolutionary biology. *Bijdragen tot de Dierkunde* 64(2): 65-74.

Nielsen, C. 2001. *Animal Evolution: Interrelationships of the Living Phyla.* (2nd edition). Oxford University Press, Oxford.

Pearse, V.B. 1989. Growth and behavior of *Trichoplax adhaerens*: first record of the phylum Placozoa in Hawaii. *Pac. Sci.* 43: 117-121.

Pearse, V.B., T. Uehara, and R.L. Miller. 1994. Birefringent granules in Placozoans (*Trichoplax adhaerens*). *Trans. Am. Microsc. Soc.* 113(3): 385-389.

Raff, R.A., C.R. Marshall, and J.M. Turbeville. 1994. Using DNA sequences to unravel the Cambrian radiation of the animal phyla. *Annu. Rev. Ecol. Syst.* 25: 351-375.

Seilacher, A., P.K. Bose, and F. Pflüger. 1998. Triploblastic animals more than 1 billion years ago: trace fossil evidence from India. *Science* 282: 80-83.

Winnepenninckx, B. M. H., T. Backeljau, and R. M. Kristensen. 1998. Relations of the new phylum Cycliophora. *Nature* 398: 636-638.

Winnepenninckx, B., T. Backeljau, L.Y. Mackey, J.M. Brooks, R. De Wachter, S. Kumar, and J.R. Garey. 1995. 18S rRNA data indicates that Aschelminthes are polyphyletic in origin and consist of at least three distinct clades. *Mol. Biol. Evol.* 12: 1132-1137.

Phylum Porifera

Phylum Porifera [po-RIF-er-a; L., *pori*, pore + L., *ferre*, bearing], or sponges, comprises a group of simple, sessile metazoans considered to have a cellular grade of construction. They are an ancient group whose geologic history extends back to before the **Cambrian Period** (Fig. 1). Sponges are either radially symmetrical or asymmetrical and have a body consistency varying from hard and stony to friable, rubbery, or gelatinous, depending upon nature and arrangement of their skeletal elements. Sponges range in size from a few millimeters to about 1 m tall. From an economic viewpoint, sponges are important as members of the marine-fouling community and continued commercial source of bath sponges. Lately the significance of sponges has increased because they are viewed as potential sources of unique biochemicals that may be important in fighting cancer.

In their simplest form, sponges resemble a tube closed at one end surrounding an inner cavity called the **spongocoel** or **atrium** (Fig. 2). The tube wall consists of two layers of cells arranged as concentric cylinders separated by a thin, noncellular, gelatinous layer, the **mesohyl**. The outer cell layer (**Pinacoderm**) is made up of flattened cells called **pinacocytes** that do not secrete a basement membrane. The inner layer consists of flagellated feeding cells called **choanocytes** or **collar cells** (Fig. 2). Sponges are supported internally by a calcareous or siliceous skeleton of **spicules**, or by protein **spongin** fibers. Some sponges have a combination of siliceous spicules and spongin. A large variety of different sizes (**mega-** and **microscleres**) and shapes of spicules has been described (Fig. 3). Spicules are absent in some sponges and a massive or reticulate, calcareous skeleton is present.

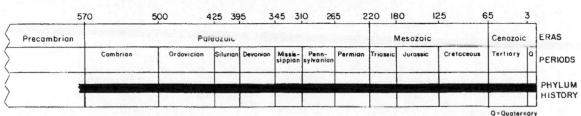

Figure 1. Geologic history of the Phylum Porifera.

From *Invertebrate Zoology*, Sixth Edition, Robert L. Wallace and Walter K. Taylor. Copyright © 2002 by Pearson Education, Inc. Published by Prentice-Hall, Inc. All rights reserved

Phylum Porifera

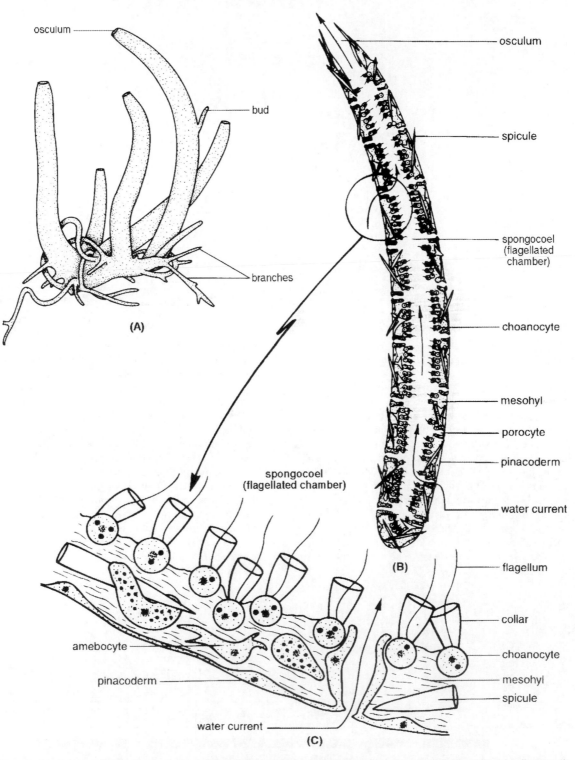

Figure 2. An asconoid sponge, *Leucosolenia*, and its canal system. A small portion of a *Leucosolenia* colony (A) and a diagramatic longitudinal section of *Leucosolenia* (B) with an enlargement of the body wall are shown (C).

Figure 3. Common spicule types.

The name "pore bearer" refers to the fact that sponges are perforated by numerous, minute, incurrent pores (**ostium**, plural **ostia**) and by one or more large excurrent pores (osculum, plural oscula). Water currents, generated by flagellar action of choanocytes, enter the sponge through ostia, pass into choanocyte (flagellated) chambers, and exit the sponge via the osculum. Viewed under high magnification of a light microscope, choanocytes appear as globular cells each with a long flagellum surrounded at the base by a collar-like extension of the cell membrane (Fig. 2). The collar is actually a ring of microvilli. Except for a recently discovered carnivorous form (Vancelet and Boury-Esnault 1995), sponges feed by screening incurrent water through a progressively finer series of filters (canals to choanocyte chambers) until the finest particles are removed by the choanocytes.

The structure of sponges may be divided into three body types, based on anatomy of choanocyte chambers and incurrent and excurrent canals. These types, in increasing order of complexity, are as follows: **asconoid**, **syconoid**, and **leuconoid** (Figs. 2, 4, and 5).

Both asexual and sexual reproduction occur in sponges. Asexual reproduction is accomplished by

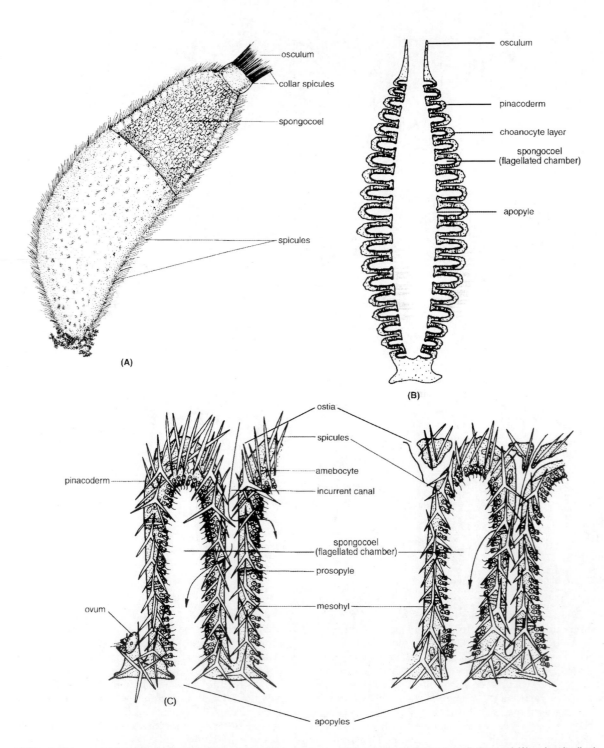

Figure 4. The syconoid sponge body plan of *Sycon*. A whole specimen with a portion of the body wall removed (A), a longitudinal section (B), and two cross sections (C) are shown.

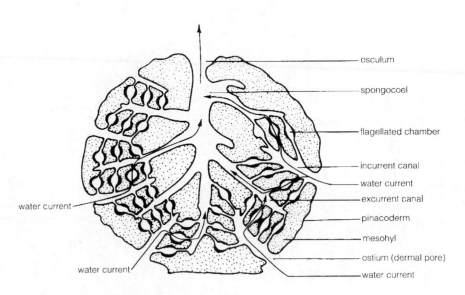

osculum

spongocoel

flagellated chamber

incurrent canal

water current

excurrent canal

pinacoderm

mesohyl

ostium (dermal pore)

water current

water current

water current

Figure 5. Diagrammatic view of a leuconoid sponge.

fragmentation and budding, and in freshwater and a few marine sponges, by production of resistant structures called **gemmules** (Fig. 6). Some sponges have remarkable powers of regeneration and reaggregation. Apparently all sponges are capable of sexual reproduction. Both hermaphroditic (**monoecious**) and **dioecious** species occur in the phylum. Fertilization and development are internal, except for some species that release fertilized eggs. Two different larvae occur in sponges. Most sponges have a **parenchymula** larva and a few an **amphiblastula** (Fig. 7). After a mobile phase of a few hours to several days, larvae attach to a suitable surface and metamorphose into young sponges.

Figure 6. Gemmules of Spongilla, a freshwater sponge.

Classification

Sponge taxonomy is based primarily on the chemical nature and morphology of inorganic and organic skeletal elements. However, reproductive features, comparative biochemistry, and ultrastructural histology also are important. Four classes of sponges are recognized. Reiswig and Mackie (1983) separate sponges into two subphyla: **Cellularia** (having discrete cells) comprise the three main classes; **Symplasma** (having a syncytium) comprise the Class Hexactinellida (cf. Vacelet 1985 and Bergquist 1985). Most of the 5,000 or more species of sponges are marine; about 150 species inhabit freshwaters.

1. **Class Calcarea.** Sponges with spicules of calcium carbonate; massive skeletal structures also are present. Microsclere spicules lacking; entirely marine, usually located in shallow water. All three body types occur. Examples include *Leucosolenia* and *Sycon*.

2. **Class Demospongiae.** Siliceous spicules (megascleres and microscleres), spongin fibers, or both present. The Family Oscarellidae lacks any skeleton. Most sponges in the this class are marine, but the freshwater Family, **Spongillidae**, belongs here. The class contains approximately 90% of all extant poriferans. Only the leuconoid body is present. Example: *Ephydatia, Spongilla, Cliona* (boring sponge), *Spheciospongia* (loggerhead sponge), and *Spongia* (bath sponge).

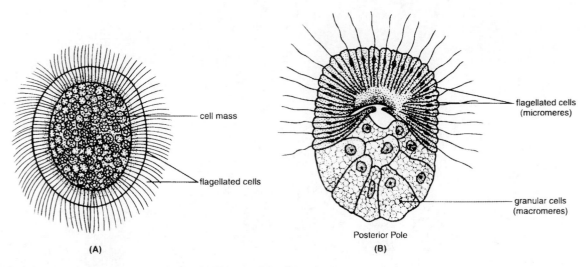

Figure 7. Parenchymella (A) and amphiblastula (B) larvae (After Hyman).

3. **Class Sclerospongiae.** Tropical to subtropical sponges usually found in cryptic habitats, and possessing massive or reticulate skeletons of calcium-carbonate with spicules of silica embedded within the matrix. Only the leuconoid body type is present. Examples are *Calcifibrospongia* and *Merlia*. Vacelet (1985) suggests that these few species (ca. 15) are members of the Calcarea and Demospongiae.

4. **Class Hexactinellida.** Deep-water marine sponges with siliceous six-pointed spicules and long siliceous fibers forming a fused lattice structure. Some glass sponges have a syconoid-like body type. A prominent example is *Euplectella* or Venus's flower basket. Because of their syncytial organization, it has been argued that hexacts should be a distinct phylum, Symplasma (Bergquist 1985).

Literature Cited

Bergquist, P.R. 1985. Poriferan relationships. *In:* S. Conway Morris, J.D. George, R. Gibson, and H.M. Platt (eds.), *The Origins and Relationships of Lower Invertebrates.* Systematics Association Spec. Volume 28, Clarendon Press, Oxford: 14-27.

Reiswig, H.M., and G.O. Mackie 1983. Studies on hexactinellid sponges. III. The taxonomic status of Hexactinellida within the Porifera. *Phil. Trans. R. Soc.* B301: 419-428.

Rützler, K., and G. Rieger, 1973. Sponge burrowing: fine structure of *Cliona lampa* penetrating calcareous substrata. *Mar. Biol.* 21: 144-162.

Vacelet, J. 1985. Coralline sponges and the evolution of Porifera. *In:* S. Conway Morris, J.D. George, R. Gibson, and H.M. Platt (eds.), *The Origins and Relationships of Lower Invertebrates.* Systematics Association Spec. Volume 28, Clarendon Press, Oxford 1-13.

Vacelet, J. and N. Boury-Esnault. 1995. Carnivorous sponges. *Nature* 373: 333-335.

■ Observational Procedure:

Caution: Please note that when you touch a sponge the tiny spicules may rub off on your hands. Therefore, never touch your eyes immediately after handling a sponge!

Class Calcarea

Leucosolenia. An Asconoid Sponge. Using a dissection microscope observe a preserved specimen of *Leucosolenia*. Keep the specimen immersed in fluid in a small shallow dish while making your observations. This small, marine sponge lives attached to rocks in the lower intertidal zone as a group of clustered, tubular structures in varying stages of growth (Fig. 2). The clusters result from budding. The body wall is quite thin and the surface has a rough texture due to spicules that project through the pinacoderm. Locate the osculum, flagellated chamber, and buds. Two types of spicules may be seen in *Leucosolenia*. Place a portion of a specimen on a glass slide, tease apart with dissection needles, and apply a small drop of bleach to the sponge. Cover the preparation with a coverslip and examine. The bleach will dissolve organic material and only spicules will remain, allowing identification of spicule types under high power (Fig. 3).

Return your microscope to low power and obtain a pair of polarizing filters. Notice how these filters stop all transmitted light when they are rotated 90° out of phase from one another. Rotate the filters so that light passes through them and place one filter above your spicule preparation (analyzer) and another on top of the light source of the microscope (polarizer). You probably will have to refocus the microscope. While observing the spicules, rotate the polarizer until it is out of phase with the analyzer. The background will be dark due to exclusion of light by the crossed filters, however, the spicules will appear to be bright. This phenomenon, called birefringence, occurs because CaCO3 spicules have two or more principal refractive indices and will rotate light themselves, thus permitting light to pass through the analyzer. What does this indicate about these spicules?

Sycon (=Scypha). A Syconoid Sponge. *Sycon* is also a marine sponge. Small buds occasionally appear at the base of mature specimens and may separate from the parent. Examine a specimen of *Sycon* using a dissection microscope and locate the osculum and the large monaxial spicules arranged around the opening as a collar (Fig. 4A). Also note that the surface is interrupted by numerous, small projections (Fig. 4B). These are the flagellated chambers (radial canals or choanocyte chambers). Using a sharp scalpel, bisect the animal along its longitudinal axis and carefully examine the spongocoel. The numerous, inner openings are **apopyles** that communicate with the choanocyte chambers.

Examine a prepared slide of a cross and/or longitudinal section of *Sycon* and with the aid of Fig. 4C identify the following structures: (1) pinacoderm, (2) choanocyte chambers, (3) choanocytes, (4) incurrent canal, (5) apopyle, (6) mesohyl, (7) spicules, (8) ostia, and (9) spongocoel. The prosopyles will be indistinct. Choanocytes will not be as neatly arranged as depicted in Fig. 4C. In a prepared cross section, note the arrangement of spicules within the sponge. Ova or embryos may be present in some preparations. How is Sycon more complex than *Leucosolenia*?

Make a spicule preparation of *Sycon* as described above and identify the spicule types seen (Fig. 3). Are the spicules of *Sycon* birefringent?

Class Demospongiae

Spongilla. A Leuconoid Sponge. Examine a preserved specimen of *Spongilla* under a dissection microscope. Remember to keep the specimen covered with fluid. You should see numerous spicules projecting through the pinacoderm. Obtain a prepared thin section of *Spongilla*

and observe the distribution of spicules in the sponge mass. Note the concentrations of spicules, called **fascicles**, that project through the pinacoderm (Fig. 8). The pinacoderm also should be visible. Choanocyte chambers are not located at the outer periphery of the sponge mass, but rather beneath the **subdermal cavity** (Fig. 8). The choanocytes are very small and it will require good observation to identify them. Compare the body form of *Spongilla* to the other species studied.

Observe a preserved specimen of *Spongilla* with gemmules. How large are these structures? Examine a prepared whole mount-slide of gemmules under high magnification, noting the tough spongin coat in which are embedded numerous spicules (Fig. 6). If live gemmules are available, your instructor will provide directions for observation of their hatching and subsequent early sponge development.

Make a preparation of *Spongilla* spicules as described above and identify the spicule types seen (Fig. 3). Are the siliceous spicules of *Spongilla* birefringent? Why does it make sense that these spicules, which are composed of silicon dioxide, have this response to the test for birefringence?

Bath Sponge. Although you may have used a natural bath sponge before, examine one this time with a critical eye. Note how light and flexible it is. Use a hand lens or dissection microscope to observe the minute, interwoven spongin fibers. This is all that remains after the tissues have decayed. Bath sponges are noted for the amount of water they can hold. Because the fibers themselves cannot imbibe significant amounts of water, how can a sponge hold water? To answer this question do the following simple exercise. Obtain a dry sponge and weigh it to the nearest tenth of a gram. Wet the sponge, wring it out, and reweigh it. How much water is the damp sponge capable of holding? Calculate how many milliliters of water are held per gram dry weight of sponge? Under a dissection microscope re-examine the spongin fibers and note the film of water that is held by capillary action between adjacent fibers.

Cliona. The Boring Sponge. Examine a mollusk shell that has been colonized by *Cliona*. What does this sponge have to do to colonize a shell composed of calcium carbonate? Are the holes regularly spaced throughout the shell? Are the holes all the same diameter? Observe a shell that has a broken edge permitting a view of the extensive network of cavities within it. What do the cavities and holes represent in terms of the biology of the sponge?

Compare several shells with various levels of damage. Are the number of holes perforating the inside of the shell equal to the number perforating the outside?

Phylum Porifera

Figure 8. A diagrammatic view of the cross section of a freshwater sponge (*Spongilla*) with a photomicrograph of the region of the subdermal cavity (Drawings after Pennak).

What might this indicate? Would you say that this sponge is parasitic? What do your observations indicate about the importance of *Cliona* in marine systems?

Class Hexactinellida

Euplectella. *Euplectella* (Venus's flower basket) is a marine glass sponge found in waters >200 m deep. Most people who have seen this sponge have viewed only the delicate skeleton. Extreme care should be taken when handling an unprotected specimen.

Observe the following aspects of general morphology (Fig. 9). The body of *Euplectella* is tubular and slightly curved. Internally, note the large spongocoel. Are remains of the commensal shrimp (*Spongicola*) present in the spongocoel of your specimen? Note that the osculum is

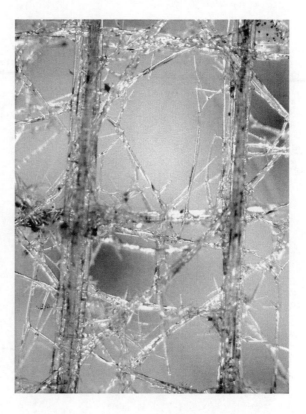

Figure 9. *Euplectella*, Venus's flower basket.

covered by a **sieve plate** of fused spicules that adds additional strength to the skeleton. Carefully examine the skeleton using a dissection microscope. Note that the skeletal framework of *Euplectella* is composed of spicules united by cross-bars of silica. Will these spicules be birefringent? Describe the shape and arrangement of spicules at the base of the sponge. Examine them using a dissection microscope. Is their surface smooth? What function might the basal spicules serve?

Other Specimens. Observe other specimens your instructor may provide. Compare the size, shape, and skeletal elements of these specimens to the others you studied in more detail. Determine whether their spicules are birefringent. If specimens of Class Sclerospongiae are available, compare their general structure to the other specimens examined in this exercise. ■

Fossil Forms

Many zoologists believe that sponges arose in the **Precambrian Era** from a group of protozoans similar to the modern choanoflagellates (Fig. 1). By the **Cambrian Period**, sponges had developed an extensive fauna.

However, in spite of their auspicious start these colonial organisms are unique and difficult to relate to other phyla.

■ Observational Procedure:

Because of the delicate nature of poriferan tissue, sponges do not preserve well and most fossil sponges are not easily recognizable. However, Cliona is easily recognizable as a fossil and fossil mollusk shells are often found riddled with cavities similar to those produced by this genus in modern shells. Compare fossil and modern shells that have been colonized by Cliona. Are there any significant differences?

Another interesting fossil organism is the sponge-like phylum **Archaeocyatha**. This group of pore-bearing organisms was unlike other sponges. **Stromatoporoids**, classified by some as colonies of fossil cyanobacteria (bluegreen algae) or cnidarians, may be another extinct sponge-like group. Examine specimens of archaeocyathids and other fossil sponges (Fig. 10). What evidence do you see in these specimens that would lead you to conclude that they are really sponges? ■

Figure 10. Examples of fossil sponges. An archaeocyathid with section cut away to view internal walls (After Moret, from Bergquist); *Astraeospongia* and *Astylospongia*, Silurian sponges; *Girtycoelia* showing repeating chambers, Pennsylvanian sponge.

Porifera	Worksheet 2
Name: _____	Date: _____
Course #: _____ / Section #: _____	Grade: _____

1. Explore the idea that a single sieve (e.g., a colander) is not an adequate model to explain the structure and function of a sponge.

2. Compare the complexity of *Leucosolenia* and *Sycon*.

3. Why use bleach and not an acid (e.g., HCl) to dissolve the sponge's organic material when you make a spicule preparation of *Leucosolenia* and *Sycon*?

4. Consider the siliceous spicules of the freshwater sponge *Spongilla* and the chemical composition of the stuff we call glass. Evaluating your own experience with polarizing sunglasses, explain why it stands to reason that the spicules of *Spongilla* are not birefringent.

5. How does *Cliona* colonize a shell composed of calcium carbonate?

THE RADIATA

The Eumetazoa is divided into two groups, one with radial symmetry called the **Radiata** and one with bilateral symmetry called the **Bilateria**. Radiata includes the Phyla Cnidaria (Coelenterata) and Ctenophora. These phyla have well-developed tissues that have the beginnings of organ functions, but they have not developed well-defined organs systems. The radiate body consists of a body wall composed of an outer epidermis, an inner gastrodermis, and a thin to thick gelatinous layer between called the mesoglea. The latter may be a noncellular, gelatinous matrix or possess amoebocytes, connective tissues, and muscle cells. The body cavity (gastrovascular cavity or coelenteron) ranges from a simple sac in the lower Cnidaria to a complex canal system in the Ctenophora, with pharynx, stomach, and other canals. In Cnidaria, the body cavity opens to the exterior through only a mouth, while in the Ctenophora both a mouth and anal pores are present.

Briggs, D. E. G., D. H. Erwin, F. J. Collier, and C. Clark, 1994. *The Fossils of The Burgess Shale.* Smithsonian Institution Press, Washington.

Harrison, F. W., and J. A. Westfall (eds.). 1991. Placozoa, Porifera, Cnidaria, and Ctenophora, vol. 2: *Microscopic Anatomy of Invertebrates.* Wiley-Liss, New York.

Muscatine, L., and H. M. Lenoff (eds.) 1974. *Coelenterate Biology.* Academic Press, New York.

Phylum Cnidaria (Coelenterata)

Hydras, jellyfishes, anemones, and corals are members of the phylum Cnidaria [ni-DAR-e-a; G., *cnide*, nettle] or Coelenterata [se-LEN-ter-a-ta; G., *koilos*, hollow + G., *enteron*, gut]. With the exception of freshwater hydras and a few jellyfishes, the approximately 9,000 species of cnidarians are marine. These carnivorous, tentaculate, multicellular animals represent the tissue level of organization; that is, organs or organ systems are lacking. This ancient phylum (Fig. 1) contains some of the most beautiful, interesting, and perhaps most dangerous of all marine invertebrates. The sea wasp (*Chironex fleckeri*), a cubomedusa of the Indo-Pacific waters, may be the most venomous invertebrate. Human fatalities have been reported from the noxious stings of this animal. The Portuguese man-of-war (*Physalia*) is less dangerous, but often becomes a nuisance when currents carry large numbers into shallow waters.

Cnidarians possess stinging organelles called **nematocysts**, the most distinguishing feature of the phylum. Each nematocyst arises from a specialized cell, the **cnidocyte** (Fig. 2A, B). Unlike sponges, cnidarians have two basic metazoan features, a **mouth** and a **gastrovascular cavity** (coelenteron or enteron) (Fig. 3). There is no anus and all materials enter and exit via the mouth. The gastrovascular cavity is a large, internal space for digestion and distribution of nutrients and other materials.

Two basic types of body forms are found in cnidarians: (1) **polyp** (**hydroid**) and (2) **medusa** (**jellyfish**). Both forms are saclike and contain a gastrovascular cavity (Fig. 3). The sessile polyp is tubular with a mouth in the **hypostome** at the distal end that is usually surrounded by tentacles. The medusa is typically free-swimming and umbrella-shaped, with tentacles extending from the outer margin of the bell. The mouth is located at the end of the **manubrium**, which hangs from the center of the subumbrellar surface somewhat like a clapper hanging from a bell. The manubrium is comparable to the hypostome of the polyp. Both the polyp and medusa are composed of the same body layers and are radially symmetrical. The medusa possesses a much thicker mesoglea than does the polyp.

Two types of medusae are found in cnidarians based upon presence (**craspedote** medusa) or absence (**acraspedote** medusa) of the **velum**, an inward projecting membrane around the margin of the bell. Rhythmic contractions of the velar musculature propel the jellyfish through the water.

The cnidarian body (polyp and medusa) is composed of three layers: (1) an outer, protective dermal epithelium (epidermis); (2) a middle mesoglea; and (3) an inner gastrodermis (endoderm) that serves in digestion and absorption. The mesoglea varies from a thin, noncellular layer to a thick, fibrous jelly-like mass with or without wandering amoebocytes. Some authors prefer the term **mesolamella** for the middle layer when it is thin and noncellular and the term **collenchyma** when the mesoglea is cellular. Regardless, the mesoglea is derived from both the epidermis and gastrodermis.

Polymorphism [G., *poly*, many + G., *morph*, shape] is common in cnidarians and is often associated with their colonial existence. Various zooids function in food procurement, reproduction, defense, or protection of the colony. A large vocabulary has been developed to describe the structure and function of zooids.

From *Invertebrate Zoology*, Sixth Edition, Robert L. Wallace and Walter K. Taylor. Copyright © 2002 by Pearson Education, Inc. Published by Prentice-Hall, Inc. All rights reserved

Phylum Cnidaria (Coelenterata)

TIME (IN MILLIONS OF YEARS)

	570	500	425	395	345	310	265	220	180	125	65	3	
Precambrian		Paleozoic							Mesozoic			Cenozoic		ERAS
	Cambrian	Ordovician	Silurian	Devonian	Missis-sippian	Penn-sylvanian	Permian	Triassic	Jurassic	Cretaceous	Tertiary	Q	PERIODS
													PHYLUM HISTORY

Q = Quaternary

Figure 1 Geological history of the phylum Cnidaria.

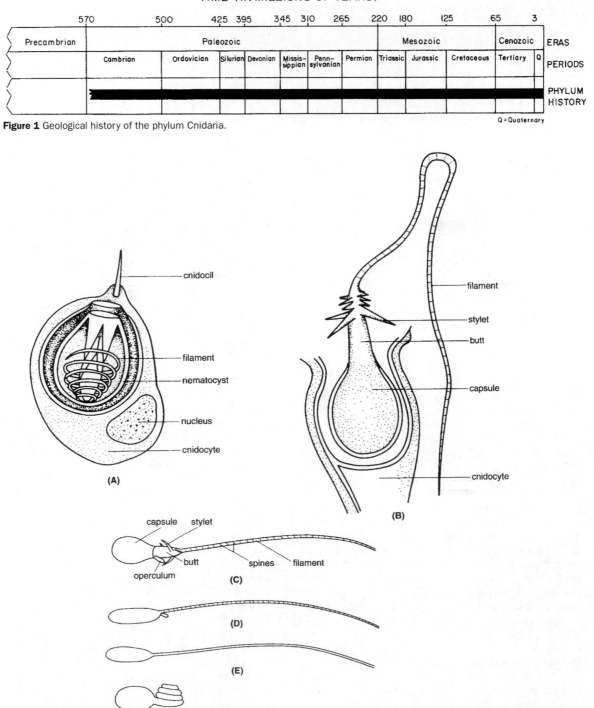

Figure 2 Cnidarian nematocysts: (A) undischarged, (B) discharged, (C) penetrant (stenotele), (D) streptoline glutinant (holotrichous isorhiza), (E) stereoline glutinant (atrichous isorhiza), and (F) volvent (desmoneme).

48

Phylum Cnidaria (Coelenterata)

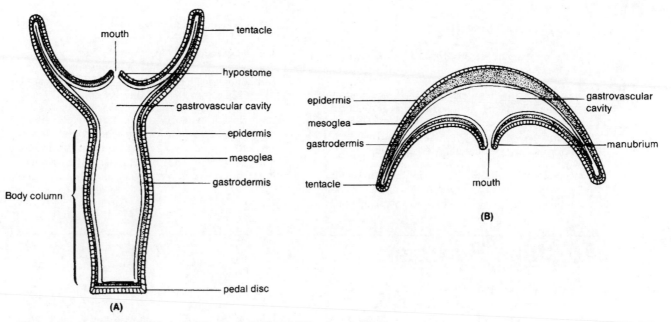

Figure 3 Two body forms of cnidarians: (A) polyp (hydroid) and (B) medusa (jellyfish).

Cnidarians are monoecious or dioecious. Reproduction is both asexual and sexual. Asexual budding or fission is generally associated with the polyp form, whereas sexual reproduction occurs in the medusa and in some polyps (e.g., *Hydra*). In the life cycle of many cnidarians, asexual reproduction in the polyp alternates with sexual reproduction in the medusa, a phenomenon termed **alternation of generations** or **metagenesis** [G., *meta*, back again + G., *genesis*, origin].

Sexual reproduction typically produces a free-swimming, ciliated larva called the **planula** (Fig. 8E). This nonfeeding, radially symmetrical larva is composed of a ciliated epidermis, mesoglea, and gastrodermis. It swims about for a time and then settles on a substrate and metamorphoses into a new individual or colony.

Classification

The phylum Cnidaria is divided into four classes.

1. **Class Hydrozoa.** Cnidarians whose life cycle includes polyp or medusa, or both. Medusa with velum. Mesoglea is noncellular. Gonads are epidermal. Both marine and freshwater forms are known. Seven orders are recognized, but only three are examined here.

    a. **Hydroida.** Polyp stage dominant. Medusa present or absent. Solitary and colonial. Examples: *Craspedacusta* (freshwater jellyfish), *Gonionemus*, *Tubularia*, *Clava*, *Halocordyle* (= *Pennaria*), *Hydractinia*, *Polyorchis*, freshwater hydras, *Obelia*, *Campanularia*, and *Plumularia*.

    b. **Chondrophora.** Polymorphic, pelagic, and polypoid colonies. Multichambered pneumatophore. Examples: *Velella* and *Porpita*.

    c. **Siphonophora.** Polymorphic, pelagic, and polypoid and medusoid individuals. Pneumatophore not multichambered. Colonies with float or swimming bells. Examples: *Physalia* (Portuguese man-of-war) and *Stephalia*.

    d. **Stylasterina.** Colonial polypoids with calcium carbonate skeletons. Examples: *Allopora* and *Stylaster*. The stinging or fire coral, *Millepora*, sometimes placed in Order Hydrocorallina or within its own Order Milleporina.

2. **Class Scyphozoa.** Cnidarians with the medusa stage dominant. No velum. Mesoglea is cellular. Gonads are gastrodermal. All species are marine. Four orders are recognized, but only two are examined here.

    a. **Semaeostomae.** Medusae bowl- or saucer-shaped with scalloped margins. Rhopalia present. Oral tentacles extend from manubrium. Examples: *Aurelia*, *Cyanea*, and *Pelagia*.

    b. **Rhizostomae.** Tentacles lacking around the bell. Oral arms of manubrium branched and fused. Filter feeders. Examples: *Cassiopeia*, *Stomalophus*, and *Rhizostoma*.

3. Class Cubozoa. (Cubomedusae). Medusa having a cuboidal shape with unscalloped margins, four rhopalia, and velum. Examples: *Chironex* and *Carybdea*. Not examined here.

4. Class Anthozoa. Cnidarians with the medusa absent. The mesoglea is cellular. Gonads are endodermal. The gastrovascular cavity is partitioned by septa (mesenteries). All marine with both solitary or colonial forms. Two subclasses are recognized.

   a. Subclass Zoantharia (Hexacorallia). Polyps with more than eight paired mesenteries. Unbranched tentacles. Solitary or colonial. Sea anemones (polyps without a hard skeleton). Examples: *Metridium*, *Calliactis*, *Cerianthus*, and *Ceriantheopsis*. Two orders of hard or stony corals (solitary or colonial polyps with calcareous skeletons and without siphonoglyphs). Examples: *Astrangia* (eyed coral), *Porites*, and *Acropora* (staghorn coral).

   b. Subclass Alcyonaria (Octocorallia). Polyps with eight pinnate tentacles and eight complete, unpaired mesenteries. Mostly colonial. Examples: *Tubipora* (organ pipe coral), *Clavularia*, *Gorgonia* (sea fan), *Leptogorgia* (sea whip), *Stylatula* (sea pen), and *Renilla* (sea pansy).

A. Class Hydrozoa

The simpler cnidarians belong to Class Hydrozoa [hydro-ZO-a; G., *hydra*, water serpent + G., *zoon*, animal]. Seven representatives of the class are described in the following exercises. One or more of these may be omitted from your study to conserve time.

Hydra

Hydras are cosmopolitan inhabitants of freshwaters, often attached to the underside of plants and twigs in the water. Three common North American species are *Hydra littoralis*, *H. oligactis* (= *H. fusca* and *Pelmatohydra oligactis*), and *H. viridis* (= *Chlorohydra viridissima*). The green color of *H. viridis* is due to numbers of the symbiotic alga, **zoochlorella** (*Chlorella*), living within its gastrodermis. The description below will apply to any of these three hydras.

Hydras are small animals (0.3–5 cm long) with four major body regions: (1) **hypostome**, (2) **tentacles**, (3) **body column**, and (4) **pedal disc** (Fig. 4). The hypostome, a conical elevation of cells at the distal end, surrounds the mouth opening. Numerous mucus-secreting gland cells in the gastrodermis of the hypostome aid the hydra in swallowing food such as water fleas (*Daphnia*), cyclops (*Cyclops*), small annelids, and insect larvae. When the mouth is closed and at rest, it is stellate-shaped, but can be greatly distended when food is swallowed.

The hypostome is surrounded by 4–10 tentacles. Tentacles are hollow and can be extended more than twice the length of the body column. Numerous clumps or batteries of cnidocytes with nematocysts inside impart a bumpy appearance to the outer surface of each tentacle. Four kinds of nematocysts occur in hydra (Fig. 2): **penetrants**, **streptoline** and **stereoline glutinants**, and **volvents**.

The main part of a hydra is the body column, a cylindrical tube that can be greatly expanded or contracted. In *H. oligactis* the column can be divided into a large gastric region and a proximal, narrow, light-colored stalk (**peduncle**). The gastrodermis of the gastric region contains flagellated epithelionutritive cells and enzyme-secreting gland cells. Most digestion occurs in this region. The gastrodermis of the stalk is composed of vacuolated cells that do not produce enzymes. In *Hydra*, but not all hydrozoans, the gastrovascular cavity extends into the tentacles. Because the cavity is filled with water, it serves as a **hydrostatic skeleton** as well as in digestion and circulation.

The base of the pedal disc forms the proximal (or aboral) end of the body. Tall epidermal cells of the disc secrete a sticky mucus for attachment and form a gas bubble that allows the animal to float.

■ Observational Procedure: *Hydra*

Living Organism. A small dish containing hydras will be provided. Examine the specimen with a dissection microscope. A hydra in the extended state may reach 5 cm in length. Locate the tentacles, hypostome, body column, and basal disc (Fig. 4). Count the number of tentacles on your specimen. Can you see the mouth? Offer the hydra a small prey (e.g., microcrustacean) and observe prey capture. If your hydra has a lateral growth from the body, it is most likely an asexual **bud**.

Observe your specimen extending and contracting. Do the tentacles extend and contract at the same time? If disturbed, the organism will contract and remain in a nonextended state for several minutes. When contracted, a hydra resembles a jelly-like ball.

Phylum Cnidaria (Coelenterata)

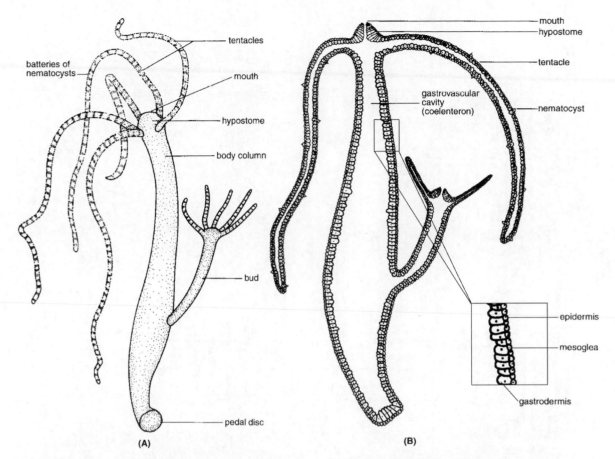

Figure 4 *Hydra.* (A) *Hydra* with a bud showing the gross external features. (B) Longitudinal section of *Hydra.*

Microscopic Study

1. With a pipette, carefully remove a hydra from the dish and place it in a depression slide, adding a drop of pond water if needed. Your instructor will provide some hints on how this may be done without damaging the specimen. Cover the preparation with a cover slip and observe under low power of the compound microscope.

2. Locate the central, light-colored gastrovascular cavity and trace the cavity as it extends into the tentacles.

3. Compare the external morphology of the tentacles with that of the body column. Locate the batteries of cnidocytes along the tentacles. Can you determine whether the cnidocytes are more numerous on the tentacles than on the body column? Are any cnidocytes located on the pedal disc? Why does this distribution make sense?

4. Place a small drop of weak acetic acid or methylene blue near the edge of the cover slip and observe what happens to the cnidocytes when the solution contacts the specimen. Can you see discharged nematocysts? Carefully focus on the nematocysts using high power and attempt to identify the different types by referring to Fig. 2.

5. Examine prepared longitudinal and cross sections of a hydra under high power of the compound microscope. Locate the three body layers: outer **epidermis**, middle **mesoglea** (mesolamella), and inner **gastrodermis** (Figs. 4 and 5). The mesoglea appears as a line wedged between the epidermis and gastrodermis. The noncellular mesoglea is secreted by both epidermis and gastrodermis; it is thinnest in the tentacles and thickest in the body column.

Study the cell types and their distribution in the epidermis and gastrodermis by examining the slide preparations under oil immersion. *If you have never used oil immersion optics before, ask your instructor for help.* With the description below and using Fig. 5 as a guide, locate the following cells and understand their functions.

Phylum Cnidaria (Coelenterata)

Figure 5 *Hydra*. (A) *Hydra* cross section. (B) Section of body wall in the region of the hypostome. (C) Section of the digestive region. (D) Section of the stalk region. (E) Section of the pedal disc. (F) Epitheliomuscular cell. (Figures B–F are after Hyman.)

Phylum Cnidaria (Coelenterata)

a. **Epitheliomuscular cells.** Most of the epidermis is composed of these cuboidal to columnar-shaped cells. The basal region is expanded longitudinally and contains contractile fibers. When contracted these fibers shorten the animal; therefore, they function as longitudinal muscles. These cells also support and provide protection for the body.

b. **Cnidocytes.** These cells contain nematocysts. They occur in groups or batteries and are most abundant on the tentacles. A few cnidocytes occur in the stalk of *H. oligactis*, but are rare in the pedal disc. None occur in the gastrodermis.

c. **Interstitial cells.** These **I-cells**, as they are often called, are found primarily in the epidermis of the gastric region, wedged between epitheliomuscular cells. I-cells occur singly or in clusters (**nests**) and have dark-stained nuclei. These cells are precursors or stem cells of all other cell types in hydras.

d. **Epithelionutritive (nutritive** or **nutritive-muscular) cells.** These tall, columnar digestive cells with food vacuoles make up most of the gastrodermis. Like their counterparts in the epidermis (i.e., epitheliomuscular cells), the base of each nutritive cell is elongated and contains contractile fibers. The fibers are oriented circularly at right angles to those of the epitheliomuscular cells. Contraction of the nutritive cells elongates the hydra and reduces the size of its gastrovascular cavity. Unlike the epitheliomuscular cells, epithelionutritive cells bear two flagella that extend into the gastrovascular cavity.

e. **Gland cells.** These large, vacuolated cells secrete digestive enzymes and mucus. They are commonly found in the gastrodermis and hypostome.

f. **Neurons and sensory cells.** These form the nerve net plexus of both epidermis and gastrodermis. They will be difficult to see.

g. **Mucous gland cells.** These tall epidermal cells do not produce enzymes. The cells are especially abundant in the pedal disc and hypostome. Those in the pedal disc produce mucus for attachment.

Reproduction. Asexual (budding) and sexual reproduction occur in hydras. Dividing epitheliomuscular and nutritive cells in the stalk initiate budding. The young polyp or bud grows until it detaches from the parent hydra in 2 to 4 days. Observe budding in living hydras or from prepared slides (Fig. 4). What is the general shape of the bud; is it identical to the parent?

Most species of *Hydra* are dioecious. The ovary and testis arise from aggregated interstitial cells in the epidermis. Unlike most cnidarians, hydras lack a medusa and a planula larva.

Examine living hydra or prepared slides (whole mounts and cross sections) showing the testis and ovary. Distinguish between the two reproductive structures. Are

Figure 6 Monopodial (A) and sympodial (B) growth patterns (diagrammatic). Age of the polyps indicated by relative size and numbers with the original polyp numbered 1.

the testis and ovary true organs such as found in higher animals? To be organs, what would these structures need to possess? ■

Pennaria

Pennaria is a colonial, shallow-water, marine hydroid that forms a minute plantlike growth on pilings, rocks, and seaweed. The pinnate colony, which may reach 15 cm in height, is attached to the surface of objects by hollow, rootlike **hydrorhiza** (stolons or rhizomes). Stemlike structures called **hydrocauli** grow upright from the hydrorhiza. The hydrocaulus buds off alternating side branches called **hydrocladia** from which are budded the terminal feeding polyps called **hydranths** (gastrozooids). The type of growth in *Pennaria* is **monopodial** because the original or primary hydrocaulus elongates throughout the colony's life. Therefore, the oldest polyp occupies the tip of the original hydrocaulus (Fig. 6A).

■ Observational Procedure: *Pennaria*

1. Obtain specimens of a preserved or living colony and prepared slides (whole mounts and cross sections) for study. Using dissection and compound microscopes, confirm that the growth of *Pennaria* is monopodial and not sympodial (Fig. 6).

2. Locate a hydranth and observe the large, conical-shaped hypostome containing the mouth (Fig. 7). Note the **capitate tentacles** on the hypostome and the ring

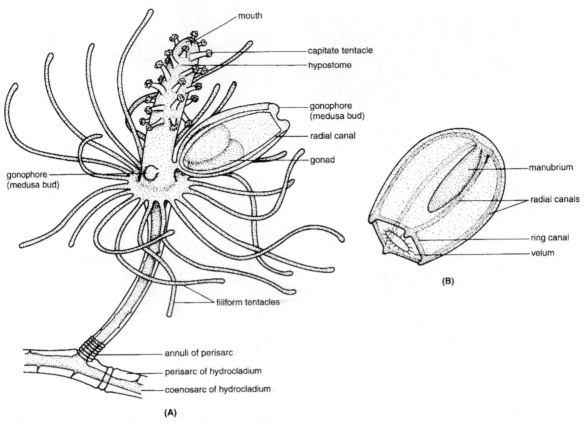

Figure 7 *Pennaria.* (A) Enlarged hydranth with medusa bud. (B) Medusa.

of **filiform tentacles** that circles the base of the gastral region. Examine both types of tentacles for cnidocytes. Are they uniformly distributed? How might this distribution be effective in prey capture?

3. Find the **coenosarc**, a living hollow tube that extends throughout all branches of the colony (Fig. 7). The coenosarc consists of an outer epidermis, a middle mesoglea (mesolamella), and an inner flagellated gastrodermis that lines the gastrovascular cavity. The cavity is continuous throughout the colony, at the base of the hydranth it enlarges as a type of stomach region. The epidermis of the coenosarc of the hydrocaulus and hydrocladium secretes an outer, protective chitinous covering, the **perisarc** (periderm).

4. In *Pennaria*, the perisarc adheres closely to the outer surface of the colony and is annulated at the base of each stem. What function(s) might these annulations serve? Carefully trace the extent of the perisarc; does it cover the entire polyp? *Pennaria* is an **athecate** (**gymnoblastic**) hydrozoan because the hydranths and gonophores (medusa buds) lack the perisarc covering.

5. Locate the small, thimble-shaped gonophores that arise by budding off the hydranth just distal to the filiform tentacles. The medusa lacks a mouth, but has a velum and four short tentacles (Fig. 7). *Pennaria* medusa are dioecious. ■

Obelia

Obelia is another colonial marine hydroid that forms a minute plantlike growth on rocks, pilings, and other substrates. *Obelia* is similar to *Pennaria* in a number of ways; however, there are important differences between the two hydrozoans.

■ Observational Procedure: *Obelia*

1. Obtain preserved or living specimens of the *Obelia* colony for study using dissection and compound microscopes. Determine the growth form of *Obelia*; is it monopodial or sympodial (Fig. 6)? Can you distinguish the youngest polyps from the oldest ones in the colony?

Phylum Cnidaria (Coelenterata)

Figure 8 *Obelia.* (A) Entire colony, (B) Longitudinal section of hydranth. (C) Single gonangium. (D) Oral view of medusa. (E) Planula larva.

2. Locate the two kinds of polyps occurring on the *Obelia* colony: **hydranth** (**gastrozooid**) and **gonangium** (**gonozooid**) (Fig. 8). Both polyps are supported by upright, stemlike, branched hydrocauli and rootlike hydrorhiza attached to a substrate. Where are the two polyp types located in the colony?

3. Observe that the entire colony is covered with a nonliving, chitinous perisarc. The perisarc covering each hydranth is bell-shaped and called the hydrotheca, whereas the perisarc of the gonangium is the gonotheca. Because the perisarc extends onto the polyps, *Obelia* is a **thecate** (calyptoblastic) hydroid, unlike *Pennaria* which is **athecate** (gymnoblastic). The perisarc of the hydrocauli is annulate at various places. Like *Pennaria*, the living coenosarc consists of epidermis, mesoglea, and gastrodermis; the hollow gastrovascular cavity is continuous throughout the colony.

4. Examine a hydranth (feeding polyp) and locate its hypostome that bears the mouth. The filiform tentacles of *Obelia* are solid and provided with cnidocytes. The tentacles can be retracted into the hydrotheca. Note that the tentacle arrangement in *Obelia* is different from that of *Pennaria* and that capitate tentacles are absent. How are the cnidocytes distributed on the tentacles in a polyp of *Obelia*?

5. Study prepared cross and longitudinal sections of *Obelia* made in the regions of the hypostome and hydrocaulus. How do these sections differ with comparable regions of hydras?

6. Examine a **gonangium** or reproductive polyp. Note that it lacks tentacles, a mouth, and hypostome. Observe the asexually produced discoid medusa buds (**gonophores**) on the club-shaped **blastostyle** of the gonangium. The blastostyle is a modified polyp and represents a continuation of the coenosarc into the gonangium. The medusa, termed a **leptomedusa**, escapes into the water from the blastostyle via the gonopore at the terminal end of the gonangium. A pelagic existence occurs before the medusa reaches sexual maturity.

7. Observe a prepared slide of a medusa of *Obelia* (Figs. 8D and 9). Note its bell or umbrella shape. The upper, convex surface is the **exumbrella** and the lower, concave surface is the **subumbrella**. The **manubrium**, comparable to the hypostome of the hydranth, hangs down from the center of the subumbrella surface. Locate the mouth in the manubrium.

8. Observe the solid tentacles around the bell's margin. Count the tentacles. Does each hydranth have the same number of tentacles? How are the cnidocytes distributed on the tentacles in a medusa of *Obelia*?

9. Locate the four **radial canals** and four **gonads** attached to them. Radial canals meet the **ring canal** that encircles the margin of the bell. Eight **statocysts** are located on the margin of the bell in the interradial areas. The gastrovascular cavity of the medusa is lined with gastrodermal cells. The cavity includes the spaces of the manubrium, radial canals, and the ring canal. *Obelia*'s medusa (Fig. 9) is atypical, compared to most hydromedusa such as *Gonionemus* because a velum is lacking (Fig. 11).

10. Locate the four gonads of the animal. Medusa of *Obelia* are dioecious. Gametes are fertilized in the water and the zygote develops into a planula larva which settles onto a substrate and metamorphoses into a sessile colony. *Obelia* is a good example for understanding metagenesis, the alternation of asexual and sexual reproduction (Fig. 8). ■

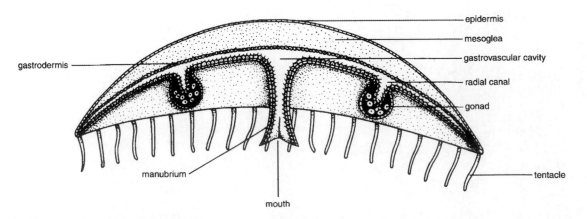

Figure 9 Oral-aboral section of *Obelia* medusa.

epidermis

mesoglea

gastrovascular cavity

radial canal

gonad

gastrodermis

tentacle

manubrium

mouth

Plumularia

Plumularia is a marine, calyptoblastic colonial hydroid with creeping hydrorhiza. Arising from the hydrorhiza are hydrocauli with attached plumelike branches (hydrocladia), each bearing on one side a series of bell-shaped hydrothecae containing the gastrozooids. The sessile hydrotheca is so small that the gastrozooid with its filiform tentacles cannot be retracted within the encasement.

■ Observational Procedure: *Plumularia*

Examine a prepared slide or preserved or living specimen of *Plumularia* (Fig. 10). Note the small dactylozooids called **nematophores** (sarcostyles) that are characteristic of *Plumularia* and its relatives. Nematophores arise from tiny thecae, the **nematothecae**, located on the hydrocaulus and on the hydrotheca of the gastrozooid. There are usually three nematophores to each gastrozooid. The nematophores are protective polyps. They have both cnidocytes and a long amoeboid process that engulfs polyps, diatoms, protozoa, and larval stages of epizoic organisms. Gonangia extend from the hydrocaulus at the point where each hydrocladium arises. No special modifications for the gonotheca exist in *Plumularia*. Compare the colony of *Plumularia* with that of *Obelia* and *Pennaria*. Can you determine the growth pattern of *Plumularia*? ■

Gonionemus

Gonionemus, containing several species, is a marine hydrozoan commonly found in shallow water attached to seaweed. The small (2 cm) medusa is the dominant stage, whereas the athecate polyp is only about 1 mm in length. The solitary polyp with its four, solid tentacles resembles a small hydra. Nonciliated, planula-like bodies called **frustules** bud from the polyp and grow into additional solitary polyps. Seasonally, medusa buds (gonophores) are formed on the column of the polyp; the buds grow into medusae.

Gonionemus is dioecious. Gametes from the gonads, which are attached to the radial canals, are shed in the water where they unite. The zygote develops into a planula larva which settles onto a substrate and grows into the small polyp.

■ Observational Procedure: *Gonionemus*

Study a medusa of Gonionemus in a small dish with water using the dissection microscope. Locate the following structures: (1) exumbrella, (2) subumbrella, (3) velum, (4) short manubrium with its four frilled lobes, (5) tentacles, (6) four radial canals with their ruffled gonads, and (7) the ring canal around the margin of the bell (Fig. 11). Can you find the mouth in the manubrium? Count the number of hollow tentacles around the bell's margin. Closely examine a tentacle, noting that the

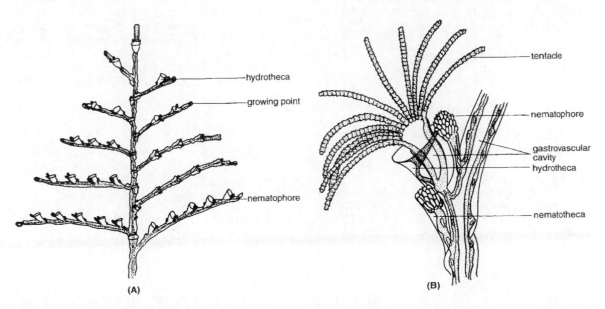

(A)

(B)

Figure 10 (A) Colony of *Plumularia* showing monopodial growth. (B) Hydranth of *Plumularia* showing two of three nematophores.

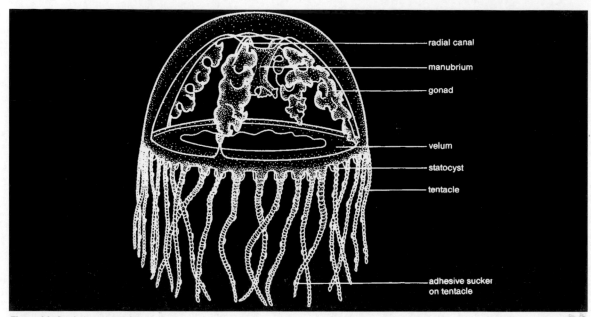

Figure 11 *Gonionemus* medusa.

cnidocytes with their nematocysts are arranged in a ring-like fashion (batteries) around the tentacles. Can you see the adhesive sucker near the distal end of each tentacle? What function might the sucker serve? At the base of each tentacle is a prominent sensory swelling called a tentacular bulb. Between the bulbs are balancing structures called statocysts. ■

Craspedacusta

Craspedacusta sowerbyi is a freshwater hydrozoan whose medusa is the dominant form (Fig. 12). The athecate, solitary polyp is very small (2 mm) and lacks tentacles.

■ Observational Procedure: *Craspedacusta*

Examine a medusa of *Craspedacusta* in a small dish with water using the dissection microscope. Compare the anatomy of the medusa to that of *Gonionemus*. How are these two organisms similar? Do you see any differences? If available, compare the polyp of *Craspedacusta* to a hydra. ■

Siphonophora

Members of the Order Siphonophora, such as the Portuguese man-of-war *(Physalia)*, are perhaps the most complex and specialized of hydrozoans. These pelagic, colonial marine animals attain the maximum development of polymorphism found in cnidarians.

The siphonophore colony originates from a planula larva. The colony consists of both modified medusoid and polypoid individuals (zooids) specialized to perform different functions. The polypoid individuals are modified for feeding, capturing prey, and producing the reproductive zooids. The medusoid individuals are concerned with locomotion, flotation, and reproduction. The different types of zooids that may occur in siphonophores are listed below.

1. Polypoid zooids

a. **Gastrozooid (trophozooid).** A feeding polyp with a mouth and one long, contractile, hollow tentacle with cnidocytes. The tentacle originates near the base of the polyp.

b. **Dactylozooid (palpon).** This tactile polypoid resembles a gastrozooid in having a long tentacle, but a mouth is lacking. The tentacle is never branched.

c. **Gonozooid.** This reproductive polyp lacks a tentacle. A mouth may be present as in *Velella*. A gonozoid usually bears several gonophores (see below).

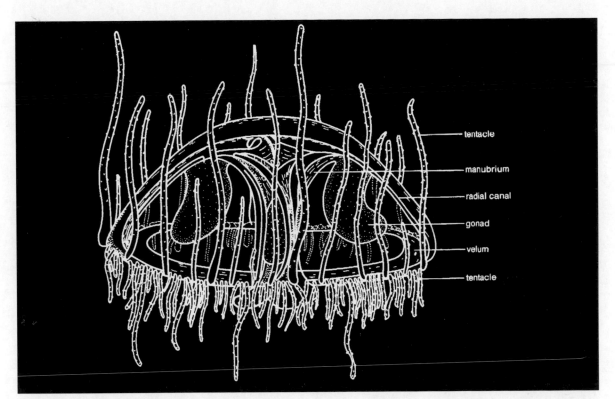

Figure 12 *Craspedacusta* medusa.

2. Medusoid zooids

    a. Nectophore (swimming bell). This modified, very muscular medusa is used for flotation. The nectophore has a bell, velum, four radial canals, and a ring canal. It lacks a mouth, manubrium, tentacles, and sense organs.

    b. Phyllozooid (bract). This leaflike zooid bears cnidocytes for protection.

    c. Gonophore. This medusoid occurs on gonozooids or branched stalks called **gonodendra**. Gonophores lack a mouth, tentacles, and sense organs. They have a bell, velum, manubrium, and radial canals. Gonophores occur singly or in grape-like clusters. Some are saclike such as the sporosacs of some hydroids. Gonophores are dioecious even though the colony is monoecious. Female gonophores are medusoid and may swim free; male gonophores are reduced.

    d. Pneumatophore. This is a float that may or may not have a pore to regulate the gas it contains.

Some workers believe that the pneumatophore is a modified polyp instead of a medusa.

Physalia. The bluish pneumatophore of *Physalia* is derived from an aboral evagination from the planula larva. The float is highly muscular, double-walled, lacks mesoglea, and lined with a chitinous epidermal secretion. The float has its greatest development in *Physalia* where it is an ovate bladder 30 cm in length. On the floor inside the pneumatophore is a modified glandular epithelium called the **gas gland** that produces gas (mainly nitrogen and carbon dioxide) contained inside the float. *Physalia*, unlike some species, lacks a pore to regulate the amount of gas within the float. Attached to the pneumatophore is an erectile, sail-like **crest** that can be lowered and raised. In the living organism the crest is blue bordered with pink.

The various zooids of *Physalia* are budded from a ventral disc area beneath the pneumatophore. The gastrovascular cavity and the coenosarc of the zooids and pneumatophore are continuous. Each group of zooids extending from the disc beneath the float is called a **cormidium**. *Physalia* possesses several cormidia, each

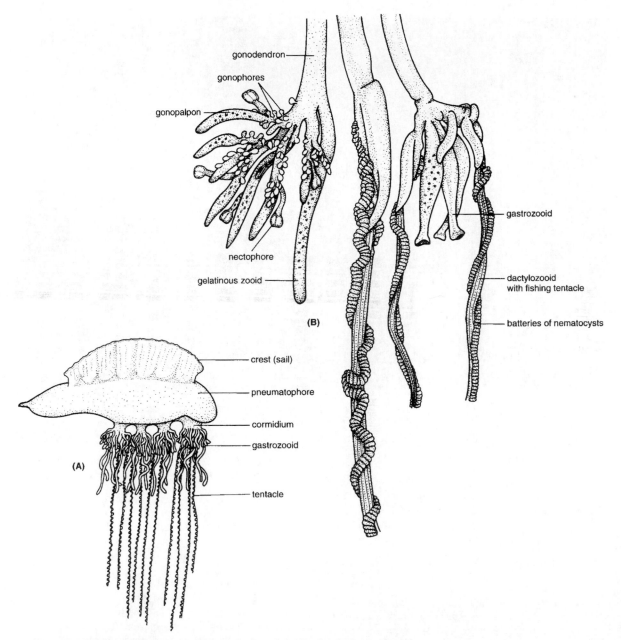

Figure 13 *Physalia.* (A) Entire colony. (B) Portion of a colony showing the types of zooids.

consisting of a gastrozooid, male and female gonozooids, and one dactylozooid with an extremely long tentacle (10 m). The dactylozooids from several cormidia form a suspended driftlike net. Contact with the tentacles results in discharge of the nematocysts. The tentacles contract and pull the prey to the gastrozooids.

■ Observational Procedure: *Physalia*

In a dish containing water, carefully examine the specimen provided. Locate the pneumatophore, crest, and gas gland (Fig. 13). The latter may be observed within

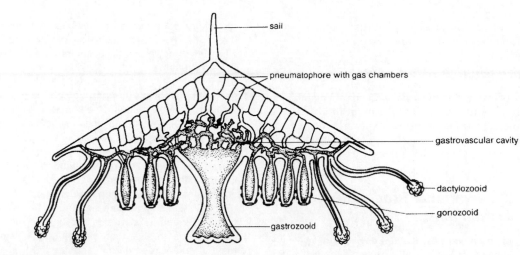

Figure 14 *Velella* colony.

the floor of the pneumatophore by holding the pneumatophore up to a bright light. Study one cormidium and identify the gastrozooid, with its mouth and long tentacle; the gonozooid, with small, grapelike, sessile gonophores; and the dactylozooid, with its long tentacle. The stem-like, branched structure bearing the gonozooid is called a **gonodendron**. A gonodendron may bear **gonopalpons** (modified dactylozooids lacking a mouth), **gelatinous zooids**, and **nectophores** (modified medusae). Each nectophore consists of a bell, velum, four radial canals, and a ring canal, but it lacks a mouth, manubrium, tentacles, and sense organs. ■

Velella. *Velella*, commonly called By-the-Wind Sailor, is a pelagic, polymorphic chondrophoran. The ovoid body is flattened with the pneumatophore on the aboral surface as a chitinous disc (Fig. 14). Arising from the aboral surface of the pneumatophore is a thin, chitinous, triangular **sail**. The living organism is bluish in color and the sail is edged with purple. *Velella* lacks control over the sail and is at the mercy of the ocean currents for movement.

Beneath the pneumatophore are three types of zooids forming the bulk of the colony (Fig. 14). Unlike *Physalia*, zooids of *Velella* are not greatly elongated. In the center of the colony is a single, large gastrozooid that contains the mouth at its free end. The mouth leads to a large gastrovascular cavity. On both sides of the gastrozooid are several gonozooids with small, grapelike gonophores that escape into the water as free-swimming medusae. Around the margin of the disc is a fringe composed of several dactylozooids.

The cavities of gastrozooids and gonozooids communicate with the cavity of the pneumatophore via ectodermal tubes. These tubes are extensions of the multi-chambered pneumatophore. *Velella* lacks swimming bells.

■ **Observational Procedure:**
   Velella

In a dish containing water, carefully examine a specimen of *Velella*. Locate the sail, pneumatophore (with gas chambers), gastrozooid, gonozooids (with gonophores), and the dactylozooids. ■

B. Class Scyphozoa

The approximately 200 species in the class Scyphozoa [sy-fo-ZO-a; G., *skyphos*, cup G., *zoon*, animal] are often called true jellyfish. The dominant body form is an acraspedote medusa (velum lacking) having a cellular mesoglea or collenchyma. The medusa may attain a diameter of 1 m such as in *Cyanea capillata*. Scyphozoans are carnivorous, feeding on a variety of marine animals:

fish, annelids, ctenophores, crustaceans, and other planktonic forms. Most scyphozoan medusae are active swimmers propelled through the water by rhythmic pulsations of the bell; however, some members are sluggish bottom-dwellers.

Two examples of the class will be studied: (1) *Aurelia aurita*, an active pelagic scyphozoan in the medusa stage;

(2) *Cassiopeia*, a sluggish jellyfish that spends most of its life on the bottom of shallow seas.

Aurelia aurita

The moon jelly, *Aurelia aurita*, is the most common jellyfish on both American and European coasts. The tetramerous medusa is relatively flat and ranges from 7 to 10 cm in diameter (Fig. 15A). Four **subgenital pits** occur on the subumbrella surface. Cilia cover both the exumbrella and subumbrella surfaces.

■ Observational Procedure: *Aurelia aurita*

1. Obtain an adult *Aurelia* in a bowl containing water and examine the specimen with a dissection microscope. Find the centrally located mouth, at the free end of the manubrium, surrounded by four long, frilly **oral arms** bearing short tentacles (**Fig. 15A**). The oral arms are extensions of the manubrium. Food trapped in mucus is transferred to the mouth by **lappets** located around the margin of the bell.

2. Follow the mouth into the central stomach that connects to four short canals, each leading to four radially arranged **gastric pouches**. The gastrodermis of the pouches bears tentacle-like projections called **gastric filaments**, chief sites of enzyme secretion and intracellular digestion. Numerous cnidocytes with nematocysts cover the filaments.

3. Observe the many radiating canals in the bell; these connect with the ring canal located around the bell's margin. The fluid-filled canals have special names depending upon their location and function: **adradial, interradial**, and **perradial** (Fig. 15A). All canals plus the stomach constitute the gastrovascular cavity.

4. Observe the fringe of numerous, short tentacles hanging around the margin of the bell. Where the perradial canal meets the ring canal is a ciliated **rhopalium** located between two rhopalial lappets (Figs. 15 and 16). *Aurelia* has eight rhopalia and sixteen rhopalial lappets. The rhopalium consists of sensory cells, sensory pits, and a statocyst, an organ of equilibrium. Unlike many of its relatives, *Aurelia* has a light-perceiving eyespot (**ocellus**) on the rhopalium.

5. *Aurelia* is dioecious. Find the four, interradial gastrodermal gonads and four well-developed genital pits. Fertilization and development to the planula larva occur in the folds of the oral arms. If small opaque patches are seen on the inner surfaces of the oral arms, carefully dissect out and open some of them and examine under high power of a dissection microscope. Do you find planulae? If so, examine them using the compound microscope. The mature, ciliated planula leaves the adult and metamorphoses into an **actinula** or **hydratuba** stage (Fig. 15C). This stubby, hydra-like body with solid tentacles settles down and develops into a polypoid stage, the **scyphistoma**.

6. Examine a cross section of a scyphistoma and observe the four septa that partition off the gastrovascular cavity. Like the medusa, the scyphistoma is tetramerous. The scyphistoma can produce additional scyphistoma by asexual budding which occurs in autumn and winter. In late winter and spring, the scyphistoma undergoes transverse fission (**strobilation**), which results in a **strobila**, a polyp resembling a stack of saucers. The saucer-shaped bodies are **ephyrae** or immature medusae (Fig. 15F). Each ephyra breaks off the strobila one at a time and eventually develops into an adult medusa. Examine prepared slides showing all stages of development in *Aurelia*. Compare the stages with Fig. 15, paying particular attention to comparison of the ephyra to the adult *Aurelia*.

The life cycle of *Aurelia* involves alternation of asexual reproduction with sexual reproduction (metagenesis). Distinguish the asexual phase from the sexual. What advantage might there be to the organism in having such reproductive cycles? ■

Cassiopeia

Cassiopeia (also spelled *Cassiopea*), was named from a mythological queen of Ethiopia. This common rhizostome scyphozoan lives in calm, shallow-water lagoons of Florida and the West Indies. The adult medusa may reach 26 cm in diameter and is unusual in its habit of living upside-down on the bottom of the seafloor. *Cassiopeia* attaches to the sea floor by having a raised circular zone around the margin of the bell thus creating a suckerlike action on the bell's aboral surface. Pulsation of the bell creates water currents that bring oxygen and food to the animal as well as carry wastes away. Small planktonic organisms are swept over the frilly oral arms, are paralyzed by discharged nematocysts, trapped in mucus strands, and then carried into the secondary, porelike mouths. Symbiotic **zooxanthellae** also live within the mesoglea of *Cassiopeia*. If disturbed, *Cassiopeia* rises off the sea floor, swims a short distance, and settles down again.

■ Observational Procedure: *Cassiopeia*

1. Obtain a specimen of *Cassiopeia* in a small dish of water and observe it with the dissection microscope. Note the flattened bell and lack of tentacles (Fig. 17). Instead of tentacles around the bell's margin as seen in *Aurelia*, *Cassiopeia* has a fringe of numerous, small **scallops**. Regularly spaced between certain scallops are

Phylum Cnidaria (Coelenterata)

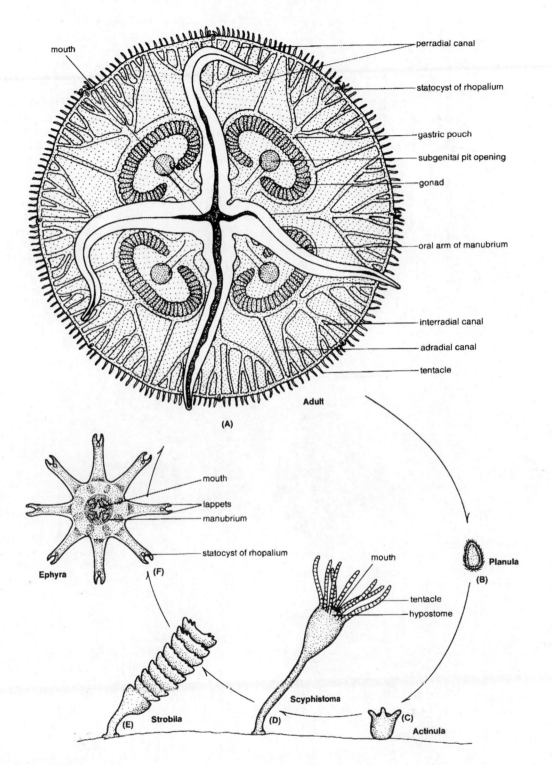

mouth

perradial canal

statocyst of rhopalium

gastric pouch

subgenital pit opening

gonad

oral arm of manubrium

interradial canal

adradial canal

tentacle

Adult

(A)

mouth

lappets

manubrium

statocyst of rhopalium

Ephyra

(F)

Planula

(B)

mouth

tentacle

hypostome

Scyphistoma

(D)

(E) **Strobila**

(C)

Actinula

Figure 15 *Aurelia* life cycle.

Phylum Cnidaria (Coelenterata)

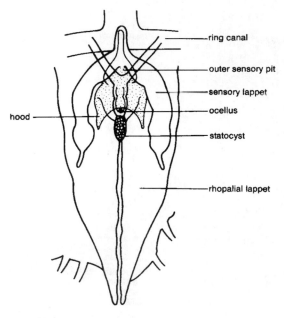

Figure 16 Rhopalium of *Aurelia*.

ring canal

outer sensory pit

sensory lappet

ocellus

hood

statocyst

rhopalial lappet

16 rhopalia. The rhopalia play an important role in controlling pulsations of the bell and in regenerating missing areas of the bell.

2. Excise a rhopalium with a sharp razor blade or needle. Place the rhopalium on a glass slide with a drop of water, cover with a cover slip, and examine with the compound microscope. A small amount of methylene blue added to the specimen may enhance your observation. Compare the rhopalium with that of *Aurelia*. Is a hood present? Unlike *Aurelia*, *Cassiopeia* lacks an eyespot.

3. Note that *Cassiopeia* lacks the distinct, central manubrium with a mouth and four separate oral arms observed in *Aurelia*. The four oral lobes are expanded and bifurcated in the adult to form eight, thick, gelatinous frilly arms. The original arm groove closes over, forming a branched **brachial canal** that opens to the oral surface by minute pores called secondary or brachial mouths. Using an illuminator, shine light through the specimen. This should permit the brachial canals to be seen. Numerous elongated appendages bearing many cnidocytes with nematocysts and mucus cells extend from the arms (Fig. 17). These are used in capturing food.

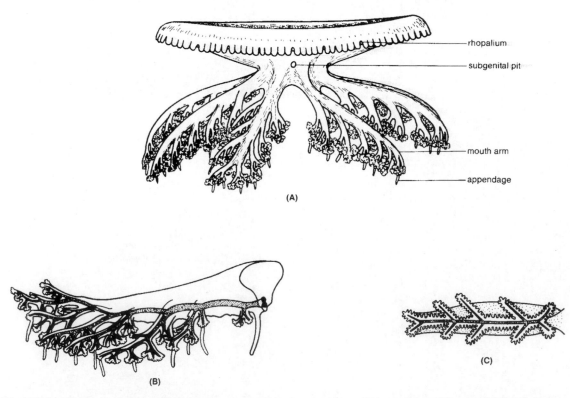

rhopalium

subgenital pit

mouth arm

appendage

(A)

(B)

(C)

Figure 17 *Cassiopeia*. (A) Lateral view of adult *Cassiopeia* with oral surface down. (B) Lateral view of *Cassiopeia*'s mouth arm showing the gastrovascular canals. (C) A mouth of *Cassiopeia* closed.

64

4. Cut off a small piece of the frilly arm at its distal end, make a wet mount, and observe under high power of the compound microscope. A small drop of methylene blue added to the specimen before the cover slip is affixed may aid your observation. You should see numerous, undischarged nematocysts.

5. Follow the brachial canals to the central stomach where extracellular digestion occurs. Numerous radial canals extend from the stomach; the canals form an anastomosing network of channels throughout the bell. A distinct ring canal, as observed in *Aurelia*, is lacking. Examine the flattened aboral surface of the bell to see the numerous radial canals.

6. Lift up the bell and locate the four openings, called **subgenital pits**, located in the stalklike area between the arms and flattened bell. The pits lead to a cross-shaped space, the **subgenital porticus**, which lies below the stomach.

7. With a sharp razor blade or scalpel, cut the flattened bell from the stalk to better observe the four gonads. Note their curved shapes. The gonads lie on the edge of the central stomach above the subgenital pits. The pits do not connect to the gonads. The gametes are discharged into the porticus.

Cassiopeia is dioecious. The planula larva settles down and develops into a scyphistoma. One ephyra at a time buds from the scyphistoma. *Cassiopeia* lacks a strobila. The ephyra settles on the sea floor when it reaches about 2 cm in diameter, and there it develops into the adult. *Cassiopeia* also buds off small planulae from the scyphistoma. ∎

C. Class Anthozoa

Over 6,000 species, including of sea anemones and corals, belong to the largest cnidarian class, Anthozoa [an-tho-ZO-a; G., *anthos*, flower + G., *zoon*, animal]. The name flower animal is appropriately assigned to these animals because many are highly colored and resemble flowering plants. These marine invertebrates occur in both deep and shallow waters of tropical and temperate seas but reach their greatest abundance in tropical areas.

All adult anthozoans are sessile polyps; there is no medusa. Anthozoan polyps may be elongated and thin-walled or short, rather squatty, and thick-walled. The polyps occur as solitary individuals (e.g., sea anemones) or as complex colonies with several hundred interconnecting polyps (e.g., corals).

The anthozoan polyp differs in a number of important features from hydrozoans and scyphozoan polyps. Instead of having a hypostome, the oral surface of an anthozoan polyp is typically expanded and flattened as an **oral disc** bearing an ovoid mouth and hollow tentacles studded with cnidocytes (Fig. 18). Radial muscles in the disc permit opening of the mouth during feeding. The number of tentacles varies from six to more than 100, and the cavities of the tentacles communicate with the gastrovascular cavity.

Anthozoans are the only cnidarians with the gastrovascular cavity divided by longitudinal (oral-aboral) **septa** or **mesenteries** and in having a pharynx (stomodaeum, actinopharynx, esophagus, gullet) (Figs. 19 and 20). The septa are composed largely of mesoglea bounded by a layer of gastrodermis on either side. The septa that extend from the body wall to the pharynx are called **primary** (perfect or complete) septa (Fig. 19). In zoantharian anthozoans, there are **incomplete** (imperfect) septa that do not meet the pharynx and according to their lengths, they are called secondary, tertiary, and quaternary septa. The free ends of the septa near and below the pharynx form coiled **septal filaments** (mesenteric filaments) containing enzyme-producing cells and cnidocytes (Fig. 19).

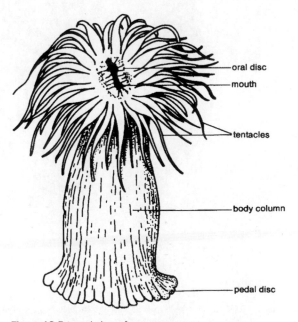

Figure 18 External view of sea anemone.

- oral disc
- mouth
- tentacles
- body column
- pedal disc

Phylum Cnidaria (Coelenterata)

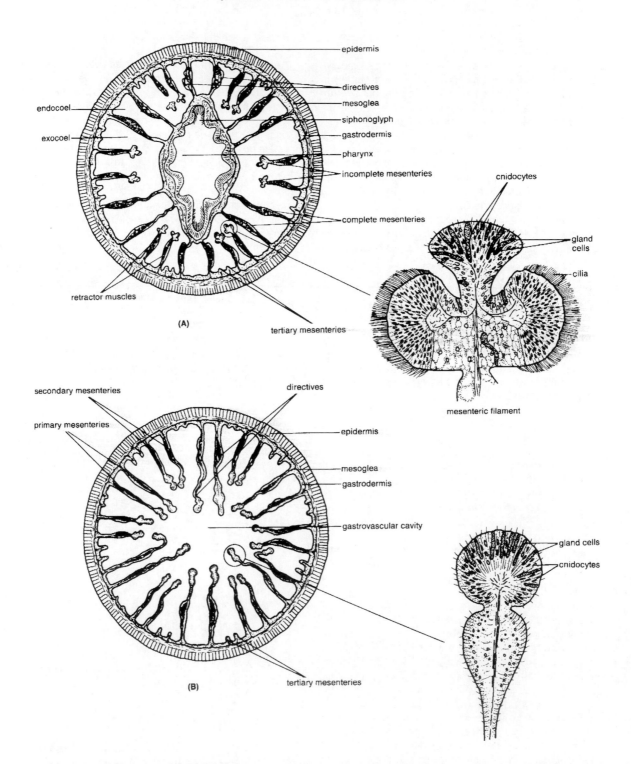

Figure 19 Sea anemone. (A) Cross section through pharynx showing two siphonoglyphs. Mesenteric filament enlarged. (B) Cross section below the pharynx. Mesenteric filament enlarged.

Phylum Cnidaria (Coelenterata)

Figure 20 Oral-aboral section of *Metridium* showing internal structures.

The pharynx is an ectodermally lined, ciliated tube chiefly for ingestion of food. The pharynx connects the mouth and gastrovascular cavity, and typically bears one or more **siphonoglyphs** (sulcuses)—ciliated grooves or gutters for moving water through the mouth and into the gastrovascular cavity (Fig. 20). Coral polyps lack the siphonoglyphs.

Two subclasses, Zoantharia (or Hexacorallia) and Alcyonaria (or Octocorallia), comprise Class Anthozoa. Zoantharians (sea anemones, stony corals) have their structures arranged in sixes (hexamerous) or multiples thereof. The several unbranched hollow tentacles are arranged in one or more circles around the mouth on the oral disc. Alyconarians (soft and horny corals) are octamerous with eight hollow, pinnate tentacles arranged around the outer margin of the oral disc. Selected examples from the subclasses will be studied.

Subclass Zoantharia

Most species of Class Anthozoa are zoantharians (hexacorallians). The 3,500 species include sea anemones and hard corals. The hexamerous symmetry and paired septa partitioning the gastrovascular cavity are two important distinguishing features of zoantharians. The pharynx bears at least one siphonoglyph in anemones, but in hard corals the siphonoglyph is absent. Tentacles of zoantharian polyps are usually simple and not like those of alyconarian anthozoans.

All septa in zoantharians are coupled, being arranged in a bilateral or biradial manner. Also, most zoanthari-ans's septa occur close together in twos and are said to be paired. The gastrovascular cavity between pairs is the **exocoel** and the cavity between members of a septal pair is the **endocoel** (Fig. 19). The exocoels and endocoels communicate with the cavities of the tentacles.

Metridium

Metridium is a common sea anemone found along the Atlantic and Pacific coasts. It belongs to the Order Actinaria which contains all typical sea anemones. *Metridium* will be studied in detail to illustrate the basic anatomy of an anthozoan polyp.

■ Observational Procedure: *Metridium*

1. Place a specimen of *Metridium* in a dissection pan and observe its general morphology (Fig. 18). Make a list of the similarities this specimen has to a hydra. In making this comparison consider size, body form, and internal structure.

2. Locate the **oral disc, body column,** and **base** (Fig. 18). The cylindrical-shaped body column can be divided into an upper, thin walled **capitulum** and a lower, thick-walled, **scapus** (Fig. 20).

3. Between the capitulum and scapus is a groove, the **fosse**, bordered by a prominent fold of the body wall called the **collar** (parapet).

4. Note how the closed, aboral base is expanded into the **pedal disc** by which the organism attaches to a substrate. Although *Metridium* is sessile, it can detach and move to another site. The oral end contains an ovoid mouth in the center of the oral disc.

5. Locate the **peristome**, an area devoid of tentacles immediately surrounding the mouth.

6. Examine the numerous hollow tentacles bearing cnidocytes that border the peristome and cover the oral disc. Are the tentacles arranged in any definite pattern? Are all tentacles on the oral disc the same length? The tentacles contain longitudinal and circular muscle fibers and can be expanded and shortened in the living animal.

7. Find the mouth and the ciliated pharynx (Fig. 20). At one or both ends of the mouth and extending down into the pharynx locate the ciliated groove or gutter called the siphonoglyph that moves water into the gastrovascular cavity. How does the position and number of siphonoglyphs in the mouth superimpose a bilateral symmetry onto this radially symmetrical animal?

8. Using a sharp scalpel, cut longitudinally a preserved specimen cleanly and evenly into two equal halves beginning at the oral end and extending through the pedal disc. With another specimen, make two clean cross sections through the body column. One section should transect the pharynx and the other section should be made below the pharynx and near the pedal disc. Locate the pharynx, siphonoglyph, and gastrovascular cavity (Figs. 19 and 20).

9. Study the location and arrangement of the paired mesenteries (or septa) in both longitudinal and cross sections. The mesenteries are paired and occur in sets or cycles. Those mesenteries that extend from the body wall to the pharynx are called primary or complete; those that extend from the body but do not meet the pharynx are incomplete (Fig. 19).

10. Locate the cycles of septa. The first cycle consists of six pairs of primary septa. The second cycle consists of six pairs of secondary septa. The third cycle consists of 12 pairs of tertiary septa. Is there a fourth cycle of quaternary septa?

11. If you have difficulty seeing the septa cycles in the preserved specimen, they will be observed when prepared slides are studied.

12. In the longitudinally halved specimen, locate a longitudinal **retractor muscle** on one face of a septum (Fig. 20). This muscle occurs on the side of each paired septum facing the endocoel, except for the septa attached at the ends of the siphonoglyphs in the pharynx. On these paired, complete septa, called **directives**, the retractor muscles face the exocoels (Fig. 19). The retractor muscles retract the oral disc. (NB: The spacial relationship of septa, the muscles, and their spaces can be seen best in a prepared slide of a cross section of *Metridium*: see steps 15–21, below). Depending on how you made the longitudinal section, one to two ostia may be seen in the septa near the pharynx and body wall at the distal end of the animal. What function might these septal perforations serve?

13. At the free end of each incomplete septum locate the longitudinal cord or ridge called the **septal** or **mesenteric filament** (Fig. 19). The filament is trilobed in the region of the pharynx; those near the base are unilobed. The detail structure of a filament will be seen in the prepared cross section.

14. Locate the many threadlike structures called **acon-**

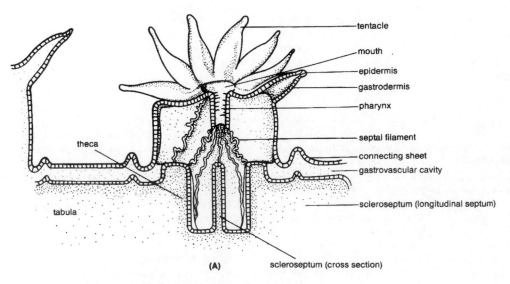

Figure 21 (A) Oral-aboral section of a hard coral polyp and its calcareous cup.

Phylum Cnidaria (Coelenterata)

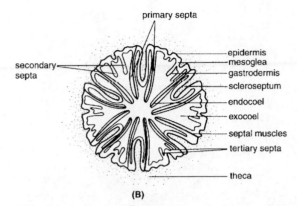

Figure 21 (B) Cross section of a coral polyp below the pharynx

tia (Fig. 20). These might be more easily observed in the longitudinal section. Acontia are continuations of the middle lobe of the lower septal mesenteries. They aid in defense and capture of prey, bear cnidocytes and enzyme producing gland cells, and can be protruded through the mouth and through minute openings, **cinclides**, located in the lower body column. When the column contracts, water is expelled through the cinclides.

Metridium is dioecious. Careful dissection and observation may reveal the gonads, which are thickened bands located behind a mesenteric filament (Fig. 20).

15. Examine a prepared slide showing a cross section of *Metridium* through the pharynx under low power of a compound microscope (Fig. 19). Locate the outer epidermis of columnar cells, the inner gastrodermis lining the gastrovascular cavity, and the middle mesoglea containing ameboid cells and muscle fibers in the body wall. The inner wall of the pharynx is folded and lined with epidermis, containing cnidocytes and gland cells. The outer covering of the pharynx is gastrodermis and the middle area is mesoglea.

16. Locate the siphonoglyph. Do you see more than one siphonoglyph? Observe the cilia of the pharynx and siphonoglyph under high power.

17. Study the arrangement of the mesenteries. Note that each mesentery consists of an inner layer of mesoglea surrounded by gastrodermis.

18. Study the structural relationship of a mesentery to the body wall from which it arises. How many pairs of primary and secondary mesenteries are present? Do you see any tertiary mesenteries?

19. Locate the retractor muscles on the secondary and primary septa. Note how the muscles face the endocoels. Do the muscles on the directives face the same way as those on the remaining septa?

20. Locate the clover-shaped mesenteric filament. The central lobe is nonciliated and contains gland cells that

produce enzymes used in digestion and numerous cnidocytes. The two lateral lobes are ciliated and lack cnidocytes. What function might the cilia serve?

21. Study a longitudinal section on a prepared slide and identify as many of the above-mentioned structures as possible. ■

Stony Corals

True or stony corals are zoantharian anthozoans of the Order Scleractinia (Madreporaria). There are two groups of hard corals: **hermatypic** and **ahermatypic**. Hermatypic corals are colonial reef builders, found in shallow tropical seas. Ahermatypic corals are noncolonial, nonreef builders, and may occur in rather deep and cold waters of higher latitudes. Most coral species are hermatypic with polyps 1–3 mm in diameter. The limy exoskeleton is secreted throughout the life of the polyp. Polyps of colonial corals are interconnected by a lateral fold of the body wall extending from the column and running along the surface of the colony. This results in the body tissues (epidermis, mesoglea, and gastrodermis) and the gastrovascular cavities of the polyps being continuous. The mesoglea is thin, but cellular.

Growth patterns and arrangement of the polyps in a colony are varied, resulting in different skeletal configurations. Coral deposits may be upright, branched, round, or flattened masses. Selected examples of common species are briefly described below. Your instructor may provide additional examples to observe.

■ Observational Procedure: Stony Corals

1. Examine the specimens available for study noting differences in density, growth form (branching or globular), and surface patterns. For example, do the specimens that branch all have the same branching patterns? How many branches occur before the patterns stop?

2. Often other sessile organisms utilize the coraline surface as a place of attachment. What evidence do you see that other organisms have attached to the specimens? What types of organisms have colonized the surface? Now reverse the question. Have any of these corals established themselves on another organism? What do these simple observations tell us about the biology of corals?

3. Each coral polyp is a miniature sea anemone fixed in a cup of calcium carbonate (Fig. 21) into which the living polyp can retract. In any specimen, what sort of variation is seen among the size of the cups? Are all of the cups of a uniform shape? How do these shapes differ?

4. The limy encasement is secreted by the epidermis

Phylum Cnidaria (Coelenterata)

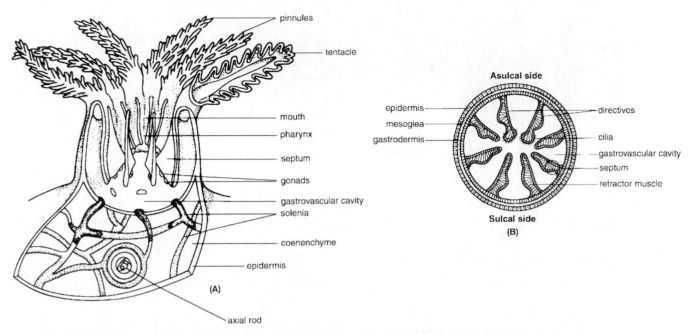

Figure 22 Alcyonarian polyp. (A) Aboral-oral section. (B) Cross section of the polyp below the pharynx.

of the polyp's base and lower area of the column. The nonliving exoskeleton of a single polyp is called a **corallite** (**calyx**); that of the colony is the **corallum**. The bottom of the corallite is the basal plate (**tabula**) and that part of the cup containing the lower part of the polyp is the **theca**. Using a dissection microscope or a hand lens identify these structures in the specimens available for your study.

5. Using a hand lens, examine the cut surfaces of several specimens. Do you see any evidence that the coral polyps are connected to one another through canals that perforate the corallum? If these cavities are not canals connecting one polyp to another, what are they?

6. Unlike sea anemones, coral polyps lack the pedal disc, siphonoglyphs, and septal perforations. The hollow tentacles occur in sets of six and the septa are usually hexamerous too. Six complete mesenteric septa typically alternate with six incomplete septa. Tertiary septa may occur. Locate the skeletal septa or ridges, called **sclerosepta**, present in each theca. These represent radial folds found between each complete septa, that are secreted by the underside of the polyp; this results in the lower part of the gastrovascular cavity divided by folds of tissue. Examine the specimens and find complete, incomplete, and tertiary septa. ■

Meandrina: Brain Coral. Note how the polyps are arranged close together in rows but that the rows are well separated. The resulting coral has ridges and valleys that appear somewhat like a human brain. The polyps of *Meandrina* are produced by intratentacular budding; however, the oral discs and columns never separate after new mouths are formed. Therefore, the polyps of a new row have many mouths, but share a common oral disc. *Meandrina sinuosa* occurs in Florida and the West Indies.

Astrangla: Eyed or Star Coral. This North Atlantic coastal coral forms small, encrusting colonies. The skeleton shows a pitted appearance because the polyps are well separated. The polyps in *A. danae* cannot withdraw into the cups. This species occurs from North Carolina to Massachusetts. Can you suggest where active budding may have been occurring in the specimen?

Fungia: Mushroom Coral. This solitary, rather deep coral has a mushroom-shaped skeleton. It is a common species of the Great Barrier Reef; *F. elegans* occurs in the Gulf of California. Individuals of *Fungia* can slide themselves over the substratum without the aid of currents. Is there a true theca in *Fungia*? Using a dissection microscope, determine the arrangement of sclerosepta. Is the arrangement in *Fungia* the same as in the other corals examined?

Acropora: Staghorn, Elkhorn, or Antler Coral. Note the branching colony form with the porous corallum of loose construction. This feature may be seen when a broken edge of a branch is examined on end. *Acropora* is a reef builder.

Phylum Cnidaria (Coelenterata)

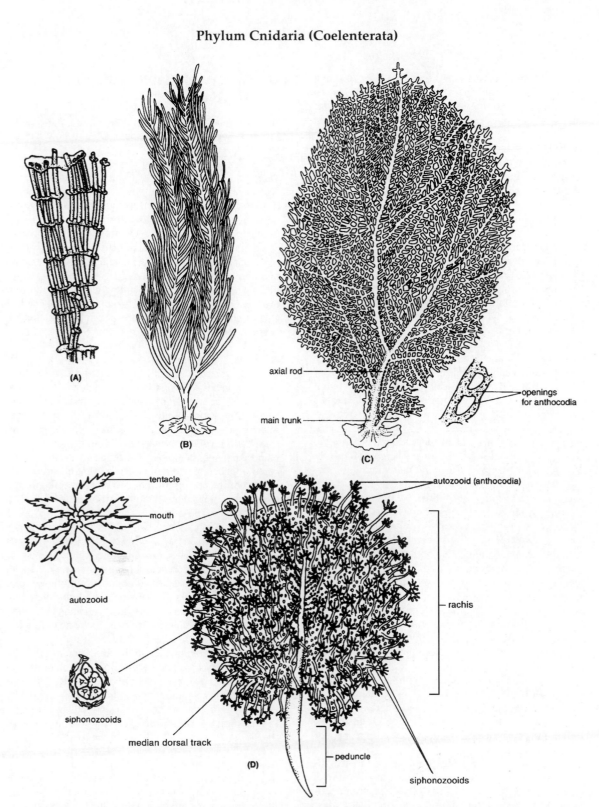

(A)

axial rod

main trunk

(B)

(C)

openings
for anthocodia

tentacle

mouth

autozooid

autozooid (anthocodia)

rachis

siphonozooids

median dorsal track

peduncle

siphonozooids

(D)

Figure 23 Selected examples of Subclass Alcyonaria. (A) Piece of *Tubipora* (organ-pipe coral) skeleton. (B) Sea whip. (C) Sea fan. *(Gorgonia);* magnified part of fan showing holes for polyps. (D) Sea pansy *(Renilla),* dorsal view. (From Hyman.)

Porites: These corals are reef builders forming branched porous colonies. Observe how the polyps are close together and that the calcareous cups are rather shallow. *P. porites* occurs in Florida and the West Indies.

Oculina: This genus forms branched, rather compact colonies. Note that the polyps are widely separated and spirally arranged. *Oculina diffusia* occurs from North Carolina to Florida.

Subclass Alcyonaria

Organ-pipe coral (*Tubipora*), sea fans (*Gorgonia*), sea pansies (*Renilla*), sea pens (*Stylatula*), sea whips (*Leptogorgia*), and their allies are alcyonarian cnidarians. All 3,000 of the known living species of alcyonarians are colonial and most abundant in warm tropical areas of the Indo-Pacific.

Unlike polyps of zoantharians, each alcyonarian polyp has eight unpaired mesentaries that connect to the body wall and a relatively short pharynx (Fig. 22). Furthermore, each polyp bears eight pinnate tentacles that are arranged symmetrically. The number of tentacles and septa and their arrangement give alyconarians an octamerous radial symmetry. The feathery appearance of the tentacles is due to many finger-like projecting **pinnules** that arise from the main part of the tentacle. The tentacles are hollow; their cavities are extensions of the gastrovascular system. Cnidocytes and cilia on the tentacles capture food.

The gastrovascular cavities of the polyps are connected by gastrodermal tubes—branched continuations of the gastrovascular walls of the polyps—called **solenia** (Fig. 22A). New polyps arise as buds or sprouts from the solenia. Arrangement of the solenia varies. The solenia are embedded in a thick mesoglea called **coenenchyme** and the entire outer surface of the colony is covered with epidermis. The thick matrix of coenenchyme also contains ameboid cells, skeletal elements (e.g., calcareous spicules and horny protein), and most of the body of the polyp. Only the oral ends of the polyps (**anthocodia**) project from the surface of the coenenchyme.

There is usually one siphonoglyph (or sulcus) located in the pharynx of the polyp. This ciliated groove, like that of other anthozoans, drives water into the gastrovascular cavity. The side of the polyp bearing the siphonoglyph is the sulcal side, and the opposite side the asulcal side.

Each septum on its sulcal side (e.g., toward the siphonoglyph) bears a strong, longitudinal retractor muscle (Fig. 22B). The free edge of each septum below the pharynx bears a septal (or mesenteric) filament.

■ Observational Procedure: Alcyonaria

The orders of Alcyonaria differ in the nature of the skeleton and mode of colony formation. Following you will study a few examples.

Tubipora: Obtain the specimen of the organ-pipe coral (*Tubipora*). The order to which this genus belongs (Stolonifera), is characterized by the lack of the coenenchymal mass (Fig. 23A). The polyps arise singly from a mat of **stolons**. Observe that the colony consists of upright parallel polyps supported by hard skeletal tubes of fused spicules giving an impression of the pipes of an organ. Using a hand lens, determine whether the tubes are solid. (NB: Back lighting will aid you in this observation.) The erect tubes are united at spaced levels by transverse platforms. Iron salts in the skeleton impart a dull red color to the organism.

Gorgonia: The sea fan (*Gorgonia*) is a horny coral of the Order Gorgonacea, which also includes the sea whips and sea feathers (Fig. 23C). These highly colored, graceful colonies occur in tropical and subtropical waters, especially in the Indo-Pacific Ocean and in the subtropical Atlantic around Bermuda, the Bahamas, and West Indies. Because of their sessile nature and firm upright position, sponges, hydroids, and other invertebrates become attached to the sea fan. The most characteristic feature of these anthozoans is the horny, protein material called **gorgonin**, located in their skeletons. The polyps secrete the gorgonin.

1. Examine a sea fan closely (Fig. 23C). Note the short main trunk to which the colony was attached to the substratum by a holdfast. Extending from the trunk is a central axial rod of gorgonin. Emerging from the axial skeleton are numerous small branches united by cross connections into a lattice network. The many branches of the colony are in one plane, thus resulting in the fan-shaped pattern. A thin layer of coenenchyme covers the colony.

2. Observe the branches of the sea fan using the dissection microscope. Locate the small polyps (**anthocodia**) scattered over the stems and branches. If you are using a dried specimen, you will see openings where the once living polyps occurred. Can you see polyps on the main stem? Do polyps occur on both surfaces of the sea fan?

Renilla: Sea pansies (*Renilla*), of the Order Pennatulacea, occur on soft bottoms of near-shore waters of the Atlantic, Gulf, and southern California coasts. The colony can uncover itself if buried by moving sediment.

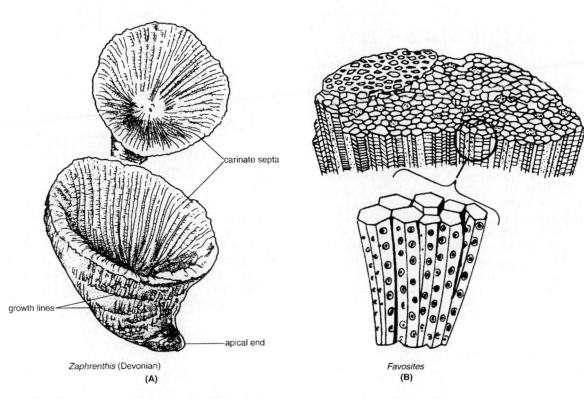

carinate septa

growth lines

apical end

Zaphrenthis (Devonian)
(A)

Favosites
(B)

Figure 24 Two examples of fossil corals. (A) Rugose coral morphology. (B) Tabulate coral morphology.

1. Obtain a preserved or living *Renilla* and observe the specimen under the dissection microscope. The primary axial polyp (**rachis**) is leaflike or somewhat heart-shaped, and is supported by a short, proximal stalk (**peduncle**) to which the colony was anchored to a substrate by peristaltic contractions of the peduncle (Fig. 23D). If the organism is dislodged, it can re-anchor itself. Note the bilateral symmetry of the colony. The symmetry is established by a stem (or track) extending from the peduncle to about the middle of the rachis.

2. Do polyps occur on the peduncle? Are there polyps on the ventral surface? Many secondary polyps are embedded in the fleshy upper surface of the rachis. The secondary polyps are dimorphic and called **autozooids** and **siphonozooids**. Autozooids are feeding polyps, containing a mouth and six pinnate tentacles. Siphonozooids are tiny, nonfeeding, warty protuberances arranged in clusters (Fig. 23D). Tentacles of siphonozooids are rudimentary. These polyps move water through the colony. The secondary polyps are formed by budding. Sexual reproduction, as in other anthozoans, results in a free-swimming planula larva.

Other Alcyonarians. Examine specimens of sea whips (*Leptogorgia*, Order Gorgonacea*)*, sea pens (*Stylatula*, Order Pennatulacea), or other examples of alcyonarians. Study these with the dissection microscope and compare their structures with members previously studied. Note the branching patterns and locations of the polyps.

Slide of a Soft Coral. Using a dissection microscope or low power only of a compound microscope examine a prepared slide of an alcyonarian branch showing a few polyps. It is a good idea to examine several slides to get a good appreciation of the form of these small polyps.

1. Count the number of tentacles on the polyps and note the short fleshy pinnules that project at right angles from the tentacles.

2. On one or more of the polyps, you should be able to find the following: mouth, pharynx, and gastrovascular cavity, with its intercommunicating canals, the solenia.

3. The most prominent internal feature of the branch is the axial rod. Locate this dark structure and check it for birefringence. What does that tell you about its biomolecular structure? ■

D. Fossil Cnidarians

Cnidarians represent an ancient group of animals dating from the **Cambrian Period** (Fig. 1). Because of the soft-bodied nature of most individuals, the fossil record of cnidarians is scant. However, individuals with chitinous perisarcs and calcareous skeletons have been preserved as fossils. Extinct individuals of Hydrozoa, Scyphozoa, and Anthozoa have been found as fossils, but the largest number of extinct cnidarians is fossil corals. The extinct **rugose** (Order Rugosa or Tetracoralla) and **tabulate** (Subclass Tabulata) corals were important reef-builders throughout most of the **Paleozoic Era** (Fig. 24). Both groups died out in the **Permian Period**. The rugose corals were mostly solitary, cone-shaped corals with an outer skeleton having a wrinkled appearance as indicated by the name rugose (Fig. 24). The tabulate corals were colonial anthozoans with calcareous skeletal tubes containing tabulae, or horizontal platforms, on which the polyps rested. These extinct corals were replaced by scleractinian and hydrozoan corals. Many well-known living genera such as *Acropora, Fungia, Favia,* and *Orbicella* have a long fossil history.

■ Observational Procedure: Fossil Cnidarians

Examine fossil specimens provided and note the similarities and differences to the present-day forms. What evidence informs you that these fossils were corals? Observe the presence of theca with sclerosepta in the specimen. In rugose corals note the wrinkled appearance of the outer skeleton. Locate the septal furrows, growth lines, septa, and fossia. In tabulate corals look for the presence of tabulae and mural pores. Your instructor will give some specific instructions to guide you further in your observations. ■

■

Phylum Ctenophora

Sea walnuts, comb jellies and sea gooseberries are common names often applied to members of the Phylum Ctenophora [te-NOF-or-a; G., *ctenos*, comb + *phora*, to bear]. The transverse, ciliary comb-shaped plates or **ctenes** located on eight bands called **comb rows** are the basis for the phylum name (Fig. 1A). The ctenes are used in locomotion.

There are approximately 100 carnivorous species in this marine group of **biradial** symmetrical invertebrates. Their biradial symmetry is established by (1) the bilateral symmetrical digestive system, which is composed of paired canals arising from a central stomach; (2) the radially arranged comb rows; and (3) the bilaterally arranged tentacles when present. Ctenophores are worldwide in distribution, and occur at all depths in the open sea as well as in coastal waters.

Ctenophora and Cnidaria are the two major phyla that constitute the Radiata because their members possess primary radial symmetry. Although both phyla have several similarities (e.g., body wall construction and gastrovascular digestive system), there are important differences. Unlike cnidarians, ctenophores are not colonial, they do not exhibit polymorphism, and lack nematocysts. Instead of nematocysts, tentaculate ctenophores have peculiar cells called **collocytes** (G., *collod*, glue) that secrete a sticky substance for catching and holding prey such as copepods and other small organisms (Fig. 1B).

Ctenophores are monoecious except for the lobate ctenophore, *Ocyropsis*. The testes and ovaries develop as two bands located within each of the eight meridional canals located beneath the comb rows. Fertilization occurs in the seawater; most forms have a free-swimming **cydippid larva** that resembles an adult ctenophore of the Order Cydippida.

Classification

The phylum is divided into two classes based primarily on the presence or absence of tentacles.

1. **Class Tentaculata.** Tentacles present. Order Cydippida: ovoid body with two branched tentacles that retract into pouches or sheaths; examples are *Pleurobrachia* and *Mertensia*. Order Lobata: compressed body in tentacular plane forming two oral lobes on either side of that plane. Tentacles are small and not located in pouches; examples are *Mnemiopsis, Bolinopsis,* and *Ocyropsis*. Order Cestida: belt-shaped body and compressed in tentacular plane; tentacles in pouches, but reduced and near the mouth; examples are *Cestum* and *Velamen*. Order Platyctenea: body flattened along an oral-aboral axis and adapted for creeping movements; examples are *Coeloplana* and *Ctenoplana*.

2. **Class Nuda.** Tentacles absent. Order Beroida: body cylindrical and compressed; mouth and pharynx enlarged; example is *Beroë*.

From *Invertebrate Zoology*, Sixth Edition, Robert L. Wallace and Walter K. Taylor. Copyright © 2002 by Pearson Education, Inc. Published by Prentice-Hall, Inc. All rights reserved

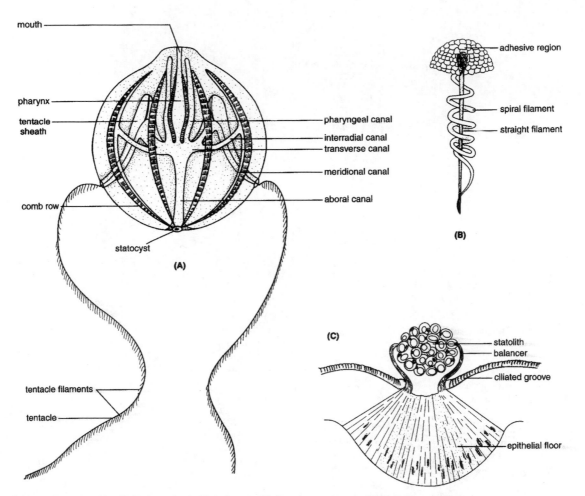

Figure 1. *Pleurobrachia.* (A) Entire animal. (B) Collocyte. (C) Aboral sense organ. (After Shelton 1982.)

Pleurobrachia

Pleurobrachia, often called the sea gooseberry, is a tentaculate ctenophore. Individuals of the genus are commonly found in coastal waters of the Atlantic Ocean.

■ Observational Procedure: *Pleurobrachia*

1. Place a preserved *Pleurobrachia* in a small dish filled with water. Using a dissecting microscope, observe the ctenophore's ovoid shape (Fig. 1A). The mouth is located at the slightly narrower (oral) end. It leads to the pharynx, stomach, and aboral canal that terminates in aboral anal pores. Arising off either side of the stom-

ach are **transverse canals** that extend as **interradial canals** connecting the eight **meridional canals**. Two **pharyngeal canals** run parallel to the pharynx (Fig. 1A). This complex of canals constitutes the gastrovascular digestive system.

2. Locate the eight radially arranged comb rows located above the meridional canals. These orally-aborally arranged rows are often whitish in color. Examine closely one comb row and locate the ctenes, each composed of fused cilia arranged like teeth of a comb. Find the openings of the two **tentacular sheaths** which are located about one third of the way to the aboral end of the animal (Fig. 1A). Preserved specimens usually have their tentacles retracted into the sheaths; however, in life the extended tentacles (up to 15 cm long) with many lateral filaments function as a fishing line to ensnare prey.

3. At the aboral end is a sense organ called a **stato-cyst,** containing a statolith that helps coordinate beating of the cilia on the comb rows (Fig. 1C). With a razor blade or sharp scalpel, cut away the aboral end and place it in a shallow dish filled with water. Examine the statocyst under high power of a dissection microscope. Can you see the four ciliary tufts that support the calcareous statocyst in its dome-shaped covering?

4. Cut away the outer wall of an aboral quarter of the body. Locate the pharynx, pharyngeal canals, and meridional canals of the digestive system. Locate the tentacular sheath. If the tentacles are retracted into the sheath, cut an entire sheath away and carefully tease the tentacle from its sheath. ∎

Beroë

Beroë, the thimble jelly, is larger (5 x 10 cm) than *Pleurobrachia. Beroë* lacks tentacles and is pinkish in color.

∎ Observational Procedure: Beroë

Obtain a specimen of *Beroë* in a small dish with water. Note its bell-shaped and laterally compressed body (Fig. 2). Observe the enlarged mouth. Locate the eight comb rows and highly branched gastrovascular cavity. ∎

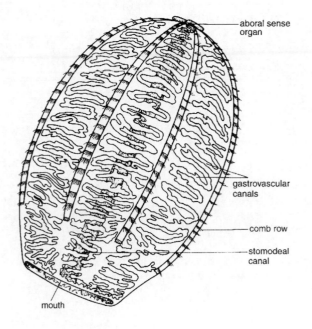

Figure 2. *Beroë.*

Phylum Ctenophora

| Cnidaria & Ctenophora | Worksheet 3 |

Cnidaria & Ctenophora   **Worksheet 3**

Name: _____   Date: _____

Course #: _____ / Section #: _____   Grade: _____

1. Why are the groups of cnidocytes said to be grouped into batteries? Discuss this use of the term in a military context.

2. Are the testis and ovary of *Hydra* true organs such as found in higher animals? To be organs, what would these structures need to possess? Discuss.

3. List the similarities between *Metridium* and a hydra.

Features	*Metridium*	a hydra
Size		
Body form		
Internal structures		

Phylum Ctenophora

4. At the base of each stem of the perisarc of a *Pennaria* colony are found several ring structures. What function(s) might these annulations serve?

5. Compare and contrast *Obelia* and *Pennaria*.

Feature	*Obelia*	*Pennaria*
Polyp		
Medusa		

6. Compare and contrast Cnidaria and Ctenophora.

Feature	Cnidaria	Ctenophora
Symmetry		
Movement		
Nutrient procurement		
Sensory		
Reproduction		

ACOELOMATE BILATERIA

The metazoans studied thus far are either asymmetrical, radially symmetrical, or biradially symmetrical. The remaining phyla to be studied are bilaterally symmetrical, although members of several phyla have undergone additional reorganization of their body plan so that they exhibit secondary radial symmetry. Bilaterally symmetrical organisms (**Bilateria**) show three levels in the organization of their perivisceral or body cavity (i.e., the space between the gut and body wall): **acoelomates** [G., *a,* without + G., *coelo,* hollow], **pseudocoelomates** [G., *pseudo,* false], and **eucoelomates**. [G., *eu,* good]. These groupings generally are not given taxonomic status, and there is some question whether the pseudocoelomate condition actually exists. In the acoelomates, derivatives of the mesoderm completely fill the space between the body wall and gut, leaving the animal without a coelom (but compare Turbeville and Ruppert 1985). The acoelomates include four wormy phyla: Gastrotricha, Gnathostomulida, Platyhelminthes, and Nemertea (Rhynchocoela).

Harrison, F.W., and B.J. Bogitsh. (eds.). 1991. Platyhelminthes and Nemertina. Volume 3. *Microscopic Anatomy of Invertebrates.* Wiley-Liss, New York, NY.

Kristensen, R.M. 1995. Are Aschelminthes pseudocoelomates or acoelomates? Pages 41-43 in *Body Cavities Function and Phylogeny.* G. Lanzavecchia, R. Valvassori & M.D. Candia Carnevali (eds), Selected Symposia and Monographs U.Z.I. 8 Mucchi, Modena.

Nielsen, C. 2001. Animal evolution: interrelationships of the living phyla. Oxford University Press, Oxford, NY.

Sterrer, W., M. Mainitz, and R.M. Rieger. 1985. Gnathostomulida: enigmatic as ever. In: *The Origins and Relationships of Lower Invertebrates.* Conway Morris, S., J.D. George, R. Gibson, and H.M. Platt. (eds.). Clarendon Press, Oxford: 181-199.

Turbeville, J.M., K.G. Field, and R.A. Raff. 1992. Phylogenetic position of phylum Nemertini, inferred from 18S rRNA sequences: molecular data as a test of morphological character homology. Mol. Biol. Evol. 9: 235-249.

Turbeville, J.M., and E.E. Ruppert. 1985. Comparative ultrastructure and the evolution of nemertines. Amer. Zool. 25:53-71.

Phylum Platyhelminthes

Members of the Phylum Platyhelminthes (PLAT-e-hel-MIN-thez; G., *platy*, flat + G., *helminth,* worm) are nonsegmented, dorsoventrally flattened worms commonly called turbellarians, flukes, and tapeworms. There are nearly 20,000 species, ranging in size from being microscopic to an incredible 15 m long or more. Most species in the phylum are parasitic. The repetition of body parts in tapeworms is not true segmentation (metamerism) as found in segmented worms of the Phylum Annelida.

Of the animals that you have studied thus far, flatworms represent the first of the **Bilateria** with a head that dominates the body. In addition, flatworms are triploblastic and the first animals to possess well-developed organ systems. Unlike most higher Bilateria, flatworms lack a true body cavity (coelom). The internal organs are embedded within a mesodermal mass of **parenchyma** that functions in secretion, storage, and regeneration. Because the coelom is absent, flatworms are commonly called **acoelomate** animals. Usually a digestive system is present in the turbellarians and flukes. The system, however, is incomplete because an anus is absent. All tapeworms lack a digestive system and are endoparasites of vertebrate animals.

Classification

Older classification schemes subdivided Platyhelminthes into three classes: Turbellaria, Trematoda, and Cestoda. However, recent work recognizes that Trematoda is more complex than originally thought and the class has been subdivided into two classes, the Monogenea and a more restrictively defined Trematoda (Subclasses Digenea and Aspidobothria or Aspidogastrea). Some schemes separate each of these two subclasses into their own class. For instructional purposes, we will use the four-class scheme.

1. **Class Turbellaria.** Relatively small flatworms with ciliated epidermis richly supplied with glands. Distinct rod-shaped structures called rhabdoids (including rhabdites) are among the glandular secretions. All possess a blind gut with oral opening usually located midventrally. Most are free-living, but some are commensal or parasitic. Twelve orders are recognized. Examples: *Dugesia* (the common freshwater planarian), *Bdelloura* (a commensal on the gills of horseshoe crabs), *Stenostomum* (a common, microscopic freshwater turbellarian), and *Bipalium* (a terrestrial turbellarian of gardens and greenhouses in the southern United States).

2. **Class Trematoda.** Moderate-sized, leaf- to wormlike parasitic flatworms, characterized by having one or more prominent ventral attachment structures. Life cycles may be simple or complex, as endo- or ectoparasites of both invertebrate and vertebrate hosts. Examples: *Aspidogaster conchicola* (freshwater clam fluke), *Clonorchis* (= *Opisthorchis*) *sinensis, Cotyaspis insignis* (freshwater clam fluke), and *Fasciola hepatica* (human and sheep liver flukes, chuman liver fluke), and *Schistosoma* spp. and *Trichobilharzia* spp. (human and bird blood flukes, respectively).

3. **Class Monogenea.** Small ectoparasites of vertebrates,

From *Invertebrate Zoology*, Sixth Edition, Robert L. Wallace and Walter K. Taylor. Copyright © 2002 by Pearson Education, Inc. Published by Prentice-Hall, Inc. All rights reserved

especially fish. A characteristic attachment organ, the opisthaptor, is located at the posterior end. Examples: *Dactylogyrus* (a pest of hatchery fish), *Gyrodactylus* (on gills of trout, bluegills, and goldfish), and *Polystoma nearcticum* (in urinary bladders of toads).

4. **Class Cestoda.** Elongate, obligate, endoparasitic flatworms lacking a gut. Most possess an anterior knoblike holdfast called the scolex. Subclass Cestodaria includes tapeworms of fish and turtles having a leaflike body shape. Example: *Gyrocotyle parvispinosa* (a parasite of fish). Tapeworms of the Subclass Eucestoda (true tapeworms) parasitize all vertebrate classes. True tapeworms possess an elongate body or strobila consisting of many repeated units called proglottids. Examples: *Dipylidium caninum* (dog tapeworm), *Moniezia expansa* (sheep tapeworm), *Taenia solium* (pig tapeworm), *Taenia pisiformis* (dog and cat tapeworm), and *Taeniarhynchus saginatus* (beef tapeworm).

A. Class Turbellaria

Turbellaria [ter-be-LAR-e-ah; L., *turbella*, a little crowd] is a moderate-sized class of flatworms comprising about 3,000 species. Many of them have an oval to elongate, dorsoventrally flattened shape and range in size from microscopic to over 50 cm long; most are less than 5 mm long. Turbellarians are predominantly free-living, although many commensal and parasitic species are known. Members of this class are found in freshwater, marine, and terrestrial habitats. All have a simple life history.

Turbellarians have a single-layered epidermis which is cellular or **syncytial**. In most species the epidermis is completely ciliated all around and amply provided with glands; some have ciliation restricted to special areas of the epidermis such as a creeping sole. One prominent secretory product in the epidermis is the **rhabdoid**. There are different types of rhabdoids, but one common type is the **rhabdite**.

A mouth opens into the gut, in most species through a simple or complex pharynx that in some forms may be protruded through the mouth to feed. The location of the mouth is highly varied within Class Turbellaria. The pharynx in turn opens into a blind gut. In some lower turbellarians a true digestive cavity is lacking. Other forms have a simple sac or complex intestine with many diverticula. Digestion begins extracellularly, and is completed intracellularly.

■ Observational Procedure: Turbellaria

Live Specimens
1. If time and climatic conditions permit, field collections of living planarians should be made. When making collections in freshwater lakes, streams, ponds, or springs, examine the undersurfaces of submerged objects such as stones, leaves, and wood. If present, planarians will be seen attached to substrates sometimes in clusters (hence the use of the Latin term *turbella*).

2. Carefully remove several collected animals from the holding jar and place them in a shallow dish containing some of the collecting water. Observe the specimens under a dissection microscope and note their locomotion and any behaviors they may exhibit when obstacles are encountered. Using a probe, turn a specimen upside down and watch how it rights itself.

3. Place a specimen in a depression slide filled with the collecting water, put a cover glass over the specimen, and observe with low power of a compound microscope. As the animal moves about, attempt to examine its dorsal and ventral surfaces. The ventral surface is ciliated and ciliary action may be observed as the animal twists and turns.

4. To aid your observation add a small amount of carmine or carbon black powder to the depression slide and observe the movement of the particles brought about by the action of the cilia.

5. If time permits, your instructor may provide instructions for observing planarian feeding habits or other behaviors, or directions for exercises in planarian regeneration. The study of other turbellarians such as *Bipalium*, and *Stenostomum* also may be undertaken.

Whole Preserved Specimens
1. Obtain a prepared slide of a whole, stained specimen of the freshwater planarian *Dugesia*. Locate the anterior and posterior ends. The earlike structures at the anterior end are chemosensory lobes called **auricles**. Near the middle of the worm is the muscular pharynx; this protrusible structure is housed in a pharyngeal cavity. In an animal that has been fed an opaque material such as carbon black, trace the outline of the intestine (Fig. 1). How many main branches of the gut are present? Note that each main branch is subbranched into numerous diverticula.

2. Locate the paired **eyespots** at the anterior end. These are special photoreceptive sensory organs and are of the inverse pigment-cup type. The shape and

Phylum Platyhelminthes

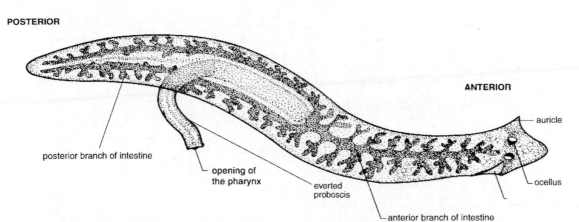

Figure 1. Dorsal view of the freshwater turbellarian *Dugesia*.

Figure 2. Dorsal view of the marine commensal turbellarian *Bdelloura*.

position of the pigment cup in relation to the photoreceptive cells give the planarian a cross-eyed appearance. Observe a cross section of a planarian at the level of the eyespots. Note the shape of the pigment cups. Which way do they face? What function does the black pigment serve?

3. Compare a whole mount slide of *Bdelloura* to that of *Dugesia* (Fig. 2). *Bdelloura* is a marine turbellarian that is commensal on gills of the horseshoe crab, *Limulus*. Attachment to the gills is allowed by a large posterior caudal sucker. At the anterior end of *Bdelloura*, note the paired eyespots, but absence of auricles. Under each eye locate a cerebral ganglion and trace the paired ventral nerve cords which leave these ganglia and run the length of the animal. In the middle of *Bdelloura* is the large pharynx and just posterior to it are various structures of the reproductive system. Note the branched digestive tract. How many major branches are there to the intestine?

Cross Sections

Examine several cross sections of *Dugesia* and make the following observations.

1. Epidermis. Observe the epidermal surfaces and locate the rhabdoids (Fig. 3). Do they have a uniform distribution? Examine the parenchyma for the presence of rhabdoids. Where are these structures concentrated? Where are they absent? Observe the lateral edges of the section. Are rhabdoids present? In this area locate the special eosinophilic glandular cells, which produce a secretion enabling the worm to adhere to surfaces.

The next observations will require the use of oil immersion techniques. If you are not familiar with these procedures ask your instructor for assistance. (NB: This is a difficult investigation; one that requires a very good slide.) Using oil immersion techniques, examine the dorsal and ventral surfaces of the cross section for the presence of cilia. Are cilia uniformly distributed on the dorsal and ventral surfaces? If not, where are cilia located?

Figure 3. Cross sections of the dorsal and ventral body wall of *Dugesia*.

2. Muscular system. Just under the epidermal basement membrane, locate the muscle layers consisting of circular, longitudinal, and diagonal muscles (Fig. 3).

3. Parenchyma. Examine the parenchymal tissue and note that this tissue completely fills the body as a loose cellular matrix (Fig. 4). However, there are cavities present in the body of the worm. What do they represent? Passing through the parenchyma locate numerous dorsoventral muscle fibers. How do they function in locomotion?

4. Gut. Locate the gut in a cross section. How many regions of the gut do you see in a single cross section of the planaria? Relate these sections of the gut to what you saw in the whole worm. Note the large vacuolated phagocytic cells of the gastrodermis. Examine the gastrodermis of your preparation carefully. In some prepa-

Figure 4. Photomicrograph of a cross section of *Dugesia* at the level of the pharynx.

rations, the gregarian parasite *(Lankesteria planariae)* may be present. This parasite may be distinguished from cells of the planarian gastrodermis by its distinct nucleation and by the larger, pear-shaped cell.

5. Pharynx. This protrusible organ can be projected through the mouth. Carefully examine cross and longitudinal sections of the pharynx. Observe how the muscular tube is located in the pharyngeal cavity. What is the relative size of the pharynx compared to the rest of the body? Find the outer ciliated layer and muscle layers of the pharynx. Compare the relative size of the muscles comprising the pharynx to that of the rest of the body. What does this comparison tell you about the feeding biology and the locomotion of this flatworm? Using a longitudinal section through the level of the pharynx, determine the anatomical relationship between the pharynx and the mouth. ■

B. Class Trematoda

Trematoda [trem-a-TO-da; G., *trema*, a hole] is a large class containing about 11,000 species of parasitic flatworms. Trematodes, or **flukes** as they are commonly called, are similar in size and shape to the turbellarians. Most are dorsoventrally flattened; however, some have a cylindrical body. As a group they range in size from microscopic to several meters in length. Flukes have enormous medical, veterinary, and economic importances. Together with the Class Cestoda (tapeworms) and Phylum Nematoda (unsegmented roundworms), flukes are the subject of the field of **helminthology** [G., *helminth*, worm + G., *ology*, study of].

Trematodes possess one or more suckers, usually an oral one surrounding the mouth and another ventral one located within the anterior one-third of the body. The suckers may be armed with many spines or hooks. The fluke body wall differs from that of turbellarians. Although once believed to be nonliving, the **tegument** is a complex, living syncytium which may be ornamented with minute spines.

Trematodes may have a simple life cycle involving a single host (Subclass Aspidogastrea) or a very complex one involving several larval stages and more than one host (Subclass Digenea). In the Digenea, development may proceed through as many as five different larval forms: **miracidium, sporocyst, redia, cercaria**, and **metacercaria**. Some of these are small free-swimming stages. Others are encysted within a host or on a substrate.

Because it is not possible to cover this diverse class completely in an introductory laboratory, exercises for a few selected species are provided here. At this point, it will be profitable if students review the life history of the digenetic fluke, *Fasciola hepatica* (Fig. 5).

■ **Observational Procedure: Trematoda**

Adults

Fasciola hepatica (Sheep Liver Fluke). *Fasciola hepatica* is a large (ca. 30 mm), leaf-shaped fluke often found in the livers of deer, goats, cattle, and sheep.

1. Observe a slide of a stained specimen and identify the anterior and posterior ends (Fig. 6). The tapered anterior end of the fluke is called the **oral cone**.

2. Locate the **oral sucker** which surrounds the mouth.

Phylum Platyhelminthes

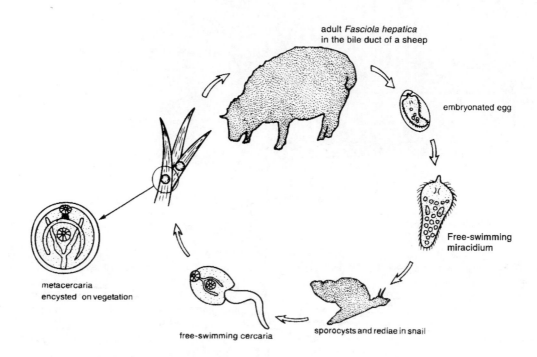

Figure 5. Life cycle of the digenetic trematode *Fasciola hepatica*.

The mouth leads to the pharynx which connects to a short esophagus and then to a biramus intestine (intestinal ceca). Trace the arms of the intestine that run the length of the fluke. Does the intestine branch into small diverticula as in *Dugesia*?

3. Just posterior to the pharynx locate the large ventral sucker called the **acetabulum**, and in front of it the common genital pore. The genital pore receives both male and female gametes. Locate the highly branched testes that lie in tandum in the central region. Bilaterally symmetrical organisms usually have paired organs on opposite sides of the body. How might this tandem arrangement of the testes affect body shape? Vasa efferentia (**vas deferens**) transport sperm from the testes to the seminal vesicle. The seminal vesicle and **cirrus sac** may be seen to one side of the genital pore.

4. Locate the tubular **uterus** that courses posteriorly from the genital pore. It may contain many eggs. Although called eggs, these are developing embryos still encased in the egg shell. The uterus terminates at the shell gland that receives yolk from the large **vitellaria** (yolk glands) located along the lateral margin of the fluke. The vitellaria (not shown in Fig. 6) may obscure the intestinal ceca.

5. On the right side of the fluke find the ovary that also terminates at the shell gland. It is branched, but darker than the testes and lies anterior to them.

6. At the posterior end of the animal, locate the excretory pore that drains the excretory vesicle. Is this structure an anus? How can you demonstrate that it is not?

7. Examine a cross section of *Fasciola*. (A longitudinal section will work for these observations.) Determine the dorsal and ventral surfaces. Is the body surface ciliated? Are rhabdites present? Locate the numerous scale like spines that are buried in the tegument. What function might they serve in this parasite?

8. Below the tegument find the muscle layers and note the dorsoventral muscles passing through the parenchyma. In cross sections from the anterior region of the worm, locate the uterus containing shelled eggs. Laterally, find the intestinal ceca and vitellaria.

9. In cross sections from the central region of the worm, locate the testis and laterally the intestinal diverticula and vitellaria.

Fasciolopsis buski (Human Intestinal Fluke). *Fasciolopsis buski* parasitizes people living in Southeast Asia. The parasite has a life history similar to that of *Fasciola* except that it occurs in the intestine. There are a few other notable differences in the body plan of these species. If slides are available, compare the general anatomy of *Fasciolopsis buski* to *Fasciola hepatica*.

1. Note that *Fasciolopsis buski* is much larger (up to 75 mm long), lacks the oral cone, and its oral sucker and

Phylum Platyhelminthes

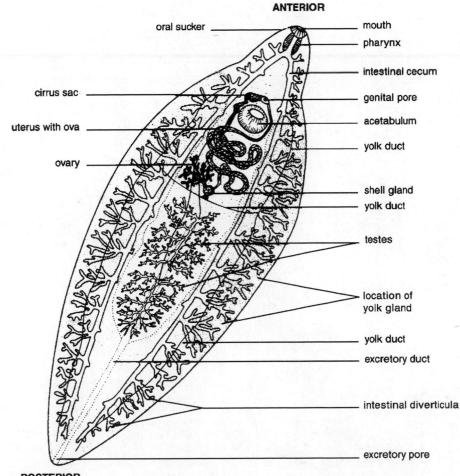

Figure 6. Ventral view of the sheep liver fluke *Fasciola hepatica*.

acetabulum are larger than those of *Fasciola*. One way to visualize the relative proportions of the oral sucker and the acetabulum in these two species is to examine their musculature for birefringence. How extensive are these structures? Considering the differences in habitat of the two species, what might be the significance of a larger (stronger) acetabulum? Using a dissection microscope, re-examine the pharynx of *Dugesia* and compare the relative size of its pharynx to that of the two flukes you have just studied. Why might the size of the pharynx in the planarian be disproportionately longer?

2. Compare and contrast the intestine of *Fasciolopsis* and *Fasciola*. How are they similar? How is the intestine of *Fasciolopsis* simpler? What might this indicate about the foods of these two parasites?

3. The reproductive systems of the two species are essentially the same. Testes lie in tandem in the central region of the body, a smaller ovary lies ahead of the testes next to the shell gland, and large vitellaria are found along the lateral margins of the fluke.

Clonorchis sinensis (Chinese or Human Liver Fluke). *Clonorchis* (= *Opisthorchis*) *sinensis*, like *Fasciola*, lives in the liver of its host (Fig. 7). However, it is a smaller fluke (ca. 25 mm long) that lacks tegmental spines. If slides are available, compare this fluke to the ones previously studied.

Note that the oral sucker is slightly larger than the acetabulum. Is the intestine most similar to *Fasciola* or to *Fasciolopsis?* Two large, branched testes lie in tandum near the posterior end, and just anterior to them, lies a small three-lobed ovary. From the ovary the uterus

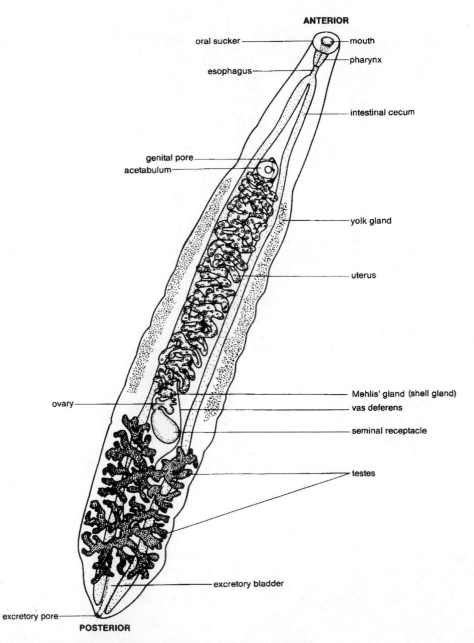

ANTERIOR

oral sucker ———

mouth

pharynx

esophagus ———

intestinal cecum

genital pore ———
acetabulum ———

yolk gland

uterus

Mehlis' gland (shell gland)

ovary ———

vas deferens

seminal receptacle

testes

excretory bladder

excretory pore ———

POSTERIOR

Figure 7. Ventral view of the human liver fluke *Clonorchis* (= *Opisthorchis*) *sinensis*.

courses anteriorly to the genital pore which lies in front of the acetabulum. To either side of the uterus are the moderately sized vitellaria.

Schistosome Flukes. Another important group of flukes are the **schistosomes** (blood flukes) including those

which afflict humans: *Schistosoma mansoni, S. japonicum,* and *S. haematobium* (Fig. 8). The first two are found in the small veins of the intestine and the latter in veins of the urinary bladder. Schistosomiasis is endemic in Africa, in parts of the Middle East, Southeast Asia, and Japan, and in eastern and northern South

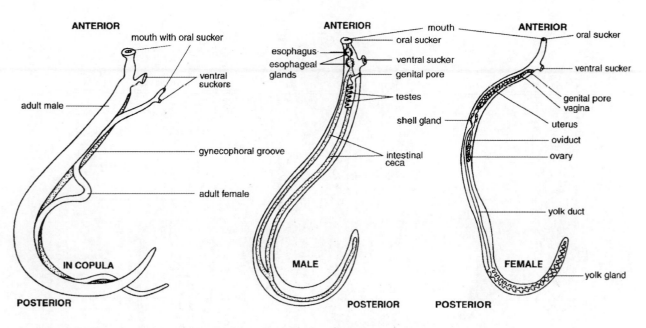

Figure 8. Generalized anatomy and morphology of male and female *Schistosoma mansoni*.

America. The following observations may be done using any of the three species noted above.

1. Observe prepared slides of *Schistosoma* (male and female). Identify the anterior and posterior ends. How does the shape of *Schistosoma* differ from the shapes of other flukes studied so far? There is a distinct size difference between the males and females; which is larger?

2. Find the oral and ventral or acetabulum suckers of the specimens. Are there differences in the sizes of the suckers?

3. Locate the **gynecophoral canal** on the male's ventral surface. Does the female have this groove? What is the significance of this structure? If available, observe a slide that shows the sexes in copula.

4. Observe a prepared slide of *Schistosoma* eggs and note the lateral **spine**. The eggs are responsible for some of the very serious pathologic aspects of *schistosomiasis*. After being liberated from the female the eggs pass through the intestinal wall where they do considerable damage. Do embryos possess any locomotory apparatus that would permit them to move through the muscle wall of the small intestine? If not, how are they capable of accomplishing this feat?

5. Eggs also may be swept into the liver through the hepatic portal system where they become lodged. Observe slides of *Schistosoma* eggs in the wall of the intestine and in the liver. Note any evidence of tissue damage done to the host's organs in the region immediately surrounding the eggs. In the liver, inflammation at the site of each egg will eventually lead to a host reaction called a **granuloma** or **pseudotubercle**.

6. Under low power, scan your slide for pseudotubercles. How many do you see in your field of view? Measure the size of the egg and compare it to the thickness of the layer of granulomatous cells produced by the host. Make a judgment of how much of the host's tissue is affected by the parasite.

7. If material is available, examine other *Schistosoma* species. How are they similar; how are they different? How do the schistosomes differ from the other flukes you have examined? Constructing a table may help you organize this comparison.

General Study of Fluke Larval Stages

Obtain prepared slides of the five larval stages from *Fasciola hepatica*, *Schistosoma*, or any other digenetic trematode (Fig. 9). The basic sequence of stages is as follows: miracidium, sporocyst, redia, cercaria, and metacercaria (Fig. 5). However, several important modifications may be found in different species. Sporocyst and redia stages may have more than one generation (mother and daughter) or may be absent; the metacercaria stage may be absent also. Depending on the quality of the preparation, the internal structures of the larval stages shown in Fig. 9 are often not visible in stained preserved specimens. Sometimes phase contrast lighting is helpful in identifying these organs. When-

Phylum Platyhelminthes

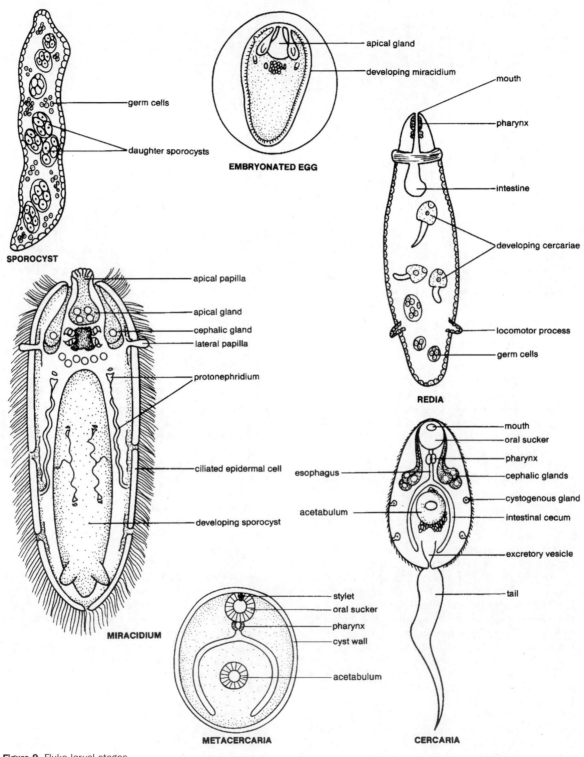

Figure 9. Fluke larval stages.

SPOROCYST
germ cells
daughter sporocysts

EMBRYONATED EGG
apical gland
developing miracidium

REDIA
mouth
pharynx
intestine
developing cercariae
locomotor process
germ cells

MIRACIDIUM
apical papilla
apical gland
cephalic gland
lateral papilla
protonephridium
ciliated epidermal cell
developing sporocyst

METACERCARIA
stylet
oral sucker
pharynx
cyst wall
acetabulum

CERCARIA
mouth
oral sucker
pharynx
cephalic glands
cystogenous gland
intestinal cecum
excretory vesicle
tail
esophagus
acetabulum

ever possible, you should first study whole mounts of the larval stages before examining sections.

1. Miracidium. The miracidium is a small, free-swimming, ciliated larva that resembles a protozoan. Observe a slide of miracidia. What evidence suggests that this organism is a metazoan and not a protozoan? Attempt to locate as many of the following features as possible: ciliated epidermis, apical papilla, apical eyespot, and developing sporocyst. Sometimes the best that one can do is to determine the anterior and the posterior ends; it all depends upon the quality of the slide.

2. Sporocyst. This larval generation absorbs nutrients directly from host tissues and reproduces another embryonic stage such as daughter sporocysts, redia, or cercaria. Look for evidence of these stages within the sporocyst. Sections of tissue parasitized by sporocysts also may be examined. Can you distinguish host tissue from that of the parasite? How can you tell the difference? Are daughter stages evident within these sections?

3. Redia. Rediae leave the sporocyst and relocate in the host's digestive gland or gonad. Note the elongate shape of this stage and the presence of embryos (daughter rediae or cercariae). At the anterior end locate the mouth and muscular pharynx that leads to a small saccate gut. Towards the posterior locate the two locomotory processes. Did the sporocyst stage possess locomotory processes? Why might redia possess such appendages while sporocysts do not?

4. Cercaria. This stage leaves the intermediate host and either locates its definitive host directly or encysts in another intermediate host, becoming a metacercaria. Note the tail used for locomotion. The nature of the tail is important in distinguishing the types of cercaria. Is the tail forked? Attempt to locate the oral and midventral (acetabulum) suckers and the biramous intestine. Are cystogenous glands present in the cercariae? These secretory structures produce the metacercarial cyst. (Phase contrast lighting may help you in these observations.)

5. Metacercaria. In most trematodes this encysted stage precedes the adult. Encystment may take place on the surface of a plant, as in *Fasciola hepatica*, or in a second intermediate host such as a fish, as happens in *Clonorchis sinensis*. In *Fasciola*, metacercariae are small, flattened, caplike structures. Scan slides of metacercariae of *Fasciola* and *Clonorchis*. In *Fasciola*, ignore the plant debris often associated with the preparation. Occasionally oral and ventral suckers, pharynx, and biramous intestine may be seen within the cyst. Unfortunately, sometimes the best you can do is to make out the cyst wall.

Observational Procedure for Live Larval Stages

Caution: All participants in this exercise are to wear rubber gloves. The cercariae isolated in the following exercise may be members of the genera of bird schisto-somes. These larvae must be considered to be a biological hazard as they cause a rash upon penetrating your skin. This condition is known as cercarial dermatitis or swimmer's itch. While not generally considered to be serious, there is an increased sensitization with successive encounters. Wash your hands and all instruments in soapy water upon completion of the observations. Spills should be cleaned up immediately; direct contact of the pond water with your skin should be attended to quickly.

Sporocysts and Rediae. Obtain a snail from your instructor and place it in a small glass dish containing a small amount of water. Using the blunt end of a metal dissection probe, crush the snail, working from the apex down the body. Do not completely pulverize the tissues as you may destroy the larval stages. Take up some of the material into a Pasteur pipette and place it into the well of a depression slide. This material will be examined for the larval stages, so the slurry should not be too thick. Dilute the preparation with water as necessary. Using low power of a compound microscope scan the slide for sporocysts and rediae (Fig. 9). Cercariae also may be present in these preparations, but they may not be mature. Once you have found these stages, repeat the observations you made on the prepared slides.

Live Cercariae

1. Place freshly collected snails or fingernail clams into separate vials (ca. 25–50 ml) filled with filtered pond water. (Do not use chlorinated tap water as the chlorine may be sufficiently concentrated to kill the mollusks. Tap water that has been aged for 2–3 days should be adequate.)

2. Examine each vial the next day for free-swimming cercariae. To do this, hold a vial in front of a piece of black paper and illuminate it from the side using a high-intensity lamp attached to a flexible arm. Try shining the lamp from different angles to achieve the best lighting. The cercariae will appear as tiny white specks moving about in the water. Use a Pasteur pipette to transfer all of the suspected cercariae to the well of a depression slide to examine them more closely.

3. Did you isolate cercariae or something else? How would you know whether the organisms are cercariae or not? If the organisms were cercariae, continue with the next two steps in the exercise.

4. How does this larval stage move? How fast do they move? To examine their internal anatomy, add a drop of a very dilution solution of neutral red or Nile blue to the depression slide. After a few minutes transfer the specimens to a regular microscope slide and add a cover slip, making sure that you do not crush the larvae. What structures can you see?

5. Were all of the mollusks examined infected with cercariae? About how many cercariae per mollusk were released? What does this indicate about the parasitic burden of these mollusks? Knowing where the snails were collected provides information on the trematode fauna of the habitat. Would you say that it is high or low?

Other Trematodes

Unfortunately, in recent years many biological supply houses have dropped a number of useful specimens from their product lines. However, the specimens available for study at your institution may include some of these interesting species. As time and materials permit, review the following specimens.

1. *Prosthogonimus.* This small digenetic fluke of the Family Prosthogonimidae is a common parasite of birds, especially ducks, living in the Great Lakes region of North America. Adults of *Prosthogonimus* parasitize the oviduct of birds, and in doing so, occasionally becomes lodged in the bird's eggs. Examine a whole mount slide of *Prosthogonimus*. Note that the adult has a wide flattened body. Based on the habitat of this species, speculate on the significance of this morphology. Because prepared specimens usually have a transparent body you should easily be able to identify all of the structures discussed in the Observational Procedure for *Fasciola*.

2. *Metagonimus.* This intestinal parasite infects a variety of mammals, including humans, in countries of the Far East and surrounding the Baltic Sea. Infections develop from eating undercooked fish. Examine available slides of whole mounts; attempt to locate the structures seen in other flukes.

3. *Echinostoma.* This species is a widely distributed parasite of the ileum of birds and mammals, including humans. Infection of the definitive host occurs by eating mollusks, fish, or amphibians infected with metacercariae. Examine available slides of whole mounts; attempt to locate the structures seen in other flukes.

4. *Paragonimus.* This small (5 x 10 mm) fluke usually lives in the lungs of humans and other mammals, encapsulated by connective tissue. However, the fluke is known to infect other organs. Infections begin by the consumption of undercooked crustaceans. Examine available slides of whole mounts; attempt to locate the structures seen in other flukes. ■

C. Class Monogenea

Monogenea [mon-o-GEN-e-ah; G., *mono*, one + G., *gene*, descent] is a relatively small class of some 1,100 species that are all parasitic on freshwater and marine ectothermal vertebrates, especially fish. They tend to be ectoparasites, but some are found in the mouth, rectum, and urinary bladders. Monogeneans are similar in size and shape to the flukes described, except for the characteristic posterior attachment organ, the **opisthaptor** or **haptor.** Anteriorly the **prohaptor** or adhesive organ, an organ of feeding and attachment, resembles the oral sucker of flukes. Monogeneans are small, ranging in size from 0.03 to 30 mm in length. Unlike the flukes, there is but a single larval stage, the oncomiracidium. This free-swimming, ciliated larva attaches to a host and then gradual develops into an adult. Few monogeneans are serious pathogens. However, under crowded conditions in fish hatcheries, massive infestations can result in serious erosion of tissues and lead to secondary infections which can cause massive die-offs.

■ Observational Procedure: Monogenea

Examine slides of *Gyrodactylus* (Fig. 10) or *Neobenedenia* (= *Benedenia*). Both are ectoparasites of fish. You may need to view several specimens to see all of the internal structures. Depending on the quality of the preparation, sometimes the best you can do is to identify the anterior and posterior ends and see that the opisthaptor is a large sucker.

At the posterior end, locate the large ventral sucker (opisthaptor). How is this sucker armed? Does it possess centrally located hooks? Are there other smaller hooks (hooklets) along the margin of the sucker? Given that monogeneans are ectoparasites that feed on their host's tissues and body fluids, how does the opisthaptor provide for an effective means of attachment? At the anterior end, locate the forked adhesive organs (head organs), large muscular pharynx, and biramous intestine. In *Gyrodactylus*, the normal oncomiracidium is not present. However, a juvenile worm may be seen developing internally in this viviparous monogenean. ■

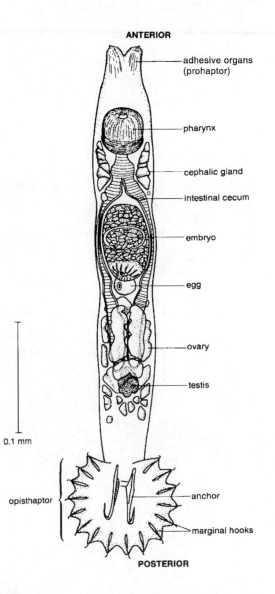

Figure 10. Ventral view of *Gyrodactylus*, a monogenetic flatworm.

D. Class Cestoda

Cestoda [ses-TO-da; G., *cest*, girdle + G., *oda*, resemblance] is a moderate-sized class comprising about 4,000 species of endoparasitic flatworms commonly known as **tapeworms**. Although they are dorsoventrally flattened, cestodes differ from other flatworms in a number of ways. Tapeworms completely lack a mouth and digestive tract. Most have a long, ribbon-like body that may be many meters in length; however, some cestodes are

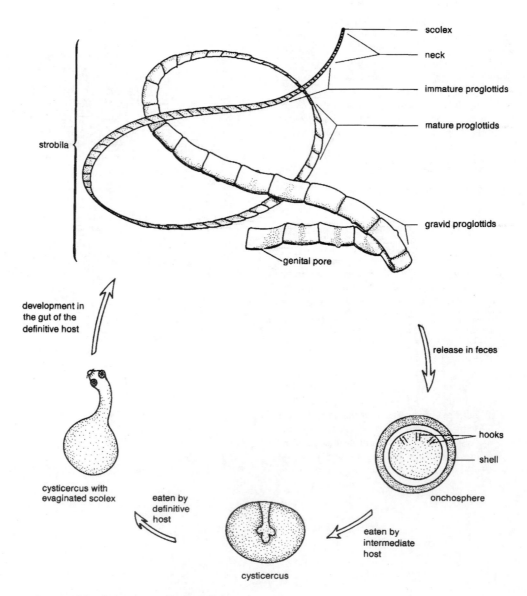

Figure 11. Life cycle of the pig tapeworm, *Taenia solium*.

Phylum Platyhelminthes

Figure 12. Representative tapeworm scolices.

less than 3 mm long. The body is usually comprised of three regions: **scolex** ("head"), **neck**, and **strobila** (body). Adults are found lodged in the intestine of a vertebrate, where they utilize the nutrients of their host. Larval stages often cause considerable damage to their intermediate hosts. Humans infected with tapeworms, normally found in animals (a condition called **zoonosis**), may have serious complications (e.g., **hydatid cysts** of *Echinococcus granulosus*). Cestodes have enormous medical, veterinary, and economic importances.

The strobila is made up of many identical units called **proglottids**, except in the Subclass Cestodaria whose members have a short undivided body. The strobila appears segmented, but tapeworms lack true segmentation. Production of proglottids is similar to strobilization of the ephyra from the strobila stage of the life cycle of the scyphozoan jellyfish, *Aurelia*. Proglottids are formed sequentially in the neck region and are at first relatively undifferentiated, but they mature as they grow older. Therefore, proglottids are progressively older and more mature the further away from the scolex. Eggs of the very oldest proglottids have been fertilized and these proglottids with expanded uteri are said to be **gravid**. There are no septa (walls) separating

proglottids and the tissues grade from one proglottid to the next. These characteristics are very different from the production of true segments in segmented phyla (e.g., Annelida).

The scolex acts as an anchor and is modified in different species to include various holdfast organs, with bulbous ends, spines, hooks, suckers, and several types of glands. The scolex also contains most of the animal's neural ganglia and sensory receptors. The tapeworm body wall is a living tissue (tegument) covered by numerous microscopic projections called **microtriches**. These microvilli-like structures are responsible for absorbing nutrients from the host's gut.

Tapeworms have an immense reproductive capacity; some may release one million eggs per day! Tapeworms usually have one or more larval stages, each with its own intermediate host. However, there are many variations in the life cycle and several different types of intermediate stages are recognized.

It is not possible to cover this diverse class completely; therefore, we will study only a few species in some detail. Other species will be introduced, if they are available. At this point it will be profitable if students review the life cycle of a typical tapeworm (Fig. 11).

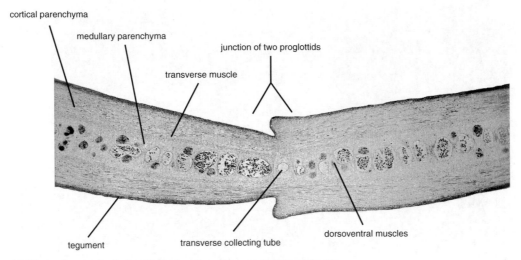

cortical parenchyma

medullary parenchyma

junction of two proglottids

transverse muscle

tegument

transverse collecting tube

dorsoventral muscles

Figure 13. Photomicrograph of a longitudinal section of two proglottids of *Taenia*.

■ Observational Procedure: Cestoda

Scolices
Obtain whole mount slides of the anterior ends of several different tapeworms (e.g., *Diphyllobothrium latum*, *Echinococcus granulosus*, *Moniezia spp.*, *Taenia solium*, *T. pisiformis*, *Dipylidium canium,* and *Taeniarhynchus saginatus*) and examine the scolices of each (Fig. 12). What types of structural adaptations do scolices have to be holdfast organs? Do all scolices have the same type of armaments? Are there any unusual structures present? Compare the scolices of *D. latum* to *T. solium*. Are they the same? Does *D. latum* have a scolex comparable to the other species studied? Formulate a table that compared the scolices of the species you examined in table format.

Strobila
Observe a whole specimen of a tapeworm.
1. As best you can, determine the length of the specimen. Is the worm of uniform width throughout? Identify the scolex, neck, and strobila of this specimen. What criteria did you use to make this differentiation? Note the individual proglottids of the strobila. How wide is the scolex compared to the width of the neck? The width of the strobila? Some tapeworms can achieve remarkable lengths, but they do not continue to increase in size indefinitely. The length of the adult worm changes: some proglottids are shed, while others are added. How does this fact and the widths of the body inform us of the rel-

ative strength of the tissues composing the scolex, neck, and strobila?
2. Return to the slides of tapeworm scolices and examine the neck regions (Fig. 12). This is the area where young proglottids are being formed. Do the proglottids begin at a specific point on the neck or do they gradually take form? Is there any differentiation of internal organs noticeable in the proglottids of the neck? Look for two strips of lighter tissue which extend posteriorly from the scolex. These are the **excretory canals**.
3. If available, examine a slide of a longitudinal section of *Taenia*. (Please note that cross sections will not do for these observations.) What structures can you see in this section (Fig. 13)? Focus your attention on the region of the junction of two proglottids. What signifies the termination of one proglottid? Are there septa between the proglottids? Consider the significance of this fact in relationship to the term segmentation? Reconsider the strobila stage of the scyphistoma polyp of the cnidarian *Aurelia*. Compare and contrast strobilization in the tapeworm and in cnidarians. How are they similar? How do they differ? (The concept of segmentation will come up again in later exercises, so it is important to begin to consider it now.)
4. Obtain a whole mount slide that includes several developmental stages of proglottids of *Taenia* (or another tapeworm), and with the aid of Fig. 14, identify the components of the male and female reproductive systems. In gravid proglottids, eggs fill the uterus and may obscure parts of the reproductive systems. Compare mature and gravid proglottids. How has the

Figure 14. Proglottids of *Taenia*. (A) Immature. (B) Mature. (C) Gravid.

morphology of the uterus been changed by the storage of eggs?

5. Obtain a slide of a whole mount of the canine or hydatid tapeworm E. granulosus. Compare the anatomy of *Taenia* with that of *Echinococcus granulosus* (Fig. 15). Note that in *E. granulosus*, the entire worm is only a few millimeters long and contains only three proglottids. The scolex has a **rostellum** [L., little beak] with a double row of hooks and four suckers. Immediately behind the scolex is a very short neck and then three proglottids. Determine which of these proglottids is immature, mature, and gravid.

6. Observe a prepared slide with cross sections of a sexually mature proglottid of *Taenia* (Fig. 16). On the surface, note the tegument and just beneath it the layers of circular and longitudinal muscle tissues. The tissue from this region inward is called the **cortex** region of the parenchyma. Look for the two parallel layers of transverse muscles which surround the reproductive systems and a less dense central parenchyma called the **medulla**. Unlike the parenchyma of turbellarians and flukes, the parenchyma of tapeworms contains few dorsoventral muscle fibers.

7. At the lateral margins of the proglottid, locate the large excretory ducts.

Figure 15. *Echinococcus granulosus.* (A) Adult. (B) Hydatid cyst.

8. Examine a slide with serial sections of a single mature proglottid, and with aid of Fig. 14, determine where the approximate position of each section would be in the proglottid. Identify the following structures in the sections: testes, ovary, uterus, vitelline gland.

Larval Stages
1. Observe a slice of **measly pork** on display and note the pits scattered throughout the meat. These are the **bladderworm** or **cysticercus** stage of the pig tapeworm (*T. solium*) (Fig. 11). Do you think that a single cysticercus could go undetected during meat processing? What about on your dinner plate? What function does thorough cooking serve here? Besides proper cooking, how do societies avoid parasitization by this species?
2. Note that some cysticerci contain a bulbous structure on the inside. This is the invaginated scolex. Describe what it looks like. Examine a whole mount of a cysticercus from *Taenia*, or another species, and locate the scolex. How does the orientation of the hooks compare to that in the adult? Why is there a difference? What process produces the reorientation (reorganiza-

tion) of the hooks from the larval to the adult condition? Where and when does this happen?
3. If available, compare cysticerci from other tapeworms (e.g., *Hymenolepis*) to that of *Taenia*. How are they similar? How do they differ? Remember your conclusions to these questions in the following study of the hydatid tapeworm.
4. Re-examine the whole mount slide of *E. granulosus*. This species demonstrates asexual reproduction in its larval stage. Once the **oncosphere** has implanted in the lungs or liver of an intermediate host, it develops into a structure called the **hydatid cyst** (Fig. 15). Eventually, inside the main portion of the cyst, many **brood capsules** are asexually produced. Within each brood capsule a dozen or more tiny protoscolices are formed. Individual protoscolices and whole brood capsules may be freed within the cyst and then are known collectively as **hydatid sand**.
5. Observe a cross section of a hydatid cyst and locate the structures indicated below (Fig. 15). The outer part of the cyst is a thick, noncellular, fibrous envelope formed from host tissues. Just inside the envelope is a

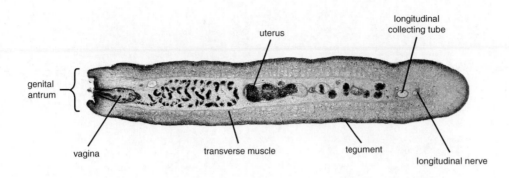

Figure 16. Cross section of a proglottid from *Taenia*.

germinal layer from which brood capsules and independent protoscolices are budded. If a hydatid cyst is ruptured by a predator during a meal, the hydatid sand (protoscolices) will be released all over the flesh of the prey. How might this event function to distribute tapeworms throughout a pack of wolves?

The zoonotic condition of having a hydatid cyst is very serious in humans. Fluid from the hydatid cyst will cause anaphylactic shock in its host if it is released due to trauma or during surgery. Consider the life cycle of this parasite and determine a scenario that would lead to human **hydatidosis**.

Other Tapeworms and Live Specimens

Compare the general morphology of other species that are available for study to the species examined in this exercise. *If exercises with live worms are to be done, follow the instructions of your instructor, explicitly.*

Exercise Review

The Platyhelminthes is a complex phylum comprised of four unique classes. To reinforce your studies, we suggest that you construct a table that compares and contrasts the distinctive characteristics of each class. ∎

Phylum Nemertea (Rhynchocoela)

Nemertea [ne-MER-te-a; G., *nemerte*, unerring] comprises about 900 species of nonsegmented, dorsoventrally flattened worms, lacking a body cavity. They are commonly known as ribbon worms because of their length and shape. Nemerteans (also nemertines) range in size from a few millimeters to an incredible 30 m in *Lineus longissimus*; the average length is <20 cm long. Most nemerteans are marine and benthic, but pelagic, freshwater, and terrestrial species are known. Most nemerteans are carnivorous; a few are parasitic.

Nemerteans have several features of turbellarians, including a ciliated epidermis, protonephridia, and a bilateral nervous system. The space between the gut and the body wall also is filled with parenchyma, but this condition may not be acoelomate in the traditional sense. Turbeville and Ruppert (1985) suggest that both nemerteans and flatworms have evolved from coelomate taxa, perhaps the annelids. Nevertheless, nemerteans are unlike flatworms in three important characteristics. (1) They possess an eversible, tubular **proboscis** housed in a special, fluid-filled cavity (specialized coelom) called the **rhynchocoel**. For this reason the alternative phylum name **Rhynchocoela** [RING-ko-SE-la; G., *rhynchos*, snout + G., *coelo*, hollow] is often used. The proboscis is used in food capture, but has a different embryological origin from the mouth. Prey is seized by the proboscis which is everted from the rhynchocoel by hydrostatic pressure created by muscular contractions. The accuracy of the proboscis is said to be "unerring," hence the phylum name, Nemertea. (2) There is a complete digestive system. (3) A closed vascular system, which may be homologous with the coelom of annelids, is present (Turbeville and Ruppert 1985).

Classification

The division of nemerteans into two classes is based on position of the mouth relative to the cerebral ganglia and on the nature of the proboscis.

1. **Anopla** [AN-o-pla; G., *anoplos*, unarmed]. Nemerteans with mouth below or posterior to the cerebral ganglia. Proboscis is unarmed. Examples: *Cerebratulus* and *Lineus*.

2. **Enopla** [EN-o-pla; G., *enoplos*, armed]. Nemerteans with mouth anterior to the cerebral ganglia. In most species the mouth and proboscis pore are united with a common opening. Proboscis is armed with one or more stylets. Example: *Prostoma*.

■ Observational Procedure: *Cerebratulus*

1. Examine a nemertean such as *Cerebratulus* and identify the anterior and posterior ends (Fig. 1). Note that the body is long, somewhat dorsoventrally flattened, and nonsegmented.

2. Locate the proboscis pore at the very tip of the anterior end. Some specimens may have the proboscis partly extended. In *Cerebratulus* the large, slitlike, ventral mouth is near the anterior end.

From *Invertebrate Zoology*, Sixth Edition, Robert L. Wallace and Walter K. Taylor. Copyright © 2002 by Pearson Education, Inc. Published by Prentice-Hall, Inc. All rights reserved

Phylum Nemertea (Rhynchocoela)

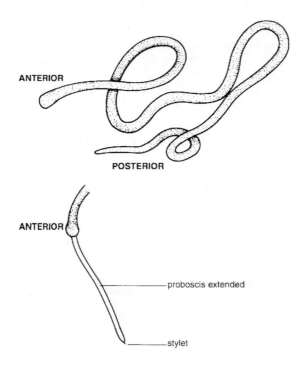

Figure 1. External view of a nemertean worm.

3. On the lateral margins just anterior to the mouth are two thin, longitudinal grooves called **cephalic slits**. These probably are chemoreceptors. At the very tip of the posterior end is the anus.

4. Examine several cross sections of a nemertean. Note that the body is covered by an epidermis of ciliated columnar glandular cells (Fig. 2). Beneath the epidermis locate a layer of connective tissue called the **extracellular matrix** or **dermis**. It occasionally has extensions that go deeper into the body. Just under the dermis locate the circular and longitudinal muscles layers.

5. Note the absence of a coelom. The body is filled with circular and longitudinal muscles and parenchymal tissue. In the central part of the animal locate the proboscis and below it the gut with its vacuolate phagocytic cells. Note that the hollow proboscis is constructed of layers of circular and longitudinal muscles. How does this tubular structure function? Surrounding the proboscis is a cell-lined, fluid-filled cavity called the rhynchocoel.

6. Also present within the body of nemerteans are lateral blood vessels, lateral nerves, protonephridia, and gonads. Attempt to locate these structures in the cross sections available for study (Fig. 2).

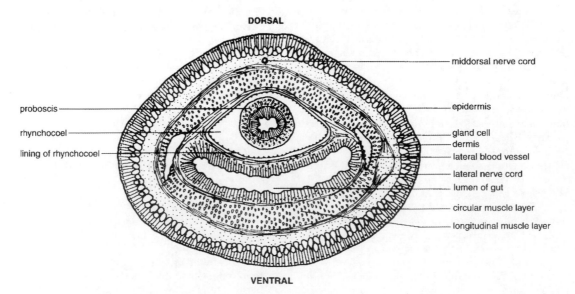

Figure 2. Cross section of a nemertean worm.

Phylum Nemertea (Rhynchocoela)

apical sense organ

midgut

foregut (stomodeaum)

lobe of pilidium

50 μm

Figure 3. Side view of a pilidium larva.

7. Examine a slide of the helmet-shaped, **pilidium larva** [G., *pilidium*, small felt cap] (Fig. 3). Note that the larva is covered with cilia, and at the aboral pole is an apical sensory organ with a tuft of long cilia. Find the foregut (**stomodeum**) flanked on either side by the oral lobes. The foregut leads to the small blind midgut. The anus develops later by an ectodermal invagination when the larva undergoes metamorphosis. The large internal cavity is the blastocoel.

Phylum Nemertea (Rhynchocoela)

1. Compare the criteria listed below for the four classes of Platyhelminthes.

Characteristics	Turbellaria	Trematoda	Monogenea	Cestoda
Mode of Life				
Body Wall Structure				
Digestive System				
Nervous System				
Excretory System				
Reproductive System				
Larval Stages				

2. What feature(s) distinguish Platyhelminthes from the Nemertea?

Phylum Nemertea (Rhynchocoela)

3. Indicate with a check which characters are associated with the particular class of Platyhelminthes.

Character	Turbellaria	Trematoda	Monogenea	Cestoda
Acetabulum				
Cercaria				
Cysticercus				
Eyespots				
Miracidium				
Onchosphere				
Oncomiracidium				
Opisthaptor				
Oral Sucker				
Pharynx				
Proglottid				
Prohaptor				
Redi				
Rhabdite				
Scolex				

4. Complete the chart for the parasitic forms of Platyhelminthes listed.

Species	Host(s)	Mode of Infection	Location of adult in host
Clonorchis sinensis			
Fasciolopsis buski			
Taenia solium			
Gyrodactylus			
Schistosoma			
Prosthogonimus			
Echinococcus granulosus			
Fasciola hepatica			
Taeniarhynchus saginatus			

PSEUDOCOELOMATE PHYLA

Traditionally a body cavity (perivisceral cavity) formed from a persistent blastocoel and lacking a meso-dermal lining (i.e., a cellular peritoneum) is called a **pseudocoelom** (pseudocoel). Using this descrip-tion, zoologists in the past grouped six phyla as pseudocoelomates: Acanthocephala, Kinorhyncha, Loricifera, Nematoda, Nematomorpha, and Rotifera. To this list some zoologists added the Phyla Gas-trotricha and Priapulida. Because these phyla possess certain similar features, some of them have been grouped within the **Aschelminthes** [AS-kel-MIN-theez; G., *ascus*, bladder + G., *helmins*, worm] or **Ne-mathelminthes** [NEE-mat-hel-MIN-theez; G., *nema*, thread]. This practice was more commonly used in European publications than in the United States.

Recent studies indicate there is no good reason to unite these taxa into a single clade. Perhaps the most significant arguments against their union is that the pseudocoel is not a persistent embryonic blastocoel and that some taxa (e.g., gastrotrichs) lack this body cavity. Thus, the pseudocoel is no longer consid-ered to be an important unifying feature. Further, some workers suggest that nematodes, nemato-morphs, and priapulids are closely related to arthropods because all possess a cuticle that is molted. One proposal is to place these animals in the clade **Ecdysozoa** [ECK-dy-SO-zo-a; G., *ecdysis*, slipping out + G., *zoon*, animal) (Aguinaldo et al. 1997). Kinorhynchs and loriciferans may be allied to Ecdysozoa. While the exact phylogenetic position of these taxa has not been firmly established, it is clear to many workers that the concept of the "pseudocoelomates" is no longer useful, except for historical consider-ations.

Given this analysis, all that remains of the old "pseudocoelomate" or aschelminth taxa are the gas-trotrichs, acanthocephalans, and rotifers, with the latter two perhaps belonging to a single taxa (Garey et al. 1996, 1998; Mark Welch 2000; Ricci 1998; Melone et al. 1998). Most of these animals are less than 1 cm long and lack a well-formed head, specialized organs for gas exchange and a circulatory system. Other important features found in many representatives of these phyla include a complete digestive tract with muscular pharynx, a protonephridial system, and eutely (consistency in the total number of cells). Three other taxa, which may be closely related to the Acanthocephala–Rotifera grouping, are the ma-rine Gnathostomulida and two new phyla: Cycliophora (Funch and Kristensen 1995) and Microg-nathozoa (Kristensen and Funch 2000). Because study material of these three taxa are not available from commercial supply houses, they are not covered in this manual.

Agree, J.R., L.Y. Mackey, J.M. Brooks, B. Winnepenninckx, and T. Backeljau. 1995. Animal phylogeny: ribosomal RNA studies of Aschelminthes. *J. Cell. Biochem.* suppl. 19B: 345.

Aguinaldo, A.M.A., J.M. Turbeville, L.S. Linford, M.C. Rivera, J.R. Garey, R.A. Raff, and J.A. Lake. 1997. Evidence for a clade of nematodes, arthropods and other moulting animals. *Nature* 387: 489–493.

Ehlers, U., W. Ahlrichs, C. Lemburg, and A. Schmidt-Rhaesa. 1996. Phylogenetic systematization of the Nemathelminthes (Aschelminthes). *Verh. Dtsch. Zool. Ges.* 89.1: 8.

Funch, P., and R.M. Kristensen. 1995. Cycliophora is a new phylum with affinities to Entoprocta and Ectoprocta. Nature 378: 711–714.

Funch, P., and R.M. Kristensen. 1997. Cycliophora. *In: Microscopic Anatomy of Invertebrates.* Volume 13. F.W. Harrison and E.E. Ruppert, (eds.). Wiley-Liss, New York, NY: 392–462.

Garey, J.R., T.J. Near, M.R. Nonnemacher, and S.A. Nadler. 1996. Molecular evidence for Acanthocephala as a sub-taxon or Rotifera. *J. Mol. Evol.* 43: 287–292.

Garey, J.R., A. Schmidt-Rhaesa, T.J. Near, and S.A. Nadler. 1998. The evolutionary relationships of rotifers and acanthocephalans. *Hydrobiologia* 387/388: 83–91.

Kristensen, R.M. 1991. Kinorhyncha. *In: Microscopic Anatomy of Invertebrates.* Volume 4. F.W. Harrison and E.E. Ruppert, (eds.). Wiley-Liss, New York, NY: 377–404.

Kristensen, R.M. 1991. Loricifera–a general biological and phylogenetic overview. *Verh. Dtsch. Zool. Ges.* 84: 231–246.

Kristensen, R.M. 1991. Loricifera. *In: Microscopic Anatomy of Invertebrates.* Volume 4. F.W. Harrison and E.E. Ruppert, (eds.). Wiley-Liss, New York, NY: 351–375.

Kristensen, R.M. 1995. Are Aschelminthes pseudocoelomate or acoelomate. *In: Body Cavities: Function and Phylogeny.* pp 41-43. G. Lanzavecchia, R. Valvassori, and M. D. Candia Carneval (eds.), Selected Symposia and Monographs U.Z.I., 8, Mucchi, Modena.

Kristensen, R.M. and P. Funch. 2000. Micrognathozoa: a new class with complicated jaws like those of Rotifera and Gnathostomulida. *J. Morph.* 246: 1–49.

Lorenzen, S. 1985. Phylogenetic aspects of pseudocoelomate evolution. *In: The Origins and Relationships of Lower Invertebrates.* Conway Morris, S., J.D. George, R. Gibson, and H.M. Platt. (eds.). Clarendon Press, Oxford: 210–223.

Mark, Welch, D. B. 2000. Evidence from a protein-coding gene that acanthocephalans are rotifers. *Invertebr. Biol.* 119: 17–26.

Melone, G., C. Ricci, H. Segers, and R.L. Wallace. 1998. Phylogenetic relationships of phylum Rotifera with emphasis on the families of Bdelloidea. *Hydrobiologia* 387/388: 101–107.

Ricci, C. 1998. Are lemnisci and proboscis present in Bdelloidea? *Hydrobiologia* 387/388: 93–96.

Rieger, R.M. 1976. Monociliated epidermal cells in Gastrotricha: significance for concepts of early metazoan evolution. *Z. Zool. Syst. Evolutionsforsch.* 14: 198–226.

Rieger, R.M., and S. Tyler. 1995. Sister-group relationship of Gnathostomulida and Rotifer-Acanthocephala. *Invertebr. Biol.* 114: 186–189.

Ruppert, E.E. 1991. Introduction to the aschelminth phyla: a consideration of mesoderm, body cavities, and cuticle. *In: Microscopic Anatomy of Invertebrates.* Volume 4. F.W. Harrison and E.E. Ruppert, (eds.). Wiley-Liss, New York, NY: 1–17.

Wallace, R.L., C. Ricci, and G. Melone. 1996. A cladistic analysis of pseudocoelomate (aschelminth) morphology. *Invertebr. Biol.* 115: 104–112.

Winnepenninckx, B. M. H., T. Backeljau, and R. M. Kristensen. 1998. Relations of the new phylum Cycliophora. *Nature* 398: 636–638.

Winnepenninckx, B. T. Backeljau, L.Y. Mackey, J. M. Brooks, R. De Wachter, S. Kumar, and J.R. Garey. 1995. 18S rRNA data indicate that aschelminthes are polyphyletic in origin and consist of at least three distinct clades. *Mol. Biol. Evol.* 12: 1132–1137.

Phylum Rotifera

Rotifera [ro-TIF-e-ra; L., *rota*, wheel + L., *ferre*, to bear] is a small phylum of some 2,000 species of bilaterally symmetrical, microscopic animals having two distinguishing features: (1) a ciliated, apical region called the **corona**, used in locomotion and food gathering (Figs. 1 and 2), and (2) a muscular pharynx (**mastax**) equipped with complex jaws of seven pieces called **trophi** (Fig. 3). The name "wheel bearer" is an allusion to the corona which resembles a rotating wheel due to the metachronal beat of its cilia. In one group of rotifers (collothecids) cilia are nearly lacking and long setae are used in prey-capture (Fig. 2).

Most rotifers are small (50–2,000 µm) and saccate to cylindrical in shape. Typically they are found in freshwater habitats where they are often very abundant, although several species are exclusively marine. Some members of Class Bdelloidea inhabit the films of water found in soils or covering terrestrial plants such as mosses. Most rotifers are free moving, either by swimming or crawling, but many sessile species live attached to freshwater plants (Fig. 2). Nearly all rotifers are solitary, but about 25 species form colonies. Although very different in size and general biology, research indicates that the rotifers and acanthocephalans are closely related.

Classification

Three classes are commonly recognized.

1. **Class Seisonidea.** Separate sexes of similar size and morphology. Gonads paired. Single Genus *Seison*, epizootic on marine crustaceans.

2. **Class Bdelloidea.** Only females. Paired ovaries. Mainly swimming and crawling forms. Many capable of becoming desiccated and then rehydrated. Examples: *Habrotrocha* and *Philodina*.

3. **Class Monogononta.** Separate sexes. Single gonads. Males rare and often structurally reduced. Reproduction mainly parthenogenetic, sexual reproduction results in a diapausing embryo. Three orders of benthic, swimming, and sessile forms. Examples: *Asplanchna*, *Brachionus*, *Collotheca*, *Filinia*, *Floscularia*, *Keratella*, *Lecane*, *Synchaeta*, and *Trichocerca*.

■ Observational Procedure:

1. Examine a culture of rotifers using a dissection microscope and describe the locomotory activities you observe. Describe the motion of the "wheel organ" at this magnification. Are the specimens you are studying monogononts (Fig. 1A) or bdelloids (Fig. 1B)? If both are available, compare their locomotion. Does each move in the same way? At this magnification can rotifers be mistaken for protozoans or gastrotrichs? How may they be distinguished?

2. Making a slide preparation of rotifers will depend on the kind available for study: for bdelloid rotifers, suck up a small amount of the debris from the bottom of the culture vessel; for free-swimming monogonont rotifers (two options), blindly suck up a small amount of culture fluid and hope for the best or attempt to pick out a single individual from the culture while observing it using a dissection microscope. Place a ring of methyl cellulose

From *Invertebrate Zoology*, Sixth Edition, Robert L. Wallace and Walter K. Taylor. Copyright © 2002 by Pearson Education, Inc. Published by Prentice-Hall, Inc. All rights reserved

Phylum Rotifera

Figure 1 Views of two common rotifers. (A) *Brachionus plicatilis*, amictic female and male (Monogononta). (B) *Philodina roseola* (Bdelloidea). Each about 300 μm in length.

on a slide and add 1–2 drops of the rotifer culture into the center of the ring. Gently mix the methyl cellulose and culture fluid with a toothpick and then carefully apply a coverslip to the preparation, avoiding the introduction of air bubbles.

3. Using low power, examine your slide for rotifers. After locating an animal, identify its anterior and posterior ends (Figs. 1 and 2). Note that the body may be divided into three general regions: head (with corona), body, and foot with toes (Fig. 1). A neck region also may be present or the foot absent. Although highly variable, the corona usually consists of two ciliated rings (trochus and cingulum) at the anterior end.

4. Switch to higher magnification and attempt to distinguish the details of the coronal ciliation, including the trochus and cingulum (Fig. 1). How do the cilia appear to move? Are cirri present? Be careful not to let the slide dry out during your examinations. This may be avoided by periodically adding a drop of culture fluid to the edge of the coverslip.

5. Turn your attention to the internal anatomy of your rotifer specimens. Under high power, locate the stomach, intestine, ovary (ovaries in bdelloids), musculature, protonephridial flame cells, foot with pedal glands, and toes (Fig. 1). As you examine the organs, look for the presence of nuclei.

6. If live protozoans or gastrotrichs are available, make a slide of that material and observe these organisms, comparing their general morphology to that of rotifers. Can rotifers easily be confused with ciliated protozoans or gastrotrichs under high power magnification? What sort of descriptive terms might be used to describe the movements of each? What distinctive anatomical features does each phylum possess?

7. Make another slide without methyl cellulose and place a small drop of food suspension (small algae or yeast) or inert material (carmine powder or latex microspheres, 1–5 μm) at the edge of the coverslip. Draw the suspension across the slide using a piece of toweling and observe the rotifers under low power. Track

Figure 2 Several common freshwater rotifers. Bars = 100 μm. All are planktonic except for *Collotheca trilobata* which is a sessile species. (After Koste 1978.)

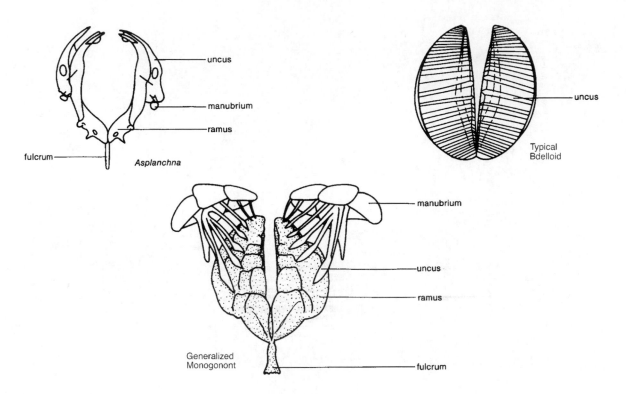

Figure 3 Rotifer trophi (not drawn to scale).

any particles that become caught in the coronal currents and follow them as they enter the mouth.

Describe the activity of the mastax during feeding. What function do the trophi serve in feeding? Can you see the particles accumulate in the gut? If you watch the animals long enough, you will see them pass the food you provided out of the anus. How long did it take from the start of feeding to first elimination of that food? This is the gut passage time. Were all the cells of the live food completely digested while in the gut? What do these observations tell you about feeding and digestion in rotifers? What are the ecological consequences of these features?

8. If additional species are available for study, examine them and compare their general morphology. What anatomical differences do you observe, especially between monogonont and bdelloid species (Fig. 1A and B, and Fig. 2)? Zooplankton samples from the field may contain a variety of species, including some with resting eggs (Fig. 4). Depending on the species avail-

Figure 4 Resting eggs of rotifers (not drawn to scale). (After Koste 1978.)

able for study, you may observe the remains of food in their guts.

9. If freshwater plants are available from a eutrophic pond or lake, examine them for sessile forms. To do this place a leaf of the plant in a small dish of water and observe it using a dissection microscope at about 30–50x. Large sessile forms (= 500–1,000 µm) such as *Collotheca* (Fig. 2) or *Floscularia* may be present. The latter resembles an elongate *Brachionus* (Fig. 1), but its corona is elaborated into large ears!

10. If time and materials permit, make another slide preparation of one or more of the available species, but add a small drop of bleach to the fluid before putting the coverslip in place. *Quickly locate a rotifer on the slide, switch to high power, and observe as the bleach dissolves the soft tissues, leaving only the trophi.* Examine the trophi and locate the various parts illustrated in Fig. 3.

11. Observe a prepared slide of preserved rotifers and compare them to the live preparations just examined. Locate as many of the features mentioned above as you can. ∎

Phylum Acanthocephala

The endoparasitic worms comprising Phylum Acanthocephala [a-kan-tho-SEF-a-la; G., *acantho*, spine or thorn + G., *cephala*, head] are distinguished by a protrusible **proboscis** covered with recurved spines (Fig. 1). The proboscis anchors adults to the mucosal lining of their vertebrate host (Fig. 2). Thorny-headed worms range from about 1 mm to more than 1 m in length depending on the species; most are about 25 mm long. Like cestodes, acanthocephalans, absorb nutrients through the porous body wall or **tegument**, a complex syncytial layer containing fluid-filled canals called **lacunae**. Because of their parasitic nature, acanthocephalans are of economic importance as they affect domestic stock and game animals. Occasionally, there are reports of human infections. In spite of a morphology and life cycle radically different from rotifers, these two phyla are clearly related for both possess a syncytial epidermis condensed into a sort of cuticle with numerous intracytoplasmic microtubules.

Classification

Four classes are recognized in this small phylum of about 700 species.

1. **Class Archiacanthocephala**. Parasites of birds and mammals. Insects and myriapods serve as intermediate hosts. Examples: *Mediorhynchus* (parasite of birds), *Moniliformis* (parasite of rats), and *Macracanthorhynchus* (parasite of pigs).

2. **Class Palaeacanthocephala**. Parasites of all vertebrate classes. Example: *Plagiorhynchus* (parasite of passerine birds).

3. **Class Eoacanthocephala**. Parasites of fish, amphibians, and reptiles. Example: *Neoechinorhynchus* (parasite of fish).

4. **Class Polyacanthocephala**. Parasites of fish and possibly crocodilians.

■ Observational Procedure: *Macracanthorhynchus*

General Morphology and the Proboscis. Observe a slide (whole mount) or preserved specimen of *Macracanthorhynchus hirudinaceus*, a parasite of pigs. Determine the anterior and posterior ends. Note the following: (1) recurved hooks on the proboscis, (2) neck, (3) trunk, and (4) genital region. Is there any evidence of segmentation in thorny-headed worms? Examine a cross or longitudinal section of *M. hirudinaceus* with the proboscis embedded in the intestine of a pig (Fig. 2). Are any spines visible in this section? Do you see any evidence of host tissue damage? How much tissue damage would you expect to find, if many of these parasites were attached to the intestinal wall?

Internal Anatomy and Reproduction. Place a specimen in a dissection pan and make an anterior-posterior incision from the region of the genital pore to the neck. Then turn the cut edges laterally and pin them to the base of the pan using fine insect pins. Using Fig. 1 as an aid,

From *Invertebrate Zoology*, Sixth Edition, Robert L. Wallace and Walter K. Taylor. Copyright © 2002 by Pearson Education, Inc. Published by Prentice-Hall, Inc. All rights reserved

Phylum Acanthocephala

Figure 1. Schematic illustration of some external and internal features of male and female acanthocephalans.

locate the following structures: male—(1) lemnisci and (2) reproductive organs; female—(1) proboscis receptacle, (2) lemnisci, (3) ligamentous sac (which posteriorly communicates with the uterine bell), (4) uterus and vagina, and (5) genital pore.

Observe the muscular complex at the anterior part of the trunk. Cut away a narrow strip of the body wall and examine it under a dissection microscope. It should appear porous. The spaces seen are the lacunar parts of the canal system in the body wall. The canal system also will be evident in prepared slides of cross and longitudinal sections of *M. hirudinaceus.*

In female specimens examine the ligament sac surface. If patches or clumps of cells are present, these probably will be egg clusters (**ovarian balls**). Examine the body cavity for eggs and/or put pressure on the uterine bell to force out some eggs for collection. Place some of them on a slide with a drop of water, add a cover slip, and examine. Note the stage of development of several eggs. If available, observe the development of acanthocephalan eggs on a prepared slide (Fig. 3) ■.

hooked (embedded in host intestinal tissue)

proboscis

tegument

Figure 2. Photomicrograph of a longitudinal section of *Macracanthorhynchus hirudinaceus* with its proboscis embedded in the intestine of a pig.

raphe

hook

acanthor

EGG WITH EMBRYO

proboscis

hook

proboscis receptacle

ACANTHELLA

hook

ACANTHOR

proboscis with hooks

proboscis receptacle

CYSTACANTH

Figure 3. Larval stages of the acanthocephalan *Macracanthorhynchus hirudinaceus*. (After Kates from Olsen.)

Phylum Acanthocephala

Gastrotricha, Rotifera, Acanthocephala	Worksheet 5
Name: _____	Date: _____
Course #: _____ / Section #: _____	Grade: _____

1. Using your textbook, laboratory manual, and other materials that your instructor permits, fill in the following chart as to whether these features are present or absent in these taxa.

Morphological feature	Gastrotricha	Rotifera	Acanthocephala
Adhesive/cement glands			
Cilia			
Foot			
Furca			
Intracytoplasmic microtubules			
Jaws			
Lacunae			
Lemnisci			
Mouth			
Ovarian balls			
Pharynx			
Proboscis			
Protonephridium			
Scales			
Toe(s)			
Uterine bell			

2. Using the data table that you developed above, develop a phylogenetic tree for these three phyla. Draw that tree on a separate piece of paper indicating where the major evolutionary steps occurred. Be prepared to discuss the phylogenetic relationships of these organisms in class.

PHYLUM MOLLUSCA

Traditionally members of Phylum Mollusca have been considered to be schizocoelomate, nonsegmented protostomes. However, to some workers, repetition of certain external and internal structures in the Classes Monoplacophora and Polyplacophora constitutes evidence of segmentation. Recent molecular studies support this idea and suggest that mollusks evolved from a segmented ancestor, probably Phylum Annelida (Aguinaldo et al. 1997, Lake 1990). Compare the coverage provided in several current textbooks of invertebrate zoology for additional consideration of this concept. We retain the pedagogical approach of covering the mollusks before the annelids so that concepts of metamerism and tagmatization can be fully understood by the student.

Two distinct features set the mollusks apart from the other phyla. (1) The ventral surface has been modified into a muscular foot or into a group of muscular arms (tentacles). (2) Tissues of the dorsal and lateral surfaces have been modified into a structure called the mantle, which in most classes secretes an external shell. In some forms the shell is internal, much reduced, or absent. In the most primitive forms there is a tendency for the pericardial cavity, the metanephridia, and the gonads to be continuous. In more advanced groups these systems, especially the reproductive, become separated and independent anatomical units. However, all systems represent parts of the embryonic coelom which originates in a schizocoelic manner. The schizocoelom does not function as a hydraulic skeleton.

Aguinaldo, A.M.A., J.M. Turbeville, L.S. Linford, M.C. Rivera, J.R. Garey, R.A. Raff, and J.A. Lake. 1997. Evidence for a clade of nematodes, arthropods and other moulting animals. *Nature* 387: 489-493.

Ghiselin, M.T. 1988. The origin of molluscs in light of molecular evidence. *In: Oxford Surveys in Biology,* Volume 5. Harvey, P.H. and L. Partridge, (eds.). Oxford University Press, Oxford.

Lake, J.A. 1990. Origin of the Metazoa. Proc. Natl. Acad. Sci. USA 87: 763-766.

Nielsen, C. 1994. Larval and adult characters in animal phylogeny. *Amer. Zool.* 34: 492-501.

Nielsen, C. 2001. *Animal Evolution: Interrelationships of the Living Phyla,* 2nd edition. Oxford University Press, Oxford.

Runnegar, B. and J. Pojeta. 1974. Molluscan phylogeny: the paleontological viewpoint. Science 186: 311-317.

Vermeij, G. 1993. *A Natural History of Shells.* Princeton University Press, Princeton, NJ.

Phylum Mollusca

Well over 50,000 living species of clams, snails, chitons, oysters, octopods, squids, and many others comprise the richly diverse Phylum Mollusca [mo-LUS-ka; L., *molluscum*, soft]. This is the second largest animal phylum as to number of species present. These highly successful, unsegmented protostomes are widely distributed in freshwater, terrestrial, and marine environments worldwide. Mollusks, however, predominately occur in marine habitats, and range in size from less than 0.5 mm to nearly 20 m long, attained by the giant squid, *Architeuthis*. Two distinct features set mollusks apart from other invertebrates: (1) The internal organs are located in a visceral mass that is enclosed by a dorsal **mantle** or **pallium** (*pallium*, L., a mantle or cloak). The mantle secretes an external calcareous shell found in most species. (2) A ventral muscular **foot** serves in locomotion and food getting. Except for some specialized members, a unique type of gill or **ctenidium** occurs in mollusks. Another unique organ found in all mollusks, except the Class Bivalvia, is the chitinous, rasplike feeding device, the **radula**, located in the buccal cavity. Most mollusks have an open circulatory system, a moderate to highly cephalized nervous system of paired ganglia and nerves, and well-developed excretory and reproductive systems. The phylum dates to the **Cambrian Period** (Fig. 1) and includes 40,000 fossil species.

Classification

Seven classes of mollusks are recognized based on morphology of the foot, and presence or absence and type of shell.

1. **Class Monoplacophora.** A small relic class of fewer than twenty species of small (less than 3 cm), nontorted, marine mollusks with a single, dorsal, caplike shell. Many fossil species are represented in this class. Examples (extant): *Neopilina* and *Vema*.

2. **Class Polyplacophora.** Mollusks possessing a creeping foot and a shell divided into eight plates. Examples: *Katharina* and *Cryptochiton*.

3. **Class Aplacophora.** Small (less than 1–5 cm), worm-like, marine mollusks with calcareous spicules in the mantle. These shell-less animals crawl on, or burrow in sediments, or are epizoic on cnidarians in deep, marine waters. They are commonly called **solenogasters** [so-LEN-o-GAS-ters; G., *solen*, channel + G., *gaster*, stomach] because some species have a ventral, longitudinal groove that runs nearly the entire length of the body. Recently a new class, **caudofoveata** [KAW-doe-fo-ve-AH-ta; (L., *cauda*, tail + L., *fovea*, pit] has been erected comprising animals formerly assigned to Class Aplacophora.

4. **Class Gastropoda.** Snails and snail-like mollusks having a well-defined head with tentacles and relatively simple eyes. Most possess a single, coiled shell. The foot is adapted for crawling, but some species can swim with the structure. Gastropods possess the greatest biological diversity and largest number of species of any molluscan class: about 30,000 extant and 15,000 fossils.

   a. **Subclass Prosobranchia.** Shelled marine gas-

From *Invertebrate Zoology*, Sixth Edition, Robert L. Wallace and Walter K. Taylor. Copyright © 2002 by Pearson Education, Inc. Published by Prentice-Hall, Inc. All rights reserved

Phylum Mollusca

TIME (IN MILLIONS OF YEARS)

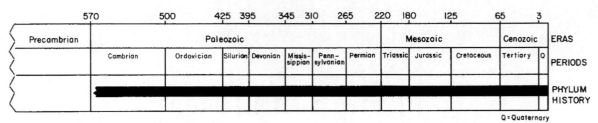

	Precambrian	Paleozoic							Mesozoic			Cenozoic		ERAS
		Cambrian	Ordovician	Silurian	Devonian	Missis-sippian	Penn-sylvanian	Permian	Triassic	Jurassic	Cretaceous	Tertiary	Q	PERIODS
														PHYLUM HISTORY

Q = Quaternary

Figure 1. Geologic history of the Phylum Mollusca.

tropods with the mantle cavity anterior. Examples: *Busycon* (whelks), *Conus* (cones), *Haliotis* (abalone), *Murex* (drills), and *Strombus* (conchs).

b. Subclass Opisthobranchia. Mostly marine gastropods with shell reduced or lacking. The mantle cavity is lacking or is on the right side, or may be partly posterior. Examples: *Aplysia* (sea hare) and *Aeolidia* (nudibranch).

c. Subclass Pulmonata. Mostly terrestrial, shelled gastropods with a mantle cavity modified as a lung. Examples: *Lymnaea* (freshwater snail) *Helix* (terrestrial snail) and *Limax* (land slug).

5. Class Bivalvia or Pelecypoda. Two shells or valves that are hinged dorsally occur in members of this class. Large curtain-like gills found in the mantle cavity are used in filter feeding. A head and radula are absent. Bivalvia is the second largest class of Mollusca with over 8,000 exant and about 20,000 fossil species present. Six subclasses of freshwater and marine species are recognized, but these are not reviewed here. Examples: *Cardium* (cockle), *Mytilus* (common mussel), *Unio* and *Anodonta* (freshwater clams or mussels), *Ostrea* (oyster), *Pecten* (scallop), *Mya* (soft-shelled clam), and *Mercenaria* (Venus clam or quahog).

6. Class Scaphopoda. A small group composed of approximately 350 species of burrowing marine mollusks with a single, dorsoventrally elongate, slightly curved, tubular shell (2–6 cm long) which is open at both ends. The shell resembles an elephant's tusk, so they are known commonly as tusk or tooth shells. A modified foot and set of delicate tentacles extend from the ventral orifice of the shell. Examples: *Dentalium* and *Cadulus*.

7. Class Cephalopoda. Elongated, free-swimming marine mollusks that are highly cephalized with a well-developed nervous system and a foot that is modified into specialized tentacles. Shell external, internal, or absent. There are about 600 living species and 8,000 fossil forms. Three subclasses are recognized.

a. Subclass Nautiloidea. Cephalopods with a multi-chambered, external shell and many arms. All forms are extinct except for four species in the genus *Nautilus*.

b. Subclass Ammonoidea. Cephalopods with coiled, multichambered, external shells. All members are extinct.

c. Subclass Coleoidea. Cephalopods with an internal shell or shell lacking. Four orders with extant species and one wholly extinct are recognized. Examples: *Loligo* (squid), *Octopus* (octopus), and *Sepia* (cuttlefish).

Of the seven molluscan classes, three (Aplacophora, Monoplacophora, and Scaphopoda) will not be covered here due to the lack of available commercial suppliers of specimens.

A. Class Polyplacophora

Commonly known as **chitons,** members of the Class Polyplacophora [POL-e-pla-KOF-o-ra; G., *poly*, many + G., *placo*, plate + G., *phora*, carry] are a small group (about 800 species) of dorsoventrally flattened marine mollusks, usually ranging in size from 1 to 10 cm long. Chitons are abundant in the intertidal zones along rocky coasts where they attach to rocks and other hard objects. Some species are found at depths greater than 5,000 m.

The ventral foot is a broad, flat, creeping sole and the shell is divided into eight partially overlapping plates or valves that articulate with one another, thus permitting chitons a certain degree of flexibility along the anterio-posterior axis. Laterally, the mantle extends beyond the plates to form a thick girdle surrounding the animal.

Chitons have an indistinct head and reduced nervous and sensory systems. They lack eyes, but have unique photosensitive structures called aesthetes (esthetes). These mantle cells occur in minute vertical canals in the upper layer of the shell plate.

■ Observational Procedure:

External Morphology

1. Obtain a specimen of the chiton *Katharina* and observe its general shape and symmetry (Fig. 2). Identify the anterior and posterior ends.

2. Place the specimen dorsal side up. Note that the shell consists of eight similar plates that overlap each other anteriorly. Portions of the plates are embedded in the fleshy mantle. The lateral, thickened part of the mantle is known as the **girdle**.

3. Observe the dorsal surface using a dissection microscope. In young individuals, aesthetes may be seen in the plates. In older specimens of *Katharina*, these and other markings on the plates are frequently eroded.

4. Place your specimen ventral side up. The most prominent feature of the ventral surface is the broad muscular foot. The indistinct head region, anterior to the foot (Fig. 2), bears the mouth, but lacks any special sense organs (e.g., tentacles and eyes).

5. Note the distinct groove between the foot and the girdle. This is the mantle cavity or **pallial groove**. It contains a single row of gills on either side of the foot (Fig. 2). Trace the gills of one side from the anterior to the posterior end. Are they the same size throughout? Approximately how many gills are there per side?

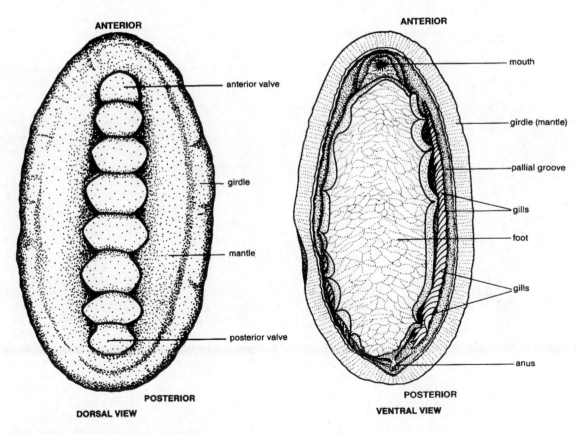

Figure 2. Dorsal and ventral views of *Katharina*.

Phylum Mollusca

6. Remove a gill and place it in a depression slide filled with a drop of water. Hold the base of the gill down with a dissection probe and gently run the point of another probe along the gill surface. Note that the gill is constructed of a series of small, rounded filaments positioned like the pages of a book. What is the significance of the serial filaments? Does this arrangement indicate true segmentation?

7. Find the anus at the posterior end of the pallial groove, just behind the foot. With a dissection microscope, locate the paired **nephridiopores** and **gonopores** that empty into the pallial groove on either side of the foot. These pores may be difficult to see. The nephridiopores are just anterior to the anus. Locate these pores by scanning the region between the gills and the foot, folding the gills aside with a probe as you proceed an-

teriorly with the search. In chitons other than *Katharina*, the nephridiopores are found on either side of the anus. The gonopore is located near and slightly anterior to each nephridiopore.

Internal Anatomy

1. To study the internal anatomy of a *Katharina*, the plates must be removed. Begin by **carefully** cutting away the mantle. Do not cut into the mantle between the plates. Cut around the plates laterally until they are nearly exposed. With a sharp scalpel, carefully remove the anterior plate by freeing it from its muscular and connective tissue attachments. When a plate is loose, carefully pry it up using a blunt probe. Working posteriorly, remove the remaining seven plates, placing each aside in order.

2. Examine the plates in their proper order (Fig. 3). The medial pigmented layer of the plate is known as the **tegumentum**, and the lateral, nonpigmented layer is called the **articulamentum**. The latter is inserted into the muscular mantle of the chiton. Note that the middle six plates are nearly identical in size and shape, but that the first (head) and last (tail) plates differ. With high magnification of the dissecting scope, look for holes in the tegmentum of an intermediate valve. These are openings to the aesthetes.

3. Examine the dorsal surface of the body and observe the thin mantle (Fig. 4). A pair of longitudinal muscles are located dorsally at the midline. What is their function? Locate the oblique and transverse muscles. What are their functions?

4. Pin the specimen to the dissection pan through the anterior and posterior ends and carefully remove the dorsal mantle without damaging the viscera beneath. Submerge the specimen in water and observe it under a dissection microscope.

5. Note the large bundles of muscles near the buccal bulb (Fig. 5) They attach to and operate the **odontophore** and **radula**. Find the salivary glands lateral to the muscular bands. Their ducts enter the buccal cavity posteroventrally.

6. Make a short incision through the dorsal surface of the buccal cavity, extending the cut laterally so as not to cut the odontophore muscles. Expose the radula and radular sac (Fig. 5); remove the radula intact and observe under the compound microscope. Are the teeth of uniform structure the entire length of the radula? Examine the morphology of the entire radula. Is it uniform from one end to the other? What does this variation indicate about the radula? Do any of the teeth have black caps? This black material is an iron salt called magnetite which makes the teeth magnetic. Find the cartilaginous odontophore over which the radula glides. Determine the action of this complex mechanism. In the

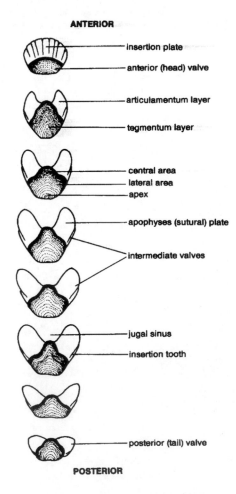

ANTERIOR

- insertion plate
- anterior (head) valve
- articulamentum layer
- tegmentum layer
- central area
- lateral area
- apex
- apophyses (sutural) plate
- intermediate valves
- jugal sinus
- insertion tooth
- posterior (tail) valve

POSTERIOR

Figure 3. Dorsal view of isolated plates of *Katharina*.

Phylum Mollusca

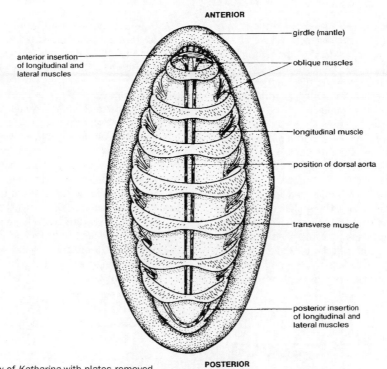

Figure 4. Dorsal view of *Katharina* with plates removed.

Figure 5. Dorsal internal view of the viscera of *Katharina*.

next part of this exercise you will compare the form of *Katharina's* radula to that of the gastropod *Helix*.

7. Without disturbing or making further incisions, locate the pharyngeal (sugar) gland, stomach, digestive gland, and intestine (Fig. 5). Note the length of the intestine. What does the length of the intestine indicate concerning the diet of this animal?

8. Located the single, mid-dorsal gonad (Fig. 5). It is a large, lobed structure that begins in the second third of the body and terminates at the posterior end. Start at the anterior end and trace the gonad until you find the genital ducts that lead to the gonopores.

9. Next locate the thin **pericardial membrane** and pericardial cavity. These are located dorsally in the hindquarter of the body under the tail valve (Fig. 5). The cavity surrounds the heart. Locate the triangular median ventricle in the posterior region of this cavity. The aorta leads from the ventricle anteriorly above the gonad. Paired thin auricles (atria) are attached to the lateral sides of the ventricle.

10. Carefully remove the digestive gland and gonad. Locate the thin, many-lobed kidneys extending nearly the entire length of the body. They drain into nephridiopores located just posterior to the gonopores.

Other Species

Observe a specimen of *Cryptochiton* and compare its external morphology to that of *Katharina*. Note the large size and apparent lack of plates. Where are the plates located? As your instructor directs, inspect other chitons. Look for differences in the size, shape, and ornamentation of the plates and girdle (e.g., granules, scales, spines). Are there any calcareous spicules on the surface of these chitons? What might their function(s) be?

If live specimens are available, observe their general movements, and feeding and homing behavior. How easy is it to remove a chiton from the substratum? If time permits, your instructor will provide instructions for observing the flow of respiratory water through the chiton's mantle cavity. ■

B. Class Gastropoda

Snails are members of Class Gastropoda [Gas-tro-POAD-a or GAS-trop-o-dah; G., *gastro*, stomach + G., *podos*, foot], a large group comprising over 40,000 extant and at least 15,000 extinct species of mollusks that vary greatly in size. Three important characteristics are seen in most gastropods. They have (1) a well-developed head, (2) a muscular creeping or swimming foot, and (3) a single asymmetrical shell of calcium carbonate and organic matter. The shell may be absent. Snail shells are usually coiled to the right (clockwise), but left-handed (counter-clockwise) shells are known (e.g., *Busycon perversum*, the lightning whelk). The shells of certain sessile gastropods (vermetid worm shells) are irregularly coiled (contorted) and generally elongated.

Students will first study shells and whole specimens of selected species to gain an appreciation of general snail morphology and of the diversity found in the class. The terrestrial pulmonate snail, *Helix*, will be dissected as a class representative.

■ Observational Procedure:

Living Gastropods

If live gastropods are available, make the following observations. Observe locomotion in a living snail. How fast does the animal move? How does the foot appear to move the animal? Describe movement of the foot when viewed from below. Determine the roles light and gravity play in movement.

Observe feeding in a living snail as it scrapes food from a glass surface. A hand lens may be helpful to make those observations. Note how the radula is applied to the glass. Is all the food removed by the animal? What marks are left by the radula after the animal passes by?

If living pulmonate specimens are available, observe functioning of the pneumostome. Does it remain open or does it periodically open and close? What is the significance of this cycle?

Diversity of Gastropods

There is a rich diversity of shelled forms in this class. Your instructor will provide you with a set of gastropod shells for you to study.

1. Place several different shells on the bench with their **apices** pointing away from you. What common features do these shells share (Fig. 6)? Are the **spires** of similar shape? Compare the relative sizes of the body whorls. Are there differences? Note the differences in shell **apertures**, size, and shape (Fig. 7).

2. On which side of the shell is the aperture found? Is this consistent in all the specimens present? Shells with the aperture on the right side are right-handed or **dextral** (L., *dexter*, right). Those with the aperture on the left side are known as left-handed or **sinistral** (L., *sinister*, left). View one shell of each type from the apex. Which way do dextral shells coil? Which way do sinistral shells coil? Are there some shells that do not conform to these descriptions?

Phylum Mollusca

Figure 6. Morphology of a generalized gastropod shell.

3. Observe that the outer shell surface may be ornamented with **lamellae, striations, tubercles, spines, and ribs**, or may be very smooth (Figs. 6 and 7). What might be the adaptive significance of these surface features? What types of colors and color patterns are found on the outer shell surface? Are these colors found through the shell? How might these color patterns be produced? (*Hint*: Consider how patterns are produced in a woven rug or mat. Is the pattern printed on at the end or is it incorporated into the rug as it is woven?) What is the significance of color and color patterns to the living snail?

4. Examine a shell that has been cut or broken in half longitudinally. The central column is called the **columella**. Is the shell divided into compartments by the columella? In life, how is the snail positioned in the shell?

5. To gain a better understanding of this point, do the following exercise. Cut a thin strip of construction paper about 10–15 cm x 0.5 cm long. Snake the paper through the whorls of the cut shell and adjust it so that the paper achieves the best possible fit. The paper strip simulates how a long bilateral organism would fit into a helical shell. Does the paper fit particularly well?

6. Repeat this demonstration, but cut the strip in the shape of a spiral. Be sure to keep the width of the spiral strip to about 0.5 cm. This simulates a spiral-shaped organism. Which of these presumptive organisms fits the gastropod shell better? Why? Based on these observations, predict the body shape of hermit crabs which inhabit old gastropod shells. Which shells (dextral or sinistral) would they fit into best? Observe the shape of the abdomen of a hermit crab that has been removed from its shell. Which way does the crab's abdomen twist? Which shell type, dextral or sinistral, will the crab fit best?

7. Not all gastropods have the typical form just studied. Many species are mistakenly identified by novice collectors as members of other molluscan classes or

Figure 7. Diversity of shell form in class Gastropoda including from left to right, top row: *Mitra* (papal miter), *Conus* (cone), V*ermicularia*, *Melongena*, *Busycon*; middle row: *Haliotis* (abalone), *Murex*, limpet; bottom row: *Polinices* (moon snail), *Architectonica*, sundial, *Clanculus* (strawberry top shell), cowrie, keyhole limpets.

even different phyla. Examine a cowrie shell. Is the spire present? What region of the shell represents the last body whorl? Note the superficial bilateral symmetry of this shell. Describe the growth pattern of this shell.

8. A very different growth pattern is exhibited by *Crepidula* (slipper shell) and *Haliotis* (abalone). Obtain a specimen of each of these species and place them open-side down. Note the growth lines in the shell surface. View these shells from above and determine whether they are dextral or sinistral. In *Crepidula*, note the shelflike **septum** that occupies about one-half of the aperture. What is its function? There is no septum in *Haliotis*, but note the large muscle scar in the central region of the interior. Find the perforations that run near the outer margin of the shell of *Haliotis*. What function do they serve? Also, observe the pearly luster of the inner nacreous or mother-of-pearl layer of a *Haliotis* shell.

9. Compare shell form of *Diodora* (keyhole limpet) to that of other gastropods. Identify the shell aperture and perforation. What function does the perforation serve? Some limpets (e.g., *Acmaea*, true limpet) lack the perforations. In these, excurrent water flow exits the shell from the right side.

10. A very different type of shell occurs in vermetid worm shells. If specimens are available, determine the apex, aperture, and direction of coiling. Can these shells be classified as dextral or sinistral?

11. Obtain a specimen of a nudibranch and place it in a dissection pan. Determine anterior and posterior ends. Note that, except for the location of the genital aperture, the animal is bilaterally symmetrical. Some nudibranchs have numerous finger-like projections on their dorsal surfaces. These are called **cerata**. The cerata apparently function in gaseous exchange by increasing the surface area. Nudibranchs that lack cerata often have other secondary outgrowths that function as gills. Living nudibranchs are often brilliantly colored. This condition is generally considered to be an example of warning coloration to potential predators. As a defense against predators many species produce obnoxious chemicals or use nematocysts obtained from their cnidarian prey. This is sort of an invertebrate recycling program.

12. Examine the sea hare, *Aplysia*. Unless instructed otherwise, only the external features will be examined. Determine the anterior and posterior ends of *Aplysia*.

Phylum Mollusca

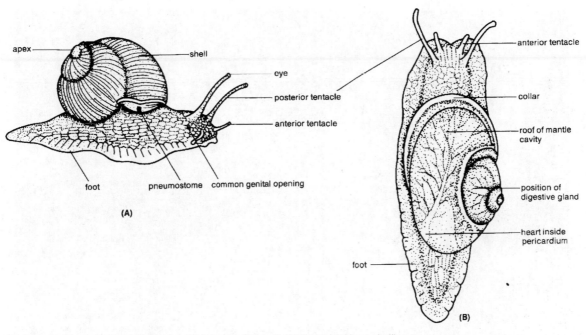

Figure 8. *Helix*, a pulmonate gastropod. (A) Lateral (with shell). (B) Dorsal (without shell).

Note the large fleshy foot and winglike **parapodia** used in swimming. At the head, locate the mouth, anterior tentacles, eyespots, and **rhinophores** (olfactory tentacles). On the right side of the head between the right tentacle and rhinophore, locate the small penis. Extending posteriorly and dorsally from the penis is the ciliated **sperm groove** that ends at the gonopore. At the posterior end locate the **anal siphon** and anus. Dorsally, find the opening in the mantle (shell aperture) under which a small, thin shell is located. Does the shell offer much protection? *Aplysia* secretes a purple dye when handled and this is said to help protect it from predators.

13. Observe other gastropods (e.g., *Busycon* and *Limax*) that are available for study. Relate the morphology and anatomy of these specimens to the ones you have just studied.

Anatomy of Helix

1. Obtain a freshly killed or expanded, preserved specimen of *Helix* and examine the shell, locating the following major features: apex, spire, suture line, and aperture.

2. Identify the head and foot of the animal (Fig. 8). The head bears two pairs of tentacles, the anterior ones being shorter than the posterior. Both pairs can be retracted. The posterior tentacles bear an eye at their distal tip. A small opening to the **common genital duct** may be found below and slightly behind the base of the right posterior tentacle. Locate the mouth with its two

lateral and one ventral lips. On the right side of the body just below the shell, locate the **pneumostome**, the opening into the mantle cavity that functions as a lung (Fig. 8).

3. The shell of *Helix* is thin compared to that of many gastropods. Does *Helix* possess an **operculum**? Carefully break the shell away from the animal. It is not necessary to remove all the shell material completely; the central portion of the shell (**columella**) may be left intact. How does the thickness of the shell of *Helix* compare to the other shells you examined? Speculate on why this difference occurs.

4. Note that the mantle is thicker along the anterior region just behind the head. This is the **collar**; it secretes shell material at the lip of the shell aperture. Carefully make a shallow cut into the lung through the pneumostome. Continue to cut the mantle cavity until the entire lung surface is exposed. Reflect the roof of the mantle cavity to one side to expose the visceral hump. Note that the floor of the mantle cavity is so thin that the internal organs may be seen underneath.

5. Carefully cut into the **pericardial cavity** and expose the heart, identifying the thin-walled auricle and the thicker-walled ventricle. The kidney is located in the roof of the mantle cavity posterior to the heart.

6. Pin your specimen to the dissection tray and immerse it in water. Cut through the floor of the mantle cavity, being careful not to damage the internal organs. Continue this cut anteriorly through the collar, extending

Figure 9. Internal anatomy of *Helix*.

it middorsally to the front of the head. With the aid of Fig. 9, locate the following structures.

7. Identify the muscular buccal mass at the anterior end and posterior to it, the nerve ring. A slender esophagus passes from the buccal mass through the ring into the expanded crop region of the gut. Right and left salivary glands will be found on the lateral surfaces of the crop. A duct from each gland extends anteriorly through the nerve ring to the buccal mass. The crop leads into the large stomach, located in the second turn of the visceral hump. Left and right digestive glands can be observed. The left gland is larger and lies alongside the

stomach; the smaller right gland occupies the apex of the visceral hump and last whorls of the shell. The intestine leads from the stomach and forms an S-shaped curve in the stomach region.

8. *Helix* has a complex reproductive system. If you are to study it, proceed through steps 8–10 with care. *Helix* is monoecious (hermaphroditic). Carefully tease apart the reproductive organs from the gut (Fig. 9) and, if possible, locate the protandrous gonad (**ovotestis**) on the inner coiled face of the right digestive gland. Trace the thin, convoluted duct (**hermaphroditic duct**) that leads from the gonad to the base of an **albumen gland**

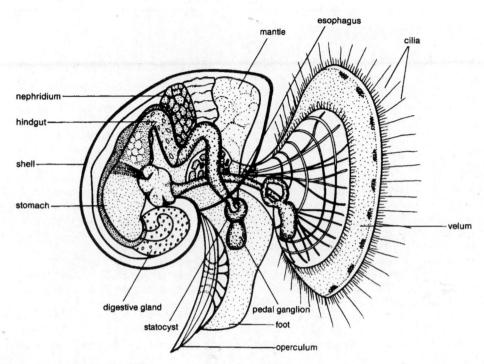

Figure 10. Typical veliger larva of a gastropod.

near the stomach region. Where the duct enters the albumen gland is a small fertilization chamber (or **talon**); here ova are fertilized prior to receiving albumen.

9. Locate the broad **spermoviduct** that has separate channels for both male and female reproductive products. It leads anteriorly from the albumen gland to a region where the duct divides into the sperm duct (**vas deferens**) and **oviduct**. The sperm duct leads to the **penis sac** and protrusible penis. Near the junction of sperm duct and penis sac is a long, thin, blind tube called the **flagellum**.

10. The oviduct leads to the vagina and a pair of branched mucus glands enter at about the same point. Nearby, a large bulbous **dart sac** enters too. The muscular dart sac secretes a calcareous needle-like dart that is plunged into the side of the partner before copulation. What purpose might this process serve? Remove the dart sac by cutting its connection to the vagina and observe its muscular structure. A long spermathecal duct joins the vagina at its posterior end. This duct ends in a spherical spermatheca that stores sperm received from another snail during copulation.

11. After you have completed your dissection, remove the buccal mass, make a longitudinal incision down its length, and with the aid of a dissection microscope, locate the radula. Remove it from the buccal mass and

examine the teeth under a microscope. How do the teeth of this radula compare to that of the chiton *Katharina*?

Gastropod Larvae

Examine a prepared slide of a gastropod **veliger larva** of *Crepidula*. Although the internal anatomy of most specimens will be difficult to interpret, attempt to locate the following structures: the double-lobed, ciliated **velum**, visceral mass, foot, operculum, and shell (Fig. 10).

The genus *Busycon* (whelks) produces young that complete their larval stages within the egg case. If available, examine a string of egg capsules of a whelk. Some whelks may produce strings of more than 175 parchment-like capsules with 100–200 eggs per capsule. How many capsules are present on the string you are examining? Note how the capsules are attached to the central cord. Are all of the capsules the same size? The first several capsules of the string are often smaller, more widely spaced, and contain no eggs. What function might the capsules in this region serve?

Examine closely several capsules and determine how young snails emerge from the capsule. If permitted, remove one or more capsules from a string and dissect them. How many young snails are present in each capsule? How big are they? In which direction do the shells of these young snails coil? ■

C. Class Bivalvia

Bivalvia [bi-VAL-ve-a; L., *bi*, two + L., *valva*, folding door] is a large class comprising more than 8,000 extant and about 20,000 extinct species of shelled mollusks. They differ from other mollusks in having a laterally compressed shell of two valves hinged along their dorsal margin. Many bivalves have a hatchet-shaped foot used in digging. This feature accounts for the alternate class name of **Pelecypoda** [pel-e-SIP-o-dah; G., *pelecy*, hatchet + G., *poda*, foot]. Bivalves lack a recognizable head and possess neither radula nor odontophore. Individual species are known commonly by many names including clams, mussels, oysters, cockles, and scallops. Many are economically important food sources and are used in jewelry and, in certain cultures, for money. The wood-boring bivalves, called **shipworms** and **piddocks**, do considerable damage to pilings, docks, ships, and other wooden structures in marine environments.

Students will study shells of a few selected species to gain an appreciation of the diversity of forms that comprise this class. The marine clam *Mercenaria* (= *Venus*) *mercenaria* will be dissected as a class representative.

■ Observational Procedure:

Live Specimens
If living bivalves are available, observe and describe the various ways they burrow. What behaviors are exhibited when a light or dark shadow strikes the edge of the mantle or siphons? What behaviors are exhibited when the mantle or siphons are touched?

If time permits and materials are available, your instructor will provide information for observing swimming movements in scallops and flow of water in and out of the siphons in filter-feeding clams.

Shell Morphologies
1. As your instructor directs, obtain shells of several different species of bivalves (e.g., *Anodonta*, *Arca*, *Crassostrea*, *Donax*, *Mercenaria*, *Mya*, *Mytilus*, and *Pecten*). Whenever possible, study specimens with both valves. Note that these shells differ widely from one another in their size and shape, but that they have several features in common. List several of these common features and

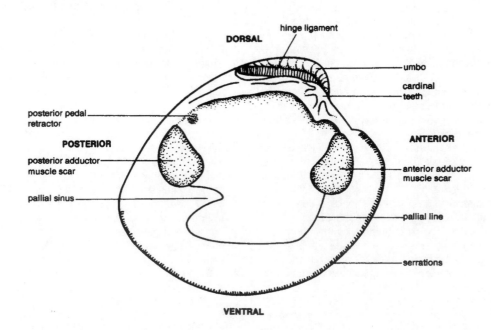

Figure 11. Inner surface of the left valve of *Mercenaria*.

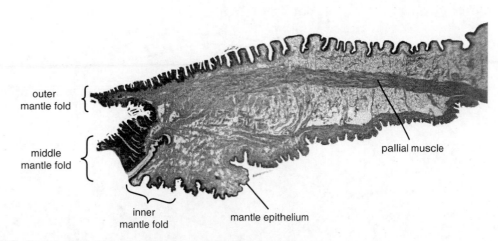

outer
mantle fold {

middle
mantle fold {

inner
mantle fold

mantle epithelium

pallial muscle

Figure 12. Cross section of the mantle margin of a clam, shell removed.

also several ways in which the shells differ. Do any have more than one type of symmetry? How would you describe shell shape in oysters?

2. Study more closely the shells of *Mercenaria* and the freshwater clam *Anodonta*. Note the thin, dark organic **periostracum** covering the outer surface of *Anodonta*. What functions might the periostracum serve? Observe the concentric lines on the external surface that recede from an elevated point near the hinged margin. These are laid down as growth proceeds. The elevation is the **umbo**, the oldest part of the shell. Umbos of opposite valves are directed toward each other and the approximating points are called **beaks**. In these clams the umbo is directed towards the anterior.

3. Orient both specimens so that the dorsal surface (hinge) is up and the umbo points away from you. Identify the right and left valves (Fig. 11). In other species this arrangement is not as clear.

4. Observe the external surface of all specimens you have assembled. Are there any ridges, spines, or folds on these species? Where are these features located? What purpose might they serve? Examine the surface of the valves closely. Is there evidence of predatory attack (e.g., drill holes or chips along the ventral margin of the shell)? Was this damage repaired before the bivalve died? Do any of your specimens show damage caused by the boring sponge *Cliona*?

5. Turn your attention to the inside of the shells and note any color patterns present. In some species such as *Anodonta* and *Mytilus* the inner surface is made up of **nacre** (mother-of-pearl). It is secreted by the entire outer surface of the mantle. Examine a prepared microscope slide of a section of mantle margin and locate the inner, middle, and outer mantle folds, pallial retractor muscle, and mantle epithelium (Fig. 12).

The shell is composed of a number of layers: inner (sometimes nacreous), middle, and outer. The whole shell is covered by periostracum. The middle and outer shell layers and the periostracum are formed at the perimeter of the mantle.

6. Using a hammer and chisel, break the shell, taking care to protect your eyes from shell fragments by wearing safety glasses. View the broken edge of the shell fragment in cross section using a hand lens or dissection microscope. Describe the cross section of the shell. Compare the similarities and differences in shell structure of various species. Are they all the same?

7. Observe the inner dorsal margins of several species and note the presence of any prominent plates or ridges (Fig. 11). These make up the **dentition** or teeth of the valves. Those that run longitudinally along the hinge line are **lateral teeth**. Those grouped near the umbo are **cardinal teeth**. Carefully move the valves, noting how the teeth on opposing valves articulate. Is the fit between valves tight in all species? Note the serrated, inner ventral margin of the valves in *Mercenaria*. How do these serrations fit when the valves close? Suggest ideas that could explain the functional significance of these serrations. Do other species have similar serrations?

8. Observe the anterior and posterior muscle scars and the pallial line on the inner surface of the valves (Fig. 11). The pallial line represents the point of attachment of the pallial retractor muscle to the shell.

Internal Anatomy

Preserved or live specimens may be used for this study. *Be sure to heed the warnings given below.*

1. Obtain a preserved specimen of *Mercenaria* in which the valves are held apart by a wooden peg. Using a heavy scalpel, carefully sever the hinge ligament that

Phylum Mollusca

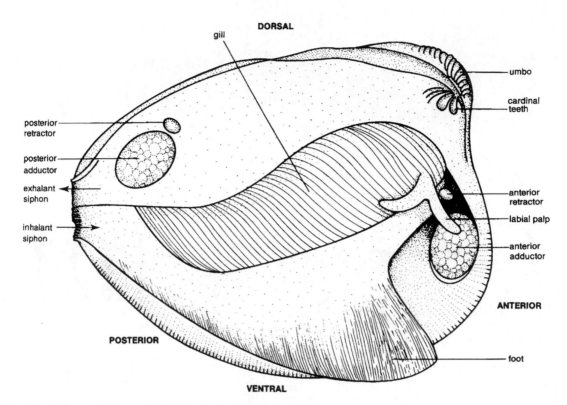

Figure 13. Anatomy of *Mercenaria* with right valve and mantle removed.

connects the valves along their dorsal margins. *Use extreme* **CAUTION** *when doing this procedure; cut away from your body and your fingers! Breaking the edge of the shell with a hammer will provide sufficient space to insert a scalpel. Be careful to protect your eyes from shell fragments when breaking the shell.*

2. With the hinge weakened, carefully insert the scalpel inside the shell at the ventral, posterior margin; separate the delicate mantle from the right valve, progressing anteriorly. Be careful not to tear the mantle. Detach the anterior and posterior adductor muscles where they insert at the surface of the right valve. Lift the right valve off the clam, carefully separating any remaining mantle tissues or muscles from the shell. After completing the separation at the hinge, the right valve should come free while the left contains the intact animal.

3. Identify the exposed muscle bundles. The large anterior muscle is the **anterior adductor**, important in keeping the valves closed. Above, and in close proximity, is the smaller **anterior pedal retractor** muscle which withdraws the foot. The large posterior muscle is the **posterior adductor** used also in closing the valves. Above it is the **posterior pedal retractor**.

4. Carefully cut away the right mantle lobe. This will expose the mantle cavity and the organs it contains.

Locate the following structures: foot, **ctenidia** (gills), visceral mass, labial palps, exhalant (excurrent) and inhalant (incurrent) siphons (Fig. 13). How many gills are present? Note the arrangement of the siphonal openings. The inhalant siphon bears the aperture through which water enters the mantle cavity. The exhalant siphon is the exit channel for water that has passed through the ctenidia, for urine expelled by the kidney, for feces from the adjacent anus, and for gametes. The visceral mass houses the digestive, excretory, and reproductive organs.

5. Examine the arrangement of the ctenidia and their connection to the foot and to the mantle. Observe how they lie in an angular position in the mantle cavity on each side of the body. Note that each ctenidium (right and left sides of the mantle cavity) is composed of two **demibranchs** (inner and outer), the former typically larger than the latter. Each demibranch is composed of two **lamellae**, ascending and descending.

6. Examine a prepared microscope slide of a section of a demibranch (Fig. 14) and locate the numerous **ostia** in the lamellae through which water enters. Water is transported dorsally within the ctenidia through numerous **water tubes**. A complex arrangement of cilia on the vertically aligned filaments that make up the sur-

Phylum Mollusca

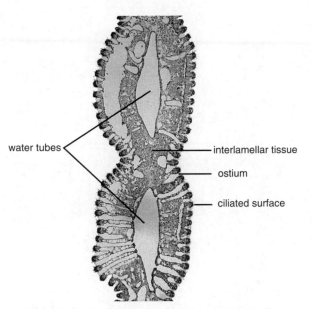

Figure 14. Photomicrograph of a section of a bivalve gill.

water tubes

interlamellar tissue

ostium

ciliated surface

face of the lamellae creates the flow of water. All tubes empty into the dorsal **suprabranchial cavity**, which in turn empties into the exhalant siphon. Blood vessels are profusely distributed throughout the ctenidia. Note the minute chitinous rods present to the inside of the ciliated surface. What is the significance of these rods? Water entering the mantle cavity also carries food particles, that are retained on the surface of the ctenidia. Ciliary action moves material to food grooves located on the ventral margin of each demibranch. Within the groove, food materials are moved toward the labial palps and into the mouth.

7. With a pair of scissors cut the mantle free from the outer demibranch. This will expose the suprabranchial cavity; some of the water tubes may be visible. Carefully remove the remaining gill parts on the right. Posteriorly there is a union of both chambers, forming a **branchial-cloacal** chamber.

8. Hold the animal with the anteriormost point of the foot directed toward you. Locate the anterior adductor muscle. Just below the muscle are the labial palps and slitlike mouth with outer and inner lips (Fig. 15). With scissors make a lateral incision and follow the mouth

Figure 15. Partially dissected *Mercenaria*, depicting internal anatomy.

pericardium   ventricle   auricle   stomach

posterior foot retractor

posterior adductor

rectum

anus

excurrent siphon

incurrent siphon

gill (cut)

kidney   gonad

VENTRAL

umbo

cardinal teeth

digestive gland

mouth

labial palp

anterior adductor

ANTERIOR

intestine

foot

serrations

cavity posteriorly for a short distance. The cavity exposed is the esophagus which opens up into an enlarged stomach. Surrounding, and opening into the stomach, is the dark **digestive gland** (Fig. 15). Also opening into the stomach from a cecum may be a long, flexible, translucent **crystalline style** that rotates against the chitinous gastric shield of the dorsal stomach wall, releasing enzymes used in extracellular digestion. The intestine is a long, coiled tube surrounded by the gonads. What does the length of the intestine tell us about the food of this organism? The later part of the intestine ascends dorsally, where it enters the anterior end of the pericardial cavity. From here the rectum passes posteriorly through the pericardial cavity, passes through the heart, and finally ends in an anus on the face of the posterior adductor muscle (Fig. 15).

9. To observe the pericardial cavity and its contents, it may be necessary to remove some of the overlying mantle tissues, if they have not been removed earlier in the dissection. Locate the region just dorsal to the suprabranchial cavity and carefully remove the mantle tissue; the pericardial cavity should then be exposed (Fig. 15). Locate the rectum surrounded by the single, median ventricle of the heart.

10. Locate the two auricles laterally attached to the ventricle and the anterior and posterior aortae. In fresh preparations the heart still may be beating. If your dissection was done properly, you may be able to see the **nephrostome** and the genital aperture, both located just ventral to the pericardial cavity.

11. Follow the rectum to the anus located on the posterior face of the posterior adductor muscle and near the exhalant siphon. Because the circulatory and nervous systems, and reproductive and renal ducts are difficult to differentiate in a general dissection, they will not be studied here.

Other Specimens

The Mussel *Mytilus*. Carefully open the shell of a mussel of the genus Mytilus. Note the reduced foot and cluster of threadlike filaments arising from the heel of the foot anteriorly. These are **byssal threads** secreted by a byssal gland. The mussel uses the threads for attachment to hard substrata. Note the difference in size of the adductor muscles.

Scallops. Along the edge of the mantle are numerous ocelli. Carefully open the shell of a scallop. Note the single, large, posterior adductor muscle. The adductor is divided into two approximately equal sections of smooth and striated muscle tissue. The latter is responsible for the rapid clapping of the valves when the scallop swims. The muscle is the part most often con-

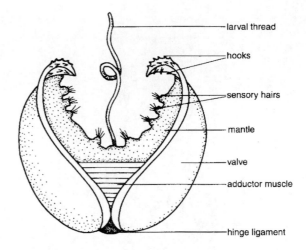

Figure 16. Glochidium, parasitic veliger larval stage of freshwater clams.

sumed. Note the orientation of the muscle fibers within the cylindrical adductor. Occasionally one is served a dish made with scallops but the muscle fibers of the flesh run from side-to-side and not top-to-bottom. How do you know that this food item is not an adductor muscle from a scallop? (Think skates.)

Wood-Boring Bivalves. Examine pieces of wood that have been colonized by wood-boring bivalves. If the bivalves are present, note the size, shape, and modifications to their shells from the basic bivalve plan. Why are these bivalves called shipworms? How is the shell modified to allow these mollusks to burrow? How is the burrow lined?

Larval Stage. Examine specimens or prepared slides of bivalve larval stages. The first larval stage is a ciliated, somewhat barrel-shaped **trochophore**. Note the position of ciliary bands. The **veliger** stage is more complex. Although the internal anatomy of most specimens will be difficult to interpret, attempt to locate the following structures of the veliger stage: ciliated **velum**, visceral mass, adductor muscles, and valves. Compare the anatomy of a free-living veliger with that of the parasitic **glochidium** larva of the freshwater clam, *Anodonta*. Attempt to locate the visceral mass, adductor muscle, hinge ligament, valves (with hooks possessing small spines), sensory cilia, and attachment thread (Fig. 16).

Fossil Specimens. Bivalves have a long geological history, dating back to the **Cambrian Period** (Fig. 1). If fossil specimens are available, examine their general shell morphology and compare them to extant species. ■

D. Class Cephalopoda

Cephalopoda [SEF-a-lo-POAD-ah or sef-a-LOP-o-da; G., *cephalo*, head + G., *poda*, foot] comprises about 600 extant and 8,000 extinct species of marine mollusks. Most cephalopods are less than 1 m long, but some very large forms are known. In general, cephalopods are adapted for swimming, although many species are bottom-dwellers, crawling about on their arms. The shell is generally reduced or even absent (e.g., octopuses) in living cephalopods, but well-developed shells were possessed by members of the extinct Subclasses Ammonoidea and Nautiloidea (represented today by members of the Genus *Nautilus*).

Cephalopods have four major features. (1) All possess a well-developed brain and complex nervous system. (2) The anterior portion of the foot is modified into a circle of prehensile, muscular arms and tentacles that surround the mouth. Except in *Nautilus*, these appendages bear numerous, muscular suckers that aid in prey capture. (3) Cephalopods have a muscular buccal apparatus containing beaklike jaws and a radula. (4) Locomotion in this group is unique. Water taken into the mantle cavity can be expelled in a forceful contraction of the mantle walls. This exhalation furnishes a type of jet propulsion.

The common Atlantic-coast squid, *Loligo pealei*, will be studied in detail as the class representative. Given the diversity within the class, *Loligo* should not be considered to be a typical cephalopod.

Figure 17. Dorsal view of the squid *Loligo pealei*, with enlargement of an arm and suckers.

■ Observational Procedure:

External Anatomy

1. Orient the squid in the dissection pan so that the arms and tentacles are directed away from you and the broad flat surface of the fins is directed up. In terms of biological function, the posterior end of the animal is now nearest you, the anterior end farthest away, and the dorsal surface is up. (Fig. 17). Now identify anterior, posterior, dorsal, and ventral surfaces in terms of the other molluscan classes. Why do these two ways of viewing the animal differ?

2. Note the finely striated appearance of the surface of the fins. These striations are muscle bundles that control fin movement. The spotted condition of the body surface is due to the presence of pigmented cells called **chromatophores**.

3. Gently scrape the surface of the body removing the transparent outer cuticle. Each chromatophore is a small membranous sac to which tiny muscle fibers are

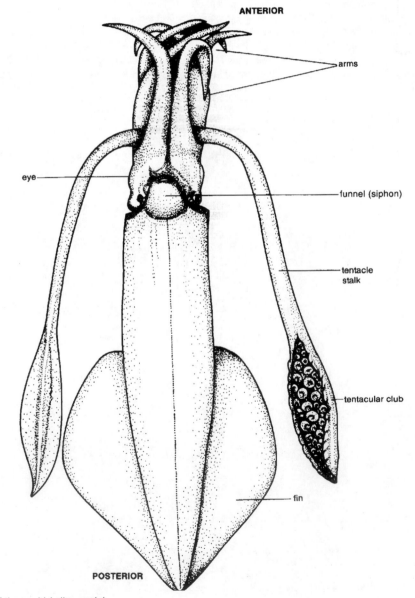

Figure 18. Ventral view of the squid *Loligo pealei*.

Figure 19. Lateral internal view of the trunk-head region of a male squid (*Loligo pealei*).

attached. Contraction of muscle fibers enlarges the chromatophore and makes the pigment visible.

4. Arrange the squid with the ventral side up and the head nearest you. The body is elongate and arrow-shaped (Fig. 18). The head region appears as though it is inserted in a central tube. This is the tough, muscular mantle.

5. Pick up the squid and view the animal from the oral aspect. While applying lateral pressure to the tube, look into the mantle cavity. The blunt lateral projections are extensions of the **mantle locking ridges**. Cartilaginous locking grooves are located on the inside surface and will be observed later. The pointed extension on the dorsal surface of the mantle marks the location of the

internal shell (**gladius**) or **pen** (Fig. 17). The cone-shaped structure extending beyond the mantle on the ventral surface is the **funnel** or **siphon**.

6. Locate the eyes on either side of the head in the region of the funnel. They will be considered in detail later.

7. Two kinds of appendages are located at the anterior end around the mouth; shorter ones are arms and the longer ones with club-shaped ends are tentacles. How many arms and how many tentacles are present?

8. Examine the arms and tentacles. How do they differ as to size and shape? Note any differences in size and position of sucker cups on the arms and tentacles (Fig. 17).

9. Remove several suckers and determine how they function. What do they resemble?

10. Locate the **aquiferous pore** at the anterior edge of the eye (Fig. 19). This pore probably equalizes pressure in the eye chamber.

11. Observe the articulation of the mantle ridges with the funnel locking cartilages on each side of the funnel. Near the eye, the integument is folded and thickened as the **olfactory crest**, under which is found the **olfactory groove** (Figs. 17 and 19).

Internal Anatomy

1. Orient the squid with its ventral side up (Fig. 18). With a sharp, heavy-duty scalpel, make an incision from the mantle aperture to the posterior end. First make a *shallow cut*; follow this by a second cut that completely separates the mantle. Make sure this cut is not so deep it disturbs the internal organs. Gently fold the two sides of the mantle laterally and, with large dissection pins, firmly attach the outer edges of the mantle to the base of the dissection pan (Fig. 20). If the mantle can-

Figure 20. Ventral view in the mantle cavity of a male squid (*Loligo pealei*).

140

not be secured with dissection pins, make a shallow longitudinal cut the length of the mantle on either side.

2. With the aid of Fig 20, determine the sex of your specimen. Sever the funnel lengthwise, exposing its cavity. The large paired glands inside the funnel are the **organs of Verrill**, whose function is not known. The lip-like structure at the forward edge of the funnel is the funnel valve that regulates water flow out of the mantle cavity. Note the fold extending from the funnel to the other side of the head. This is one of the **lateral valves** that prevents water from exiting the mantle cavity along the same path from which it came. Water exits only through the funnel. Describe the functional morphology of the structures involved with circulation of water through the mantle cavity.

3. Locate the **rectum** and the anal opening at the end. The anus bears two flaplike valves. How do they function; are they active or passive? Why does the anus possess valves of this sort?

4. Below the rectum and opening into it just behind the anus is the ink sac (Fig. 20). This small sac is filled with a black pigment called **melanin**. When the squid is alarmed, the ink is released through the anus. Observe the membranous tissue binding the ink sac to the rectum. Using sharp, fine-pointed scissors and a scalpel, carefully separate and remove the ink sac from the rectum.

5. Open the sac in a small dry dish. Remove some of the thick, dark ink with a pipette or syringe and place a drop into some water. Note how deeply the ink stains the water.

6. Two pairs of large muscles are found in the area of the ink sac. Locate the **siphon retractor muscles** that extend dorsally from under the siphon and dip strongly under the central organs. Beneath these muscles and still larger in size are the paired **cephalic retractor muscles** (Figs. 19 and 20).

7. The paired, large, pinnate structures in the mantle cavity are the gills (Figs. 19 to 21). In specimens injected with latex, the gills will be colored, usually red with some blue. Dorsally the gills are attached to the mantle by the gill mantle membrane.

8. Follow the gills to their proximal junction with the other viscera. Along the outer edge of each gill is a large blood vessel (**efferent branchial vein**). Oxygenated blood is returned through this vessel from the gill to the **systemic heart**.

9. Between the bases of the gills is a pair of elongate, sponge-textured organs. This is the region of the kidney or nephridium. It appears as if the branchial veins are directly connected to the kidneys. Actually they pass under the organs and connect to the systemic heart (Fig. 21). This connection will be better observed later. At the base of each gill is a bulblike **branchial heart**.

The branchial hearts collect venous return and pump blood into the vessels of the gills.

10. Extending back from the branchial hearts are two elongated conelike structures with broadened bases. They lie next to the branchial hearts. These vessels vary in size according to the amount of blood contained. They are the **posterior vena cavae** (posterior mantle veins). It will be revealed by later dissection that each posterior vena cava gathers venous blood from the far part of the body opposite the head and empties it into the branchial heart.

11. Coming from the opposite area of the body is another venous vessel that forks in the region of, and courses through, the kidney. Because of the close association of the forks, the vessels are hard to see. Each fork is described as the **nephridial portions of the anterior vena cava**. The venous blood in these vessels empties into the branchial hearts. With blood from both the anterior and posterior vena cava, each branchial heart functions as an accelerating pump that forces blood into the gills for aeration.

12. In addition to the larger vessels that empty into the branchial hearts, there are three smaller vessels that bring blood directly from the mantle (**anterior** and **medial mantle veins**) and from the gonad (**gonadal vein**). The latter vein will not be seen at this time. The anterior and medial mantle veins may be seen lateral to the branchial hearts.

13. Arrange the squid so that the head is nearest you. Take the head in your hand and spread the arms and tentacles. Observe a ring of small finger-like projections, **buccal lappets**, surrounding the mouth. Note their arrangement and the suckers they bear. The buccal lappets are united with the buccal membrane which they support. Inward to and below the buccal lappets surrounding the mouth is another membrane, the **peristomial membrane**. The margin of this membrane forms a rugose collar (Fig. 22A).

14. Grasping the free edge of the siphon with a pair of forceps, lift the siphon and sever the two small siphon protractor muscles extending between the head and siphon. Also cut the lateral siphon valves.

15. Separate the pair of arms immediately below the siphon by making a medial lengthwise incision at the base of the arms. Again note the buccal and peristomial membranes. As the arms are separated, notice their arrangement around the buccal mass. The general muscular organization of the specialized foot is complex and will not be studied.

16. Apply slight pressure to this region of the body to flatten the arms and tentacles thereby revealing the **buccal bulb** (Fig. 22A).

17. Examine the buccal bulb. How muscular is this structure?

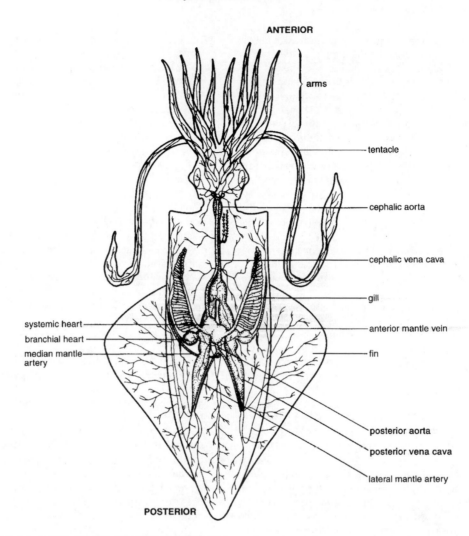

ANTERIOR

arms

tentacle

cephalic aorta

cephalic vena cava

gill

anterior mantle vein

fin

systemic heart
branchial heart
median mantle artery

posterior aorta

posterior vena cava

lateral mantle artery

POSTERIOR

Figure 21. Circulatory system of *Loligo*. (Modified after Williams.)

18. Cut the peristomial and peripheral buccal membranes, exposing a compact body with the end displaying dark chitinous jaws (mandibles) that are similar to an inverted parrot's beak. The upper jaw is overlain by the lower jaw (Fig. 22B). What function do the mandibles serve?

19. Using a sharp scalpel make a midsagittal cut through the buccal bulb. Locate the jaws and, in the floor of the mouth, a structure called the **tongue**. A duct from the median posterior salivary gland opens at the tip of the tongue.

20. With forceps, grasp the distal end of the tongue and bend it backwards until the radular area is exposed. The radula is surrounded by the upper jaw and is easily identified by having numerous teeth. Note the flaplike plates at the side of the radula. The lower (ventral) edges

of the paired flaps lead to the esophagus. With the dissection microscope, study the dentition of the radula. How does the radula of *Loligo* compare to those of the other mollusks you studied? The space enclosed between the jaws is the buccal cavity; it communicates with the esophagus.

21. To locate the esophagus, it will be necessary to make a deep, medial incision on the surface of the head at the base of the arms. The incision must be exact as the esophagus is a relatively small tube. As you dissect, a hardened structure, the **cephalic cartilage**, will be encountered at about the level of the eyes. Also exposed are whitish, pulpy masses, on either side of the tubular esophagus. These two tissue masses are the **cerebral** and **pedal ganglia**. The pedal ganglion is on the same side of the esophagus as the siphon.

Figure 22. *Loligo.* (A) Base of arms sagittally separated to expose the buccal bulb. (B) Midsagittal diagrammatic section of the head region.

22. Follow the esophagus from the buccal bulb attachment to the place where it penetrates the cream-colored **digestive gland** (Fig. 23).

23. Remove the digestive gland and expose the esophagus, which lies in a groove between the digestive gland and the body wall. The digestive gland also surrounds the elongated median posterior salivary gland. Anterior salivary glands are embedded in the buccal bulb and may be found with careful dissection. The anterior glands produce a lubricating secretion and the posterior salivary gland a poison and **hyaluronidase**. What are the functions of the poison gland and the enzyme hyaluronidase? The small vessel, located alongside the esophagus and connected to the systemic heart, is the **cephalic aorta** (Fig. 21).

Study of the digestive system will be temporarily discontinued and attention given to the circulatory and the reproductive systems. It is difficult to dissect the digestive canal at this point and still leave the circulatory and reproductive systems intact.

24. Two types of hearts (branchial and systemic) have been mentioned (Fig. 21). The branchial hearts are venous and the systemic heart is arterial. The systemic heart receives aerated blood from both gills. Blood moves from the systemic heart to the body via the cephalic aorta, posterior aorta, and genital artery. Valves in each vessel prevent blood from flowing back into the heart. Blood returns to the central circulatory system through a complex system of veins. The cephalic vena cava and posterior vena cava are enlarged portions of this system. Blood in the vena cava passes to the gills via the branchial hearts. Blood vessels leaving the branchial hearts possess valves that prevent return of the blood.

25. Locate the small vessel that extends between and slightly posterior to the branchial hearts. This is the **posterior aorta**, which communicates with the systemic heart. It is three-pronged, with two lateral vessels and one medial vessel. The central one is the **median mantle (pallial) artery**. The other two forks are the

ANTERIOR

- buccal bulb
- anterior salivary gland
- posterior salivary duct
- posterior salivary gland
- digestive gland
- anal valves
- rectum
- ink sac
- pancreas
- stomach
- cecum

esophagus

POSTERIOR

Figure 23. Schematic view of the digestive organs of *Loligo*.

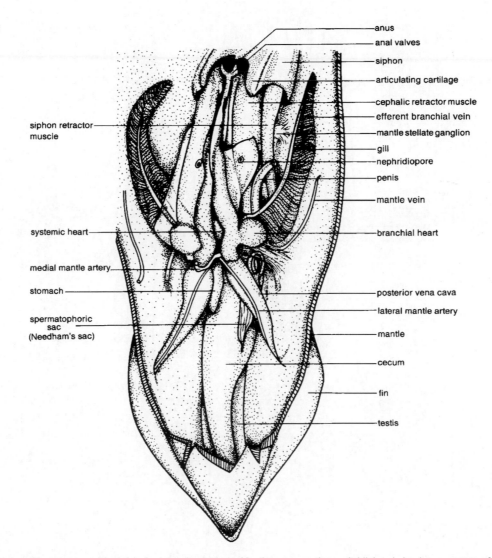

Figure 24. Central visceral mass with perivisceral membrane turned back to expose the nephridial and circulatory organs of a male *Loligo*.

lateral mantle (pallial) arteries. That portion of each posterior vena cava in close association with the kidney before entering the branchial heart is known as the **nephridial portion of the posterior vena caval vein**. The right and left lateral mantle arteries run along the inner margins of each posterior vena cava (Fig. 21).

26. Using a broad-blade scalpel, gently scrape away the nephridial tissue between the bases of the gills. A somewhat convoluted mass of tissues beneath the kidney is the digestive duct appendages. When additional pancreatic tissue is removed, the quadrate-shaped systemic heart can be seen (Fig. 21). The forwardmost corner of the systemic heart is the part communicating with the anterior aorta, supplying the head and foot. Large lateral vessels running to the inside of the gills are the efferent branchial veins. Smaller blood vessels may be found attached to the systemic heart. They are very small and only careful dissection will insure their being located. These vessels carry arterial blood to the branchial hearts.

27. Locate the **genital artery** arising from the systemic heart. The dorsal corner of the heart leads into the conspicuous short posterior aorta that subsequently branches into the three mantle arteries mentioned previously.

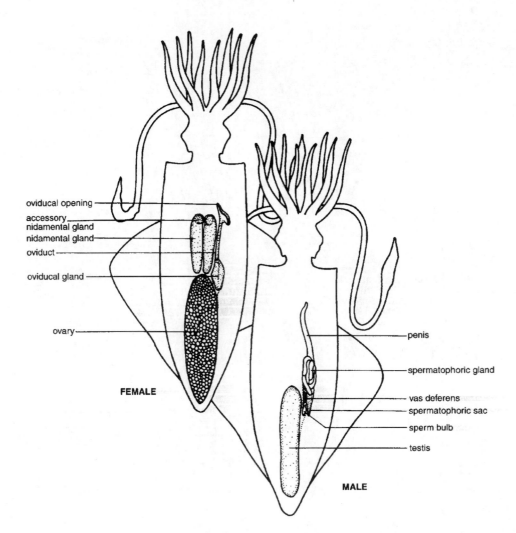

Figure 25. Female and male reproductive systems of *Loligo*.

28. Turn your attention to the remainder of the digestive system and trace the esophagus posterior to the large, muscular stomach. Attached to the stomach is a thin-walled, saclike organ, the **spiral cecum** or **gastric pouch**. Both stomach and cecum may vary in size depending on the amount of food eaten before the animal was preserved. Inside the cecum, located on the proximal wall, is a large, spiral system of folds. These **ciliary leaflets** sort minute food particles sent from the stomach.

Reproductive System: Male

1. Using the handle of your scalpel, gently lift and reflect the cecum laterally.

2. The large, somewhat firm but flattened, light colored organ in the dorsal part of the cavity and under the cecum is the whitish testis (Fig. 25). It is enclosed by the perivisceral (peritoneal) membrane. Sperm are passed freely into the cavity surrounding the testis. The sperm exit from the testis through a slit-like opening on its surface.

3. Locate on the right side below the gill the spindle-shaped organ, the **spermatophoric sac** or **Needham's sac** (Figs. 24 and 25). Alongside the sac is the coiled vas deferens. The free end of the vas deferens is enlarged as the **sperm bulb** (ciliated funnel). Sperm are swept by ciliary currents into the bulb. After entering the bulb they pass into the convoluted vas deferens.

4. The vas deferens connects to an enlarged convoluted tubule, the **spermatophoric gland** or seminal vesicle. These glands provide secretions that package the sperm in **spermatophores** (Fig. 25). Spermatophores exit the spermatophoric glands by way of the spermatophoric duct to the spermatophoric sac (Needham's sac) where they are stored. Exclusive of the testis, Needham's sac, when filled with spermatophores, is the largest structure of the male reproductive system. The spermatophores exit to the mantle cavity through the muscular penis that extends anteriorly from Needham's sac.

5. Remove some of the spermatophores from the sac or from the penis and examine them under the low power of the compound microscope. Study the shape and size of the spermatophores.

Reproductive System: Female

1. Examine a female squid. If your specimen is a mature female, note the prominent paired **nidamental glands** (Fig. 25). They secrete the outer coverings for the egg masses.

2. The nephridia, rectum, ink sac, and part of the heart region are covered by these glands. The anterior **accessory nidamental glands** are enlarged when the female is mature. However, they are usually small, rounded bodies located just below (as you view the specimen) the nidamental glands on the anterior side. The accessory glands secrete an elastic membrane about each egg.

3. Remove the nidamental glands by separating them with the blunt end of a scalpel, and lifting them from the body. Be careful not to disturb the ink sac if it has not been removed. The large oviduct lying parallel to the rectum should be evident.

4. The ovary lies in the coelomic cavity in the same position as the testis. Note how the perivisceral membrane encloses the ovary.

5. Locate the large oviducal opening of the oviduct by following the course of the oviduct forward.

6. In the region of the branchial heart, the oviduct is dilated and is called the oviducal gland. It secretes the capsules of the eggs. The capsule covering is elastic and hardens somewhat upon contact with water. The oviduct at this point turns down for a short distance and then reverses direction toward the ovary.

The Eye and Shell

If time permits, examine the squid's eye. Remove one eye from its cavity by severing the nerve connection at the base of the cavity. With forceps remove the outer covering or false cornea of the eye. The true cornea lies underneath the false one. Remove the cornea. The opaque, ball-like structure is the lens. Surrounding the lens is the iris. Under the iris the surface of the eye is dark in color. Remove this membrane. The ciliary muscles controlling the lens may be seen as a concentric ring around the lens. By holding the lens and its band of ciliary muscles to the light, one will discover that what appears as a single band is really made up of several colored bands. Remove the inner lining or retina of the eye and examine it with the aid of a dissection microscope. Your instructor will provide additional information if you are to compare the eye of a squid to that of a vertebrate.

Push the viscera to one side and carefully dissect free the translucent, amber-colored gladius or pen (internal shell) embedded within the mantle.

Other Specimens

Sepia. Cuttlefish (*Sepia*) and its allies are not as streamlined and as rapid swimmers as *Loligo*. The European cuttlefish (*Sepia officinalis*) is found in shallow waters where it lies buried just under the surface of the sediment during the day. At night *Sepia* becomes a free-swimming predator. A brief study of the external anatomy of *Sepia* will be made and compared to that of *Loligo*.

1. Obtain undissected specimens of *Sepia* and *Loligo* and determine the anterior-posterior axis of each specimen. How does the body shape of these two cephalopods differ? Compare and contrast other features of the two specimens.

2. Observe how the head of *Sepia* is inserted into the muscular mantle tube.

3. Locate the fins of both specimens. How do they compare? Do they have the same shape? How might these structural differences be manifest as functional differences in swimming?

4. As in *Loligo*, the extension of the mantle margin on the dorsal surface is the extension of an internal shell.

5. Examine a specimen of the internal shell of *Sepia*. This structure is known as the **cuttlebone**. Describe its shape. How does this shell compare to the pen of *Loligo*? Of what is it composed? Using a dissection microscope or hand lens, examine the inside of a piece of cuttlebone that has been cut in cross section at an oblique angle. Note the thin septa. How could this shell add buoyancy to the animal? (*Hint*: Examine the form of the shell of *Nautilus*.)

6. Locate the eyes and chitinous jaws (mandibles).

7. Note that *Sepia* has short arms and long club-shaped tentacles. How many arms and how many tentacles does *Sepia* have? Examine closely the arms and tentacles. How do they compare to the squid? Unlike *Loligo*, the two long tentacles of *Sepia* can be retracted into sheaths and become invisible when not in use.

Octopus. Octopuses are very different types of cephalopods from those studied so far. Though

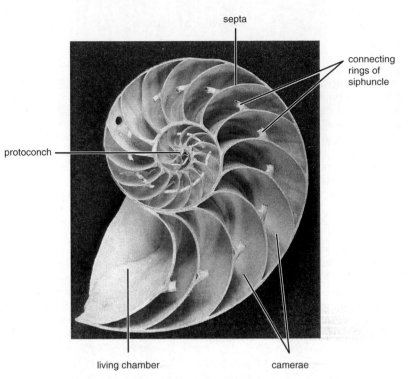

septa

connecting rings of siphuncle

protoconch

living chamber

camerae

Figure 26. Photograph of the internal structure of the shell of *Nautilus*.

capable of swimming by jet propulsion octopuses more often crawl along the bottom in search of prey or hide, waiting for prey. *Octopus* is capable of learning simple tasks and may be one of the most intelligent of all invertebrates. A brief comparison will be made of the general morphology of *Octopus* to that of the other cephalopods studied.

Obtain undissected specimens of *Octopus*, *Sepia*, and *Loligo*, and compare their general external anatomy. Identify the anterior and posterior ends of *Octopus*. Locate the siphon of the specimen. Where is water taken into the mantle cavity in this organism? How is it expelled? Is there any noticeable internal shell as in *Loligo*? (NB: *Octopus* has paired internal shell vestiges called **stylets**.) How many arms does *Octopus* have? Compare the suckers to those of *Loligo* and *Sepia*. How are they different? Locate the eyes on *Octopus*.

If available, examine a female specimen of the pelagic octopod, *Argonauta*. Note the paired dorsal arms with their broadly expanded membranes. The membranes secrete the shell that functions as a buoyancy organ and also as an egg case. Examine the shell of *Argonauta*. Note that it has a general spiral shape.

Nautilus. *Nautilus* is the only extant cephalopod with a well-developed external shell. This species lives in the tropics of the western Pacific ocean, ranging from the surface to depths of about 500m. *Nautilus* is an active diurnal hunter, grasping prey with its 90 or so suckerless tentacles.

1. Obtain shells of *Nautilus* and a few gastropods that have been cut in a medial longitudinal section. Compare the external morphology of the *Nautilus* to that of the gastropods. Is shell coiling the same in both of these shells? What type of coiling is found in *Nautilus*? Note that each successive whorl is in the same plane as previous ones.

2. Examine the outer surface of *Nautilus* and note any external color patterns that may be present. Also note the central depression called the **umbilicus**. This represents the axis of coiling that develops because the body whorls do not fully reach the axis. Is there external evidence of internal septa?

3. Examine the inner cut face of the Nautilus shell (Fig. 10.26) and locate the aperture septa, the internal chambers called **camerae**, nacreous layer, and connecting rings of the **siphuncle**. The siphuncle is a slender cord of tissue that emerges from the visceral mass and passes through each chamber posteriorly. The siphuncle produces a gas which makes the shell buoyant.

4. What do the different-size camerae represent? Where was the major portion of the body of the living organism located?

5. Where is the perforation of the siphuncle located on the septal face?

6. In the axis of coiling, locate the umbilical perforation. This is the internal manifestation of the umbilicus noted above.

7. Also locate the **protoconch**, a small camera that is the initial chamber of the shell.

Figure 27. Examples of fossil cephalopods.

8. *Nautilus* regulates its buoyancy by altering the relative volumes of liquid and gas in the camerae through action of the siphuncle. Given this information, describe how *Nautilus* is oriented in the water. In which direction does it swim? How does this buoyancy system relate to the one in the cuttlefish?

9. If available, examine a preserved *Nautilus* and observe the position of hood, eyes, tentacles, funnel, and shell.

10. Examine the surface of the tentacles noting the lack of suckers.

11. Determine the thickness of the hood. What is the function of this structure?

12. Compare the general anatomy of *Nautilus* to that of the three other cephalopods studied. Note that the funnel in *Nautilus* is not a closed tube, the edges only overlap.

Fossil Forms

Examine the fossilized cephalopods on display. In coiled forms, what type of coiling is exhibited? In ammonoids note the suture pattern formed by the septa where they meet the outer margin of the shell. How would you describe these patterns? In a sectioned specimen locate the camerae. Compare shells of ammonoids with that of *Nautilus*. Are there any similarities or differences? Do any of the fossil specimens exhibit evidence of the siphuncle (i.e., septal neck)? The internal anatomy of these forms is believed to be similar to that of *Nautilus*.

Not all fossil cephalopods had coiled shells, some were loosely coiled, arc-shaped, or even had straight shells (Fig. 27). Examine a fossil species which had a straight shell (e.g., *Geisenoceras*). Where were the camerae located with respect to the living animal in these forms? How did straight-shelled species maintain a balanced horizontal position in the water? Or did they? Is there any evidence of **cameral** or **siphonate deposits** that could help counterbalance the animal? How would that make the animal like to teeter-totter? ■

Phylum Mollusca	Worksheet 6
Name: _____	Date: _____
Course #: _____ / Section #: _____	Grade: _____

1. Using examples of a chiton, snail, clam, and squid, briefly describe the foot of each in relation to the shape and modifications for locomotion and food procurement.

2. Compare the structure of the radula of the chiton (*Katharina*) to those of the snail (*Helix*) and squid (*Loligo*).

Phylum Mollusca

3. Indicate with a check which characters are associated with the particular class of Mollusca.

Character	Polyplacophora	Gastropoda	Bivalvia	Cephalopoda
Aesthetes				
Beak				
Camera				
Cardinal teeth				
Chromatophore				
Columella				
Costae				
Crystalline style				
Funnel cartilage				
Glochidium				
Inhalent siphon				
Ink sac				
Labial palps				
Operculum				
Pallial line				
Pen				
Periostracum				
Pneumostome				
Radula				
Rhinophores				
Siphuncle				
Spermatophore				
Spire				
Sugar gland				
Umbo				

Phylum Mollusca

4. Do any mollusks studied in this exercise show evidence of segmentation? Give examples and support your conclusions by briefly noting the evidence for segmentation.

5. From studying various representatives of Mollusca you are cognizant of the tremendous diversity exhibited by members of the phylum. As to their life modes, there are grazers (e.g., chitons, snails, and slugs), filter-feeders (e.g., clams and oysters), and predatory carnivores (e.g., squid, cuttlefish, and octopus). Write a short essay relating the adaptive features (structural and physiological) possessed by individuals of each group that allow them to carry out their life modes.

PHYLUM ANNELIDA

Members of Phylum Annelida are schizocoelomate, segmented protostome worms. The most striking feature of annelids is their body construction which consists of a series of similar compartments called **segments** or **metameres**. This feature is called **segmentation** or **metamerism** [me-TAM-er-ism; G., *meta*, after + G., *mere*, a part]. Annelida is the first phylum to be covered in this manual that exhibits this characteristic in an unequivocal way. The repetition of body units in cestodes is **strobilization** and not segmentation, and the interpretation of segments in some mollusks is not clearly defined. Metamerism is probably the greatest advancement displayed by annelids. In two of the three classes (Polychaeta and Oligochaeta), the external rings generally correspond to an internal division of the body. In the third class (Hirudinea or leeches), external annulation does not correspond to internal segmentation. Most major organ systems are affected by metamerism (e.g., body wall musculature, nervous, excretory, and vascular). Metamerism is important in burrowing activities of annelids. The schizocoelom acts as a hydrostatic skeleton when circular and longitudinal muscles of the body wall contract alternately. This is because the volume of each segment remains relatively constant despite variations in their linear proportions. Two other groups, which traditionally have received the rank of phylum (**Echiura** and **Pogonophora**) are treated by some authors as Annelids. Due to the lack of readily available study material these taxa will not be studied.

Brinkhurst, R.O. 1982. Evolution in the Annelida. *Canadian J. Zool.* 60: 1043–1059.

Cutler, E.B. 1975. The phylogeny and systematic position of the Pogonophora. *Syst. Zool.* 24: 512–513.

Eernisse, D.J., J.S. Albert, and F.E. Anderson. 1992. Annelida and Arthropoda are not sister taxa: a phylogenetic analysis of spiralian metazoan morphology. *Syst. Biol.* 41: 305–330.

Harrison, F.W., and M.E. Rice. (eds.). 1993. Onychophora, Chilopoda, and Lesser Protostomata. Volume 12. Microscopic Anatomy of Invertebrates. Wiley-Liss, New York, pp. 327–369 [Pogonophora]; 371–460 [Vestimintifera].

McHugh, D. 1997. Molecular evidence that echiurans and pogonophorans are derived annelids. *Proc. Natl. Acad. Sci. U.S.A.* 94: 8006–8009.

Siddall, M.E., K. Fitzhugh, and K.A. Coates. 1998. Problems determining the phylogenetic position of echiurans and pogonophorans with limited data. *Cladistics* 14: 401–410.

Trueman, E.R. 1975. *The Locomotion of Soft-bodied Animals.* Edward Arnold, London.

Zrzavy, J., S. Mihulka, P. Kepka, A. Bezdek, and D. Tietz. 1998. Phylogeny of the Metazoa based on morphological and 18S ribosomal DNA evidence. 14: 249–286.

Phylum Annelida

Members of the Phylum Annelida [an-NEL-ee-da; L., *annellus*, ring] represent the highest development and advancement of worm-like animals. This diverse and highly successful phylum contains over 12,000 species that are widely distributed in marine, freshwater, and terrestrial habitats. Both free living and parasitic forms are present. The chief anatomical feature of these worms, from which the phylum named is derived, is that their body is composed of a series of similar cylindrical compartments called **segments** or **metameres**. Segmentation or metamerism is prominent in the animal kingdom in only two other phyla, Arthropoda and Chordata. In addition to being segmented, a spacious schizocoelom that is compartmentalized by septa occurs in polychaetes (Class Polychaeta) and oligochaetes (Class Oligochaeta). Unlike these two classes, leeches (Class Hirudinea) have many external rings called **annuli**; groups of annuli correspond to internal segmentation, but not in a simple fashion. Also, the schizocoelom in leeches is filled with connective tissue and reduced to a complex system of sinuses. Many polychaetes have well-developed, fleshy, lateral locomotory appendages called **parapodia** that exhibit a high degree of neuromuscular organization. Parapodia are lacking in the other classes. In the polychaetes and oligochaetes, bristle-like **setae** are present on most segments; setae are absent in most leeches.

Classification

In some classification systems Classes Oligochaeta and Hirundinea are grouped in the **Subphylum Clitellata**, because both possess a clitellum and other similarities. Polychaetes are then placed in the **Subphylum Aclitellata**. At one time, Archiannelida was employed as a separate class; however, these highly modified forms are now placed within Polychaeta. Some schemes include the echiurans and pogonophorans as separate classes within the Annelida.

1. **Class Polychaeta.** This very diverse class consists mainly of marine worms distinguished by having paired, lateral appendages called parapodia bearing numerous setae. Most polychaetes possess a distinct head with eyes, palps, tentacles, antennae, and cirri. Examples: *Aphrodita* (sea mouse), *Lepidonotus* (the scale worm), *Nereis (= Neanthes)* (sand or clam worm), *Eunice (= Palola)* (Samoan palolo worm), *Chaetopterus* (parchment tube worm), *Arenicola and Abarenicola* (lugworms), *Sabella* (fanworm), *Glycera* (beak-thrower or bloodworm), and *Amphitrite* (spaghetti worm).

2. **Class Oligochaeta.** These are terrestrial (e.g., earthworms) and aquatic annelids with external and internal segmentation. Parapodia are absent, but setae are present. A distinct, band-like clitellum is formed on several anterior segments in sexually mature individuals. Examples: *Tubifex*, (aquatic tubificids), *Eisenia foetida* (manure worm), and *Lumbricus terrestris* (the night crawler).

3. **Class Hirudinea.** Predominantly freshwater, leeches are also terrestrial and marine. Many leeches are blood-sucking parasites, but a large number are not

From *Invertebrate Zoology*, Sixth Edition, Robert L. Wallace and Walter K. Taylor. Copyright © 2002 by Pearson Education, Inc. Published by Prentice-Hall, Inc. All rights reserved

parasitic. The body of a leech has conspicuous, superficial external annulation that is not reflected internally as segmentation in any simple fashion. Parapodia are lacking and setae are usually absent, but a clitellum is present. Examples: *Hirudo medicinalis*, *(medicinal leech)* and *Glossiphonia complanata*.

Fossil Forms. Annelids do not fossilize well because they have few hard parts. Most putative fossils consist of trails and burrows. However, several good specimens of the Class Polychaeta are represented in the Burgess Shale Fauna. Therefore, this class dates at least to the mid-Cambrian Period and probably earlier (Fig. 1).

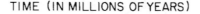

TIME (IN MILLIONS OF YEARS)

Figure 1. Geologic history of the Phylum Annelida.

A. Class Polychaeta

The largest class of annelids is Polychaeta [POL-ee-KE-tah; G., *poly*, many + G., *chaeta*, hair or bristle] comprising more than 8,000 species that range in length from a few millimeters to more than 3 m. Two groups of polychaetes, though not completely clear-cut, were previously recognized: free-moving forms, the **Errantia** [er-RAN-she-ah; L., *erran*, wander], and sedentary tube-dwelling forms, the **Sedentaria** [sed-en-TAR-re-ah; L., *sedent*, sit]. Modes of food procurement also show great diversity and include raptorial predators, herbivores, scavengers, and sediment and filter feeders. Few polychaetes are parasitic.

The body comprises a series of similar cylindrical segments, each having a pair of lateral appendages called parapodia, that are important in locomotion and gaseous exchange (Fig. 2). The schizocoelom is compartmentalized by intersegmental septa that are perforated to allow the coelomic fluid to pass from one segment to another. Many of the same body functions are performed in each segment. Not all polychaetes are uniformly segmented and the parapodia may be grouped into regions that differ in size, shape, and function. These specialized, functional regions are called **tagmata** [TAG-ma-ta; G., *tagma*, a division]. Tagmatization is often quite pronounced in some forms.

■ Observational Procedure:

Nereis
Members of the Genus *Nereis* (= *Neanthes*), commonly known as rag, sand, or clam worms, are found in shallow marine and estuarine waters worldwide.

Live Specimens
1. Obtain a live *Nereis* or similar species. Do you see any color patterns? Gently run your fingers down the side of the worm. What do you feel? These paddlelike structures are the **parapodia**. Place a *Nereis* on a piece of wet paper that you have previously marked with a grid of lines 1 cm apart; this will help you observe movement of the animal better. How does the animal move? What role do the parapodia play in locomotion? Is their movement synchronous? Do the parapodia move in a coordinated fashion? If so, describe that coordination. Are the parapodia in contact with the surface at all times? How do they grip the surface? How do the parapodia function as a series of lever arms? Determine how fast *Nereis* can move. Stimulate the animal with a gentle prod from the rear. Does the pattern of locomotion change when *Nereis* is crawling fast? Determine how *Nereis* moves around obstacles.

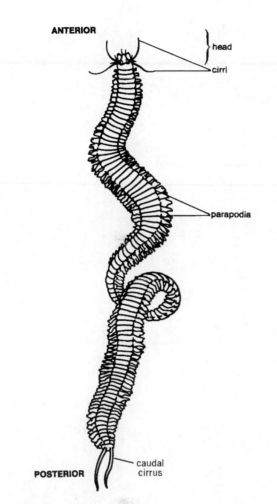

ANTERIOR

head

cirri

parapodia

caudal
cirrus

POSTERIOR

Figure 2. Dorsal view of *Nereis*.

2. Place *Nereis* in a clear glass tube filled with seawater having a diameter only slightly wider than the width of the worm. Put the tube in a dish filled with seawater. How does the worm react to this habitat? Does the worm remain in the tube? What function do the parapodia play under these circumstances?

3. Remove the worm from the tube and place it in a tank of seawater. Can *Nereis* swim? Describe the swimming movements. How do the movements of *Nereis* compare to those of planarian and nematode worms?

External Morphology

The following dissection of *Nereis* may be done with a freshly anesthetized worm or one that has been preserved. In either case, the worm should be kept submerged during the dissection. In general razor blades do not work well on a fresh worm; very fine scissors should be used. If an anesthetized worm is used for dissection, be sure that it is killed at the end of the exercise. If a preserved worm is to be used for the following observations, return the live *Nereis* to the holding tank.

1. Obtain a specimen of *Nereis* and examine both surfaces. There is a slight, midventral depression that runs the length of the worm. Observe the distinct segmentation with paired, lateral parapodia, and the appendages on the head region (Fig. 3). Is this segmentation uniform?

Examine the anterior region and locate the **prostomium**, **eyes**, **palps**, and **antennae**, **peristomium** (segments 1 and 2), and **peristomial cirri**. The mouth is on the ventral side of the peristomium. The terminal, unsegmented region, the **pygidium** [p-JID-e-um; G., *pyg*, rump], bears the anus and **caudal cirri**. Are parapodia found on the peristomium and pygidium?

2. If you are examining a preserved worm, determine whether the pharynx is extended or retracted. If muscles can only contract, how can a worm extend its pharynx? Examine an extended pharynx and locate the jaws and pharyngeal **paragnaths**.

3. Observe the worm under a dissection microscope. Do the segments vary in size or morphology along the length of the worm? The first parapodia-bearing segment (number 3) is called the first **setiger**.

4. Using a scalpel, remove several parapodia from different places along the worm's body. Make sure they are cut close to the body. Place the parapodia in a watch glass, cover with water, and examine them using a dissection microscope. Locate the **notopodium**, **neuropodium** with extra processes or **ligules**, setae, and dorsal and ventral cirri (Fig. 4). Do the various parapodia differ greatly from one another? Is there evidence for tagmatization in *Nereis*? What would you have to see to conclude that tagmatization was present?

5. Compare a prepared whole mount of a parapodium with your specimen (Fig. 4). Species may be differentiated on the basis of morphological details of their parapodia. How does your specimen differ from the prepared whole mount obtained commercially?

6. Note that both the notopodium and neuropodium are supported internally by a stiff, chitinous rods called the **acicula**.

7. Remove a few setae from several parapodia, place them in a drop of water on a slide, add a cover slip, and observe under a microscope. Note that the setae are not just uniform rod-shaped structures. How do the setae function in locomotion? Are they birefringent?

Phylum Annelida

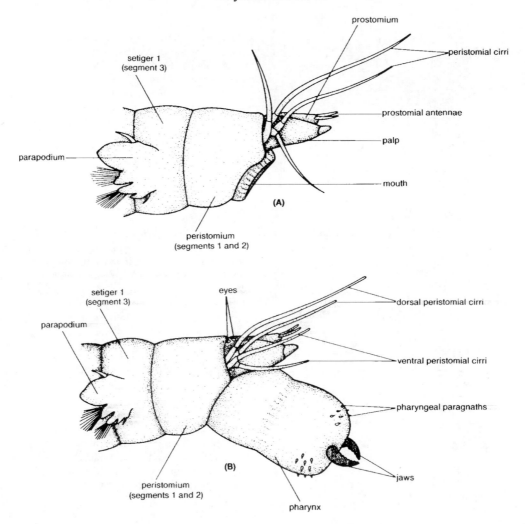

Figure 3. Lateral anterior view of the anterior end of *Nereis*. (A) Pharynx retracted. (B) Pharynx extended.

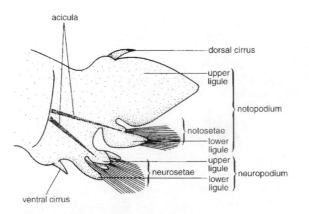

Figure 4. Typical *Nereis* parapodium.

Internal Anatomy

1. With a scalpel carefully make a parasagittal, shallow incision from the dorsal side, about one-third of the way from the anterior end.

2. With a small water dropper, siphon some liquid from the coelomic compartments of several segments. Examine this fluid by placing several drops on a glass slide, cover with a coverslip, and view under low power of the compound microscope. Gametes may be present, depending on the season the worm was collected. Abundant corpuscles should be seen. Following your examination of the coelomic fluid, cover the worm with water and proceed with the dissection.

3. Continue the dissection forward until the peristomium (segments 1 and 2) is reached. Pin the body wall to the bottom of the dissection pan as the incision is made.

Phylum Annelida

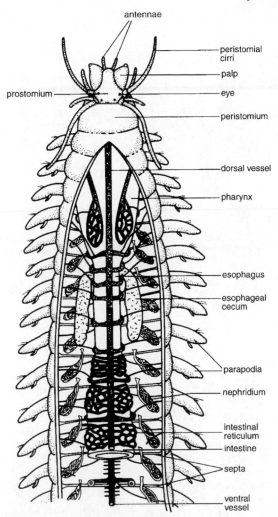

antennae

peristomial cirri

palp

eye

prostomium

peristomium

dorsal vessel

pharynx

esophagus

esophageal cecum

parapodia

nephridium

intestinal reticulum

intestine

septa

ventral vessel

Figure 5. Internal dorsal view of *Nereis*.

4. Observe the numerous **septa**. These may have been torn during the parasagittal incision.

5. Count the segments posteriorly from the peristomium to the seventh segment (fifth setiger). Note the enlarged pharyngeal region (segments 3–6, setigers 1–4) and the absence of septa. Locate the **dorsal blood vessels** that runs longitudinally over the gut (Fig. 5). Coming off the vessel are paired lateral vessels that communicate with the parapodia and body wall. The lateral vessels may be difficult to observe.

6. Trace the gut toward the posterior end. The **esophagus** occurs in segments 7–11 (setiger 5–9). In the region of the esophagus, paired **esophageal cecae** are attached laterally to the gut. Posterior to the esophagus the gut is designated as the **stomach-intestine**. In each segment are paired **nephridia** located ventrolaterally (Fig. 5).

7. Sever the gut between the fifteenth and twentieth segments. Carefully remove the gut up to the **pharynx** and sever again. Make sure that you do not damage the ventral nerve cord.

8. Once the pharyngeal region is reached, continue to remove the gut and note the position of the nerve cord. Just above the nerve cord the **ventral blood vessel** may be found. Locate the **circumpharyngeal connectives**; these encircle the pharynx and communicate with the **dorsal ganglia** or **brain**.

9. Find the nerves which extend anterior from the brain to the prostomium.

10. Observe the nerve cord along its length. How are the ganglia arranged in each segment?

11. Obtain a prepared slide of a cross section of *Nereis*. The body wall consists of an outer, thin cuticle that is produced by the epidermis below. Note the thick circular muscle layer and the dorsal and ventral longitudinal muscle masses. Locate the gut, dorsal mesentery, dorsal and ventral blood vessels, and ventral nerve cord (Fig. 6).

Aphrodita

Observe a specimen of the sea mouse, *Aphrodita*. The dorsal side appears hairy because of fine setae arising from the notopodia. Turn the specimen over and identify the anterior and posterior ends. Locate the terminal anus. Does *Aphrodita* exhibit tagmatization?

Arenicola

This worm, commonly known as the lugworm, lives on both U.S. coasts at about the low-tide mark where it burrows in sandy to muddy sediments.

1. Observe a specimen of *Arenicola*. There is a shallow, narrow, linear depression running along the entire ventral length of *Arenicola*. Locate the terminal anus.

2. Note that the parapodia are modified and reduced in size compared to those of worms just studied (Fig. 7).

3. *Arenicola* also has distinct **annulation** between segments. Body segments extend from the first annulation behind a parapodium to the first annulation behind the next parapodium.

4. At the anterior end, a fleshy pharynx and buccal mass, covered with small papillae, may be extended from the mouth (Fig. 7). Just behind the pharynx is the minute prostomium that lacks appendages. The peristomium, the first annulus, may be seen behind the prostomium.

5. Note that the body appears to be divided into three distinct tagmata: (a) anterior, pre-branchial; (b) branchial; and (c) posterior, post-branchial (Fig. 7). The first tagmata past the peristomium has reduced notopodia. They increase slightly in size towards the posterior end. The neuropodia are very difficult to see in this region. Segments in the next tagmata have biramous parapodia

Phylum Annelida

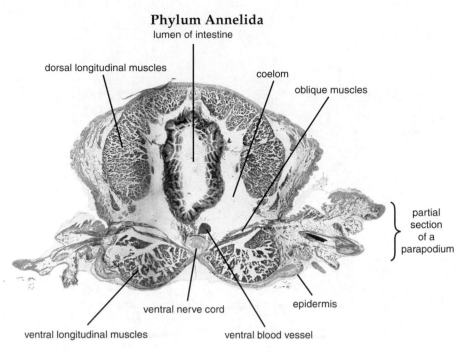

lumen of intestine

dorsal longitudinal muscles

coelom

oblique muscles

partial section of a parapodium

ventral nerve cord

epidermis

ventral longitudinal muscles

ventral blood vessel

Figure 6. Cross section of N*ereis*.

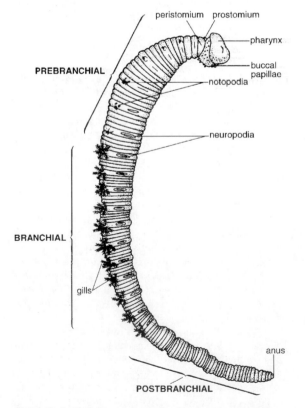

peristomium prostomium

pharynx

buccal papillae

notopodia

PREBRANCHIAL

neuropodia

BRANCHIAL

gills

anus

POSTBRANCHIAL

Figure 7. Lateral view of *Arenicola* with pharynx extended.

and possess gills, branched outgrowths of the body wall. In this region the neuropodia appear as slightly raised welts with slits. Appendages are lacking beyond the last gill-bearing segment.

Chaetopterus

Chaetopterus, the parchment tube worm, lives in **U-shaped** tubes that are opened at both ends. These worms occur in marine mudflats, but their tubes are only exposed during the lowest tides.

1. Obtain a specimen of *Chaetopterus* which has been removed from its tube. Locate the spatulate anterior end. There is a small, dorsal, ciliated groove at this end. The outer lip of the mouth is the **peristomal collar**.

2. Beginning anteriorly, observe that the segments and parapodia are not of a uniform morphology. Rather, the animal's body is differentiated into three tagma: (a) anterior with uniramous parapodia, (b) middle with greatly modified parapodia, and (c) posterior with biramous parapodia (Fig. 8). Water containing food and oxygen is drawn into the tube at the worm's anterior end and forced out the posterior vent. This movement is accomplished by special, modified parapodia called **fans** (segments 14, 15, and 16). Notopodia of segment 12 collect food. They are long and winglike (**aliform**) and contain mucus glands that produce a film of mucus that stretches between the notopodia forming a bag-like structure.

3. At segment 13 is a cup-shaped structure where food is concentrated and formed into small balls. These

160

Figure 8. Dorsolateral view of *Chaetopterus*.

balls are passed anteriorly along the small, dorsal ciliated groove that extends to the mouth, a shallow, funnel-like depression.

4. Note that parapodia posterior to the fans are well developed and similar in shape, although they decrease in size at the posterior end. The anus is terminal.

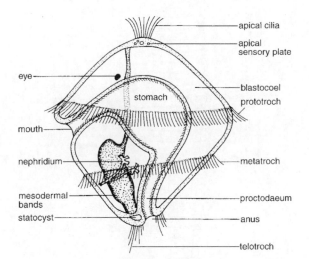

Figure 9. Typical polychaete trochophore larva.

Other Polychaetes

Diversity is very great in Polychaeta. One should not have the impression that the few specimens reviewed here give a complete view of the diversity of this class. Other polychaetes may be available for your study, and you should examine additional specimens as your instructor directs. For example, free-moving forms such as *Glycera* (beak-thrower or bloodworm) and *Lepidonotus* (scale worm) and sedentary species such as *Pectinaria* (= *Cistenides*) (trumpet worm or ice-cream-cone worm), *Diopatra* (plume worm), *Sabella* (fanworm), *Sabellastarte* (feather-dusters), and *Spirorbis* (calcareous tube worms) may be available for observation.

Larvae

Sexes are separate in most polychaetes, though distinct gonads are not usually present. Seasonal outgrowths of the coelomic lining in the ventral part of many segments form the gametes that are released into the body cavity where they mature. The gametes are released to the environment when the body wall bursts, or via the excretory system, or via the gonoducts. In many species the embryo develops into a **trochophore larva** (Fig. 9), whereas in other species development is direct. After metamorphosis the young worm settles on the substratum and develops into an adult. If available, examine a prepared slide of a trochophore larva. ∎

B. Class Oligochaeta

Oligochaeta [o-LEE-go-KEY-tah; G., *oligo*, few + G., *chaeta*, long hair or bristle] is the second largest class of annelids, containing more than 3,000 species. Although oligochaetes are commonly called earthworms, this term is technically incorrect because most species inhabit fresh waters, and there are many microscopic marine species. Most feed on dead and decaying materials, but earthworms ingest soil to feed on the microfauna and microflora. The night-crawler represents a group that browses on grass and leaves on the surface of the soil. Oligochaetes range in length from less than 0.5 mm to more than 7 m (e.g., giant Australian earthworm, *Megascolides australis*).

The oligochaete body consists of a series of uniform, cylindrical segments. As in polychaetes, many of the same bodily functions are performed in each segment. However, the extensive tagmatization of segments present in some polychaetes is absent in oligochaetes. Parapodia are absent; setae often occur on the lateral surface of each segment in many oligochaetes. Compared to most polychaetes, oligochaetes have few setae, hence the literal meaning of the class name. One prominent region of the epidermis in sexually mature individuals is the **clitellum**, a bandlike, glandular structure that may be one to many cells thick. The size of the clitellum varies depending on the species and the time of the year. The clitellum produces mucus during copulation and later secretes a **cocoon** or capsule where embryonic development takes place.

Because of some uniformity in individuals of earthworms and leeches, one can use a single species to learn the basic structural makeup of each class. In this exercise the readily available *Lumbricus terrestris* will be studied in detail, although it is not a typical oligochaete.

■ Observational Procedure:

Live Specimens
If possible begin your studies with a live specimen. Do not be put off by the slimy feel of the organism, and do not waste the opportunity of learning new things about *Lumbricus* by wearing latex gloves.
1. Obtain a live *Lumbricus*. Note any differences in the color pattern on the dorsal and ventral surfaces. Gently hold opposite ends of the worm in each hand noting the strength the worm exhibits upon contraction. Gently run your fingers down the length of the worm while holding on to one end. What do you feel? Are the setae as numerous as in *Nereis*? Run your fingers down the worm again, first in one direction then in the other. Is there a difference in the feel of the setae? What accounts for the difference and what function might this feature serve in locomotion?
2. Place the worm on a piece of wet paper that you have previously marked with a grid of lines 1 cm apart; this will help you observe the movement of the animal better. How does *Lumbricus* move? Does locomotion in *Lumbricus* resemble in any way that of *Nereis*? Describe how these movements are like peristalic waves.
3. Move the worm to a sheet of wet glass. Does movement still occur? How is this organism better suited to crawl through something (e.g., soil or mulch) than over a flat surface?
4. Drop *Lumbricus* into a tank of freshwater. Can it swim? Compare the locomotory abilities of the earthworm to *Nereis*. How are they similar? How are they different? How does movement in *Lumbricus* compare to other wormlike organisms that you have studied?

External Morphology
The dissection of *Lumbricus* described may be done with a freshly anesthetized worm or one that has been preserved. Some anatomical details are best seen with a live worm, including viewing all the stages of the parasite, *Monocystis*. An excellent view of the functioning of the dorsal vessel and hearts also is possible. In both cases, the animal should be kept submerged during the dissection. In general razor blades do not work well on a fresh worm. Very fine scissors work better than razor blades when fresh worms are dissected. If an anesthetized worm is used for dissection, be sure that it is killed at the end of the exercise.

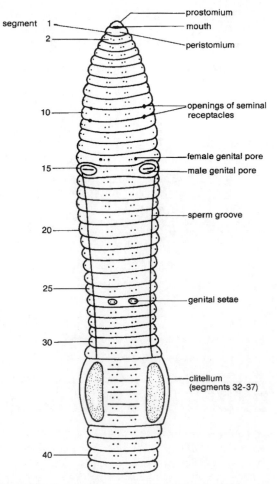

Figure 10. Ventral anterior view of *Lumbricus terrestris*.

Phylum Annelida

1. Obtain a preserved specimen of *Lumbricus* or one that has been recently anesthetized. Note the lack of any tagmata in this species. Identify the worm's anterior and posterior ends. At the anterior end is the mouth, located on the ventral portion of segment 1 (peristomium). The short, knoblike, mid-dorsal projection is the prostomium which is not considered to be a true segment (Fig. 10). Is the earthworm's prostomium similar to that of *Nereis?* Are setae present?

2. At the posterior end locate the pygidium bearing the anus.

3. Again, gently pull the animal between your fingers to feel the setae. Eight setae in four pairs are found on every segment except the first and last. Are the setae randomly scattered around the animal or is there a pattern to their placement?

4. *Slide:* Select a cross section of *Lumbricus* which shows setae. Note the position of the setae and the muscles attached to them (Fig. 11). Setae are highly birefringent and may be easily identified in the section by examining it for birefringent structures.

5. Arrange the worm so that the dorsal surface is uppermost. Starting at segment 1, count posterior to segment number 31. Note the bandlike clitellum, which covers segments 32–37 and forms the cocoon from secretion by large gland cells.

6. *Slide:* Examine a cross section of *Lumbricus* at the level of the clitellum. Note that the clitellum is a thickened region of glandular cells. Is the clitellum of uniform thickness around the worm? Which part is the thicker? Under high magnification, observe the large, globular secretory cells that make up the bulk of the clitellum. The darkly-staining cells closest to the surface secrete mucus and cocoon material; those cells with less stain secrete albumin for nourishing the developing worm while in the cocoon.

7. Turn the worm ventral surface uppermost and count the segments from the prostomium until you reach segment 15. In this segment find the paired male **genital pores**, each of which bears a distinct swelling resembling a pair of lips.

8. On segment 14 locate a pair of extremely small

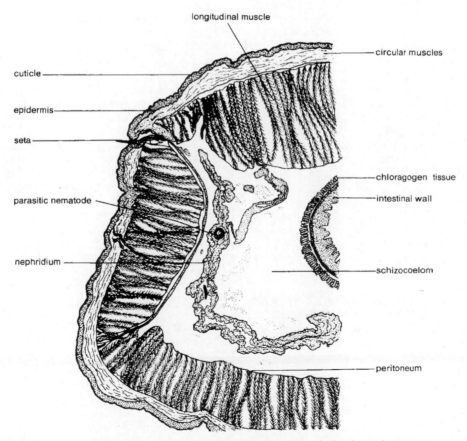

Figure 11. One-half of a cross section of *Lumbricus terrestris* showing the seta and other internal structures.

openings in the same position as the male pores. These are the external pores of the **oviducts** (Fig. 10). The paired openings of the **seminal receptacles** are located between segments 9 and 10, and 10 and 11, but they are very small and difficult to find.

9. On the ventral side locate the two **sperm grooves** and trace them from each male gonopore to the clitellum. Review in your textbook about copulation and reproduction.

10. Two other types of pores, though difficult to locate, may be seen on the surface of *Lumbricus:* **nephridiopores** and **coelomic pores**. Nephridiopores are paired in the segmental furrows just anterior and slightly above the ventrolateral setae.

11. Coelomic pores are single and release fluid which helps keep the worm's surface moist. They are located middorsally in the intersegmental furrows in the middle and posterior body.

Body Wall

The outermost layer of the body wall is the noncellular **cuticle**, which is secreted by special cells in the epidermis. Microscopic pores present in the cuticle allow epidermal secretions to pass to the outside of the body.

1. Scrape some cuticle from the epidermis. Place the sample on a glass slide, add a drop of water, and apply a coverslip. Observe under low power of the compound microscope. What do you observe? The smooth texture of the cuticle plus mucoid secretions give the characteristic slippery feel to the worm's surface. Immediately below the cuticle is the epidermis, composed of several kinds of columnar epithelial cells.

2. *Slide*: Obtain a median longitudinal section of *Lumbricus* and examine the body wall using high magnification. Note the different cell types found in the epidermis. Inward from the epidermis are two muscle-tissue layers. The outermost of these is the circular muscle layer. Scattered among the fibrils are brownish pigment granules. Note that the circular muscles are not continuous with the muscles in other segments.

3. The innermost muscle layer consists of longitudinal muscle cells that are continuous from segment to segment.

4. Just below the longitudinal muscles is the very thin peritoneum. This mesodermal layer lines the schizocoelom and is continuous with the septa.

5. Locate a septum between each pair of segments.

Internal Anatomy

1. Extend the worm full length with the ventral surface down. Fasten the specimen to the bottom of a dissection pan by placing pins through the prostomium and the pygidium.

2. Using a razor blade or very fine scissors, make a shallow, midsagittal incision through the anterior third of the body wall. Be very CAREFUL not to cut too deeply thereby disturbing the underlying viscera. *Work slowly and patiently; a rushed dissection can render the specimen useless for detailed anatomical study.*

3. About halfway along the cut, start to turn the body wall over laterally and pin it to the pan. Work posteriorly, continuing to pin the body wall to the pan as you cut.

4. Note the septa that connect the gut to the body wall. The schizocoelom is found between each pair of septa.

5. Add water to the pan to immerse the worm completely. All observation should be made with the worm submerged to prevent drying and to allow structures to float freely for better observation.

6. Several organ systems are now exposed. Study your dissection with a dissection microscope. Some structures, such as the seminal funnels and the vas deferens, may be difficult to locate. However, students who are patient will be successful at locating them. These structures also should be observed in prepared microscopic sections.

Circulatory System (Fig. 12)

1. The dorsal blood vessel is located on the upper surface of the gut. In preserved worms this vessel usually appears as a light brown to gray line. Close examination will reveal the small vessels joining the main vessel at right angles in each segment. The dorsal vessel is a collecting and pulsating tube; therefore it is actually the heart of the worm because it moves the blood from posterior to anterior.

2. In segments 7 through 11 locate five pairs of hearts that extend dorsoventrally around the esophagus, connecting the dorsal and ventral vessels (Fig. 12). These hearts also pulsate, contracting in coordinated rhythm with the dorsal vessel. The ventral blood vessel will be observed when the gut is removed later in the dissection.

3. *Slide*: Obtain a cross section of *Lumbricus* at the level of a heart. Note the position and size of the heart(s) and the thin muscular wall. In most sections, connections to the dorsal and ventral vessels will not be evident. Why?

Reproductive System (Fig. 12)

1. Posterior to the second pair of hearts in segment 8 are three pairs of large, light-colored structures that almost fill the whole area of the worm in this region. These are the seminal vesicles. Their bases are attached ventrally, but they expand dorsally to occupy space in segments 9–12.

2. *Slide*: Obtain a cross section of *Lumbricus* at the level of the seminal vesicles and observe the large size and general construction of these structures. Note that they are not just large sacs. What is their function?

3. Using a scalpel, remove a small portion of one seminal vesicle and macerate it on a microscope slide in a small amount of water. Add a coverslip and observe this preparation using a compound microscope. Scan the seminal vesicles for gametocysts of the gregarine protozoan parasite *Monocystis* (the Protozoa, Exercise 1D). Gametocysts resemble a small sphere filled with many minute spindle-shaped structures, the sporocysts (Fig. 13). If you macerated your preparation very well, most of the sporocysts will probably be free of their gametocyst. You also should examine the prepared cross section of *Lumbricus* for *Monocystis*.

4. Under the lobes of the two anterior pairs of seminal vesicles (segments 9 and 10) are the paired, spherical seminal receptacles (Fig. 12) where sperm are stored.

5. *Slide*: Obtain a cross section of the **seminal receptacles (spermatheca)**. The vesicles are located ventrolaterally and may contain many spermatozoa. Testes are found near the nerve cord in the anterior of segments 10 and 11, and the ovaries similarly in segment 13.

6. Near the bases of the middle seminal vesicle and located midventrally are the first pair of testis sacs (segment 10). The second pair is located in segment 11. The **sperm funnels** are buried under a membrane, the testis sac, and may be difficult to locate.

7. If this is the case, turn your attention to segment 15 and locate the vasa deferentia which run anteriorly along the body wall. Follow that tube anteriorly as it leads to a funnel.

8. *Slide*: View a cross section at the level of the sperm funnels. Sperm funnels may be located easily as the sperm stain darkly. In longitudinal section, sperm funnels appear to be highly convoluted.

9. Ovaries are located in the anterior part of segment 13. Eggs set free in the coelomic cavity are collected by the **ovarian funnels**. Oviducts open to the outside of the body in segment 14. The oviduct will not be easily seen, but the area of the ovarian funnel may be identified by the button-like opening on the septum directly posterior to the ovary.

10. *Slide*: Examine cross sections of *Lumbricus* at the levels of the testes and ovaries and locate these structures. Note their small size compared to seminal vesicles.

Digestive System (Fig. 12)

Buccal Cavity and Pharynx. The digestive system is a straight tube with a few specialized regions.

1. Locate the peristomium of your specimen. At this level a buccal cavity opens into the pharynx (segments 4 and 5).

2. Note the size and shape of the pharynx, and observe the numerous muscle fibers that connect the pharynx to the body wall. Take care not to damage the brain that is located dorsally at the anterior junction of the buccal cavity and pharynx in segment 3 (Fig. 12).

3. Gently press your finger on the pharynx and feel the general texture of the organ.

4. *Slide*: Examine a cross section of the pharynx and note the distribution of the powerful pharyngeal muscle. What is the function of this muscle?

5. Observe a medial section through the anterior end of the worm and locate the pharynx.

6. In this section note the **pharyngeal dorsal diverticulum**. What function might this structure perform?

7. Note the muscle fibers that connect the pharynx dorsally to the body wall.

Esophagus. The esophagus is a long tube (segments 6 to 13) that carries food from the pharynx to the crop (segments 14 and 15).

8. Follow the pharynx posteriorly where it opens into the esophagus (Fig. 12).

9. On either side of the esophagus are two pairs of bulbous evaginations (segments 11 and 12) called **calciferous glands**. One function of their secretions is regulation of calcium concentration in bodily fluids, thereby maintaining ionic and pH balance.

10. *Slide*: Locate these glands in a cross section of the esophagus. Note the cavities between elongate cells of the gland.

Crop and Gizzard. From the esophagus, food passes into a thin-walled storage organ called the **crop** (segments 14 and 15) and then into a muscular, cuticle-lined **gizzard** (segments 16–19), a food-grinding organ (Fig. 12).

11. Locate these organs in your specimen. Using your finger or probe, gently press on the crop and gizzard and compare the general texture of these organs. What does this indicate about the functions of these two organs?

12. *Slide*: With an anterior medial section of *Lumbricus*, locate the crop and gizzard. How can you tell these organs apart in this section?

13. Also observe these two organs in cross section. Are muscles present in the walls of the crop or gizzard? How are the muscles distributed in the crop?

14. Observe the inner lining of the crop and gizzard. Why would the gizzard have a thick cuticular lining?

Stomach-Intestine. After being processed in the gizzard food passes into the stomach-intestine.

15. Continue the midsagittal incision of the body wall for the full length of the worm, pinning the body wall to the

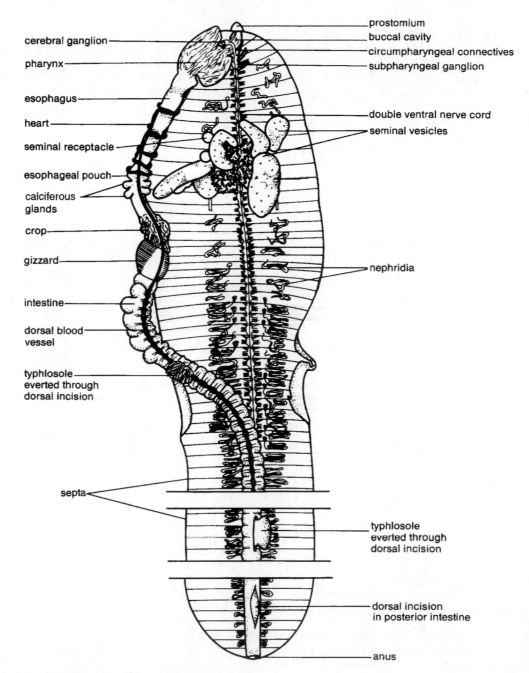

cerebral ganglion

pharynx

esophagus

heart

seminal receptacle

esophageal pouch

calciferous glands

crop

gizzard

intestine

dorsal blood vessel

typhlosole everted through dorsal incision

septa

prostomium

buccal cavity

circumpharyngeal connectives

subpharyngeal ganglion

double ventral nerve cord

seminal vesicles

nephridia

typhlosole everted through dorsal incision

dorsal incision in posterior intestine

anus

Figure 12. Schematic internal dorsal view of *Lumbricus terrestris.*

dissection pan as you proceed. Trace the intestine from the gizzard to the anus (Fig. 12).

16. Observe the external morphology of the intestine along its length. Externally there is only minor specialization of the gut past the gizzard.

17. Remove 1-cm sections from anterior, mid, and rectal portions of the intestine. Cut these sections open lengthwise, place them in small glass dishes, and observe the lining under a dissection microscope.

18. In the anterior section, note the presence of the

Figure 13. Cross section of *Lumbricus terrestris* at the level of the seminal vesicles.

seminal vesicle

wall of intestine

gametocytes of *Monocystis* containing many sporocysts

nephridium

Excretory System (Fig. 12)

A pair of **nephridia** (or **metanephrida**), one on each side, is located in the lateral area of each body segment, with the exception of the first two segments and pygidium.

1. In the region of the gizzard and posterior to it, examine the inner body wall surface of each segment and locate the metanephridia.

2. Using a dissection microscope examine a nephridium in situ. The nephrostome and nephridiopore will be difficult to locate.

3. *Slide*: Compare this structure to a whole mount slide of a metanephridium. Locate the convoluted tubules, bladder, and the vessels of the circulatory system.

4. Locate the nephridiopore in a prepared cross section. What other structures of the nephridium do you observe? *Lumbricus* is a host to a parasitic nematode, *Rhabditis maupasi*, which is believed to enter the worm via nephridiopore or genital openings (Phylum Nematoda).

typhlosole. Is the typhlosole found in the other sections of the intestine? What does it look like in each section? What is the function of the typhlosole? Was a typhlosole present in the cross section of the Polychaete *Nereis*?

19. *Slide*: Examine a cross section of the intestine. The intestine is just below the dorsal blood vessel. Both are surrounded by a special tissue called **chloragogen**. Suspended from the dorsal side of the intestine is the typhlosole (Fig. 14). From what region of the intestine was your section made? How can you tell?

20. Note that chloragogen tissue also is found inside the typhlosole. Locate the thin layer of cells between the intestinal epithelium (gastrodermis) and the chloragogen tissue. This layer is sometimes called the **submucosa**, but it is actually a layer of circular muscle.

Nervous System (Fig. 12 and 14).

1. Dorsal to the buccal cavity, at a point where the buccal cavity and the pharynx meet, locate the **brain** (or **suprapharyngeal ganglia** or **cerebral ganglia**) in segment 3. Projecting anteriorly into the prostomial region are the prostomial nerve fibers. Extending laterally from each cerebral ganglion are the **circumpharyngeal connectives** that lead to the **subpharyngeal ganglia**.

2. Using scissors, carefully cut through the pharynx and esophagus and remove that section to expose the circumpharyngeal connectives and the subpharyngeal ganglia.

3. Observe the size difference between the supra- and subpharyngeal ganglia. Note the ring form made by the circumpharyngeal connectives.

coelom

chloragogen cells

dorsal blood vessel

longitudinal muscles

wall of intestine

typhlosole

lumen of gut

circular muscles

setae

Figure 14. Cross section of *Lumbricus terrestris* at the level of the intestine.

4. *Slide*: Locate the suprapharyngeal and subpharyngeal ganglia in cross sections made at the appropriate levels.

5. Trace in your specimen the **ventral nerve cord** as it extends posteriorly from the subpharyngeal ganglia. Just above the nerve cord is the ventral blood vessel.

6. In each body segment locate a ganglionic enlargement of the nerve cord.

7. Find the three pairs of lateral nerves which arise from the nerve cord in each segment. Lateral nerves are more or less independent in all their sensory and motor functions, allowing localized action to one segment or several widely separated or even contiguous segments.

8. *Slide*: Examine several cross sections of *Lumbricus* below the level of the subpharyngeal ganglion and locate the ventral nerve cord. (Continue your observations of this slide in steps 9 and 10).

9. Just above the nerve cord locate the ventral blood vessel and within the nerve cord find the **midventral subneural blood vessel** and two **lateral neural blood vessels**.

10. In the dorsal area of the nerve cord note a centrally placed tubelike body with two smaller ones subequal in size to either side. These are **giant fibers**. Giant fibers are large neurons that transmit impulses unimpeded the full length of the worm, thereby permitting a sudden withdrawal of the worm down its burrow.

11. *Slide*: Compare the structure of the supra- and subpharyngeal ganglia to the ventral nerve cord using cross sections. Below the giant fibers are two circular structures that are composed of motor and sensory neurons. In some cross sections you may be able to locate lateral nerves that leave the ventral nerve cord in each segment.

12. *Slide*: In medial sections, the ventral nerve cord may be traced posteriorly for some distance. Occasionally segmental ganglia and lateral nerves may be seen.

Other Species

Lumbricus terrestris is not a typical oligochaete, but it is a fairly easy one with which to work. If time permits, your instructor may provide specimens of *Aeolosoma*, *Enchytraeus*, *Dero*, *Stylaria*, *Tubifex* and other oligochaetes to observe. ■

C. Class Hirudinea

Leeches, members of the Class Hirudinea (or Hirudinoidea) [hi-ru-DIN-e-a; L., *hirudin*, leech], are a small group of about 600 species of highly specialized annelids. They are mainly freshwater, but terrestrial and marine forms are known. Most leeches range in length from less than 1 mm to over 5 cm. The very largest may reach more than 0.25 m. The Amazonian leech, *Haementeria ghiliani*, is 30 cm in length. Leeches are popularly identified as blood-sucking parasites; however, many are predaceous or scavengers. Medicinal leeches, *Hirudo medicinalis* (native to Europe) and *Macrobdella decora* (native to the U.S.) were used in bloodletting during the eighteenth and nineteenth centuries. Leeches are used in hospitals today, after performing microsurgeries on reattachment of fingers, hands, ears, and other organs, to restore blood flow to the reattached organs. Patients with severe bruises may have leeches applied to remove clotted blood. In natural habitats and fish hatcheries, heavy infestation of leeches on individuals is not uncommon and these infestations may cause anemia or even mortality. Most leeches are temporary parasites, abandoning their host after becoming engorged with blood.

Leeches have fewer segments than do other annelids. What appear to be segments in leeches are **annuli**, which are surface subdivisions of individual segments.

This is similar to what was observed in the polychaete *Arenicola*. Unlike other annelids, the number of segments in leeches is fixed at 34 (some accounts, which do not count the prostomium, report 33). The body is rounded to flattened and may be divided into five regions. Traditionally the segments within these regions are given Roman numerals: (1) head (segments I to VI), (2) preclitellum (segments VII to IX), (3) clitellum (segments X to XII), (4) trunk (segments XIII to XXIV), and (5) a terminal region (segments XXV to XXXIV), with an anus (segments XXV to XXVII) and posterior sucker (segments XXVIII to XXXIV).

■ Observational Procedure:

Live Specimens

Leeches may be capable of sucking your blood, but if you handle them with a quick hand they will not have an opportunity to sample your blood.

1. What types of color patterns are present on the dorsal and ventral slides of the animal? How do they compare to those of *Nereis* and *Lumbricus*? Are they cryptic?

2. Gently run your fingers down the side of the worm. Are setae present? How does setation compare to the polychaetes and oligochaetes studied previously? Gently pick up the leech and permit it to attach to a glass

Phylum Annelida

Figure 15. Dorsal and ventral views of *Hirudo medicinalis*. (After Sherman and Sherman.)

slide. Invert the slide and determine how strong the suckers are in making the attachment. Wait until the leech is attached with both suckers and gently prod its anterior end with a probe so that it releases its hold from that end. How does the leech react? Describe how it re-establishes its hold. Now do the same thing, but to the posterior sucker. How does the leech react? Are these reactions different? Place the leech onto a flat sheet of glass and observe its locomotory abilities. How does the leech move when out of water?

3. Drop the leech into a tank of freshwater. How does it swim? Does it swim in the same manner as *Nereis*? Is the entire body involved in this movement? Notice in particular the plane of undulations of the body. Compare the locomotory abilities of the leech with the other annelids you have observed. How are they similar? How are they different?

External Morphology

1. Obtain one or two preserved leeches such as *Hirudo medicinalis* and *Haemopis grandis*. Observe the elongated body with the numerous annuli. Note any patterns in body pigmentation.

2. Place the leech on a dissection tray and identify the dorsal and ventral surfaces (Fig. 15). The dorsal surface is usually darker. Why might this be advantageous to the animal in its natural habitat?

3. Locate the anterior and posterior **suckers**. The anterior sucker is the smallest and surrounds the mouth. Note the general shape of the posterior sucker.

Phylum Annelida

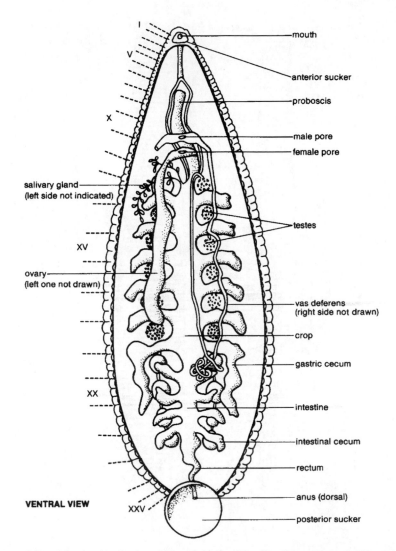

Figure 16. Ventral view of *Glossiphonia*, showing the relative positions of the digestive and reproductive systems.

4. Several minute eyespots are located on the dorsal surface at the anterior end just above the mouth. Observe the eyespots with the dissection microscope or hand lens.

5. On the mid-dorsal surface of the worm, just anterior to the posterior sucker, is the anus. It is often helpful to dry the surface of the animal with a paper towel to see the anus. Why is the anus not at the very posterior part of the animal and within the sucker?

6. Turn the worm over on its dorsal side. About one-fifth to one-fourth of the way from the anterior end in the ventral midline are two small **gonopores**; the male gonopore is anterior to the female gonopore. In some

specimens, the penis may be everted from the male pore. It is easier to locate these pores if the surface is dry.

7. Although sensory papillae are difficult to see on preserved worms, attempt to locate them. They occur on the dorsal and ventral sides of the body. The annulus on which sensory papillae are found marks the middle of a segment that extends through several annuli (Fig. 15).

8. On the second annulus of each segment, almost in the depression between the annuli, are the paired nephridiopores (Fig. 15). There are five annuli per segment in the midsection of *H. medicinalis*.

Phylum Annelida

Internal Anatomy

Glossiphonia complanata

Stained prepared microslide mounts of *G. complanata* will now be observed. Under both low and high powers of the dissection microscope locate the following anatomical features: annuli, paired eyespots, muscular proboscis and proboscis cavity, salivary gland, crop, gastric ceca, intestine, intestinal ceca, rectum, anus, posterior sucker, ovary, and testes (Fig. 16). Although the various anatomical parts shown in the illustration are not exactly the same for all leech species, the basic structure is similar.

Hirudo medicinalis

Leech dissection is difficult, but care and patience will provide you with a greater appreciation for these complex organisms.

1. Place a specimen of *H. medicinalis* in a dissection pan on its dorsal surface. Firmly pin the leech to the pan by inserting a dissection pin through the tip of the anterior sucker and another pin through the tip of the posterior sucker. Cover the specimen with water.

2. *Carefully* cut away the lower lip to expose the three jaws, arranged as a triangle; two jaws are lateral and one is dorsal. Observe the position of the jaws and the numerous dilator muscles connected to the pharynx. Care-

fully remove one jaw with a fine-pointed scalpel. Place the jaw in a drop of water in a depression slide and examine under a compound microscope. Note the numerous minute serrations along the cutting edge of the jaw.

3. Set aside your specimen and obtain a cross section of a leech at the level of the pharynx and observe the very muscular, triangular lumen of the pharynx. What is the functional significance of a triangularly shaped pharynx?

4. Return to your specimen and turn it over on its ventral side. Pin the specimen firmly to the dissection pan. Make a shallow medial incision from about the level of the anterior sucker posteriorly for about 25 annuli. At the posterior and anterior limits of this incision, make two lateral cuts. Using a sharp scalpel, cut the body wall from the fibrous internal mass of tissue. Pin the flap to the dissection pan. Note that complete, internal septa and a spacious body cavity observed in the other annelids are absent. Throughout the coelom is a loose mesenchymal mass called **botryoidal tissue**. This is a highly vascularized mass of tissue whose main component is pigmented cells. Spaces, called **coelomic sinuses**, between the loose-connected mass of fibers are the remains of the coelom.

5. Obtain a cross section of a leech at the midbody level and note the position of the botryoidal tissue. Also note the relative positions of the gut and sinuses (Fig. 17). ■

Figure 17. Interior view of the oral region of *Hirudo medicinalis* (After Sherman and Sherman).

Phylum Annelida

Phylum Annelida   Worksheet 7

Name: _____   Date: _____

Course #: _____ / Section #: _____   Grade: _____

1. Using one or two words or short phrases, differentiate or characterize the three classes of Annelida for each structure listed below.

Structure	Polychaeta	Oligochaeta	Hirudinea
Septa			
Clitellum			
Parapodia			
Schizocoelom			
Tagmatization			
Larva			
Segments			
Setae			

Phylum Annelida

2. Refute or support the statements: Adapative advantages occur in animals whose bodies are segmented compared to those that lack segmentation. What relationship is there, if any, between metamerism and tagmatization?

3. Refute or support the statement that Oligochaetes are more closely related to leeches than to Polychaetes.

4. Why does an earthworm have a well-developed, muscular gizzard, and not the leech?

5. During the exercise on the Class Polychaeta, you learned that members of this class were formerly divided into two groups: Errantia and Sedentaria. Do you think, now that you have performed the exercise, that using these two terms to differentiate and analyze the polychaetes is accurate and has any advantage? Discuss. Consider any disadvantages to using this approach.

ARTHROPODOUS PHYLA

Termed **Ecdysozoa** by Aguinaldo et al. (1997) seven phyla (Nematoda, Nematomorpha, Onychophora, Tardigrada, Kinorhyncha, Priapulida, and Arthropoda) comprise a group of schizocoelomate protostomes that possess a **cuticle** which is periodically shed or **molted** by ecdysis. While this organization is still controversial and seems unlikely because it unites **metameric** (segmented) taxa with those that are not, the arrangement is supported by a phylogenetic analysis of 18S ribosomal DNA sequences. We will not study the Kinorhyncha and Priapulida due to the lack of suitable study material from commercial supply houses.

Nematodes and nematomorphs resemble one another, and based on some molecular analyses are probably closely related. Both onychophorans and tardigrades have been allied with arthropods; recent molecular analyses support this view.

Arthropods are metameric with a strong tendency for reduction in number of appendages and segments, and for **tagmatization** of segments. Their cuticle is often strengthened with calcium deposits into an exoskeleton, but it is not equally thickened in all regions of the body. Separate plates are associated with each body segment or **somite** (G., *soma*, body) and these are connected to one another by flexible, thinner regions called **articulating membranes**. Periodically the arthropod forms a new exoskeleton underneath the old, which is then shed in a molt. The new, flexible exoskeleton is then stretched to a larger size before hardening. In primitive arthropods, each segment possesses a pair of appendages, but this condition does not hold for most species. The schizocoelom is much reduced; it does not function as a **hydraulic skeleton** as occurs in annelids. The large body cavity in arthropods is actually a **hemocoel** (a modified blastocoel).

Some workers believe that the Arthropoda may have arisen several different times (i.e., polyphyletic arthropodization) from the annelid-arthropod line. However, most argue that the phylum is monophyletic. The parasitic **Pentastomida**, once given phylum status, are now considered to be arthropods closely related to Class Branchiura.

Aguinaldo, A.M.A., J.M. Turbeville, L.S. Linford, M.C. Rivera, J.R. Garey, R.A. Raff, and J.A. Lake. 1997. Evidence for a clade of nematodes, arthropods and other moulting animals. *Nature* 387: 489-493.

Ballard, J.W., G.J. Olsen, D.P. Faith, W.A. Odgers, D.M. Rowell, and P.W. Atkinson. 1992. Evidence from 12S ribosomal RNA sequences that onychophorans are modified arthropods. *Science* 258: 1345-1348.

Boudreaux, H.B. 1979. *Arthropod Phylogeny with Special Reference to Insects*. John Wiley and Sons, New York, NY.

Briggs, D.E.G., D.H. Erwin, and F.J. Collier. 1994. *The Fossils of the Burgess Shale*. Smithsonian Institution Press, Washington.

Chen, J.-y., G.D. Edgecombe, L. Ramsköld, and G.-q. Zhou. 1995. Head segments in early Cambrain *Fuxianhuia*: implications for arthropod evolution. *Science* 268: 1339-1343.

Conway Morris, S. 1998. The *Crucible of Creation*. Oxford University Press. NY.

Eernisse, D.J., J.S. Albert, and F.E. Anderson. 1992. Annelida and Arthropoda are not sister taxa: a phylogenetic analysis of spiralian metazoan morphology. *Syst. Biol.* 41: 305-330.

Garey, J.R., M. Krotec, D.R. Nelson, and J. Brooks. 1996. Molecular analysis supports a tardigrade-arthropod association. *Invertebr. Biol.* 115: 79-88.

Manton, S.M. 1973. Arthropod phylogeny—a modern synthesis. *J. Zool.* 171: 111-130.

Manton, S.M. 1977. *The Arthropoda: Habits, Functional Morphology and Evolution*. Clarendon Press, Oxford. UK.

Orr, P.J., D.E.G. Briggs, and S.L. Kearns. 1998. Cambrian Burgess Shale animals replicated in clay minerals. *Science* 281: 1173-1175.

Storch, V. 1991. Priapulida. *In*: Harrison FW and Ruppert EE (eds.) *Microscopic Anatomy of Invertebrates*. Wiley-Liss, NY.

Wills, M.A. 1996. Classification of the Arthropod *Fuxianhuia*. *Science* 272: 746-747.

Winnepenninckx, B., T. Backeljau, L.Y. Mackey, J. M. Brooks, R. De Wachter, S. Kumar, and J.R. Garey. 1995. 18S rRNA data indicate that aschelminthes are polyphyletic in origin and consist of at least three distinct clades. *Mol. Biol. Evol.* 12: 1132-1137.

Phylum Nematoda (Nemata, Nema)

Phylum Nematoda [nem-a-TOD-a; G., *nema*, thread] is a large group of some 20,000 species of threadlike "pseudocoelomate" worms known commonly as roundworms. Free-living species have been found in every habitat examined, e.g., arctic ponds, hot springs, all soils (including mountain and desert), deep sea marine muds, rotting apples and unpasteurized vinegar. Diversity of animal and plant parasitic nematodes is tremendous. Every vertebrate species may serve as a host to one or more nematodes. On a global scale, humans are infected commonly by about 15 species of nematodes, but an additional 15 species may occasionally parasitize humans, a condition called **zoonosis**.

Despite of their breadth in nutritional habits and geographic distribution, all nematodes have the same basic body structure. Typically they are cylindrical worms tapering at both ends (Fig. 1) and ranging in size from less than 1 mm to several meters long. Nematodes are covered by a resistant **cuticle**; the cuticle is composed of three layers (**cortical, matrix**, and **fibrous**). Nematodes have a straight digestive tract consisting of a mouth, buccal cavity, pharynx, intestine, rectum, and anus. The buccal cavity, pharynx, and rectum are lined with cuticle. (NB: The term esophagus is routinely used by nematotologists in reference to the pharynx.) The nematode mouth is surrounded by up to six **lips**, but these may be fused into three lips or may be absent totally. Some nematodes, especially those that parasitize plants, are armed with a long **stylet** which is used in feeding (Fig. 1).

Nematodes lay eggs which may be released from the female or may hatch in *utero*. Hatchlings are usually called larvae. However, except for an immature reproductive system, they possess most adult structures; thus they are really juveniles. As the young grow they undergo four molts, at which time the entire cuticle is shed. However, unlike arthropods which also molt, individuals grow in size during intermolt periods. Larvae of some parasitic forms are given specific names: **rhabditiform, filariform**, and **microfilaria**. Parasitic nematodes may have a life cycle which is direct (**monoxenous**), having only one host, or indirect (**heteroxenous**), having two or more hosts.

The main objective of the following study is to direct student attention to the general structure and diversity of free-living and parasitic nematodes, and to review the life cycle of some species important as human parasites. Owing to time constraints, it is probable that only a few of the following studies may be done in your laboratory.

Classification

Two classes and 20 orders of nematodes are recognized.

1. **Class Adenophorea** (Aphasmida) 12 orders. Predominantly free-living nematodes lacking phasmids; amphids located behind the anterior end. Males lacking lateral extensions of the tail. Examples: *Trichinella spiralis* (trichina worm), *Trichuris trichiura* (whipworm), *Metoncholaimus* (free-living in mud on North American coasts).

From *Invertebrate Zoology*, Sixth Edition, Robert L. Wallace and Walter K. Taylor. Copyright © 2002 by Pearson Education, Inc. Published by Prentice-Hall, Inc. All rights reserved

Phylum Nematoda (Nemata, Nema)

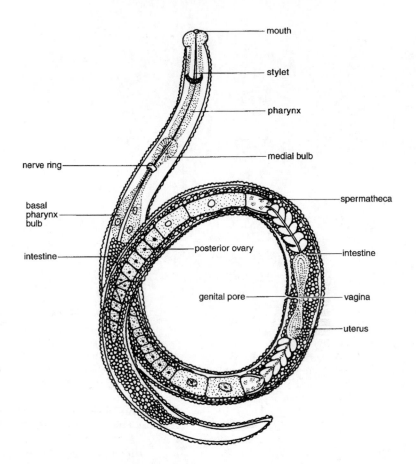

Figure 1. Typical female nematode, *Tylenchorhynchus cylindricus*.

2. **Class Secernentea** (Phasmida) 8 orders. Predominantly parasitic or free-living terrestrial nematodes having phasmids; amphids are located forward in the anterior end. Males often have lateral extensions of the tail. Examples: *Ascaris lumbricoides* (intestinal roundworm), *Dracunculus medinensis* (Guinea worm), *Dirofilaria immitis* (dog heartworm), *Enterobius vermicularis* (pinworm), *Necator americanus* (American hookworm), *Rhabditis maupasi* (earthworm parasite), and *Wuchereria bancrofti* (filarial worm), *Turbatrix aceti* (vinegar eel).

■ Observational Procedure:

Free-Living Nematodes

Using a dissection microscope and a Pasteur pipette, remove some of the nematodes from a culture containing the vinegar eel, *T. aceti* (Fig. 2), or another appropriate species (e.g., *Caenorhabditis*, *Chiroplacus*, *Rhabditis*). Place your sample on a concave microscope slide and examine it for specimens. Describe how these animals move. What other animals move in this fashion?

Remove a few specimens, place them on a microscope slide, add a drop of water and a coverslip, and examine under low and high magnifications. Identify the anterior and posterior ends. How does this species feed? Can you see the pharynx or any other internal organs, especially of the gut? Note that the thick cuticle may make identification of internal organs difficult.

Occasionally, you may see copulating pairs of worms. What region of his body does the male use to grasp the female? What region of her body does the male grasp? If the culture is actively growing, all developmental stages should be present. What types of evidence can you provide to suggest that your culture is growing? Are any of the worms molting? Each successive molt stage is larg-

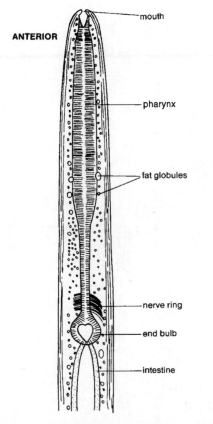

Figure 2. Anterior end of the vinegar eel, *Turbatrix aceti*, a free-living nematode.

er than the previous one, but does growth occur between molts? How can one go about determining this without observing worms during their entire intermolt period?

Examine a prepared slide of *Turbatrix* or the species you examined alive and locate the pharynx, the remainder of the gut, and reproductive system. Attempt to trace the digestive tract from mouth to anus. Determine the length and diameter of these specimens. This information will help you when you study the other specimens.

Parasitic Nematodes

Nematodes are some of the most important parasites affecting the lives and general welfare of humans, including domestic and game animals and crops. Only a few of the better known animal parasites have been selected for this exercise. For each species studied, a brief description of the life history will be given followed by directions for the observations to be made. *If live specimens are to be studied, be very careful not to infect yourself with infective stages (eggs, larvae, adults).*

Pinworm (Fig. 3). Pinworm (**Enterobius vermicularis**) or seat worm is a cosmopolitan oxyurid parasite of humans having a direct life cycle. Fertilized females migrate from the colon (usually at night) and lay thousands of eggs in the perianal region. The embryonated eggs contain rhabditiform larvae which may enter the digestive tract either by inhalation of dust contaminated by the eggs, or through direct ingestion. Once embryos reach the intestine, they hatch and after several successive molts the adults mate and become attached to the colon wall. It is estimated that 500 million people worldwide have **enterobiasis**.

Examine a prepared slide of pinworms and with the aid of Fig. 3 identify the anatomical structures of the specimen. Determine the size of this parasite and compare it to the free-living specimen just studied. Examine a slide of pinworm eggs. Note their oval shape and flattened side. Your instructor may discuss the clinical methods used for obtaining and identifying pinworm eggs.

Hookworms (Fig. 4). One of the most devastating cosmopolitan diseases of human's is **ancylosotomiasis**, more commonly known as hookworm disease. Several species of hookworms may be studied with equal educational value; *Ancylostoma duodenale* (Old World hookworm), *Ancylostoma caninum* (domestic dog and cat hookworm), and *Necator americanus* (New World or American hookworm) are examples. New World hookworm is believed to have been brought to the Americas by the slave trade. Most hookworms have a direct life cycle. Adults live attached to the mucosal lining of their host's intestine and feed on blood and tissue fluids. Embryonated eggs are passed in the feces and the first two developmental stages take place in the soil. Third-stage larvae burrow into skin and are transported via the bloodstream to the lungs where the larvae burrow into the alveoli. They are then carried up the trachea and are swallowed. Final molt and sexual maturity are achieved in the small intestine.

Examine a whole-mount slide of a hookworm and note the structures in the mouth region, including a large buccal cavity with **cutting plates** or teeth. Examine a longitudinal section of a hookworm in *situ* and note how the worm is attached to the mucosa. In a whole-mount slide of a male, note the **copulatory bursa** and **spicules**. Determine the size of these intestinal worms. Compare the size and general morphology of A. *duodenale* rhabditiform (free-living) and filariform (infective) larvae. How do hookworms compare in size and general morphology to pinworms?

Filarial Worms (Fig. 5). Adults of the human filarial worm, *Wuchereria bancrofti*, live in the lymph nodes of

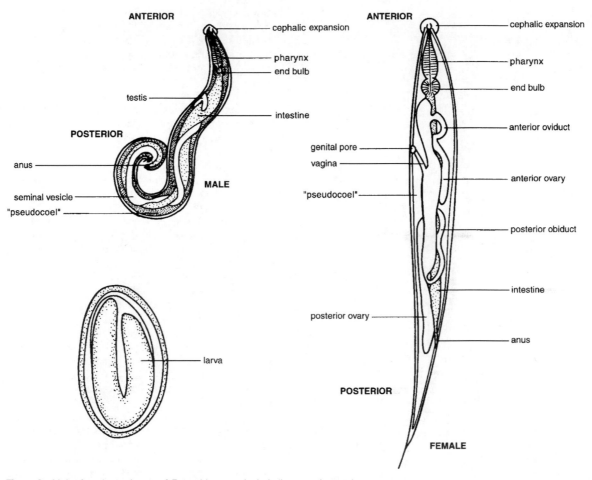

Figure 3. Male, female, and eggs of *Enterobius vermicularis* (human pinworm).

humans where **ovoviviparous** females release thousands of motile embryos known as microfilaria. These make their way to the peripheral blood of humans where female mosquitoes pick them up while taking a blood meal. The larvae migrate to thoracic and leg muscles of the mosquito where they continue to grow. Upon reaching a certain stage of growth (ca. 2–5 weeks), they migrate to the mosquito's mouthparts and enter the human body when the mosquito takes another blood meal. In humans, the microfilaria find their way to the lymphatic system and attain maturity in about a year. Lymphoid tissues increase in size in response to microfilaria parasitization. If, after repeated attacks, sufficient worms are present in the human host, an enlargement of certain body appendages (e.g., lower limbs, scrotum) occurs producing the disease inappropriately called **elephantiasis**. Other disease produced

by filarial worms include river blindness (*Onchocerca volvulus*) and dog heartworm (*Dirofilaria immitis*) which is common in North America. Specimens of all three species discussed here will be studied.

Observe a preserved specimen of *Dirofilaria immitis*, noting its long, thin form. How can such a long worm develop in a dog's heart? What problems would this cause Fido? Examine slides showing blood smears of *D. immitis* and/or *W. bancrofti* microfilaria. Compare the relative sizes of the microfilaria and red blood cells. Could these worms be mistaken for other blood parasites such as *Plasmodium* or *Trypansoma*? Why or why not? Examine a cross section of a nodule produced by the worm, *O. volvulus*. What evidence do you see that the worm is present in the nodule? How can a worm which parasitizes adipose tissue in the human midregion cause blindness?

Phylum Nematoda (Nemata, Nema)

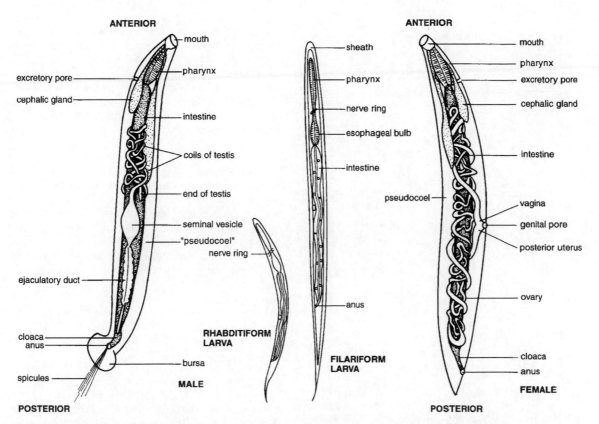

Figure 4. Male, female, and larval stages (rhabditiform, filariform) of *Necator americanus* (American hookworm).

Trichina Worm (Fig. 6). **Trichinosis** is acquired by eating insufficiently cooked meat contaminated with the encysted stage of *Trichinella spiralis* (Fig. 6). Digestive juices in the gut liberate the larvae from the meat and then by removing the cyst wall. Worms achieve adulthood in about 3 days. After mating the male worms die and females penetrate the intestinal mucosa where they release juvenile worms. One female may liberate as many as 2,000 larvae into the host's blood stream before she dies. The larvae are transported throughout the body and become lodged in skeletal muscle and other muscles with a rich blood supply such as the diaphragm and tongue. Soon after the muscles are invaded, the worms enlarge and encyst, causing harmful tissue damage. In the past, the usual source of human infection was contaminated pig meat. However, bear meat is now a source of infection, but any carnivore, especially rats, may be infected.

Figure 5. Microfilarial stage of *Wuchereria bancrofti* (human filarial worm).

Phylum Nematoda (Nemata, Nema)

Figure 6. Photomicrograph of the juvenile stage of *Trichinella spiralis* (trichina worm) encysted in muscle tissue.

Examine a section of muscle with encysted larvae. Note the size of the cysts and their general frequency in the tissue. Estimate the number of trichina cysts per cm^3 of muscle tissue. How can you go about making the appropriate calculations to do this estimation? Is there any evidence of damage to the muscle tissue by the cysts? How might a heavy infection affect host muscle function? Examine a slide of adult *Trichinella* and compare their general anatomy with the other nematodes you have observed. How are they similar; how do they differ?

Whipworm (Fig. 7). The life cycle of the human whipworm (*Trichuris trichiura*) is direct. Eggs, ingested via fecal contamination, hatch in the small intestine, and in about 2 weeks the juvenile worms migrate to the colon where they attach permanently to the mucosa and feed on blood cells. Whipworms reach sexual maturity in about 3 months. It has been estimated that more than 350 million people worldwide are infected!

Examine a whole mount slide of a whipworm. Describe the shape of the worm. Why are these worms given their common name? The pharynx is a long, thin-walled, multiglandular tube called the **stichosome**. There are no lips. The buccal cavity is armed with a minute **stylet** which may be seen under high magnification. Determine the size of these worms. Examine a whole-mount slide of whipworm eggs. Note their oval shape with the characteristic bipolar plugs (Fig. 7). Compare the eggs of whipworms to pinworms. Take some notes describing how they are similar and how they differ.

Earthworm Parasite (Fig. 8). Adults of the species *Rhabditis maupasi* are free-living, soil nematodes, but earthworms (*Lumbricus terrestris*) play host to juveniles. When the earthworm dies the larvae mature by feeding on bacteria which grow in the decaying tissues. Larvae are believed to enter the earthworm through the nephridiopore or genital openings. If time permits, complete one of the following exercises.

Culture:
1. Dissect an anesthetized earthworm. Make a longitudinal cut in the earthworm's muscular body wall and pin back its edges to the dissection pan.
2. Carefully remove the digestive tract from the posterior two-thirds of the body.
3. Remove the viscera anteriorly, cut it into small sections of about 1 cm in length. Place these in separate petri dishes containing 3% sterile agar. Label the plates with the date and the approximate location of the worm section.
4. Cut similar sections from the muscular body wall and prepare similar agar cultures with these.
5. Set the cultures aside at room temperature. In about 3 days examine the cultures using a dissection microscope and estimate the number of nematodes per section. Which part of the worm housed the greatest number of nematodes? Transfer some specimens to a microscope slide; add a drop of water, a coverslip, and observe under higher magnification.

Dissection (may be done as a team exercise):
1. As described above, dissect an anesthetized or preserved earthworm.
2. Carefully remove the entire digestive tract, but not the seminal vesicles which are located in segment 8. Use them to provide a landmark to enumerate the segments.
3. Locate the paired nephridia in each segment of the worm. Carefully excise them, paying attention to their segment number and their location on the right and left sides of the worm. As you remove the nephridium place each in a drop of water on a microscope slide. Cover with a coverslip and examine for nematodes.

Phylum Nematoda (Nemata, Nema)

Figure 7. The human whipworm *Trichuris trichiura* (male, female, and bipolar eggs).

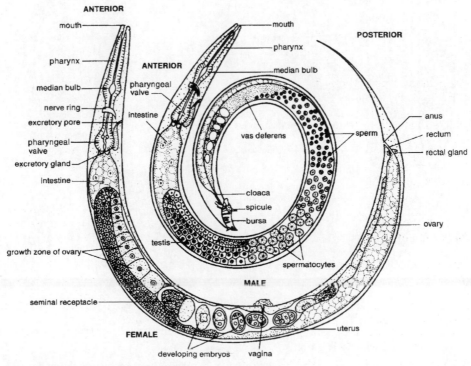

Figure 8. *Rhabditis maupasi*, a parasite of the earthworm (male and female).

Phylum Nematoda (Nemata, Nema)

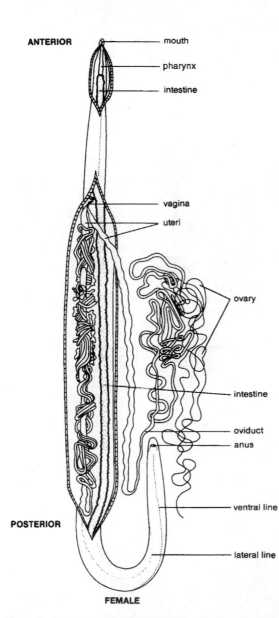

Figure 9. *Ascaris lumbricoides*: internal longitudinal view of an adult female.

Figure 10. *Ascaris lumbricoides*: cross section of an adult female worm showing parts of the reproductive and digestive systems. (The body form is not circular in this preparation due to distortion during fixation and sectioning.)

Fertile (embryonated)

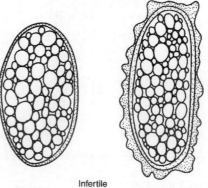

Infertile

Figure 11. *Ascaris lumbricoides*: fertile and infertile eggs. Eggs are about 60 μm long and 40 μm wide.

Phylum Nematoda (Nemata, Nema)

Figure 12. *Ascaris lumbricoides*: internal longitudinal view of an adult male.

Figure 13. *Ascaris lumbricoides*: cross section of an adult male worm showing parts of the reproductive and digestive systems. (The body form is not circular in this preparation due to distortion during fixation and sectioning.)

4. Have each member of the team report the number of nematodes in the nephridia from the left and right sides of the body. Plot these data on X-Y coordinates. Is there a pattern to the distribution of *Rhabditis*? Develop a null hypothesis that considers the numbers of nematodes in nephridia from the left and right sides of the body. How can this hypothesis be tested with the data you possess?

Intestinal Roundworm (Figs. 9–12). From a morphological point of view, *Ascaris lumbricoides* is not a typical nematode. Nevertheless, it is important to examine it more closely because **ascariasis** remains a public health problem in the United States. Older estimates suggest a childhood prevalence of about 15% in certain regions (Darby and Westphal, 1972). The size of *Ascaris* makes it suitable for dissection and its reproductive system is often used to demonstrate mitosis and gametogenesis. Specimens you dissect may be from the pig, *A. suum*. This species is similar morphologically to the one found in humans, differing only in the minute details of the lips and in aspects of its physiology.

Phylum Nematoda (Nemata, Nema)

Ascaris has a direct life cycle. When embryonated eggs are swallowed, they hatch in the small intestine where the young worms penetrate the wall and pass into the bloodstream. Upon entering the lung the worms break out into the alveoli where they develop to the fourth stage. Then they are carried up the trachea to the pharynx where they are swallowed. The worms mature in the small intestine where they mate and begin releasing eggs in the host's feces. Two related species, *Toxocara canis* and *Toxocara cati* (parasitizing dogs and cats, respectively), can cause a serious disease of humans known as **visceral larval migrans**.

General Morphology
1. Note the four thin, longitudinal strips of lighter-pigmented cuticle along the length of the worm: two strips are lateral, one dorsal, and one ventral. The lateral strips are broader and seen more easily than the other two. These are external manifestations of internal structures, the **hypodermal cords**.
2. Examine the cuticular covering under a dissection microscope and note that it appears to be finely segmented. This is not true segmentation, but superficial striations of the cuticle.
3. Locate the terminal mouth and the subterminal and ventral anus.
4. Observe the anterior end in a head-on position under a dissection microscope to see the single dorsal lip and the two subventral lips surrounding the mouth. Note the somewhat dentate condition of the inner surface of the lips.
5. At the periphery of the dorsal lip locate the two cephalic papillae which house special sensory organs.
6. *Ascaris* is sexually dimorphic. In males the posterior end is curved ventrally. Are any of the specimens in the class male? Occasionally a pair of **penial spicules** (copulatory structures) can be seen protruding from the male's cloaca. Females are usually larger than the males.
7. Examine the cuticle surface of a female under the dissection microscope and find her genital pore which is located ventrally about one-third of the body length from her mouth.

Female Reproductive System (Figs. 9 and 10).
1. Place a female specimen ventral surface down in a dissection pan and orient the specimen and pan so that you may easily observe the worm through a dissection microscope. Pin the anterior and posterior ends of the worm to the pan, cover the specimen with water, and dissect the worm as follows.
2. Make a shallow incision in the outer body wall the full length of the worm. Take care not to disturb the internal viscera. After an incision of some 6–8 cm has been made, carefully pin the body wall to the pan. Con-

tinue the dissection and pinning until the entire length of the worm has been exposed (Fig. 9).
3. Observe the outer body wall just cut. It surrounds a central digestive tract and other organs located in the spacious "pseudocoel."
4. Note the highly convoluted pair of tubules that wind about the intestine in the posterior part of the body cavity. The tube varies in dimension and constitutes the female reproductive system (Fig. 9).
5. Locate the most anterior part of this structure which appears to penetrate the body wall; this is the **vagina**. The vagina bifurcates forming the two **uteri**.
6. Follow one uterus as it grades into the **oviducts**. Although there is an appreciable decrease in tube diameter, there is no obvious external change in the morphology from oviducts to the ovary which ends blindly.
7. Obtain a prepared slide of a cross section of a female worm showing the reproductive tract. Locate the uterus filled with eggs and the smaller oviducts and ovarian loops in the section (Fig. 10). The upper part of the oviduct contains eggs without shells, but the lower portion should have shelled eggs indicating that fertilization has taken place. Some of the eggs may be in early stages of cleavage.
8. Examine slides fertilized and unfertilized of *Ascaris* eggs. Note the egg's thick, bumpy (mammillated) coat (Fig. 11). How can one tell the difference between fertilized and unfertilized eggs? Humans infected with *Ascaris* often have only unfertilized eggs present in their stools; what simple fact would account for this situation? Why might it be important for a physician to know whether a person has fertilized or unfertilized eggs in his or her stools? Compare the eggs of pinworm, whipworm, and *Ascaris*. Develop a simple chart or a dichotomous key that will permit you to tell them apart.

Male Reproductive System (Figs. 12 and 13).
1. Complete a dorsolongitudinal incision of a male *Ascaris* in the same way that was done for the female. Use Fig. 12 to assist in the location and identification of the following structures.
2. The male's genital and anal openings open posteriorly into a region called the **cloaca**. Why is the term cloaca used to describe this cavity? The female lacks a cloaca.
3. Locate the single highly contorted tube in the male. The threadlike distal part of the tube constitutes the **testis** and is located forward in the pseudocoel. Like the female oviduct, the gradation from testis to **vas deferens** is not visible externally.
4. As the vas deferens approaches the region of the cloaca, there is a distinct enlargement of the tube. This is the beginning of the **seminal vesicle** which stores sperm.

Phylum Nematoda (Nemata, Nema)

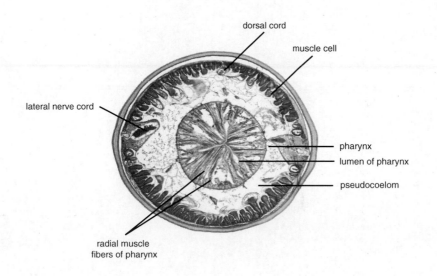

Figure 14. *Ascaris lumbricoides*: cross section of a worm at the level of the pharynx.

5. Beyond the seminal vesicle is the ejaculatory duct. It connects the reproductive tract with the cloaca.

6. Obtain a cross section of a male worm showing the reproductive tract (Fig. 13). Locate the testis, vas deferens, and seminal vesicle. The seminal vesicle is much larger in diameter than either the testis or vas deferens. It may be possible to find mature sperm cells in slide preparations that show portions of the ejaculatory duct and/or cloaca.

Digestive System and Other Internal Structures of *Ascaris* (Figs. 9 and 12).

1. In your dissected specimen, examine the digestive system: pharynx, intestine, rectum, cloaca (male), and anus. It may be necessary to move parts of the reproductive system to expose the digestive tract.

2. Observe a prepared slide showing a cross section of the body of *Ascaris* made through the region of the pharynx (Fig. 14). Note the three powerful muscle units which produce the sucking action when food is obtained from the host. Note the glandular bodies in the muscle tissue of the esophagus.

3. Strip a section of cuticle from the body and mount it on a slide with a drop of water; add a coverslip. Observe the superficial striation of the cortical (outside) layer and the crosshatched fibers of the fibrous layers. Estimate the angles the fibers make with the longitudinal axis of the worm. How do these fibers aid the muscles in locomotion?

4. Observe a prepared slide showing a cross section of the body wall. Use either sex. Observe the close associ-ation between the muscle cell bases and the **syncytial hypodermis**. The muscles at the inner body wall are in four quadrants, divided by the four **cords** (see below). Note that in the cross section being examined, the muscle cells have been cut transversely, which makes it somewhat difficult to visualize their proper arrangement. There are about 150 cells per quadrant and each cell is a very elongated body with a narrow, spindle form.

5. Locate the dorsal, ventral, and lateral cords. The dorsal and ventral cords contain the nerve trunks. Just inside the lateral cords you should be able to see the lateral excretory canals.

6. Examine the intestine. The outermost perimeter of the intestine is called the basement membrane. Just inward from the basement membrane is a layer of columnar epithelial cells. These epithelial cells are elongated and bear distinct nuclei at their bases. On the side opposite the nuclei, a fuzzy coat may be seen on these cells. This coat is actually made up of many microvilli which extend into the lumen of the intestine.

If you are to work with live Ascaris *eggs, your instructor will give detailed instructions to avoid accidental contamination.*

Plant Parasites. If time and materials permit, your instructor will provide information for the study of some plant parasites. As you follow those directions, be sure to compare these parasites to the ones just studied. How are they similar and how do they differ? The preparation of a simple chart may help you organize your findings about the nematodes. ■

Phylum Nematomorpha

Nematomorpha [NE-mat-o-MOR-fa; G., *nema*, thread + G., *morpha*, form] comprises about 230 species of thread-like "pseudocoelomate" worms that lack a functional gut. They range in length from 10 to 100 cm, but are only 1 to a few millimeters in diameter. As juveniles they parasitize arthropods, while the adults are free living. The common name, **horsehair worms**, comes from myths that said these worm's arose from horse hairs that had fallen into water. The body wall of nematomorphs consists of a (1) thick **cuticle** often containing plates called **areoles;** (2) single-layered, cellular **hypodermis;** and (3) muscle layer whose fibers are oriented longitudinally as in nematodes. Emergence of adults from the host that housed the juvenile stage takes place in or near water and mating begins soon thereafter.

Classification

Two classes are recognized based on external morphology and aspects of the cuticle: **Nectonematoida** (marine nematomorphs) and **Gordioida** (freshwater, most nematomorphs).

■ Observational Procedure:

Examine a whole worm while keeping it immersed in a shallow dish of water. Determine the length and diameter of the specimen. Locate the anterior and posterior ends. The mouth will be located either terminally or subterminally. The head is called the **calotte** and usually has a darker colored area below it. The posterior end may be unlobed, bilobed, or trilobed, with a subterminal, ventral anus (cloacal aperture). Are any other structures visible on the external surface of the animal?

Observe a slide of a cross section of a horsehair worm (Fig. 1). First become familiar with the position of the section on the slide. Determine the dorsal and ventral sides. How can you do that? Once you are familiar with the section, locate the structures indicated in Fig. 1.

How do these parasites compare to nematodes? Develop a table that compares the two phyla. How are they similar and how are they different in size, shape, life cycle, and internal anatomy? ■

From *Invertebrate Zoology*, Sixth Edition, Robert L. Wallace and Walter K. Taylor. Copyright © 2002 by Pearson Education, Inc. Published by Prentice-Hall, Inc. All rights reserved

Phylum Nematomorpha

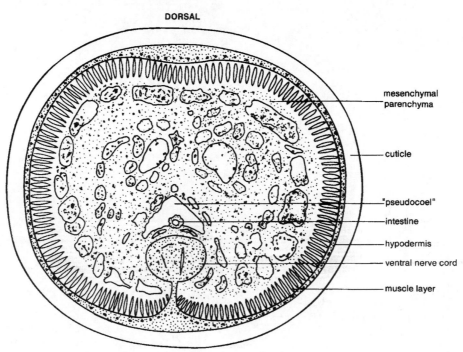

Figure 1. Cross section of a horsehair worm.

Phylum Nematomorpha

Phyla Nematoda & Nematomorpha	Worksheet 8
Name: _____	Date: _____
Course #: _____ / Section #: _____	Grade: _____

1. In nematodes each successive molting stage is larger than the previous one, but does growth occur between molts? How can one go about determining this without observing worms during the entire intermolt period?

2. (a) Assuming that a sample of muscle tissue infected with trichina cysts has been sectioned at a thickness of 10 μm and that there are 100 cysts in the section which measures 1 x 1 cm. Estimate the number of trichina cysts per cm^3 of muscle tissue. *Show all your calculations in making this estimation.*

    (b) What assumptions are you making in this problem that need to be considered?

3. Is there any evidence of damage to the muscle tissue by the cysts? How might a heavy infection affect host muscle function?

Phylum Nematomorpha

4. Complete the following table that compares the Nematoda and Nematomorpha.

Characteristic	Nematoda	Nematomorpha
Size range		
General shape		
Approximate number of species		
Development of the gut		
Mode of nutrient procurement		

5. What features do Nematoda and Nematomorpha both possess? Develop an argument that would support the idea that these two phyla are related. Which would have evolved first? WHY?

Phylum Onychophora

Phylum Onychophora [o-NEE-kof-or-ah; G., *onychos*, claw + G., *phora*, to bear] comprises some 70 species of small (2–5 cm long) wormlike organisms that resemble caterpillars. Onychophorans, called velvet worms or walking worms, have features similar to both arthropods and annelids. Because of this, some authors have regarded onychophorans to be a sort of missing link between Arthropoda and Annelida. Arthropod characteristics include an open circulatory system with a dorsal tubular heart bearing ostia, a large hemocoel, a reduced schizocoelom that is limited to small sacs associated with the gonads and nephridia, a respiratory system of tracheae and spiracles, and a pair of modified appendages (e.g., **mandibles**) for feeding. The presence of ciliated **nephridia** (coelomoducts), lack of jointed appendages, and structural configuration of the body wall are annelidan in character. Although the body appears to be unsegmented, the nervous system and nephridia are segmented and the position of the legs indicates segmentation. All onychophorans are dioecious, with males being smaller and having fewer legs than do females. A larval stage is absent; development is direct.

Distribution of onychophorans is discontinuous in both tropical and southern temperate regions. The animals are nocturnal and most are tropical, living in moist areas under leaves, rocks, and logs. A fossil specimen from the **Burgess Shale Fauna** of the **Cambrian Period** indicates the phylum is ancient (Fig. 1). Present distribution of the phylum can be explained by continental drift.

Classification

Onychophora is divided into two families. Peripatidae contains members having primarily an equatorial distribution. Example is *Periparatus*. Peripatopsidae, exemplified by *Peripatopsis*, is limited to the southern hemisphere.

■ Observational Procedure:

Peripatus
1. Observe one or more preserved specimens of *Peripatus* under the dissection microscope. The elongate body has two indistinct regions: a head and a trunk of 14 to 43 fused annulated regions. Gentle pressure applied to the outside of the body with a blunt probe will demonstrate that the animal is covered with a thin, flexible chitinous **cuticle**. Note the short, unjointed, paired legs on the trunk (Fig. 2). How many pairs of legs are on your specimen? The number varies with the species and sex. Examine closely the pair of curved terminal claws and **transverse pads** on each leg. Note the **tubercles** and their arrangement on the legs and body. Using high power of the dissection microscope, attempt to see the **nephridiopore** on the ventral surface near the inner base of each leg. The anus opens on the ventral side of the posterior end. Attempt to see the gonopore just anterior to the anus (Fig. 2).

From *Invertebrate Zoology*, Sixth Edition, Robert L. Wallace and Walter K. Taylor. Copyright © 2002 by Pearson Education, Inc. Published by Prentice-Hall, Inc. All rights reserved

Phylum Onychophora

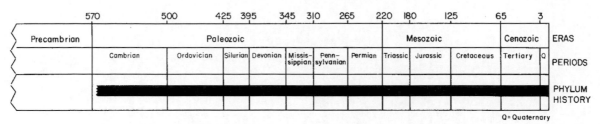

Figure 1. Geologic history of Phylum Onychophora.

2. Locate the two annulated **antennae** (preantennae) on the head (Fig. 2). Sensory bristles cover the antennae. A small ocellus may be seen near the base of each antenna. Posterior to each antenna and on the ventral surface are two **oral papillae**. Glands in each papilla discharge a secretion that hardens, forming a net of adhesive threads that catch prey such as worms, insects, and other small invertebrates. Between the oral papillae is the mouth, containing paired mandibles. Note the

peribuccal lobes or lips surrounding the mouth.

3. Obtain a slide of a cross section of *Peripatus* and examine it under low power to become familiar with the orientation of the animal on the slide. Switch to high power and locate the cuticle. It will be darkly stained. Note that the papillae are evident and that they are tipped with numerous spines. Find the following layers in order of their position: cuticle, epidermis, dermis, and circular and longitudinal muscles (Fig. 3).

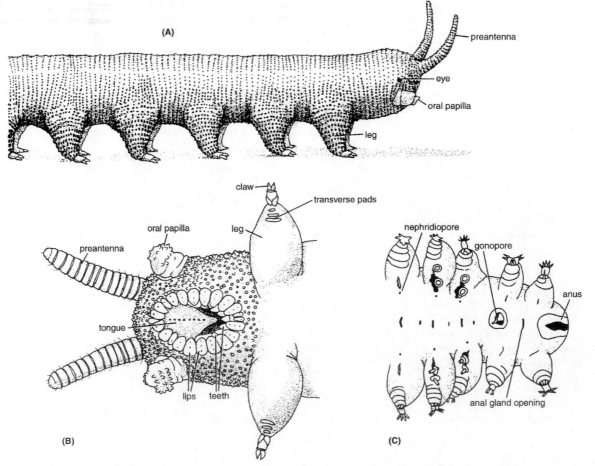

Figure 2. *Peripatus*. (A) Side view of body. (B) Anteroventral area. (C) Posteroventral area. (After Sherman and Sherman.)

Phylum Onychophora

4. Depending on the manufacture of slide, your preparation may have more than one section. Scan all sections in an attempt to understand the anatomy of *Peripatus*; it may take the examination of several slides to find all of the structures discussed below (Fig. 3).

On the legs, look for evidence of claws and transverse pads. Locate the gut, noting that the intestine is composed of columnar cells. The nervous system consists of a **brain,** two **circumpharyngeal connectives**, and two ventrolateral **nerve cords**. Observe the latter in the cross section. The paired ovaries or testes also may be seen in a cross section. Located near the gut, attempt to find the slime glands (dorsolateral to lateral in position) and salivary glands (lateral to ventrolateral in position). You also may be able to make out the dorsal heart and, running tangentially, dorsoventral muscles strands.

Now that you have observed several annelids and an onychophoran, compare the overall morphology and internal organization of both kinds of organisms. What features do onychophorans share with annelids? What characteristics are unique to each? You may wish to organize your conclusions into tabular form and save it so that you may add similar observations concerning the arthropods. ■

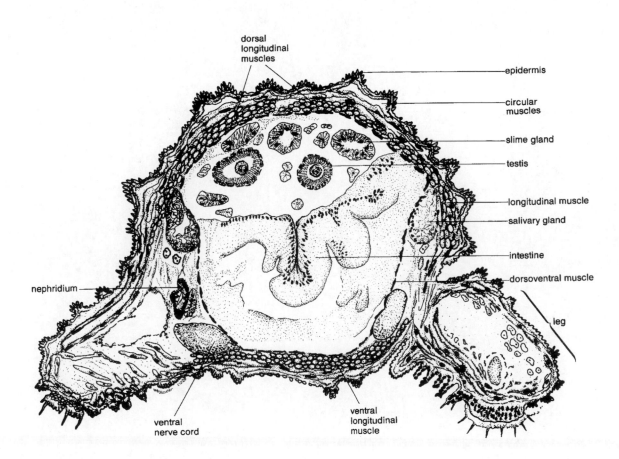

Figure 3. Cross section of *Peripatus* through the level of the testes.

Phylum Tardigrada

Phylum Tardigrada [TAR-di-grad-a; L., *tardi*, slow + L., *grada*, walk] comprises a small group of bilaterally symmetrical, arthropod-like animals. About 400 species of tardigrades, or water bears as they are commonly known, are recognized. These minute (50–1,000 μm) protostomes possess short cylindrical bodies with four pairs of short, stubby, nonjointed legs extending ventrolaterally as if they were attached to a fat little bear (Fig. 1). Each leg has two or more toes, claws, or a combination of both at the distal end for grasping the substrate. Many semiterrestrial species have eyespots anteriorly. The bearlike image in tardigrades is reinforced when one observes the slow pawing motion that they make with their legs when moving.

Tardigrades are principally freshwater, but marine species have been found in the littoral area and at considerable depths (5,000 m). Semiterrestrial forms often are found in the thin water films in soils or covering mosses, lichens, and liverworts. In both freshwater and marine habitats, tardigrades may be found on surfaces of aquatic plants and in interstitial spaces among sedimentary particles. Many species have a cosmopolitan distribution.

Classification

Two classes are recognized based on presence or absence of cephalic appendages, Malpighian tubules, morphology of solid supports in the pharynx, and types and number of claws and toes.

1. **Class Heterotardigrada.** Armored tardigrades. Example: *Echiniscus*.

2. **Class Eutardigrada.** Unarmored tardigrades. Example: *Macrobiotus*.

■ Observational Procedure:

Observe the movements of a live tardigrade under a compound microscope. Note the four pairs of legs, each of which possesses a set of claws. Describe the locomotory activity of your specimen. How fast does the animal move? Does the specimen stop to feed? How is feeding accomplished?

Using live or preserved specimens, attempt to locate the following internal structures: (1) muscular sucking pharynx, (2) salivary glands, (3) esophagus, (4) midgut, (5) Malpighian tubules, (6) rectum, (7) anus, and (8) unpaired gonad (Figs. 1 and 2). Eggs may be present in the ovaries of females. Locate several of the body muscle fibers. Trace a muscle from its attachment to the body wall at one point to another. What is the net result of the contraction of this single muscle fiber?

If time and specimens are available for experimental work, follow the directions given by your instructor to initiate and revive animals from the anabiotic resting state. One way to undertake this study is to rehydrate small samples of dried moss using aged tap water. Then, over the next few days, periodically examine the moss for active tardigrades using a dissection microscope. ■

From *Invertebrate Zoology*, Sixth Edition, Robert L. Wallace and Walter K. Taylor. Copyright © 2002 by Pearson Education, Inc. Published by Prentice-Hall, Inc. All rights reserved

Phylum Tardigrada

Figure 1. Dorsal internal view of a female tardigrade of the genus *Macrobiotus*.

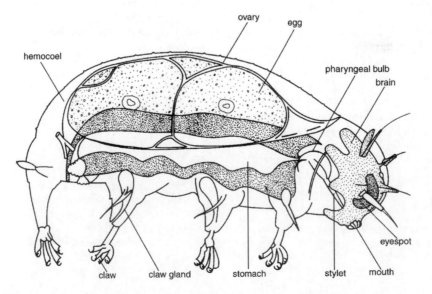

Figure 2. Lateral internal view of a female marine tardigrade of the genus *Styraconyx*. (After Kristensen and Higgins.)

Phylum Tardigrada

Phyla Onychophora & Tardigrada   **Worksheet 9**

Name: _____   Date: _____

Course #: _____ / Section #: _____   Grade: _____

1. Complete the following table that compares the Onychophora and Tardigrada to the Annelida and Aerhropoda.

Characteristic	Annelida	Onychophora	Tardigrada
Appendages (kinds; variety)			
Tagmatization (present/absent)			
Cuticle (magnitude)			
Feeding (examples)			
Distribution (habitats)			
Movement (examples)			

Phylum Tardigrada

2. Briefly describe how movement is accomplished in the Onychophora, Tardigrada, and Annelida. How is the biomechanics of movement similar in each of these? How are they different?

3. How many tagma are present in onychophorans and in tardigrades? Defend your answer by providing a simple diagram of each.

Phylum Arthropoda

Arthropoda [ar-THROP-o-dah; G., *artho* , joint + G., *pod*, foot] is an enormous phylum of segmented (metameric), schizocoelomic protostomes possessing an exoskeleton with jointed appendages. Arthropods range in size from microscopic to several meters in length. Estimates of the number of described species range from 750,000 to 1 million. However, it is predicted that up to 10 million or more species of insects are extant, but perhaps one species per day becomes extinct due to clearcutting the Brazilian rain forests. Arthropods are found from the ocean depths to mountain peaks, and even several thousand meters in the air. They have enormous medical, veterinary, ecological, and economic importance. Some of the most virulent diseases to plague humans are carried by arthropod vectors: the mosquito *Aedes aegypti* transmits the virus causing yellow fever, the flea *Xenopsylla cheopis* carries the bacterium causing black death, and the mosquito *Anopheles* spp. carries the protozoan causing malaria. The immense size of this phylum precludes anything but a brief overview to be presented in the following exercises.

Arthropods possess four important features. (1) A unique **exoskeleton** or **cuticle** made of **chitin** and **scleroprotein** completely covers the body. The exoskeleton is often strengthened by deposits of calcium salts. (2) Primitively, arthropods possess one pair of jointed appendages per body segment (**somite**), but as segments have been lost or fused in the evolution, this condition is lost. (3) The arthropod body can usually be divided into two or three distinct **tagmata**. (4) Cilia are nearly absent.

Additional features of the phylum include: (1) presence of a reduced coelom, (2) presence of a modified blastocoel (a **hemocoel**) that functions as an open circulatory system, (3) absence of a nephridial excretory system, (4) a high degree of cephalization, and (5) sexual reproduction with development characterized by distinct morphological stages, (6) a remarkable array of pigments in the cuticle. Arthropods have a geologic history dating from the **Cambrian Period** (Fig. 1).

Classification

Four major lines of arthropods are commonly recognized; here we treat them as Subphyla Trilobita (extinct), Chelicerata, Crustacea, and Uniramia.

1. **Subphylum Trilobita or Trilobitomorpha.** Extinct arthropods possessing three longitudinal lobes (two pleural and one axial) and three tagmata (head, thorax, and abdomen). Trilobite systematics is based on external features alone. Examples: *Elrathia, Diacalymene, Peronopsis,* and *Placops.*

2. **Subphylum Chelicerata.** Arthropods possessing two body regions, or with the entire body fused into a single unit, and no antennae. The first pair of appendages are called chelicerae. This subphylum is divided into three classes: Merostomata, Pycnogonida, and Arachnida.

   a. **Class Merostomata.** Two subclasses of mostly extinct aquatic chelicerates having book gills and a posterior telson: Order Xiphosura (containing the horseshoe or king crab, *Limulus polyphemus*); Order

From *Invertebrate Zoology,* Sixth Edition, Robert L. Wallace and Walter K. Taylor. Copyright © 2002 by Pearson Education, Inc. Published by Prentice-Hall, Inc. All rights reserved

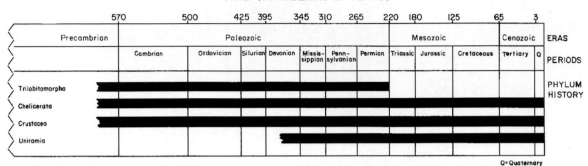

Figure 1. Geologic history of the four subphyla in Phylum Arthropoda.

Eurypterida (entirely extinct group of aquatic chelicerates known as giant water scorpions).

b. **Class Pycnogonida** (**Pantopoda**). Spider-like marine chelicerates with 4–6 pairs of very long legs. Examples: *Achelia, Pycnogonum,* and *Nymphon.*

c. **Class Arachnida**. Most chelicerates are arachnids. There are 12, predominantly terrestrial, orders. Examples: Scorpiones (scorpions), Araneae (spiders), Opiliones (harvestmen or daddy longlegs), and Acarina (mites and ticks).

3. **Subphylum Crustacea.** Mainly aquatic arthropods with biramous appendages and two pairs of antennae. One classification scheme (Schram 1986) presents four classes: Remipedia, Phyllopoda, Maxillopoda, and Malacostraca. Other schemes divide crustaceans into about a dozen classes. Collectively all but one of these classes are sometimes referred to as the lower crustaceans or **entomostracans** [en-to-MOS-tra-kans; G., *entom*, insect + G., *ostracum*, shell]. Examples: Branchiopoda—*Artemia* (brine shrimp), *Branchinecta* (fairy shrimp), and *Bosmina, Daphnia* (water fleas); Ostracoda—*Cypris*; Copepoda *Calanus*; Cirripedia—*Balanus* and *Lepas* (barnacles). The remaining single class, **Malacostraca** [mal-a-KOS-tra-ka; G., *malac*, soft], is then referred to as the higher crustaceans. Examples: Isopoda—*Oniscus* (pill bugs) and *Limnoria* (wood lice); Amphipoda—*Gammarus*

(freshwater scuds) and Orchestoidea (beach fleas); Euphausiacea—*Euphausia* (krill); Decapoda—*Penaeus* (shrimp), *Callinectes, Cancer, Paralithodes, Pagurus, Uca* (crabs), *Cambarus* (crayfish), and *Homarus* (lobsters).

4. **Subphylum Uniramia.** Arthropods with appendages of one branch and a single pair of antennae. The subphylum contains three major classes (Insecta, Chilopoda, and Diplopoda) and the two minor ones, Symphyla and Pauropoda.

a. **Class Insecta (Hexapoda)**. Arthropods having three body regions (head, thorax, and abdomen), a single pair of antennae (rarely absent), and wingless or with one or two pairs of wings borne on the thorax. Two subclasses are recognized: **Entognatha** (primitive insects, with mouthparts in a pouch) and **Ectognatha** (winged or wingless insects divided into two divisions, Exopterygota and Endopterygota, based on the type of metamorphosis). The first division includes dragonflies, grasshoppers, cockroaches, termites, and bugs. The second division includes beetles, butterflies, flies, fleas, and ants.

b. **Myriapodous Arthropods**. Myriapods comprise four classes, two of which are of some importance: Chilopoda (centipedes) and Diplopoda (millipedes).

A. Subphylum Trilobita or Trilobitomorpha

Trilobita [tril-o-BI-tah; L., *tri*, three + G., *lob*, lobe] is a moderately sized group of over 10,000 extinct species of primitive, dorsoventrally flattened arthropods with a chitinous exoskeleton strengthened with calcium and phosphate deposits. These marine animals were most abundant during the **Cambrian** and **Ordovician Periods** of the **Paleozoic Era**, but were extinct by its end (Fig. 1). Although a few large species are known to reach nearly 1 m, most adult trilobites were small (less than 10 cm long). The name trilobite refers to their oval body being longitudinally divided into three lobes: two lateral **pleural lobes** and one medial **axial lobe**. The body consisted of three tagmata: **cephalon** (head), **thorax, pygidium**.

Although extinct for over 200 million years, trilobites possessed many features common to the Phylum Arthropoda. As in other phyla with a rich fossil history, a complex nomenclature has been developed by paleontologists. Here students will study only the basic morphology of these remarkable arthropods.

■ Observational Procedure:

1. Observe specimens of several species and identify the anterior and posterior ends, the three lobes (axis and two pleural), and the three tagmata (cephalon, thorax, and pygidium) (Figs. 2 and 3).

2. The cephalon of several fused segments forms a large dorsal head shield that is divided into various parts by **facial sutures** and **furrows**. Trace the central **axial furrow** that delimits the axis from the pleural lobes through all three tagmata.

3. Examine specimens to see if their cephalons are divided into a central region, the **cranidium** (Fig. 3) and lateral **cheeks** (Fig. 2). In the center of the cranidium, often elevated above the cephalon, locate the **glabella.** This structure probably housed intestinal diverticula, stomach, and provided a broad surface to which muscles attached.

4. Lateral to the glabella find the compound eyes. In some species you may be able to see the functional units of the eye, the **ommatidia** (e.g., *Phacops rana*). In many fossils the ommatidia will not be visible.

5. At the posteriolateral corners of the cephalon locate the **genal angles.** If elongated, these are called **genal spines.**

6. The thorax consists of 2–42 unfused, articulating segments each bearing a pair of appendages similar to those on the cephalon. The thorax was capable of flexing so that many trilobites were able to fold over like a pill bug, a process called **enrollment** or **conglobation** (Fig. 4). Presumably this protected the vulnerable (thinner) ventral surface called the **doublure.** Do any of the specimens exhibit enrollment?

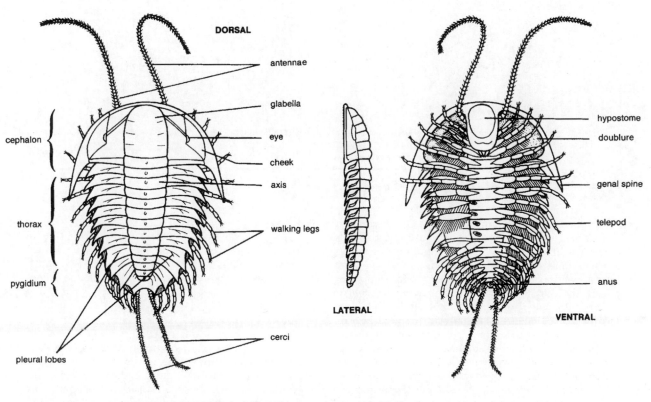

Figure 2. Schematic diagram of a generalized trilobite (dorsal, ventral, and lateral views).

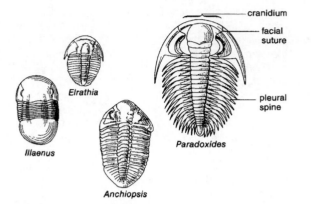

Figure 3. Examples of trilobites.

7. The pygidium was usually constructed of 2–30 fused segments with the anus located at the end of the last segment. Are the pygidia well defined in the specimens? In some species the axis is ribbed in the pygidium, giving a false impression that it was articulate in this tagma.

8. Although appendages are very infrequently preserved, examine the study specimens for them.

9. The entire **tergal** [L., *tergum,* back] exoskeleton, particularly the cephalon, may be ornamented with bumps, granules, tubercles, lines, and other markings. Using Fig. 2 as an aid, identify any other anatomical features exhibited by the specimens.

10. If a whole-mount slide of a trilobite larva from a horseshoe crab is available, compare the larva to the drawings of trilobite larval stages (Fig. 5) and to the adult specimens. What similarities are found in these specimens; how do they differ? ■

Figure 4. Enrollment (conglobation) of *Placops.*

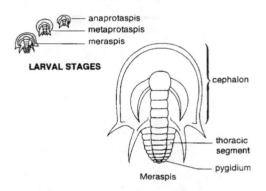

Figure 5. Trilobite larval stages (protaspis and meraspis).

B. Subphylum Chelicerata

Members of Subphylum Chelicerata [ke-LIS-e-ra-tah; G., *chela,* claw + G., *cera,* horn] are distinguished from other arthropods by having two important features. (1) Chelicerates do not possess antennae. (2) The first pair of appendages are modified distally to form opposing clawlike legs called **chelicerae.** Following the chelicerae are the **pedipalps,** and posterior to these are four pairs of walking legs. Mandibles are lacking. The body is divided into two tagmata: anterior **cephalothorax** or **prosoma,** and posterior **abdomen** or **opisthosoma.** All appendages are associated with the prosoma; the opisthosoma lacks appendages except in the Xiphosura. Most of the 75,000 species of chelicerates are predaceous or parasitic on arthropods or other invertebrates.

Class Merostomata

Two subclasses comprise the Class Merostomata [mer-o-STO-mah-tah; G., *mero,* part + G., *stoma,* mouth], Xiphosura (including horseshoe crabs) and the extinct Eurypterida.

Subclass Xiphosura. Horseshoe crabs, members of the subclass Xiphosura [ZIF-o-SU-rah; G., *xiphos,* sword + G., *oura,* tail], have existed since the **Ordovican Period,** but only four marine species are extant. *Limulus polyphemus* is widely distributed along the Gulf of Mexico and east coast of the United States. The other species occur along coasts in the far east Pacific.

Phylum Arthropoda

In some ways *Limulus* resembles a trilobite. *Limulus* possesses three indistinct longitudinal lobes and has a convex dorsal shield covering the ventral appendages (Fig. 6). However, *Limulus* possesses only two tagmata. From above, *Limulus* resembles an upside-down shovel. Specimens may reach more than 50 cm in length, including the tail spine or **telson**. The sexes are separate and mating pairs may be observed along U.S. coasts in the spring. *Limulus* has a commercial importance because of its use in the *Limulus* Amebocyte Lysate (LAL) Assay. This test indicates the presence of minute amounts of the outer cell wall or (LPS) of Gram negative bacteria in spinal and other fluids.

■ Observational Procedure: *Limulus*

1. Place a specimen of *Limulus* dorsal side up with the telson to one side. Identify the anterior and posterior ends. Note the shovel-shaped prosoma. How is *Limulus* adapted for shallow burrowing? Notice the general resemblance of *Limulus* to that of a trilobite. How does tagmatization in *Limulus* differ from that of the trilobites? Are the ventral sides of the two organisms similar (compare Figs. 2 and 6)?

2. Return the animal to its dorsal side and examine the **medial** and **compound eyes** with a hand lens. Of

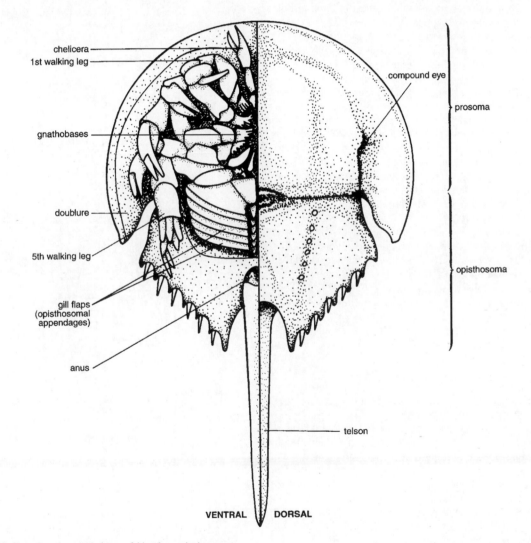

Figure 6. Dorsal and ventral views of *Limulus polyphemus*.

what type of eye does this remind you? What defensive structures does *Limulus* possess on its dorsal surface? Examine a molted exoskeleton (**exuvia**) and identify the **suture line** that breaks open when the animal molts.

3. Examine the ventral surface of a preserved specimen. As in the trilobites, the ventral extension of the carapace is called the **doublure.** Locate the seven pairs of prosomal appendages. The first pair are chelicerae, followed by five pairs of **walking legs.** The first of these being the **pedipalps.** Finally, there is a short, unsegmented pair of appendages called **chilaria.**

4. Trace each leg from its distal end to the point where it attaches to the doublure. How do these seven legs differ?

5. The pedipalps of adult males are different. The chelate ends have a curved claw that is used to hold females while mating. How does this clasping organ function? Is there anything unusual about its size?

6. Observe that the bases of the walking legs, but not the chelicerae, possess spined **coxae** called **gnathobases.** They are grinding organs, processing food to be swallowed by the mouth located posterior to the chelicerae. The chilaria also function as gnathobases.

7. The fifth pair of walking legs are modified in two ways. Observe that they are not chelate, but at their distal end is a structure with four, spatulate blades capable of spreading apart like legs of a tripod. *Limulus* uses these to push against the sediment during locomotion. Also on the lateral side of the same leg, near the doublure, locate the spatulate **flabellum.** This structure is used in cleaning the gills.

8. Observe the opisthosomal region of *Limulus* and examine the six pairs of tough, flaplike appendages that are fused medially. The first pair is thicker and called the **genital opercula.** Move these out of the way and find the next five opercula. These are gill opercula, each possessing many soft, leaflike lamellae known as a **book gill.**

9. In a preserved specimen tease apart some of the gill folds and note their delicate nature. How many gill folds are present?

10. Find the anus at the base of the telson. Carefully move the telson and determine its range of motion. From that observation do you think that the telson is a particularly good defensive structure?

11. Examine a whole-mount slide of a **trilobite larva** of *Limulus.* Note that the larva looks like a minature adult. All the legs are present, but some of the gills are still absent and will be gained in subsequent molts. The medial and compound eyes should be visible through the thin exoskeleton. *Limulus* larvae superficially resemble larval and adult trilobites. Compare the general morphology of a *Limulus* larva to larval and adult trilobites (Figs. 2 and 3).

12. If live animals are available for study, note how they move, burrow, and right themselves when turned over. Examine adult *Limulus* for the commensal flatworm, *Bdelloura* (Platyhelminthes), on the ventral side, especially on the legs.

Subclass Eurypterida (Gigantostraca). Eurypterida [U-rip-TER-ee-dah; G., *eury,* wide + G., *pteron,* wing] is a group of extinct chelicerates that lived during the **Paleozoic Era** (Fig. 1). They are sometimes referred to as sea scorpions because the chelicerae and long abdomen resemble that of true scorpions. The etymon, wide wing, refers to the paddle-like swimming legs. Most specimens are less than 30 cm long, but some giant forms reached nearly 3 m, hence the alternate name **Gigantostraca** [JI-gan-tos-tra-kah; G., *gigantos,* giant + G., *ostraca,* shell]. ∎

∎ Observational Procedure:

If specimens are available for examination, note the general body size and shape of fossil eurypterids (Fig. 7). Usually only parts of the organism are present in the sedimentary rock for study. Do eurypterids resemble trilobites or xiphosurans such as *Limulus*? Does the study specimen exhibit any evidence of tagmatization?

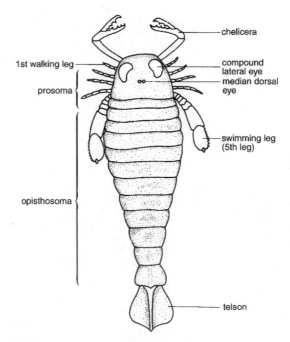

Figure 7. A fossil eurypterid (sea scorpion).

Class Pycnogonida (Pantopoda)

The Pycnogonida [pik-no-GON-ee-dah; G., *pycno*, thick + G., *gony*, knee or joint] comprises nearly 1,000 species of spiderlike marine chelicerates with very long legs. It is their long-legged condition that provides their other name, **Pantopoda** [pan-to-POD-ah; G., *panto*, all + G., *poda*, feet]. Pycnogonids are common in benthic communities, where they prey on soft-bodied animals such as cnidarians and bryozoans by sucking the body fluids or consuming bits of tissue. Some are not predaceous, but feed on algae accumulated on the surface of sessile organisms. Most pycnogonids are less than 10 mm long, but some have very long legs (ca. 75 cm).

■ Observational Procedure:

Examine a preserved pycnogonid under a dissection microscope and note the narrow body, composed of a prosoma with cephalon and trunk, and a small, unsegmented abdomen (**opisthosoma**) bearing a terminal anus (Fig. 8). Locate the proboscis at the anterior end and, on the anterior dorsal part of the cephalon, find a small tubercle that bears **ocelli.** The number of appendages differs among species; *Nymphon* has seven pairs. Locate the chelicerae that lie alongside the proboscis. Also locate the pedipalps, the second pair of appendages near the chelicerae. The third pair of appendages are the very slender **ovigerous legs** that normally are used by males to carry eggs; females of many species lack these legs. Note that the remaining four pairs of walking legs are long (Fig. 8). Does *Nymphon* exhibit any evidence of tagmatization?

Your instructor will assist you in making observations, should live specimens be available for study.

Class Arachnida

Class Arachnida [ah-RAK-nid-ah; G., *arachne*, spider] comprises the vast bulk of chelicerates (more than 80,000 species) and is of great importance because many are parasitic on plants and animals, or prey upon agricultural pests. Arachnids range in size from minute (200 μm) to nearly 20 cm long. The class dates to the **Silurian Period** from which the first aquatic scorpions are known.

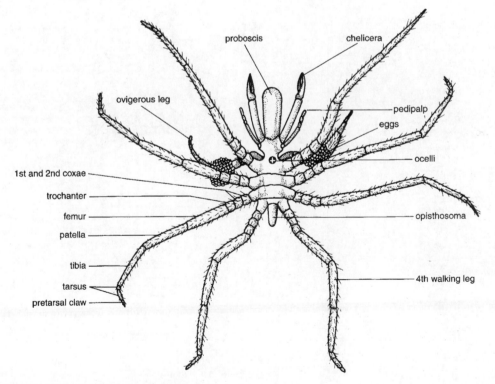

Figure 8. Dorsal view of the pycnogonid, *Nymphon*.

The opisthosoma of arachnids lacks locomotory appendages, while the prosoma possesses six pairs: a pair of chelicerae, a pair of pedipalps, and four pairs of walking legs. Of the 12 orders in this class, seven will be studied here. They represent greater than 99% of arachnids. The remaining five minor orders, Amblypygi, Cyphophthalmi, Palpigradi, Ricinuclei, and Schizomida, will not be studied unless your instructor has specimens for examination.

Order Scorpiones. Order Scorpiones [skor-pi-O-nez; G., *skorpios,* scorpion] is a well-known group of relatively large (<1 cm to nearly 21 cm) chelicerates with a long mobile tail that terminates with a poisonous **sting.** Some fossil species were very large (greater than 0.5 m). The prosoma bears chelicerae, pedipalps, and four pairs of walking legs. The chelate pedipalps are used to hold prey and are used in courtship. Pedipalps also have a sensory function. The opisthosoma is elongate and of two parts, a mesosoma (preabdomen) and a metasoma (postabdomen). The latter is a segmented tail that possesses the sting. Scorpions are viviparous and are common in tropical, subtropical, and south temperate zones where the climate is warm. In North America, scorpions occur as far north as southern Canada; they also live in parts of central Europe. *Centruroides* is a common genus found in the southwestern United States; it also occurs in the central United States, as far north as Illinois. Some species of *Centruroides* occur in Florida. The species *C. exilicauda* (=*sculpturatus*) can be dangerous to humans, especially children.

■ Observational Procedure: *Centruroides*

1. Examine a specimen of *Centruroides* or of another genus available for study (Fig. 9). At the anterior end of the scorpion examine the chelicerae and large pedipalps; behind the pedipalps locate the walking legs.

2. Dorsally the prosoma is covered by a subquadrate plate or **carapace,** that bears, at the anterior end, three groups of simple eyes. The prosoma comprises six somites, with the 7th having been resorbed in the embryo.

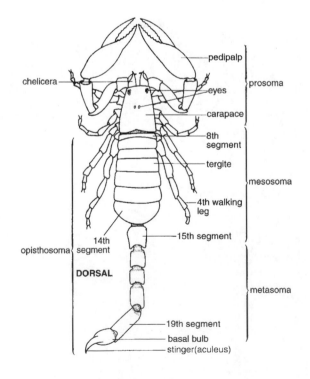

Figure 9. Dorsal view of a scorpion.

Figure 10. Ventral view of a scorpion, prosoma and mesosoma.

3. Immediately behind the carapace is a short segment (eighth) that begins the opisthosoma. Observe that the opisthosoma is divided into two sections. The first is a broader region called the mesosoma (preabdomen) comprising segments 8–14. The second part (metasoma or postabdomen) is thinner, tail-like and comprises segments 15–19.

4. Locate the **telson** with the curved **stinger** or **aculeus** which is attached to segment 19. The sting is capable of injecting a neurotoxin into prey from a gland located in the **basal bulb**.

5. Examine the chelicerae closely. Note that there are two major tines at the end of the movable finger, one major tine at the end of the fixed finger, and that the margins of both fingers bear cusps. How do these features aid in chewing prey? Observe that the legs end in a single pair of dorsal tarsal claws and a single ventral medial claw. What is the functional significance of this arrangement?

6. Turn the animal ventral side up (Fig. 10). Most of the ventral prosoma is covered by the first joint (**coxae**) of the walking legs. Find the ninth body segment. It may be recognized by the presence of **pectines**, comblike sensory structures unique to scorpions. Given their location and morphology, speculate on the function of the pectines.

7. Just anterior to the pectines locate the genital operculum of the eighth segment.

8. Find segments 10–13 just posterior to the pectines and, at their lateral margins, locate the spiracular openings to the respiratory organ called the **book lung**. ■

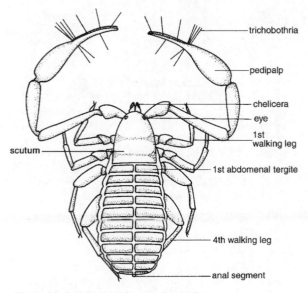

Figure 11. Dorsal view of a pseudoscorpion.

Order Pseudoscorpiones. Order Pseudoscorpiones [SU-do-SKOR-pi-O-nez; G., *pseudo*, false] comprises about 3,000 species of small (less than 10 mm) chelicerates that resemble true scorpions. Book lungs are also missing; gas exchange takes place through a tracheal system. These animals are common occupants in nests of ground–inhabiting animals as well as in organic debris. *Chelifer* is commonly found in houses. Pseudoscorpions feed on other small arthropods by grasping them and injecting a poison from glands in the pedipalps.

■ Observational Procedure:

Examine a whole-mount slide of a pseudoscorpion, noting their general resemblance to scorpions (Fig. 11). What characteristic scorpion features are missing in the pseudoscorpion? Locate the chelicerae, pedipalps, and four pairs of walking legs. The dorsal surface is covered by a carapace or **scutum.** The segmented opisthosoma is broader than the prosoma and rounded at its posterior end. As in scorpions, coxae cover most of the ventral surface of the prosoma. Note that the bulbous pedipalps are chelate and bear several sensory hairs, called **trichobothria,** scattered over their surfaces. Eyes may be present at the anteriolateral regions of the carapace. ■

Order Araneae. Order Araneae [a-RA-ne-ah; L., *arane*, spider] comprises over 30,000 species of true spiders. Spiders differ from most other chelicerates in that the prosoma and opisthosoma are connected by a short, narrow isthmus called the **pedicel**; both body regions are unsegmented in the adult. The opisthosoma, usually referred to as the abdomen, contains the majority of the viscera, including the silk-spinning organs. Spiders range from less than 1 mm to nearly 10 cm long and are found in most habitats, including the tropics, deserts, arctic and alpine regions, dorm rooms, and at several thousand meters in the air.

■ Observational Procedure:

1. Obtain several specimens for study (e.g., *Argiope*, orb weaver; *Latrodectus*, black widow; *Tarantula*, tarantula) and examine them, locating the prosoma, opisthosoma, and pedicel (Fig. 12).

2. Find the four pairs of walking legs and pedipalps on the prosoma. Note the two-jointed chelicerae with **fangs** (Fig. 12). The basal joint is the larger and the second joint is composed of a dagger-like claw or fang. In males the terminal joint of the pedipalp is modified as an organ by which sperm are conveyed to the female's genital receptacle.

Phylum Arthropoda

Figure 12. Frontal, dorsal, and ventral views of a generalized spider. Ventral is of a female.

3. Note the dorsal shield or carapace that covers the prosoma. Locate two rows, of four eyes each, at the anterior end.

4. Find the pedicel, the first segment of the opisthosoma (Fig. 12). Ventrally, segment 2 possesses the genitalia as well as openings to the book lungs. The latter may be found by locating a transverse line called the **epigastric furrow** or fold. The lateral extensions comprise the openings (**spiracles**) to the book lungs. Male spiders also have a genital pore which is covered by a small plate.

5. Medial and slightly anterior to the furrow, find the genital opening. In the vicinity of the genital opening of most female spiders is the **epigynum** that contains the opening to the seminal receptacles.

6. Find the **spinnerets** on the posterioventral surface of the opisthosoma near the anal lobe (Fig. 12). There are 4–6 spinnerets depending on the species. Spinnerets are silk-producing glands and are considered appendages of the ventral body segments 10 and 11.

7. Near the spinnerets, locate another one or two spiracle openings. In primitive spiders (mygalomorphs), the posterior spiracles are paired and lead to book lungs. In advanced forms the respiratory organs are trachae, most often with a single spiracle which is often very difficult to locate.

8. If live spiders are available, observe web-building and prey-capturing behaviors according to directions provided by your instructor. ■

Order Opiliones. The familiar daddy longlegs or harvestmen comprise the Order Opiliones [o-pil-ee-O-nes;

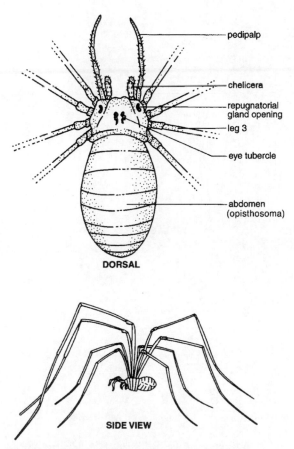

DORSAL

SIDE VIEW

Figure 13. Dorsal and lateral views of a daddy longlegs.

L., *opilio,* shepherd] or Phalangida [fa-LAN-ji-da; G., *phalange,* spider], about 5,500 species of arachnids noted for their long legs although not all of them possess long legs. Opiliones have the prosoma and opisthosoma more-or-less fused into an egg-shaped body (5–20 mm long) that is elevated above the substratum by four pairs of very long legs. They have a cosmopolitan distribution, but are abundant in moist regions.

■ Observational Procedure:

Obtain a daddy longlegs and note that the prosoma and opisthosoma appear to be fused (Fig. 13). As in other chelicerates, the prosoma, termed the carapace, supports the appendages. The opisthosoma may be identified by the presence of 10 weakly lined segments. Examine the anterior end and locate the chelicerae and leglike pedipalps. Locate the eyes and anteriolaterally the opening to the stink gland on the central region of the dorsal carapace. ■

Order Acarina. Acarina [AK-a-RI-na; G., *akari,* mite] comprises about 40,000 species of small (less than 1 cm) chelicerates commonly known as ticks and mites. Acarines are of great medical, veterinary, and economic importance, because many are vectors or intermediate hosts of disease-causing organisms (e.g., Lyme disease and Rocky Mountain spotted fever). The standard tagmatization of chelicerates is not present in acarines. The tagma are fused into a dorsoventrally flattened, ovoid body of several arbitrarily defined regions.

Of the seven suborders, five are parasitic or vectors of other parasites. Anatomical differences that separate ticks and mites are relatively minor. All ticks (Suborder Metastigmata) are blood-sucking parasites. Parasitic mites feed on blood or burrow through epidermal tissues or internal organs (e.g., respiratory system). The common dust mite (*Dermatophagoides*) is not parasitic, but releases materials that may cause severe allergic reactions in humans. However, many mites are free-living with diverse feeding habits (e.g., predation, scavenging). Students will examine several examples of ticks and mites for an understanding of their diversity of form.

■ Observational Procedure: Ticks

Hard Ticks (Family Ixodidae): *Dermacentor* spp.

1. Examine male and female specimens of either *Dermacentor andersoni* (Rocky Mountain wood tick) or *D. variabilis* (American dog tick) (Fig. 14A). Identify the two body regions: the body or **idiosoma** consists of a region bearing the legs (**podosoma**) and one in which legs are missing (**opisthosoma**).

2. Locate the anterior **capitulum** (**gnathosoma**) bearing the feeding appendages, including the toothed **hypostome,** chelicerae, and pedipalps. Note that the capitulum may be seen in a dorsal view. This feature distinguishes hard from soft ticks.

3. On the ventral side of the opisthosoma, find the genital pore, anus, stigmal plates with spiracle, and marginal **festoons.** The latter have taxonomic importance.

4. Also observe the four pairs of walking legs, each bearing a terminal tarsus with apotele and tarsal claws. At the tip of the tarsus of the first walking leg find **Haller's organ,** which is sensitive to humidity and odors.

5. Compare the dorsal idiosoma of a male and female and note the difference in the size of the **scutum** (Fig. 14B).

6. Examine larval and nymph stages of *D. andersoni.* Note that the larval stage is much smaller than the adult and possesses only three pairs of legs. The nymph is larger than the larval stage and resembles the adult, except for lacking the genital opening.

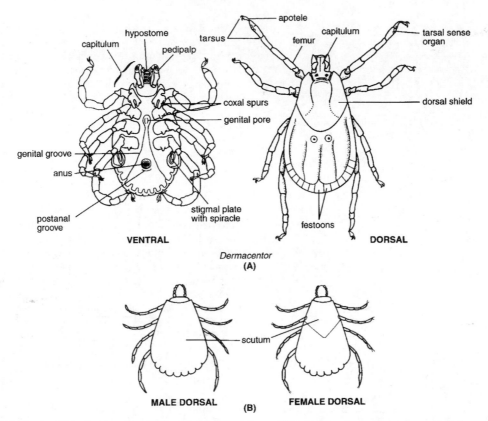

Figure 14. The hard tick, *Dermacentor*. (A) Dorsal and ventral views. (B) Dorsal view comparing male and female ticks.

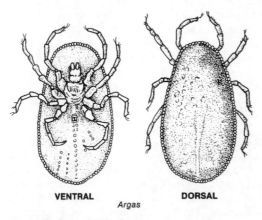

Figure 15. The soft tick, *Argas*.

7. For more advanced study, examine other examples of hard ticks: for example, *Haemaphysalis leporispalustris* (rabbit tick); *Amblyomma americanum* (lone star tick); *Rhipicephalus sanguineus* (brown dog tick); *Boophilus annulatus* (American cattle tick). Compare these species to *Dermacentor*. How are their body plans similar to that of *Dermacentor*? How do they differ?

Soft Ticks (family Argasidae): *Argas persicus.*
Examine a specimen of *Argas persicus*, the fowl tick, a vector of relapsing fever in birds. Observe the sculptured cuticle. Note that the capitulum is obscured by the idiosoma in dorsal view (Fig. 15). How would the body regions be designated in this tick? ■

Mites. Representatives of three of the four Suborders comprising the mites may be studied depending on the time available.

■ Observational Procedure: Mites

1. *Dermanyssus gallinae* (Chicken Mite): Suborder Mesostigmata. These mites parasitize chickens, hiding in the roosts by day and coming out to feed at night. Large infestations may be sufficient to kill the hosts from loss of blood. Examine a specimen of *Dermanyssus gallinae* (Fig. 16). Locate the capitulum with unarmed

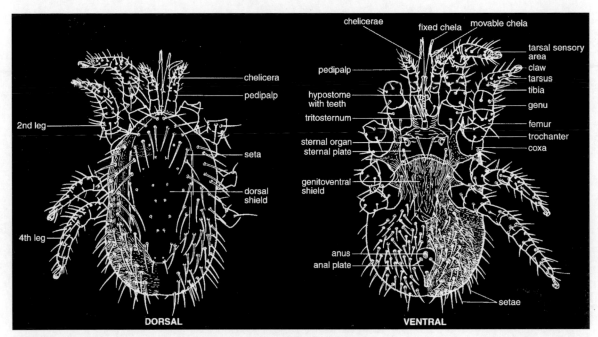

Figure 16. Dorsal and ventral views of *Dermanyssus gallinae*. (After T.M. Evans.)

hypostome, chelicerae, and pedipalps. Note that the chelicerae are needle-like; if you examine them under high magnification you may be able to see their minute chelate ends.

2. *Sarcoptes scabiei* (Human Itch Mite): Suborder Astigmata. These small mites (less then 500 µm long) cause **scabies** in humans. Females burrow through the skin, depositing eggs and excreta that cause itching and may lead to secondary infection by bacteria. Examine a

Figure 17. Dorsal view of a female *Sarcoptes scabiei*.

specimen of *S. scabiei* noting the rounded body and fine striations on the cuticle (Fig. 17). Also, note the position of the four pair of stubby legs, presence of long setae, and dorsally, a central region of raised scales that extend posteriolaterally. Observe the legs of your specimen. The first and second pairs possess extensions called **pulvilli** just proximal to the tarsal leg segment. Females lack pulvilli on the rear pairs, but males have them on the fourth pair. What might the function be of these structures?

Examine a section of the epidermis from a mammal that had **sarcoptic mange** and attempt to locate adult females in their winding burrows. You may also be able to locate eggs, unhatched embryos, and ecdysed cuticles. What sort of tissue damage do you see in this preparation?

3. *Dermatophagoides* (House Dust Mite): Suborder Astigmata. Most species of this genus are not parasitic; however, certain forms produce powerful allergens causing allergic reactions in sensitive people. Examine a specimen of the house dust mite, *Dermatophagoides* sp., noting the ovoid body, long setae, and fine striations present on the cuticle as in *S. scabiei*. If time permits, you will be instructed on how to collect your own specimens.

4. *Demodex folliculorum* (Follicle Mite): Suborder Prostigmata. The follicle mites, *D. folliculorum* and *D. brevis,* live in human follicles and sebaceous glands, respectively, usually without causing serious damage.

They are small (less than 500 μm) mites with short legs and an elongated, annulated opisthosoma. Examine a specimen of a follicle mite, noting the four pairs of short legs with claws and the elongate, annulated opisthosoma. What is the significance of the elongated body? Also, examine a cross section of *D. folliculorum* in situ and locate the mites in the hair follicles. Do you notice anything unusual about the orientation of these organisms in the follicle? If time permits, you will be instructed on how to collect specimens from your own eyebrows. Are you parasitized by *Demodex*? ■

Order Solifugae. The Solifugae [so-LIF-u-je; L., *soli,* sun + L., *fug,* flee], also Solpugida [sol-PU-ji-dah; L., *solpug,* venomous spider], is a group of relatively large (1–7 cm), aggressive chelicerates. They are commonly known as sun, camel, soldier, or wind spiders. Solifugids feed on arthropods and vertebrates, tearing prey apart with large, stocky chelicerae. They have a cosmopolitan distribution in tropical, subtropical, and warm, arid temperate regions. They are abundant in desert regions of the southwestern United States. Respiration in the entire order is accomplished by trachea.

■ Observational Procedure:

1. Examine a specimen of a solifugid (Fig. 18). Observe that the hirsute (hairy) body appears to be divid-ed into three divisions. Actually the prosoma has a constriction that separates it into two regions of three somites each: head and thorax (or anterior and posterior carapaces, respectively). In nonburrowing species, the head and thorax sections articulate. How can that be advantageous?

2. Note that the thorax has dorsal transverse lines that indicate the position of the three somites. Four to six simple eyes are present on the head, depending on species. Locate the large chelicerae and determine in which direction they articulate. How does this differ from the other chelicerates studied so far?

3. Note the robust nature of the pedipalps and the relatively delicate first legs. The pedipalps are not chelate but they are used in prey capture. The first pair of legs are not used in locomotion but are tactile organs. On the coxae of the posterior legs are the **racquet organs** whose function is unknown. The segmented opisthosoma is broadly joined to the prosoma and comprises 10 segments. ■

Order Uropygi. The Uropygi [U-ro-PI-ge; G., *uro,* tail + G., *pyge,* rump] contains moderately sized chelicerates (a few mm to about 7 cm) that are flattened both in the prosoma and opisthosoma. They are commonly called whip scorpions because of the long **flagellum** or **whip** at the end of the opisthosoma. They are also called **vinegaroons** due to their ability to spray a defensive fluid

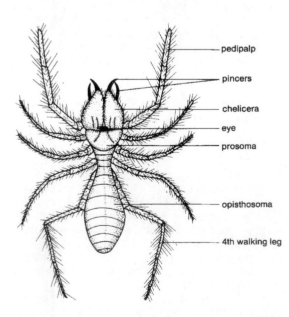

Figure 18. Dorsal view of a solifugid. (Total body length ≈ 2.5 cm.)

Figure 19. The American uropygid, *Mastigoprocetus giganteus.*

composed mainly of acetic acid from a pair of glands on either side of the anus. Whip scorpions have a worldwide distribution, but tend to be common in tropical, subtropical, and warm temperate regions. The world's largest species (ca. 6.5 cm), *Mastigoproctus giganteus,* is found in the southern parts of the United States.

■ Observational Procedure:

Examine a specimen of *Mastigoproctus*, noting the flattened body and long flagellum (Fig. 19). At the anterior end distinguish the small, stout chelicerae from the larger, chelate pedipalps used in prey capture. The first pair of legs are thinner and sensory, but the remaining three pairs are used in walking. Note that the opisthosoma is segmented and is attached to the prosoma by a wide pedicel. The opisthosoma is composed of a larger mesosoma of eight somites and a shorter metasoma of three narrow segments before the flagellum. Find the paired openings to the defensive **anal glands** located on the ventral side of the opisthosoma near the anus. ■

C. Subphylum Crustacea

Shrimps, crabs, crayfish, lobsters, barnacles, and pill bugs are members of a large, diverse subphylum of arthropods called Crustacea [krus-TA-shi-ah; L., *crusta,* crust or rind]. Over 40,000 species are recognized, most of which are aquatic. Crustaceans are unique arthropods possessing two pairs of antennae, biramous appendages, and mandibles (jawlike appendages). They range in size from minute (less than 500 µm) to extremely large; the lobster *Homarus americanus* may reach more than 0.5 m long. Many crustaceans are commercially important to the shellfish fishery (e.g., shrimps, crabs, lobsters in marine coastal waters and crayfish in fresh waters). Small free-swimming crustaceans, their larvae, and the larvae of larger forms, collectively called **zooplankton,** are very important ecologically as they constitute a trophic level intermediate between single-celled organisms and zooplanktivorous fish.

Primitively, the crustacean body is composed of a series of segments each possessing a pair of biramous appendages. In advanced forms there is a strong tendency towards tagmatization, loss and fusion of segments, and loss of appendages. Three tagmata are usually recognized: head, thorax, and abdomen. The head and thorax may be fused into a single cephalic region called the **cephalothorax** (prosoma). Many crustaceans possess a shieldlike extension of the cephalothorax called the **carapace,** which may surround the animal entirely except for a small ventral gap. Most members of the Class Malacostraca have a shrimplike body form with obvious tagmatization (Fig. 20). This arrangement is called the **caridoid facies** [L., *carid,* shrimp + L., *facies,* appearance].

Typical crustacean appendages are paired and biramous (Fig. 21), consisting of a proximal **protopod** (or

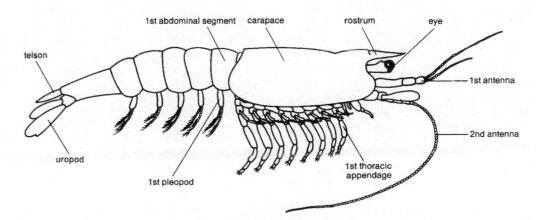

Figure 20. Generalized malacostracan crustacean which is illustrative of the caridoid facies.

protopodite) with two distal rami: the **endopod** (inner or medial branch) and **exopod** (outer or lateral branch). The protopod may be composed of three units (precoxa, coxa, and basis) and have other outgrowths on the lateral side (**epipodites** or **exites**) and on the medial side (**endites**).

Different classification schemes for the crustaceans are found in general and advanced texts, and your instructor may choose to discuss the merits of these various schemes. However, for purposes of laboratory study, taxonomic position is not particularly important, so the following exercises do not emphasize taxonomy. The crustaceans available for study are to be considered only as representatives of this very diverse group. Your instructor may provide additional representatives or substitute others for study.

Class Branchiopoda

Cladocera [kla-DOS-er-ah; G., *cladus*, branch + G., *cera*, horn] is an important suborder of predominantly freshwater crustaceans of Class Branchiopoda [brank-ee-o-PO-dah; G., *branchium*, gill + G., *pod*, foot]. Other branchiopods with whom you may be familiar are fairy and brine shrimp. Feeding on algae and bacteria, the cladocerans represent an extremely important link in the food web of freshwater systems. Cladocerans are commonly called water fleas because planktonic forms perform an unusual jump or hop followed by a slow sinking movement. Most individuals are 200–3,000 µm long and possess a transparent, laterally flattened, nonhinged carapace that extends ventrally beyond the body, covering the legs. There is a ventral gap between right and left valves that allows water to pass between them.

■ Observational Procedure:

Live Specimens

1. Observe the hop-sink motion of live *Daphnia* in a culture vessel under low light. How is the hop motion accomplished? How does drag and the center of gravity of the animal affect the orientation of the animal as it sinks?

2. How does *Daphnia* respond to light shined from above? From the side? From beneath the vessel?

3. Place a single specimen into a drop of pond water on a shallow depression slide and cover it with a coverslip.

4. Observe the beating heart located dorsally near the midpoint of the body. Under high magnification you may be able to see blood cells coursing through the **hemocoel.**

5. Observe feeding activity of *Daphnia* by adding a small drop of a suspension of food particles. Can you

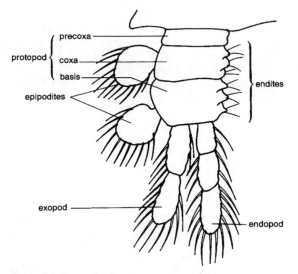

Figure 21. Generalized crustacean appendage. (After Schram.)

see feeding currents? How does *Daphnia* process food particles? How do the mandibles work? Is food present in the food groove? Attempt to observe rejection of food by *Daphnia*. How is this accomplished? Does the postabdomen have any function in food processing? Remember that your observations do not reflect the normal feeding conditions of *Daphnia.* In your preparation the animal is confined in a small amount of water with abnormally high levels of food.

Morphology

The following observations of *Daphnia* morphology may be made using live or preserved specimens. Live specimens will require an anesthetic or methyl cellulose to slow them down.

1. Examine a cladoceran such as *Daphnia* under a compound microscope (Fig. 22). Examine the ovoid body and identify the anterior, posterior, dorsal, and ventral ends.

2. Observe the prominent second antennae and the single compound eye enclosed within a head shield at the anterior end. The prominant muscles that originate on the inner surface of the head shield and insert on the inner surface of the second antennae are birefringent and may be visualized using crossed polarizing filters. In some populations, the size and shape of the head shield undergoes a dramatic variation (**cyclomorphosis**) depending on season.

3. Find the first antennae, located just beneath the **rostrum,** and the small, pigmented **ocellus,** just posterior to the compound eye.

4. Also, locate the mandibles, posterior to the insertion of the second antennae. Using crossed polarized fil-

Phylum Arthropoda

Figure 22. Lateral view of the freshwater cladoceran, *Daphnia*.

ters may help you locate the mandibles as their striated grinding surfaces are birefringent.

5. Note the spine at the posterior end of the carapace. What function might the spine serve? Does the specimen have an enlarged dorsal **crest** or **helmet** above the compound eye? If so, examine the musculature that originates at the crest and inserts on the second antennae. Compare the development of this musculature with a nonhelmeted form. How do they differ? What function(s) might the helmet serve?

6. Find the gut, which first courses anteriorly and then curves posteriorly, proceeding through the central part of the body. Is food in the gut? The gut exits the body after passing through the flexible **postabdomen**.

7. Locate the thoracic legs within the **branchial chamber.** Note the numerous comblike setae on each leg. In life, the legs are almost constantly in motion, producing a water current that flows between the valves of the carapace, bringing food to the animal.

8. Dorsal to the gut is the **brood chamber** that may contain developing embryos. How many embryos are present in your specimens? At what stage of development are the embryos? If sexual eggs have been fertilized, they undergo **diapause** within a thick-walled brood chamber called an **ephippium** [G., saddle-shaped]. Are any of the specimens ephippiate? How many diapausing embryos are present in each ephippium? What are the consequences to the female of her ephippium being dark? ■

Class Ostracoda

Ostracoda [os-tra-KO-dah; G., *ostracum*, shell], is a class of small, bean-shaped crustaceans, commonly called seed shrimps. Most are less than 1 to about 3 mm long, although some larger (greater than 2 cm) marine forms are known. Ostracods resemble bivalves in possessing a dorsally hinged carapace of right and left **valves,** with an adductor muscle for closure. Resemblance to bivalves provides another common name, mussel shrimp. The valves are reinforced with calcium carbonate, except at the hinge. Ostracods have a cosmopolitan distribution in benthic freshwater and marine environments; several terrestrial genera are known. As with the cladocerans, ostracods use their antennae for locomotion. Many ostracods are omnivorous.

■ Observational Procedure:

Live Specimens

Observe the locomotory activities of ostracods in a small culture vessel or beaker. How do they move about? What appendages appear to be most important for locomotion? Using a dissection microscope observe the movement of ostracods in a small Petri dish. Compare locomotion in ostracods to that of cladocerans (e.g., *Daphnia*). Do ostracods swim as much of the time as the cladocerans you just studied? If they don't, where do they spend much of their time?

Morphology

The following observations of ostracod morphology may be made using live or preserved specimens. As with cladocerans, live ostracods may require an anesthetic or methyl cellulose to slow them down.

1. Obtain an ostracod and observe it under a compound microscope (Fig. 23). Note the ovoid body and determine the anterior, posterior, dorsal, and ventral ends.

2. Observe at the anterior end the prominent, paired first and second antennae. How do these differ from those of *Daphnia*? Note how the valves surround the body and the appendages except for the flagella of the antennae.

3. Unfortunately, much of the internal anatomy of ostracods is obscured by the valves. However, you should be able to observe the single compound eye just posterior to the insertion of the first antennae.

4. In the central region of the valve, locate the adductor muscle.

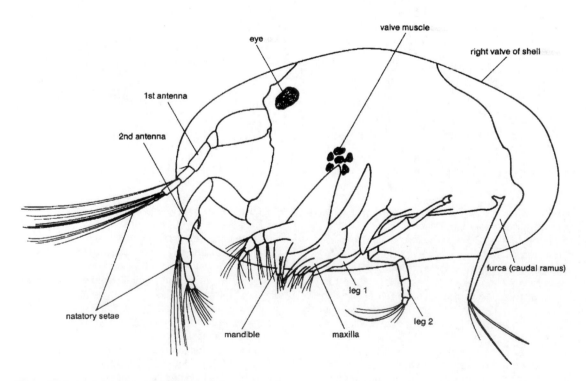

Figure 23. Lateral view of generalized ostracod.

5. Attempt to locate the gut. Occasionally, portions of the gut may be identified by the presence of food material. The mandibles may been seen about one-third of the way back from the anterior end near the ventral margin of the valves. ■

Class Copepoda

Copepoda [ko-PEP-o-dah; G., *kope*, an oar + G., *podos, foot*] is a large class (more than 8,000 species) of small bullet-shaped crustaceans with prominent first antennae. Like herbivorous cladocerans, copepods represent an extremely important link in aquatic food chains. They range in size from less than 1 mm to several millimeters long. Copepods have three tagmata, including a cephalothorax (head plus 1–2 thoracic segments), the remaining thorax, and an abdomen. Each tagma is comprised of a few to several rigid, cylindrical segments joined by somewhat flexible joints. There is a major junction within the body dividing it into two parts: **metasome** and **urosome**.

Copepods have a cosmopolitan distribution in freshwater and marine environments occurring in both benthic and planktonic habitats. Herbivorous, predaceous, and parasitic forms are known. Ectoparasitic copepods often look very similar to free-living species, but some endoparasitic forms are so modified that they hardly resemble other copepods at all.

■ Observational Procedure:

Live Specimens
1. Observe the locomotory activities of copepods in a small culture vessel using a dissection microscope. How do they move about? What appendages appear to be most important for locomotion? Attempt to capture an individual using a wide-mouth Pasteur pipette. Is this an easy task? What does it indicate about copepods? Compare locomotion in copepods to that of cladocerans and ostracods.

2. Place a single specimen into a drop of pond water on a shallow depression slide and cover it with a coverslip. The specimen should be restrained as much as possible, but not crushed.

3. Note that there is no heart as in the cladocerans and ostracods. Are there any colored materials present outside the gut? Colored lipid drops are often found in the hemocoel of copepods (and other microcrustaceans) as forms of stored energy.

4. Occasionally, the exoskeleton will be covered with sessile protozoans or algae. Are any present on your specimen? How might these phoretic [G., *phora*, to bear] organisms influence copepod swimming? ■

Morphology
The following observations of copepod morphology may be made using live or preserved specimens. As with the other microcrustaceans studied, live copepods may require an anesthetic or methyl cellulose to slow them down.

1. Obtain a copepod and observe it under a compound microscope (Fig. 24). Examine the bullet-shaped body and identify the anterior, posterior, dorsal, and ventral ends. Also determine the metasome and urosome.

2. At the anterior end observe the long uniramous first antennae and the shorter second antennae. The first antennae are not used in locomotion but are important in sensory reception. Locate the compound **nauplius eye** at the very tip of the head region.

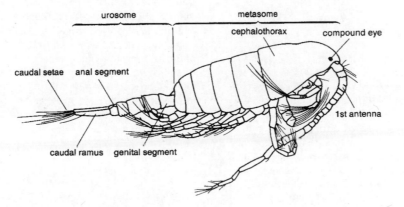

Figure 24. Lateral view of typical free-living copepod.

cirri
tergum
scutum
penis
testis
mandibular palp
(mandible below)
anus
adductor muscle
labrum
mouth
supraesophageal
ganglion
digestive ceca
stomach
carina
intestine
oviduct
ovary
stalk (peduncle)
cement gland
antennule

Figure 25. Lateral view of the stalked, thoracican barnacle, *Lepas.* (After Sherman and Sherman.)

3. Other appendages that should be found include the feeding appendages, the paired swimming legs (in the thorax), and a pair of setaeous **caudal rami** at the posterior end of the urosome.

4. Females may carry a pair of egg sacs near the junction of the metasome and urosome. Are egg sacs present on your specimen?

5. Internally, look for prominent bands of longitudinal and circular muscles. ■

Class Cirripedia

Cirripedia [ser-ree-PED-ee-ah; L., *cirrus,* curl of hair + L., *pedis,* foot] is a small class of about 1,000 species of sessile, marine crustaceans commonly called barnacles. Barnacles hardly resemble crustaceans at all. In fact Carl von Linn (a.k.a. Linnaeus) classified barnacles with the Mollusca where they remained until 1830, when their larvae were discovered and it was deduced that they were crustaceans. Barnacles have tremendous economic importance, chiefly by fouling ocean-going vessels.

Most people are familiar with free-living thoracican barnacles, which are separated into two groups: (1) stalked or goose-neck barnacles (*Lepas*) and (2) stalk-less, or sessile barnacles (*Balanus*). Parasitic barnacles, which will not be studied here, have a morphology that is very much different from the thoracicans.

■ Observational Procedure:

Live Specimens

Examine a living barnacle in a small dish filled with seawater and observe movements of the rakelike structure that is periodically exposed. These are the legs or **cirri** and they are involved in feeding. The rate of movement of the cirri and the way in which they are used to filter particles from the water depends on factors such as temperature, water movement, and concentration of food. Place a drop of milk near the cirri and observe the movement of milk. How do the cirri respond to the presence of the milk suspension? At the direction of your instructor attempt feeding the barnacles other materials.

Morphology

1. Obtain a specimen of *Lepas*, a stalked barnacle, and place it in a dissection pan with the muscular peduncle towards you. Distinguish the **peduncle** from the laterally compressed **capitulum** (Fig. 25).

3/4 side view

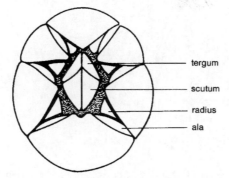

tergum

scutum

radius

ala

Figure 26. External plates of the sessile barnacle, *Balanus*.

2. On one edge of the capitulum, locate the **aperture** and on the opposite edge (dorsal) locate an unpaired, keel-like plate called the **carina.**

3. On either side of the capitulum and near the peduncle, locate a pair of large, broad plates, the **scuta.** Above the scuta is another pair of smaller plates, the **terga.**

4. Remove the mantle and plates from the right side of the animal. Pin the animal to the dissection pan and cover it with water.

5. The most conspicuous structures are six pairs of biramous **cirri** (legs) with numerous setae. The cirri curl towards the mouth and increase in size posteriorly. How is the setation distributed on the cirri? To understand this question you will need to examine the cirri using a dissection microscope.

6. Posterior to the cirri, locate the long, segmented penis and at its base, the posterior anus.

7. At the anterior end, locate the adductor muscle that connects the right and left sides of the mantle. Posterior to this muscle find the mouth and accompanying mouth appendages. The mandibles will be easily recognized by their strong dentition. Other appendages will not be identified.

8. Obtain a specimen of a sessile barnacle such as *Balanus*. Dried specimens will suffice, unless the specimen is to be dissected (Step 10).

9. Determine the anterior-posterior orientation of the barnacle and the various plates (Fig. 26). Note that the operculum is composed of two pairs of movable plates (terga and scuta).

10. The internal anatomy of *Balanus* is similar to that of *Lepas*. If advanced dissection is to be done, your instructor will provide additional directions.

Larva

1. Obtain a prepared slide of a **nauplius larva** of a barnacle under a compound microscope and examine the shield-shaped body.

2. Determine the anterior and posterior ends, and dorsal and ventral sides. At the anterior end locate the first antennae, nauplius eye, and frontal horns.

3. Two prominent bulges may be seen on either side of the ventral surface. These are the second antennae, which possess **cement glands**.

4. Towards the posterior part of the body a metameric tail-like structure may be seen. These metameres will develop into the thoracic legs in subsequent molts. ■

Class Malacostraca

Class Malacostraca [MAL-ah-co-STRAK-ah; G., *malaco*, soft + G., *ostracum*, shell] encompasses three-quarters of the crustaceans, including those most favored on the dinner table: shrimp, crab, and lobster. The body plan is of two tagma: anteriorly a fusion of the cephalon and thorax into the cephalothorax and posteriorly an abdomen.

Order Amphipoda. Amphipoda [am-FIP-o-dah; G., *amphi*, double + G., *podus*, foot] is a large order (about 6,000 species) of shrimplike malacostracans that range in size from fewer than 1 mm to nearly 30 cm in a deep-sea benthic form. Most amphipods are marine, but many freshwater species and a single terrestrial group are known. Amphipods are commonly called **scuds**, indicating a swift swimming movement, but benthic burrowing and crawling forms are common. The laterally flattened body is slightly rounded on the dorsal side. Three tagmata are recognized: head, thorax (preaeon), and abdomen with pleon plus urosome. Amphipods lack a carapace.

■ **Observational Procedure:**

Live Specimens

If available, observe locomotory activities of amphipods in a small dish with the aid of a dissection microscope. How do the animals move about? What appendages appear to be most important for locomotion? Compare locomotion in amphipods to that of the other crustaceans examined so far.

Phylum Arthropoda

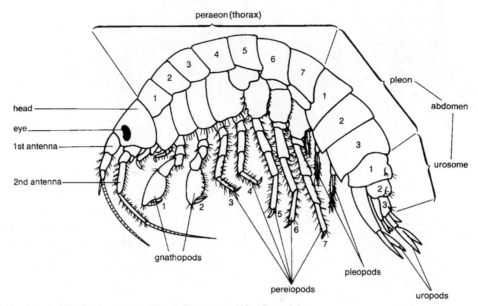

Figure 27. Lateral view of the freshwater amphipod, *Gammarus*. (After Pennak.)

Morphology

1. Obtain an amphipod such as *Gammarus* and observe it under a compound microscope (Fig. 27). Determine the anterior, posterior, dorsal, and ventral ends of the organism.

2. Locate the paired, prominent first and second antennae at the anterior end. Note the well-defined head with paired, sessile compound eyes.

3. Find the feeding appendages in the buccal region. They are usually small and hidden from view. Locate the two pairs of subchelate **gnathopods** that are used in grasping food and, by males, in holding the female during copulation. Gnathopods are the second and third pairs of thoracic legs called **pereiopods** [G., *pereio*, on the other side; also peraeopods]. The third through seventh pereiopods are unspecialized ambulatory limbs.

4. **Coxal gills** are difficult to locate, but may be seen as ovoid sacs on the inner surface of the coxae of legs 2–6.

5. In the pleon region of the abdomen, locate the three pairs of setous **pleopods** [G., *pleo*, swim + G., *podos* foot] used in swimming.

6. Posterior to the pleon is the urosome of three segments, each with paired uropods.

Order Decapoda. Crayfish, crabs, and lobsters are members of the Order Decapoda [DEC-ah-poad-ah; G., *deca*, ten + G., *podos,* foot] by virtue of having five pairs of pereiopods. We will study the crayfish as a representative decapod. The study of the blue crab, which then follows, may be substituted for that of the crayfish or these two decapods may be compared. ■

Crayfish. Crayfish, crawdads, or crawfish are commercially important as food, especially in Louisiana. However, crayfish often are considered to be pests. In some regions they consume young crops and their burrows interfere with cultivation, while in other regions their feeding habits deteriorate habitat previously suitable for game fish.

■ Observational Procedure:

General Anatomy

1. Obtain a preserved crayfish and place it in a dissection pan dorsal side up with the anterior end facing away from you (Fig. 28A). At first glance it is obvious there has been considerable fusion of segments.

2. The large dorsal, saddle-like structure is the carapace. It represents fused segments of the head and thoracic regions into a single unit, the cephalothorax.

3. Locate the transverse **cervical groove** that divides the cephalothorax into its anterior and posterior regions. Anterior to this groove is the head, and posterior, the thoracic region. In the mid-dorsal region of the thoracic portion of the carapace and bounded by the **branchiocardiac grooves** is the **areola**.

4. The fused terga of the carapace curve ventrolaterally to form a rooflike cover known as the **branchiostegite.** The space underneath it is the branchial chamber.

5. Turn the specimen over and reflect to one side one of the branchiostegites (Fig. 28B). Observe the branchial chambers containing the gills.

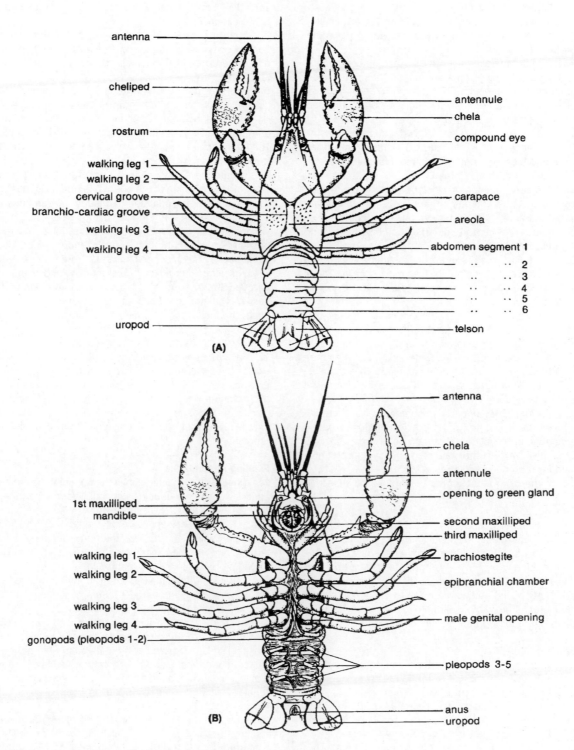

antenna

cheliped

rostrum

walking leg 1
walking leg 2
cervical groove
branchio-cardiac groove
walking leg 3
walking leg 4

uropod

antennule
chela
compound eye

carapace
areola
abdomen segment 1
.. .. 2
.. .. 3
.. .. 4
.. .. 5
.. .. 6
telson

(A)

1st maxilliped
mandible

walking leg 1
walking leg 2

walking leg 3
walking leg 4
gonopods (pleopods 1-2)

(B)

antenna

chela

antennule
opening to green gland

second maxilliped
third maxilliped

brachiostegite

epibranchial chamber

male genital opening

pleopods 3-5

anus
uropod

Figure 28. Male crayfish. (A) Dorsal view. (B) Ventral view.

Phylum Arthropoda

6. Return the specimen to its dorsal side and locate the **rostrum.** To each side of the rostrum are located the stalked compound eyes that are set in ocular depressions (Fig. 28A).

7. Turn the specimen ventral surface up and find the biramous **antennules** (first antennae). These are the anteriormost appendages.

8. Just behind them are the elongate **antennae** (second antennae).

9. The next six pairs of appendages surround the mouth. These feeding structures are, from front to rear, the **mandibles,** first and second **maxillae,** and the first, second, and third **maxillipeds.**

10. The next five pairs of appendages are termed pereiopods. The first pair of pereiopods (**chelipeds**) are large and stout, distally bearing massive chelae. They are used in prey capture, defense, and aggression, and in manipulation of food.

11. The next two pairs of appendages posterior to the chelipeds are also chelate, but are much smaller. These and the following two nonchelate pairs are the walking legs.

12. Turn your attention to the abdomen. There are six abdominal segments (**tergites**). The first five are somewhat bandlike and extended laterally over the sternal plates. The sixth segment is flattened and broader than the others, and bears the tail, consisting of two fanlike biramous appendages called **uropods** and a central plate, the **telson.**

13. Ventrally, the abdomen is somewhat flattened and possesses six pairs of lateral appendages called **pleopods.** In the female the first pair of appendages is diminutive, while in the male the first two pairs are modified for reproductive purposes.

14. In the central part of the telson find the anus.

Appendages

This section gives direction for a detailed study of crayfish appendages. In each instance, observe the appendages in place before they are removed, noting their position, movements, and relationship to other appendages. Each appendage will be compared to the hypothetical biramous crustacean limb (Fig. 21). As the appendages are removed from one side of the body, lay them out in their proper sequence.

Sensory Appendages

1. Manipulate the first antennae (antennule) and determine what its range of motion is. Two **flagella** of unequal length and a **protopod** of three segments compose the first antennae (Fig. 29). The proximal, single segment of the protopod is the coxa. The next two distal segments are a basis of two parts. The flagella attach to the distal joint of the basis. The shorter,

inner flagellum is the **endopod** and the longer, outer one is the **exopod.**

2. The dorsal surface of the coxa of the first antennae when viewed under magnification will show a depressed area. This is the external opening to the **statocyst.**

3. Observe the second antenna, manipulating it to determine its range of motion.

4. Using a scalpel, carefully remove the second antenna, making sure that the coxa remains attached. The large leaflike structure is the exopod, also termed the **squame** or **antennal scale** (Fig. 29).

5. Locate the slightly elevated structure on the coxa and note the opening at the apex. This opening leads to the excretory organ commonly called the **green gland.**

6. Anterior and lateral to the coxa there is the broad second joint of the protopod, the basis. Inward to the basis is the first joint of the endopod, called the **ischiopodite.** The endopod consists of three joints. First is the ischiopodite, next the **meropodite,** and then the **carpopodite.** The latter supports the many-jointed flagellum. The straight margin of the squame is the outer edge; the inner margin is clothed on its margin with a fringe of long setae. Examine the distribution and kinds of setae on all parts of the second antenna.

7. Remove one eye, including the **peduncle** (stalk) and examine it under a dissection microscope.

8. Scrape a portion of the eye's surface and place the scraping on a slide. Add a drop of water and a coverslip; examine under low power of a compound microscope. What pattern do you see? What does this represent?

Feeding Appendages

1. Observe the appendages in the region of the mouth and move them about using a probe. Observe how they articulate and nest together. It is easier to study the crayfish mouthparts by carefully removing the third maxilliped and then proceed anteriorly, appendage by appendage, until the mandibles are reached. The following procedures use this approach.

2. Locate the three maxillipeds. The third maxilliped is the largest and most posterior feeding appendage. It is located anterior to the base of the chelipeds. Lying just anterior to the third maxilliped is the second and ahead of it the first. Carefully remove all three maxillipeds by grasping and pulling each firmly at its base with forceps. Observe that the second and third maxillipeds are similar, being composed of an outer exopod with an extension called the flagellum and an inner endopod of several joints (Figs. 29 and 30).

3. Examine the first maxilliped. The elongate, basal rectangular piece of the first maxilliped is the epipodite, which fits into the gill chamber and assists in water

Phylum Arthropoda

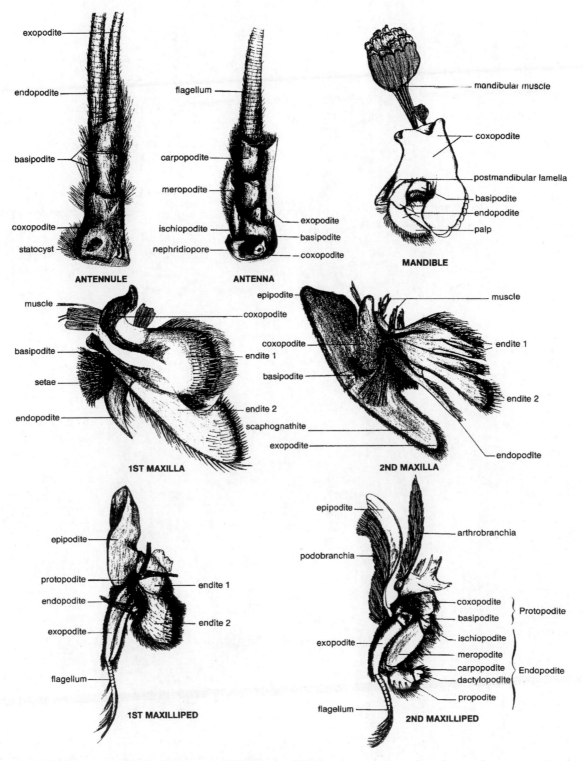

Figure 29. Crayfish appendages: first antennae through second maxilliped.

Phylum Arthropoda

Figure 30. Crayfish appendages: third maxilliped through uropod.

Phylum Arthropoda

movement (Fig. 29). Anterior to the epipodite is the long, narrow, and medially grooved exopod. Distally the exopod has a many-jointed filament called the flagellum. The large, leaflike inner structure is divided into two parts, endite 1 proximally and endite 2 distally. At the base of and in between endite 2 and the exopod is the relatively diminutive endopod. As with the second maxilla, the coxa and basis are not distinctly separated. The central complex of chitinized structures represents a fusion of parts and constitutes the protopod. A large epipodite is attached to a coxa, as are the endites. The endopod and exopod are attached to the basis.

4. Locate the second maxilla. The largest part is the **scaphognathite** or **gill bailer** (Fig. 29). The narrower part lies next to the mandible, while the broader portion extends into the branchial chamber and assists water movement in the chamber. The lateral (inner) part of the second maxilla is divided into four narrowly foliaceous subdivisions. The anterior pair is considered to be endite 2 and the posterior endite 1. The slender, elongate appendage between endite 2 and the scaphognathite is the endopod. The basis and coxa are not distinguishable as separate components.

5. The first maxilla is leaflike (Fig. 29). The smaller, pointed part is the endopod. The two parts lateral to the endopod are endites; the broadest one is endite 1 and the longest is endite 2.

6. Locate the anteriormost feeding appendages, the mandibles, composed of broad, smooth, convex surfaces, with an inner sawlike edge and a blunt finger-like process (Fig. 29). The basal part of the mandible is the coxa and the finger-like structure the **palp**, comprised of three joints. The first joint of the palp is considered the basis and the outer two segments compose the endopod. The exopod is not present on the mandible.

Walking Appendages The first, second, and third maxillipeds are considered the first appendages of the thorax. The next five to be studied are the pereiopods.

1. Locate the first pair of pereiopods, the chelipeds (Figs. 28 and 30). They are the largest of the appendages and are used to capture prey and to tear food apart. Are there major differences between the left and right chelipeds? The remaining four pairs of pereiopods are the walking legs. Of these, only the first two pairs are chelate.

2. Carefully remove all the pereiopods from one side of the body, severing them from the body at the coxa. Note that the exopod is not present in these appendages.

3. On the posteriormost part of the cheliped is a bilamellate, folded **podobranch gill** (arthrobranchia). The lamellated epipodite is membranous and folded as in the second and third maxilliped. The upper lamella is covered with the gill filaments. Near the point where the long, threadlike coxal filaments are located, the plumose arthrobranchia are attached. Even with the greatest of care, the arthrobranchia may be difficult to remove intact.

4. Observe that the chela is made up of the propodite and dactylopodite (Fig. 30). The propodite is extended finger-like at its outer edge, while the dactylopodite is moveable and opposes the propodite, forming a pincer-like structure.

5. Remove a chela from one of the large chelipeds. This is best done by severing the appendage at the carpopodite joint (Fig. 30).

6. Remove the exoskeletal covering from one side of the chela. Judicious use of a nutcracker will be helpful. Note the two sets of muscles. The larger is the adductor muscle; it inserts on the inner edge of the dactylopodite and is instrumental in pulling the dactylopodite toward the propodite, thus providing the pincer action. The smaller abductor muscle reverses the movement.

7. Pereiopods 2 and 3 are chelate and other than in size are very similar to the cheliped. The female crayfish has a **genital operculum** on the inside surface of the coxa of the third pereiopod. The male genital opening is located on the inner surface of the coxa of the fifth pereiopod (Fig. 28).

8. Identify the sex of your specimen, and be able to identify specimens of the opposite sex.

9. The fourth and fifth pereiopods are strictly ambulatory appendages and are nonchelate. Between the coxopodites of the fifth pereiopods, the sternum in some female crayfish is modified as a **seminal receptacle.** This structure is termed the **annulus ventralis.** Sperm released from the receptacle at egg-laying time fertilize the eggs, which are then retained on the under surface of the tail region.

10. The remainder of the crayfish appendages are located on the abdominal region and are called pleopods or **swimmerets** (Figs. 28 and 30). Some of them are similar in structure, but others differ considerably, depending on the sex.

11. Compare the position and morphology of the pleopods on the first and second abdominal segments in male and female crayfish.

12. In the male, the first pair of pleopods are closely associated, directed forward, and modified for sperm transport to the female during copulation. They are called **gonopods** (Fig. 30).

13. In the female the first pleopod is small and is composed of a single stalk (of two joints) with a flattened, distal flagellum. The second female pleopod is the typical biramous appendage characteristic of most abdominal segments (Fig. 30). The sternite to which the pleopod is attached is narrow and ringlike.

14. The remaining pleopods are the same in both sexes

(Fig. 30). The coxa is a small ringlike structure and may be lost unless the limb is carefully removed. The endopods and exopods are flattened, setose, and flagellate. They arise from the stocky basis.

15. The sixth pair of pleopods is the **uropods**. They are similar in both sexes, but radically different in shape compared to the other pleopods. The exopod and endopod are large paddle-like flaps (Fig. 30). The exopod is divided into two sections along a broad joint. The coxa and basis are fused into a large, angular segment from which the exo- and endopods arise.

16. The **telson** is not considered to be an appendage in the same sense as the others studied here. Note that the anus opens through the telson's ventral surface (Fig. 28). The uropods and the telson comprise the tail fan. This structure is used for rapid backward movement.

Gill Chamber Cut away the carapace which covers the gills on the side where appendages are still intact. Be careful to cut only the branchiostegite, not the gills within the chamber. The entire gill system should be exposed undisturbed. Starting at the anteriormost gill,

note how the gills are arranged. Using dissection needles, tease the gills apart to understand their places of attachment and serial arrangement. Resolve: are the gills placed internally or externally?

Internal Anatomy

1. Make a very shallow, midsagittal incision through the carapace, beginning at the posterior dorsal margin, and extend it to the rostrum. Avoid damaging the muscles and other internal organs just beneath the carapace. Remove the carapace anterior to the **cervical groove** (Fig. 28A).

2. With the carapace removed, several muscle groups and other internal organs are exposed. Extending to the rostrum from the stomach are the **anterior gastric muscles** (Fig. 31). The two large muscles at the lateral edge of the stomach are the **mandibular adductors,** and those attached to the posterior dorsal margin of the stomach are the **posterior gastric muscles.** One of the mandibular muscles may have been removed previously when the appendages were being studied, but there should be one left in position. The anterior and posterior set of muscles are important in the mechanical operation of the

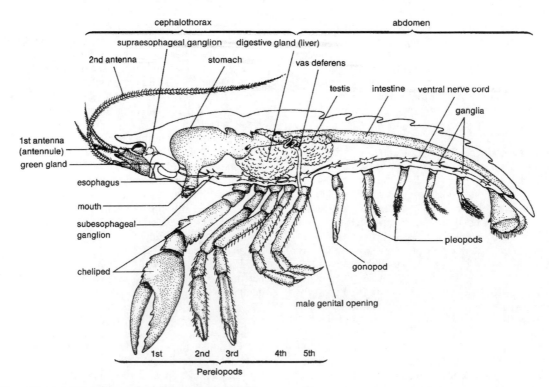

Figure 31. Internal anatomy of the crayfish (diagrammatic).

Figure 32. An internal, ventral view of the gastric mill.

stomach. Dissection a little later will show an intricate set of **ossicles** in the stomach that are moved by muscles assisting in grinding food that enters the stomach.

3.   Gentle movement of the mandibular muscles to one side will reveal the dorsal anterior portion of the digestive gland (Fig. 31).

4.   Cut away the carapace posterior to the cervical groove. This will expose the heart and the principal arterial vessels, reproductive bodies, and the remainder of the hepatic bodies. On each side of the heart are the elongate extensor muscles that manipulate the abdomen. Closely examine the heart and note the **ostia** [L., opening]. If the specimen is a female, the ovary will be found directly in front of and slightly below the heart. If the sex is male, the testes will be located in about the same position.

5.   Remove the right lateral wall of the cephalothorax to the base of the legs. The expansive liver is best shown by this dissection. Identify the green gland (Fig. 31).

6.   Remove the stomach by severing the esophagus from the intestine. Place it in a dissection pan, partially filled with water. Turn the stomach ventral surface up-

ward. Examine the organ with the dissection microscope. Make a longitudinal midsagittal incision and then pin the stomach membrane aside. Identify the several sets of ossicles (Fig. 32) in the stomach called collectively the **gastric mill.**

7.   Also note the unusual lining of portions of the stomach. This serves as a filtering mechanism. In the anterior, lower portion of the stomach, there may appear rounded, flattened structures on each side. These are **gastroliths.** They occur seasonally and will not be present in recently molted individuals.

8.   Now that the stomach and other viscera in the cephalothorax have been removed, direct your attention to the nervous system (Fig. 31). Locate the stub of the esophagus and posterior to it find the **subesophageal ganglion.** Extending around the esophagus are single nerve connectives that communicate with the **supraesophageal ganglion.**

9.   Follow the nerve tract posteriorly to the abdomen. This will necessitate careful dissection as the nerve trunk is closely associated with the inner surface of the exoskeleton.

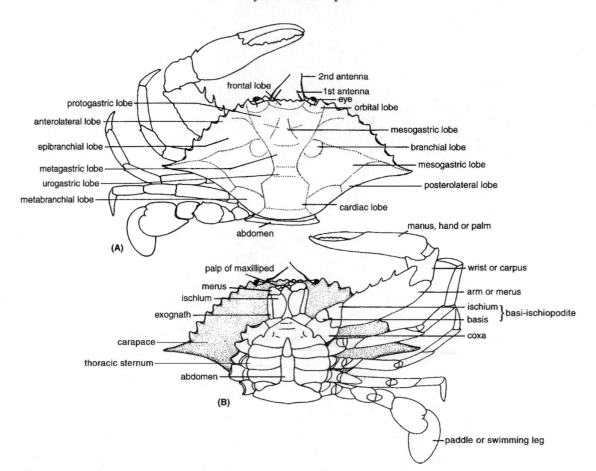

Figure 33. The blue crab, *Callinectes.* (A) External dorsal view. (B) External ventral view of male.

10. Remove the upper exoskeletal surface of the abdomen to the telson (Fig. 31). Locate the hindgut and the superior abdominal artery with its lateral branches. Note the arrangement and distribution of the abdominal flexor muscles.

Live Specimens
Observe the live crayfish on display. How do they move about the aquarium? How does the crayfish react when threatened? As your instructor directs, observe the feeding behavior of crayfish.

Blue Crab. The blue crab, *Callinectes sapidus,* is a common Atlantic and Gulf coast inhabitant of the United States, ranging from Massachusetts Bay to the northern shores of South America. It is commercially important to the fishing industry in the United States. This crab lives in waters ranging in salinity from brackish to normal sea water.

■ Observational Procedure:

External Morphology
Obtain a specimen and compare its morphology with that of the crayfish (see Figs. 28 and 33A,B).
1. Place the crab dorsal side up in a dissection pan. Note that, unlike the crayfish, the blue crab is compressed dorsoventrally and is greatly expanded laterally. The crab is very broad and the legs are spread comparatively farther apart than in the crayfish.
2. Turn the crab ventral side up and find the abdomen, which is folded under the thorax (Fig. 33B). Note that the abdomen is proportionally smaller than that of the crayfish. The abdomen consists of six segments and is narrow and T-shaped in males, triangular in immature females, and broad in mature females.
3. What is the sex of your specimen? Be able to identify crabs of the opposite sex. Find the tubercles on the fifth thoracic sternum of males and immature females that lock the abdomen to the thorax.

4. Locate the anus on the ventral side of the abdomen at its distal end.

5. The ventral side is divided into several regions (Fig. 33B). The area reflected around from the spines to the legs is called the **sub-branchial carapace.** Most of the ventral surface is composed of the **thoracic sternum,** separated from one another by distinct suture lines. The thoracic sterna are more or less covered by the abdomen, depending on the sex.

6. Although the position and anatomy of the gills will be considered later, locate the right and left **inhalant** and **exhalant apertures,** through which water enters and leaves the branchial chambers. The inhalant apertures are located anterior to the coxae of the chelipeds; the exhalant apertures are on either side of the mouth.

Appendages

1. Identify the first antennae (antennules), second antennae, and eyes noting their size, shape, and relative position (Fig. 33A and B). Compare these structures to those of the crayfish. Determine the movements of which each are capable. Locate the depression into which the first antennae fold. What is the significance of the ability to protect the antennae in this way?

2. The feeding appendages are similar to those of the crayfish. Remove a set from one side of the crab and compare them with those of the crayfish. As in the crayfish, it is best to locate the three pairs of maxillipeds in reverse order, followed by the two pairs of maxillae, and then the mandibles.

3. The third maxillipeds are the largest feeding appendages. Progressing towards the mouth, locate the second and third maxillipeds.

4. On each maxilliped, locate the long, setous epipodite called the **flabellum,** that enters the branchial chamber. The three flabella are fringed with setae and function to clean debris from the surface of the gills.

5. Find the second and first maxillae. The second maxillae has a large, platelike exopodite called the **scaphognathite** or **gill bailer.** The scaphognathite beats back and forth to circulate water through the branchial chamber.

6. Locate the mandibles surrounding the mouth. Note their broad, smooth, heavily calcified surfaces. These appendages are used to cut, crush, and hold food, while other appendages process it.

7. The pereiopods are similar in crabs and crayfish, although the basis and ischium are fused into a single unit called the **basi-ischiopodite.** As in the crayfish, the first pair of pereiopods (chelipeds) are chelate and are used to obtain food and for defense. Are these major differences between left and right chelipeds in the crab?

8. Note how the articulation of this pereiopod permits it to be folded closely against the body. The next three pairs of pereiopods are not chelate and are used for walking. If a leg is caught or damaged, it is cast off or **automized** by the crab at the basi-ischiopodite and is later to be regenerated.

9. Find the last pair of pereiopods (Fig. 33). How do they differ from the other pereiopods? These paddle-shaped legs are used in a sculling fashion for swimming.

10. On the ventral surface of the abdomen, locate the pleopods. Only the first two pairs of pleopods are present in the male. They are highly modified and used in copulation. The first pair is larger and possesses an elongate, hollow spine (endopod). The second pair is similar to the first, but its spine is shortened and not hollow.

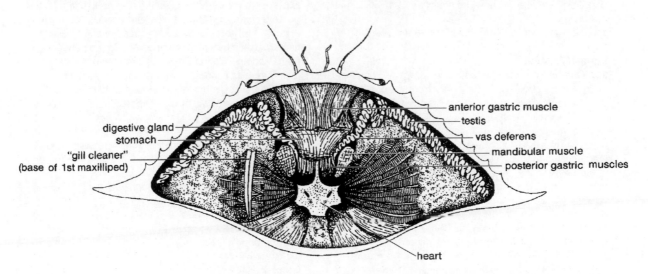

Figure 34. Dorsal internal view of *Callinectes.*

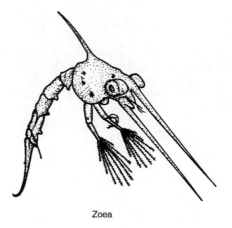

Megalops

Zoea

Figure 35. Zoea and megalops larvae of a crab.

11. Observe that the spine of the second pleopod enters the first pleopod through a hole (anterior foramen) at its base. Spermatophores are pushed through the hollow spine of the first pair by the spine of the second.

12. Examine the pleopods of a female crab. In the female the first pleopods are absent, but the second through the fifth pairs are present and similar. The long endopod and exopod of these appendages possess many setae. These setae help hold the numerous embryos while they develop.

13. Examine a female specimen in **sponge.** The spongy material, composed of hundreds of small balls, is the egg mass. Determine how the eggs are held in place. Occasionally a specimen will be found with 2–3 large roundish masses where the eggs should be. These are the reproductive organs of *Sacculina,* an unusual parasitic barnacle. Review the life cycle of this unusual barnacle.

14. Note that uropods are absent in both sexes.

Internal Anatomy

1. Carefully remove the top of the carapace by making an incision a short distance inward from the dorsal border of the carapace and separate the underlying tissues from the exoskeleton.

2. Locate the heart enclosed within the pericardial cavity by the translucent pericardium and the vessels leading from the heart (Fig. 34). The circulatory system is almost identical to that of the crayfish. The most noticeable organ exposed at this point is the large **digestive gland** (**hepatopancreas**) with left and right lobes.

3. Carefully determine what the extent of the digestive gland is without damaging other tissues (Fig. 34).

4. Find the gonads on the surface of the digestive gland and trace their ducts ventrally just anterior to the heart. Ovarian size may vary considerably in different specimens.

5. Paired **antennary glands** that are excretory in function lie just lateral to the cardiac stomach; they usually are difficult to find.

6. Locate the eight pairs of gills on either side of the crab. The anterior four pairs may be obscured by the digestive gland and gonad (Fig. 34).

7. Remove a gill and examine it using a dissection microscope. Each gill has a central axis and consists of an anterior and posterior row of lamellae.

8. The gut is similar to that of the crayfish. Locate the esophagus, cardiac stomach, pyloric stomach, and intestine. Find the long, narrow midgut cecum extending from the pyloric stomach.

9. Remove the stomach region and identify the nerve ring around the esophagus and the nerves that radiate from it.

10. Locate the cerebral ganglion anteriorly and a large, posterior concentration of ganglia around the sternal artery. From this conspicuous mass radiate separate nerves to all mouthpart appendages, to the pereiopods, to the abdomen, and to a pair of circumesophageal commissures that connect with the cerebral ganglion.

11. If advanced study is to be done of blue crab anatomy, your instructor will provide the necessary directions.

Crab Larval Stages

1. Examine prepared slides of **zoea** and **megalops** larvae (Fig. 35). In each locate the carapace, abdomen, rostrum, and stalked compound eyes.

2. Find the biramous thoracic appendages in the zoea. These will develop into the maxillipeds.

3. Locate the chelipeds and walking legs in the megalops. This is the last stage before final metamorphosis into the adult crab.

Other Specimens

Examine any other malacostracans that your instructor

has provided for study. What similarities do they possess? What differences do you see? How do these other specimens conform (or not) to the idealized of the caridoid facies? Is left and right handedness evident in any of these specimens? Is it exhibited to the same degree?

Live Specimens

1. Observe the live specimens of crabs on display. How do they move about the aquarium? How do the various species react when threatened? Can you observe the bailing activity of the scaphognathites? As your instructor directs, place a small piece of shrimp to one side of the crab. How does the crab respond? Observe the elaborate movements of the mouthparts during feeding.

2. Some crabs will become rigid when they are held by a leg. This phenomenon, aptly termed freeze behavior, is very evident, for example, in the genus *Uca*, especially when the large claw is held. As your instructor directs, attempt to induce freeze behavior in one or more species of crab. Caution: in doing this take extreme care with those animals with strong pinching claws; we recommend the use of tongs or gloves that cannot be pierced by the animal's chelipeds! In doing this exercise consider the following questions. Is freeze behavior evoked to the same extent when different appendages are held? Which appendages summon the strongest freeze response? Which the weakest? Speculate on the functional significance of freeze behavior. Why might it be evident in some species and not in others or for some appendages and not others? ∎

D. Subphylum Uniramia

Class Insecta (Hexapoda)

All insects belong to the Class Insecta (in-SEC-tah; L., *insectum*, insect). These arthropods are the dominant and most successful group of all invertebrates, especially in the invasion of terrestrial habitats. Insects are the only invertebrates capable of flight. There are probably not less than 750,000 described insect species; however, some recent estimates of the actual number of extant insect species may reach 10 million. The ecological and economical impacts insects have on local and worldwide populations of plants and animals are tremendous. The study of insects is called **entomology** [G., *entomon*, insect + G., *logy*, study], often with emphasis in medical entomology and economic entomology.

The bodies of adults are divisible into three **tagmata:** an anterior **head,** middle **thorax,** and posterior **abdomen.** The head typically bears two antennae, five eyes (two compound and three ocelli), and mouthparts. Six legs and usually two pairs of wings in the adults are attached ventrolaterally and dorsolaterally to the thorax, respectively. The thorax is always composed of three segments.

Classification

Class Insecta is often divided into two large subclasses based primarily on the structure of the mouthparts. Each subclass is further divided into orders based on features including internal anatomy, modes of development, and presence or absence of wings. Familiarity with the principal characteristics of the orders is a necessity for the beginning student of insect biology.

Some of the more common orders are characterized below.

1. Subclass Entognatha. Mouthparts in a pouch; wingless insects lacking metamorphosis.

a. Order Collembola. Springtails. These small insects possess an abdominal organ for jumping and chewing mouthparts. They are found in leaf litter.

2. Subclass Ectognatha. Mouthparts not in a pouch. Except for two orders, primarily winged insects; the wingless condition, if present, has been secondarily acquired. Metamorphosis present or absent depending on the group.

a. Order Thysanura. Silverfish and bristletails. These fast-moving insects possess two or three styliform appendages on the abdomen and chewing mouthparts. They are destructive to clothing and books.

b. Order Ephemeroptera. Mayflies. The first pair of net-veined wings are larger than the second pair. Animals possess two or three caudal appendages. Mouthparts of short-lived adults are a vestigial chewing type. Metamorphosis is gradual.

c. Order Odonata. Dragonflies and damselflies. Wings are long and net-veined. Mouthparts are chewing type. Dragonflies possess a stout body and are stronger fliers than are damselflies. Metamorphosis is gradual.

d. Order Orthoptera. Grasshoppers, katydids, crickets, roaches, and allies. The winged forms of this large order generally have the membranous hind wings folded beneath the leathery forewings (tegmina). The femur of hind legs is enlarged in many species. Mouthparts are chewing type. Metamorphosis is gradual.

e. **Order Isoptera.** Termites. The abdomen is broadly joined to the thorax. Bodies are soft and often whitish. These colonial, social insects have winged and wingless individuals. Wings are equal in length. Mouthparts are chewing. Metamorphosis is gradual.

f. **Order Hemiptera.** True bugs. The basal part of the forewings is thickened, while the distal part is membranous, overlapping at rest. The hind wings are membranous. Piercing-sucking mouthparts form a beak arising at the front of the head. Metamorphosis is gradual.

g. **Order Homoptera.** Aphids, cicadas, and leaf-hoppers. Both winged and wingless individuals are known. The forewings are membranous unlike those of Hemiptera. (Many entomologists make this order a suborder of Hemiptera.) Piercing-sucking mouthparts form a beak arising from back of the head. Metamorphosis is gradual.

h. **Order Neuroptera.** Lacewings, ant lions, and dobsonflies. Both pairs of wings are veined and membranous. Mouthparts are a chewing type. Metamorphosis complete. Larva of ant lions commonly called doodlebug; larva of dobsonfly is a hellgrammite; larvae of one family (Sisyridae) live in and eat freshwater sponges.

i. **Order Coleoptera.** Beetles. Anterior wings are thick and hard and called **elytra**. Membranous hind wings, when not in use, are folded under the elytra. Metamorphosis is complete. Mouthparts are a chewing type. This is the largest insect order, with over 300,000 species. The larva stage commonly called a grub.

j. **Order Lepidoptera.** Butterflies and moths. Body and wings in the adult are covered with minute scales. A coiled proboscis is used for sucking nectar from flowers. Metamorphosis is complete. The larva is commonly called a caterpillar.

k. **Order Diptera.** Flies and mosquitoes. Hindwings reduced to knoblike **halteres**. Mouthparts are piercing-sucking and lapping types. Metamorphosis is complete. The larva is commonly called a maggot.

l. **Order Hymenoptera.** Ants, bees, wasps. Winged and wingless species occur in this large order. The wings are transparent with few veins. Both solitary or social species are known. Mouthparts are modified for chewing, lapping, or sucking. Metamorphosis is complete.

m. **Order Siphonaptera.** Fleas. The bodies of small, wingless insects are compressed laterally. The legs are modified for jumping. Adults possess piercing-sucking mouthparts. Metamorphosis is complete.

■ Observational Procedure: *Romalea*

The grasshopper or locust (Order Orthoptera) will be used to illustrate basic insect anatomy. Obtain a large specimen such as the lubber grasshopper (*Romalea*), a common species found in the southern United States.
1. Observe the body markings, coloration, and reduced wings that are characteristic of the species (Fig. 36). Note that the grasshopper is segmented. Is there evidence of tagmatization? How many tagma do you see?
2. As in all insects, the external, protective covering is a tough, nonliving **cuticle** or **exoskeleton** containing **chitin**. The hardened sclerotized plates of the cuticle are called **sclerites**. The major sclerites are typically separated by membranous areas called sutures that permit movement of body parts. A dorsal sclerite is the **tergum,** a ventral one the **sternum,** and a lateral one the **pleuron.** In areas (e.g., head) where individual segments are fused, the terga (or tergites) are fused as a solid hardened mass. The sclerites also may be divided into subplates.
3. Locate the three tagmata composing the grasshopper's body: (1) anterior head, (2) middle thorax, and (3) posterior abdomen (Fig. 36).

Head
1. The head is in the form of a capsule (Figs. 36 and 37A). The upper part is heavily sclerotized and the ventral area contains the mouth surrounded by several mouthparts used in feeding. Exact agreement by entomologists does not exist as to the number of segments in the insect head. Note the shape of the head and its position in relation to the long axis of the body. The mouthparts of the grasshopper are directed downward, a position called **hypognathous**.
2. The head capsule is divided by sutures into several regions. It is often difficult to discern where one region begins and the other ends. The dorsum of the head between and behind the eyes is the **vertex** (Fig. 37A). The frons is the anteriofrontal region. Note on the **frons** the two arms or forks of the Y-shaped **epicranial su-**

ture whose stem begins on the back of the head. The forks are called the **frontal suture** and the stem the coronal suture. The epicranial suture represents a line of weakness that splits the head capsule at molting.

3. Find the **gena** or cheek, which is located at the lateral lower part of the head posterior to the **frons** and below the eyes. The back of the head is the occipital that contains the **occipital foramen** (or foramen magnum).

4. Examine the anterior face of the head (Fig. 31). Locate the liplike sclerite, the **clypeus**, below the frons to which it is attached. Hanging down from the clypeus is the **labrum** or upper lip.

5. Lift the clypeus with forceps to fully expose the bilobed labrum (Fig. 37B). Does the labrum articulate directly to the clypeus? A swollen area, the **epipharynx**, is prominent in many insects on the ventral or posterior side of the labrum. Does the grasshopper have an epipharynx?

6. Behind the labrum are paired, unsegmented **mandibles**. Lift up the labrum with your forceps to expose these paired, hard mouthparts with teeth used to cut, chew, and grind food. The mandibulate insects include other orthopterans, odonates, isopterans, and coleopterans.

7. Behind the mandibles are the paired maxillae. These masticate and manipulate food. Note the antenna-like, segmented **palps** attached on top of the maxillae. How many segments compose a palp? The palps are sensory structures.

8. Other parts of a maxilla are as follows: the basal **cardo**, the **stipes** with a palp, the outer **galea**, and the inner jawlike **lacinia**. These areas are best observed when the maxillae are dissected out (Fig. 37B). Although the **labium** is a single structure, it represents fused paired second maxillae. The labium also manipulates food and has paired sensory palps. Note the three regions on the labium: basal **postmentum** (divided into a basal submentum and distal mentum), middle **prementum** with palps, and distal **ligula** with apical lobes.

9. The labium should be dissected from the grasshopper and observed with the dissection microscope (Fig. 37B).

10. Locate the median, unpaired tongue-like **hypopharynx** that protrudes in the preoral cavity. The hypopharynx is closely associated with the base of the labium. Your instructor may have you dissect out all of the mouthparts and examine them under the dissection microscope (Fig. 37B).

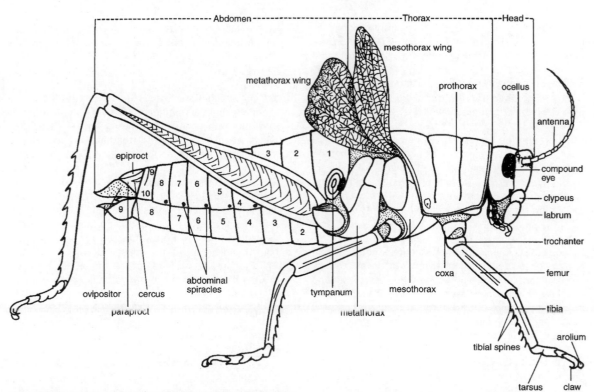

Figure 36. Lateral view of a female lubber grasshopper, *Romalea*.

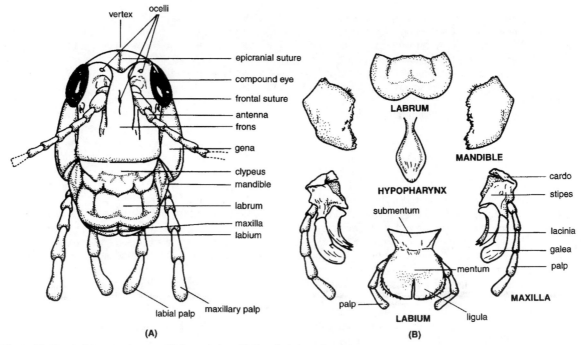

Figure 37. Head of the grasshopper. (A) Frontal view. (B) Detailed view of mouthparts.

11. Note the shape and position of the two large immovable **compound eyes** (Fig. 37A). Examine an eye under the dissection microscope. How does it compare to the eyes of the other arthropods that you have examined? Note the many hexagonal **facets**. Each facet is a lens to an **ommatidium**, the basic structure of the eye. The number of ommatidia varies; some dragonflies have up to 30,000.

12. Between the compound eyes and on the frons are three single-faceted simple eyes or **ocelli**. Note that the arrangement of the ocelli forms a triangle. The ocelli apparently perceive changes in light intensity, whereas the compound eyes form images.

13. Below the two lateral ocelli are two antennae (Fig. 37A). These movable sensory appendages articulate in antennal sockets. A variety of shapes and sizes of antennae occurs in insects. They function in touch, smell, and hearing. The grasshopper's antennae are thread-like or **filiform**. Remove an antenna from its socket and examine it under the dissection microscope. Note the tiny sensory hairs on the antenna. Locate the basal scape, the middle **pedicel**, and the long **flagellum** consisting of many segments (Fig. 38).

Cervix or Neck

Connecting the head and thorax is a membranous region called the **cervix** or **neck.** It is not a separate body

segment, but a contribution from the labial segment and the prothoracic segment. The cervix allows flexibility of movement between the head and thorax regions.

Thorax

1. All insects have three segments to the thorax: anterior **prothorax,** middle **mesothorax,** and posterior **metathorax** (Fig. 36). Each bears a pair of legs. The parchment-like forewings (or **tegmina**) are attached to the mesothorax and the hind wings are attached to the metathorax.

2. Observe the wing coloration and the folded shape of the hind wings (Fig. 36). Flight is primarily by the hind wings. Note the many veins in the wings. What function might they perform? The venation pattern is important in insect taxonomy. Both wings are outgrowths of the body wall and lack internal muscles.

3. Examine the sclerites of the thorax. Each tergum or dorsal plate on the thorax is called a **notum.** The wings are attached to the lateral margins of the nota.

Figure 38. Insect antenna.

Figure 39. Insect leg.

4. Note the greatly sclerotized sterum. The different specialized plates and sutures of the notum and sternum will not be studied.

5. Each pleuron is divided by a suture forming two sclerites. The anterior sclerite is the **episternum** and the posterior one the **epimeron.** Observe these with the dissection microscope.

6. Two pairs of **spiracles,** external openings to the tracheal respiratory system, occur on the thorax above the attachments of the second and third pairs of legs. You will observe that these locations are between the prothorax and mesothorax and between the mesothorax and metathorax, respectively.

7. Observe the legs. Each leg consists of six parts: **coxa, trochanter, femur, tibia, tarsus,** and **pretarsus** (Fig. 39). The short basal coxa articulates with the body.

8. Note the shape of the greatly enlarged femur of the last pair of legs. What adaptation might this enlarged part serve?

9. Note the two rows of spines on the tibia. Are the spines of both rows equal in size and number? Why are the spines located on the dorsal surface of the tibia instead of the ventral surface? What function do they serve?

10. Count the segments of the tarsus. Note the tarsal pads or **pulvilli.** How many are there and what function might the pads serve? The short pretarsus also has an adhesive pad, the **arolium,** and a pair of **claws.**

Abdomen

1. Observe that the abdomen is distinctly segmented and lacks jointed appendages (Figs. 36 and 40). Count the abdominal segments. The first segment bears a **tympanum,** an oval membrane covering the organ of hearing. The last pair of segments is reduced and limited to a tergite, the **epiproct,** below which lies the **anus.**

2. Observe the tergite and anus under the dissection microscope. Note the small spine or **cercus** projecting behind the tenth segment. The plate below the cercus is the **paraproct.** Although reduced in size, the cercus is one of the few appendages found on the abdomen.

The other appendages on the abdomen are reproductive in function.

3. At the end of the abdomen in female grasshoppers is a pincer-shaped **ovipositor** for digging a hole in the ground for deposition of eggs. Observe the bladelike structures (**valvulae**) that compose the ovipositor (Fig. 40).

4. Male grasshoppers lack the ovipositor. Note that the expanded sternum of segment 9 (the **subgenital plate**) encloses the male copulatory organs.

5. Observe the terga and sternal plates of the abdominal segments. Note their arrangement. Are pleural sclerites present?

6. On the lower anterior edge of each abdominal tergite of segments 1 to 8 is a small oval spiracle that leads to an internal trachea of the respiratory system (Fig. 40). Observe the spiracles with the dissection microscope. Some may be situated in a pigmented area and be difficult to see. Counting those on the thorax and those on the abdomen, the grasshopper has 10 pairs of spiracles. The first four pairs are used in inspiration and the remaining pairs function in expiration.

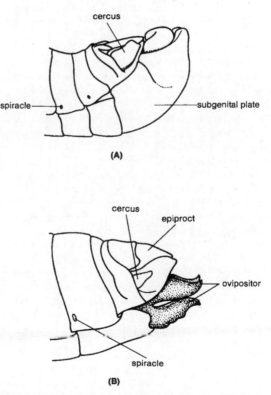

Figure 40. Posterior end of the grasshopper. (A) Male. (B) Female.

Phylum Arthropoda

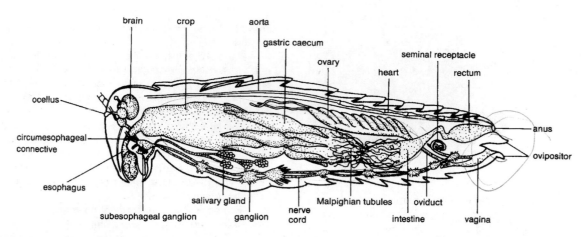

Figure 41. Internal anatomy of a female grasshopper.

Internal Anatomy

Much of the internal anatomy of the grasshopper will be difficult to observe. Therefore, exercise care in dissection and observation.

1. With a pair of fine-pointed scissors, clip off the wings close to the body. Make a very shallow midsagittal cut through the dorsal body wall beginning at the head and ending at the posterior end. Pin down the two halves of the body wall to the dissection tray.

2. The large cavity exposed and containing the internal organs is the **hemocoel** (Fig. 41). This is not a true body cavity or coelom but part of the **open (lacunar)** circulatory system. The hemocoel is filled with blood or **hemolymph.** The **heart** is an elongated slender tube in the dorsal part of the abdomen. It extends anteriorly as an aorta. Although the heart is difficult to see, make an attempt to locate it.

3. Note the muscles along the body wall, especially those in the thorax associated with the legs and wings. The muscles of the grasshopper are in bands.

4. Note the whitish, delicate tubes extending from the body wall to the viscera. These are **tracheae.** Prepare a wet mount of a piece of a trachea and examine it using a compound microscope. Describe the appearance of the tracheae. How are they constructed?

5. Components of the digestive system are the most conspicuous of the internal organs. Much of the hemocoel is filled with the digestive system (Fig. 41). Locate the tube-shaped **esophagus** leading from a short **pharynx** that connects to the mouth. The esophagus enlarges posteriorly as a thin-walled **crop** in the thorax. The crop leads to a narrow **proventriculus** (or **gizzard**) with internal gastric teeth for shredding food.

6. You may see salivary or labial glands below the crop, with a duct opening in the preoral cavity between the labium and hypopharynx. The components above compose the foregut (or **stomodeum**) of the grasshopper's digestive system.

7. Posteriorly the proventriculus leads to an elongated **stomach** or **ventriculus.** Much of the stomach is concealed by finger-shaped **gastric ceca.** These are involved in nutrient absorption. How many are present? The stomach and gastric ceca constitute the midgut (**mesenteron**).

8. Connecting to the stomach posteriorly is an **intestine,** with an enlarged anterior component and a slender posterior component, an enlarged **rectum** and the **anus.** The intestine, rectum, and anus constitute the hindgut (**proctodeum**).

9. The many threadlike excretory organs called **Malpighian tubules** and other organs such as those originating from the reproductive system may conceal parts of the hindgut. Care must be exercised not to destroy these structures.

10. Grasshoppers are dioecious. Females possess the egg-laying ovipositor, whereas males lack this structure and thus have a rounded posterior end (Fig. 40). Females lay their eggs in the ground in late summer or early fall. In the following spring, the eggs hatch into immature grasshoppers (or **nymphs**). They undergo several molts before attaining the adult form.

11. Examine a male grasshopper and locate as many of the following parts as possible (Fig. 42). The two fused **testes** of the male lie dorsal to the intestine. A slender tube, the **vas deferens,** extends from each testis. The tube passes posterioventrally and becomes enlarged as a reservoir, the **seminal vesicle,** before uniting to form a common **ejaculatory duct** that enters the **penis.** Two **accessory glands** that secrete a fluid join the ejaculatory duct.

12. Examine a female grasshopper. Several tapering **ovarioles** or egg tubes where eggs are produced from an

Figure 42. Reproductive systems of the grasshopper. (A) Male. (B) Female.

ovary. Extending from each ovary is an **oviduct.** The two oviducts join to form the **vagina,** an egg-holding chamber located under the intestine. Two **accessory glands** and a **seminal receptacle** (or **spermatheca**) enter the vagina separately. Sperm received from the male during copulation are stored in the receptacle.

13. Insects possess a highly developed nervous system (Fig. 41). It is similar to that of the crayfish and, for the most part, the system lies below the digestive system. Attempt to observe the following components of the grasshopper's nervous system. The central nervous system consists of a **trilobed brain** located in the head above the esophagus. Extending off the brain is a pair of **circumesophageal connectives** that connect to a **subesophageal ganglion.** The ganglion innervates the mandibles, maxillae, and labium. Extending posteriorly in the insect is the paired **ventral nerve cord** with one pair of ganglia per segment.

Adaptability of Structure

Insects provide excellent opportunities for students to study specializations and adaptability of structures. Morphological modifications in insects can be seen in most structures, but especially in the mouthparts, legs, antennae, and wings. Selected examples of insects showing adaptations and specializations of these structures will be observed.

Mouthparts Insect mouthparts are adapted for feeding on different types of food. As a result, different methods are employed for food procurement. Some of the major types are biting and chewing, chewing and sucking, lapping (sponging), piercing and sucking, and siphoning. The grasshopper and cockroach (Order Orthoptera) are good examples of insects with biting and chewing mouthparts. Many zoologists believe the other specialized mouthparts observed in many insects have evolved from the biting-chewing type. As you study the following examples, it is important that you keep in mind the mouthparts of the grasshopper previously examined as a basis for making comparisons.

1. Chewing and sucking: honeybee (*Apis*). The mouthparts of the honeybee (Order Hymenoptera) are used for biting and chewing wax and sucking or lapping nectar from flowers. Examine a preserved honeybee or prepared slide of the insect's mouthparts (Fig. 43). Note the arrangement of hairs on the head and mouthparts. Below the clypeus is the narrow **labrum** and a smaller fleshy **epipharynx.** Note that the **mandibles** project laterally alongside the labrum. Are teeth similar to those observed on the grasshopper's mandibles present? Locate the medial, hairy **labium.** The specialized labium, also called the **glossa** or **alaglossa,** forms an extensible organ for probing into flowers. **Labial palps** and **maxillae** occur on each side of the tongue-like labium. These fit against the labium, forming channels through which saliva is discharged and food drawn up to the mouth.

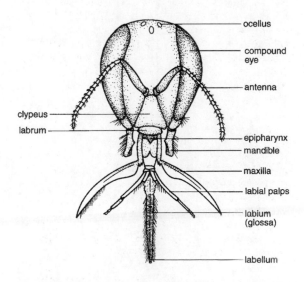

Figure 43. Mouthparts of the honeybee.

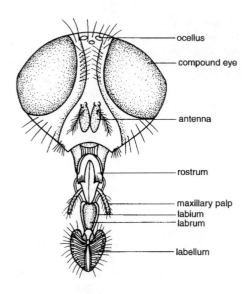

Figure 44. Mouthparts of the housefly.

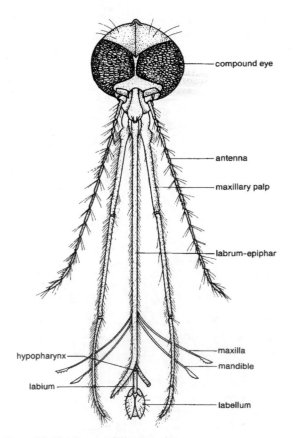

Figure 45. Mouthparts of the mosquito.

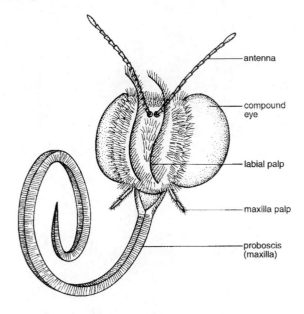

Figure 46. Mouthparts of the butterfly.

2. Lapping (sponging): housefly (*Musca*). The non-biting fly (Order Diptera) extrudes saliva onto food and then sponges or laps the dissolved food-saliva mixture into the mouth. Examine the mouthparts of a housefly from a preserved specimen or prepared slide. The feeding part is a highly modified **proboscis** with a basal rostrum and a distal labium which is modified at the extreme end as a sponge-like, bilobed **labellum** (Fig. 44). On the anterior face of the proboscis is the **labrum-epipharynx**, which covers a labial groove in which lies the bladelike **hypopharynx**. The epipharynx and hypopharynx interlock, forming a food tube to the esophagus. **Mandibles** are lacking as are most of the **maxillae** except for two maxillary palps. Unlike the housefly, other dipterans, such as horseflies and deer flies, have sharp, bladelike mandibles to cut flesh and maxillae serve as long probing styes. These flies are blood feeders. In contrast to the mandibulate insects with mandibles designed for cutting, grinding, and chewing, the housefly has **haustellate** mouthparts, in which the mandibles are stylelike for sucking or are completely absent.

3. Piercing and sucking: mosquito (*Anopheles*). The haustellate mouthparts of the female mosquito (Order Diptera) are elongated for piercing and sucking. Except for the paired maxillary palps, the mouthparts collectively form a **proboscis**. Examine a prepared slide of a female mosquito's mouthparts that have been teased apart (Fig. 45). The largest mouthpart is the hairy **labium**, with a flexible tip called the **labellum**. Note the central groove of the labium, into which the other needle-like mouthparts lie when not in use. Alongside the labium are two hairy, segmented sensory **maxiliary palps**. These are as long as the labium in *Anopheles*, but generally shorter in *Culex*. The non-hairy **labrium-epipharynx** and narrow ribbon-like **hypopharynx** form a tube for drawing blood into the mouth. The hypopharynx contains a small tube for ejecting saliva into the puncture and thus prevents clotting of the blood. The flexible labellum of the labium guides the piercing mouthparts. Observe the thin, flat paired **maxillae** and paired **mandibles** also used in piercing. The maxillae bear teeth on one edge of a narrow fin-shaped tip. The mandibles are similar but are more delicate, with finer teeth.

4. Siphoning: butterfly. Moths and butterflies (Order Lepidoptera) have mouthparts designed for siphoning nectar and juices from flowers. Examine a preserved specimen or prepared slide of the mouthparts of a butterfly **(Fig. 46)**. The long siphoning tube is the **proboscis**, fused galeae of the maxillae. When not in use, the proboscis is held coiled between the sensory labial palps.

Legs Although the insect legs are composed of six basic parts (Fig. 39), many modifications and specializations of these appendages can be observed. Certain insects possess legs designed for performing more than one type of locomotion. For example, the first and second pairs of legs of the grasshopper are used in walking or crawling, whereas the third pair is designed for leaping. Selected examples of insect legs that illustrate adaptations to different types of locomotion will be available for your study. Your instructor will direct your study.

1. Ambulatory (e.g., walking, running, crawling): cockroach, walkingstick (Order Orthoptera), butterfly (Order Lepidoptera), stink bug (Order Hemiptera), ant (Order Hymenoptera), and termite (Order Isoptera). Describe the function of these legs in terms of a tripod.

2. Grasping and holding prey: first pair of legs of a praying mantis (Order Orthoptera), ambush bug, and giant water bug (Order Hemiptera). What crustacean has similar grasping legs?

3. Swimming (flattened parts with long brushes of hair): third pair of legs of a backswimmer, water boatman (Order Hemiptera), and diving beetle (Order Coleoptera). How are these legs like paddles?

4. Digging: first pair of legs of the mole cricket (Order Orthoptera) and digger wasp (Order Hymenoptera). Are these legs like shovels or rakes?

5. Clinging or holding by suction: housefly (Order Diptera). How are connections to surfaces maintained by housefly legs?

6. Hopping, leaping, or jumping: third pair of legs of a cricket, grasshopper, katydid (Order Orthoptera), flea (Order Siphonaptera), and leafhopper (Order Homoptera). Describe the springlike mechanisms of these legs.

7. Floating or skimming on water surface: water strider (Order Hemiptera). How are these legs like oars?

8. Gathering and carrying pollen: honeybee (Order Hymenoptera). Where is the pollen held?

9. Sound production: file on inner surface of hind femur of an acridid grasshopper (Order Orthoptera). Are the spines the noise-making devices (i.e., do they vibrate) or do they pluck something that vibrates?

Antennae Other extremely varied appendages of insects are the antennae. These delicate structures range in size from very short (e.g., housefly, Order Diptera; dragonfly, Order Odonata; giant water bug, Order Hemiptera) to being very long (e.g., camel cricket and true katydid, Order Orthoptera; longhorn beetle, Order Coleoptera). In the latter, the antennae may be longer than the insect's entire body. Antennae even vary in shape between the male and female of the same species. For example, female mosquitoes have beadlike antennae, whereas the male's antennae are plumose. The antennae of males in many of the giant silkworm moths (Order Lepidoptera) are feathery and larger than those of the females. Within large orders of insects such as Hymenoptera and Coleoptera, great variations in the shape, number of segments, and size occur in the antennae. Some of the more common and perhaps striking types of antennae are shown in Fig. 47 and listed below along with representative adult insects. Observe these and other examples with the dissection microscope.

1. Filiform (threadlike). The segments have a uniform size. Examples: silverfish (Order Thysanura), dytiscid and ground beetles (Order Coleoptera), vespid wasp (Order Hymenoptera), mole cricket (Order Orthoptera).

2. Setaceous (tapering). The segments become more slender distally. Examples: dragonfly and damselfly (Order Odonata), lacewing (Order Neuroptera).

3. Serrate (sawlike). The segments are triangular in shape. Examples: click beetle and firefly (Order Coleoptera).

4. Clavate (clubbed). The segments increase gradually in diameter distally. Examples: ladybird and June beetles (Order Coleoptera).

5. Capitate (having a head). The terminal segments enlarge suddenly. Example: histerid beetle (Order Coleoptera).

6. Lamellate (leaflike). The terminal segments form oval lobes. Examples: June, dung, and unicorn beetles (Order Coleoptera).

7. Pectinate (comblike). Most segments have long lateral processes. Examples: male European sawfly (Hymenoptera), fire-colored beetle (Order Coleoptera).

8. Plumose (feathery). Most segments have many hairs. Examples: males of chironomids, mosquitoes

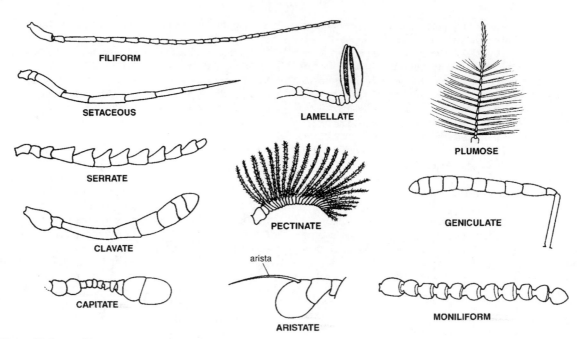

Figure 47. Types of insect antennae.

(Order Diptera); giant silkworm moths (Order Lepidoptera).

9.   Aristate. The last segment with a dorsal bristle (arista). Examples: housefly and syrphid fly (Order Diptera).

10. Geniculate (elbowed). The first segment is long and the following smaller segments are at an angle. Examples: ant (Order Hymenoptera), stag and histerid beetles (Order Coleoptera).

11. Moniliform (beadlike). The segments resemble a string of similar-shaped beads. Examples: wringled bark and tenebrionid beetles (Order Coleoptera).

Wings The presence of wings undoubtedly is a major feature that has contributed to the success of insects. Most insects have two pairs of wings. Insect wings are outgrowths of the body wall and structurally unlike those of bats and birds, which are modified forelimbs. Considerable variation in the size, texture, shape, number, venation, and position held at rest exists in insect wings. Examples of these variations will be observed in selected representative insects.

1.   Size. The more primitive winged insects have both pairs of wings equal or nearly equal in length. Observe a dragonfly or damselfly (Order Odonata). Note the size of the wings in relation to the body length. Unlike many insects, mayflies (Order Ephemeroptera) and dragonflies and damselflies cannot fold their wings over the abdomen when at rest. Examine the wing lengths of other insects

from different orders. How do they compare?

2.   Texture. Many insects, such as the dragonfly, have all four wings of the same membranous texture. Members of the Orders Orthoptera and Coleoptera have the first pair of wings parchment-like or hard, respectively. The grasshopper's forewings are called **tegmina** because of their leathery texture. Examine other orthopterans, such as the field cricket and American cockroach. Note the texture of the forewings compared to that of the hind wings. The hard forewings of beetles are called **elytra**. Observe examples of beetles showing variations of the elytra; note how the membranous hindwings are folded under the forewings. True bugs of the Order Hemiptera have the proximal part of the forewings harden and the distal part membranous. This half-wing condition (**hemelytron**) is reflected in the ordinal name, Hemiptera. Butterflies and moths (Order Lepidoptera) have wings covered with numerous **scales**, hence the name Lepidoptera. The scales easily rub off when the wings of these insects are held by the fingers. The different types and arrangement of scales give the different patterns observed in these insects' wings. Examine several scales from different moths or butterflies under the compound microscope. Describe the patterns you observe. Are all of the scales of the same type on a given individual?

3.   Number. Most adult insects have four wings. Adult members of the Order Diptera (two wing) are unique in having only one pair of well-developed wings. The second pair, called **halteres**, is reduced and knoblike. Examine representative flies or mosquitoes with a dissection microscope to see the halteres. What function might these reduced wings serve?

4.   Venation. One of the most important features of insect wings used by the taxonomist is the venation pattern. An extensive terminology, which will not be elaborated on, has been developed to describe the number and arrangement of the veins in insect wings. The more primitive insects have a larger number of veins than do the advanced forms. Compare the venation of a dragonfly or damselfly (Order Odonata) with that of a wasp or bee (Order Hymenoptera). Examine the venation in the wings of insects representing different orders. Can you determine whether a basic pattern exists in the venation? The veins are tracheae that extend into the wing. The areas between the veins are called cells. ∎

Myriapodous Arthropods

The myriapodous (G., *myrias*, number 10,000 + G., *podos*, foot) are wormlike, uniramous arthropods that live in moist dark places such as beneath wood, rocks, leaf litter, and in unused parts of buildings. The 10,500 species are divided into four classes: Chilopoda (ki-LOP-o-dah; G., *cheilos*, lip + G., *podos*, foot) the centipedes; Diplopoda (dip-LOP-o-dah; G., *diplos*, double + G., *podos*, foot) the millipedes; Pauropoda (paur-OP-o-dah; G., *pauros*, small + G., *podos*, foot) the pauropods; and Symphyla (sim-PHY-la; G., *symphylos*, of the same race + G., *phylon*, a tribe) the symphylans.

Two tagmata, the head and trunk, compose the bodies of these arthropods. The head bears a pair of segmented antennae, a pair of mandibles, an upper lip (labrum), a tongue-like hypopharynx, and one (in millipedes and pauropods) or two (in centipedes and symphylans) pairs of maxillae. Some species of millipedes and centipedes have nonimage-forming ocelli or compound eyes on the head. Pauropods and symphylans lack eyes.

Most people are familiar with centipedes and millipedes, that comprise the vast majority of myriapods. However, the pauropods and symphylans are seldom observed; the former at 2 mm or less in length, and the latter are no more than 8 mm in length. Here you will study only centipedes and millipedes.

Classification

The four classes of myriapods are probably polyphyletic and may be related to insects. Pauropods and diplopods are considered closely related, whereas chilopods and symphylans form another group of similarity.

(1) Class Chilopoda. Centipedes. Myriapods with flattened bodies. Trunk with many segments each possessing one pair of legs. The first pair of trunk appendages (maxillipeds) are poisonous. Head with two pairs of maxillae. A genital opening is located at the posterior end. Most centipedes are swift-moving, carnivorous predators. Examples: *Scolopendra* and *Scutigera*.

(2) Class Symphyla. Symphylans. Myriapods with a small, flattened body. The trunk is composed of 12 segments, with one pair of legs per segment. Head with two pairs of maxillae. A genital opening is located on the third trunk segment. Symphylans are plant feeders and are often found in greenhouses. Examples: *Scutigerella* and *Scolopendrella*.

(3) Class Diplopoda. Millipedes. Myriapods with a cylindrical body. The trunk is composed of diplosegments each with two pairs of legs. Head with one pair of maxillae (gnathochilarium). A genital opening is located anteriorly on the trunk. Most millipedes are slow-moving herbivores. Examples: *Julus* and *Spirobolus*.

(4) Class Pauropoda. Pauropods. Small, soft-bodied myriapods with biramous antennae and one pair of maxillae (gnathochilarium). The trunk is composed of 11 segments, but legs are absent on segments 1 and 11. Pauropods are vegetarians and inhabitants of leaf litter and soil. Examples: *Pauropus* and *Allopauropus*.

∎ Observational Procedure:

1.   Obtain a specimen each of a centipede and a millipede (Figs. 48 and 49). Compare the shapes of their bodies, the number of segments, and number and arrangement of legs attached to the segments.

2.   Note the less flexible and harder body of the millipede compared to that of the centipede. Calcium salts in the millipede's procuticle harden the sclerites, especially the tergites.

3.   What type of segmentation occurs in the two animals? Are all segments the same size? Compare the tergites, pleurites, and sternites of the two animals. Are intergites present? What adaptations might be correlated with a flattened body as in the centipede and the cylindrical body of the millipede?

4.   Observe the specimens under the dissection microscope. Locate the anterior **head** and the posterior **trunk** (Figs. 48 and 49). The greater part of the body of both animals is the trunk. The first four trunk segments of millipedes are often called collectively a

Figure 48. Millipede body form. (A) Anterior lateral view. (B) Cross section. (C) Posterior view of head. (D) Posterior lateral view.

Figure 49. Centipede body form. (A) Dorsal view. (B) Ventral view. (C) Anterior lateral view. (D) Lateral view of trunk, showing location of a spiracle.

thorax. The first thoracic segment is called the **collum** and is legless (Fig. 48). Segments 2 to 4 bear one pair of legs. Locate these segments. Note the flattened head of the centipede and the round head of the millipede. The individual segment composing the heads of both arthropods is not readily discernible.

5. Examine with the dissection microscope the legs of both animals. Are all of the legs on each animal of the same size? Note the **diplocondition** in the millipede; this results from fusion of two originally separate segments.

6. Are claws or pads present similar to those on the grasshopper's legs? Are the number of leg segments for both animals the same? In centipedes the last pair of legs are longer than the others and are sensory or defensive in function.

7. Locate the **spiracles**. Look for the small openings in the pleural membrane dorsal to each leg (except the first and last three segments) of the centipede (Fig. 49). In the house centipede (*Scutigera coleoptrata*) each spiracle is centrally placed on a tergum and opens to a saclike tracheal lung. Millipedes have two spiracles per segment on the sternal plate near the base of the legs. How does this relate to the diplocondition? It may be necessary to remove carefully two or three pairs of legs to clearly reveal the spiracles. In some millipedes there are paired lateral openings on the terga that communicate with internal **repugnatorial glands** that secrete hydrogen cyanide, iodine, and phenol.

8. Now locate the **gonopores** behind the second pair of legs in the millipede. The gonopore of centipedes is on the last trunk segment, that also bears the anus (Fig. 49). In some millipedes the legs of segment 7 or 8 may be modified for reproductive purposes.

9. Examine the centipede's head with the dissection microscope (Fig. 49). Observe the two antennae and paired, nonimage-forming eyes. How many pairs of eyes are on your specimen? Not all centipedes have eyes,

and some centipedes (e.g., Order Scutigeromorpha) have clusters of ocelli that form compound eyes.

10. Observe the ventral area of the head and locate the paired **forcipules** (Fig. 49). Each is composed of an enlarged basal coxa and poison claw or fang; internally, a poison gland and duct are present. The forcipules represent the first trunk appendages or maxillipeds. A centipede's bite, inflicted by the fang, can be painful.

11. Carefully remove both forcipules with your scissors. This will expose the leglike second maxillae (**palpognaths**) with paired palps. Lift up these maxillae with a probe to see the smaller first maxillae. Below the first maxillae are paired mandibles with distal teeth, between which is located the mouth. Anterior to the mouth and mouthparts is a hard plate, the **clypeus,** bordered anteriorly by the **epistome**.

12. Observe with the dissection microscope the round head of your millipede. Locate the broad epistome, that at its ventral margin is inseparably connected to the labrum.

13. Find the paired antennae, segmented, teeth-bearing mandibles, and the broad ventral plate called the **gnathochilarium** formed by fusion of the first maxillae (Fig. 48). Note that the lateral mandibular bases are large and immovable. The flexible cutting edges of the mandibles are covered by the gnathochilarium. The gnathochilarium in some species is divided into a medial **mentum** and lateral **stipes** (Fig. 48). Unlike centipedes, millipedes lack second maxillae.

14. Are eyes present on your specimen? Some species of millipedes have ocelli that are grouped together and give the impression of being compound.

15. Locate the anus of the millipede at the posterior end between two **paraproct plates** (Fig. 48). Ventral to these is a single plate, the **hypoproct**. Find the anus of your centipede on the ventral area of the last trunk segment (Fig. 49).

Phylum Arthropoda

Phylum Arthropoda				Worksheet 10	
Name: _____			Date: _____		
Course #: _____ / Section #: _____			Grade: _____		

1. Fill out this table.

Group Habitats	Cultural significance	Ecological importance	Economic importance	Parasite forms	Other medical importance
Trilobites					
Chelicertes					
Crustaceans					
Insects					
Myriapods					

Using the information you provided in your table, write an essay on the topic "some arthropods have a significant impact on humans."

Phylum Arthropoda

1. Students often remark how similar the general body form of the horseshoe crab *(Limulus)* is to that of trilobites. How are trilobites and horseshoe crabs similar? How are they dissimilar?

2. Lobster, fiddler crabs, hermit crabs, other crabs, and certain shrimp have one claw larger than the other one. Of what significance is handedness in crustaceans?

3. Given the location and morphology of pectines in scorpions, speculate on the function of these structures.

4.   Discuss how ticks are adapted to take blood meals.

5.   Provide a brief sketch of a *Daphnia* showing the spatial relationship among the following features: helmet, second antennae, and musculature of the antennae. Using the concept of a working lever arm system, indicate the location of the Fulcrum (Δ), place where the Force (F) is applied, and point where the Work (W) is done in a *Daphnia* which is doing its hop-sink swimming movements. (NB: This question is not as straightforward as it seems. Consider carefully, for example, the same question but in terms of a canoe or rowboat.)

6.   Copepods have a slow cruising speed and also can make very rapid jumps, yet their antennae are not involved. What two features possessed by copepods are used in performing these two different types of movements? Discuss.

7. What end is up on a barnacle like *Lepas?*

8. Are the gills of crayfish, lobsters, and crabs located inside or outside of the body of the animal? Discuss.

9. What is the function of the scaphognathite or gill bailer in crustaceans?

Phylum Arthropoda

10. Assume a fellow student asked you this question. Why does the Earth have so many insects as to both number of species and individuals? Write your answer as a concise essay covering at least five strong reasons where you account for this tremendous diversity.

11. Support or refute the statement that myriapods are more closely related to insects than to crustaceans and arachnids.

OTHER PROTOSTOME PHYLA

Three small, schizocoelomate, protostome phyla are listed here as a matter of convenience: Echiura, Priapulida, and Sipuncula. Priapulida is believed by some zoologists to be a member of the pseudo-coelomates, while others place it near to the arthropods and their allies. Thus, the best we can say at this time is that the specific relationship of these phyla within the protostome line is uncertain. Only the Sipuncula are studied here due to lack of readily available study material.

Cuttler, E.B. 1994. *The Sipuncula: their Systematics, Biology, and Evolution.* Cornell University Press, Ithaca.

Kohn, A.J. and M.E. Rice. 1971. Biology of the Sipuncula and Echiura. *BioScience* 21: 583–584.

Rice, M.E. 1985. Sipuncula: developmental evidence for phylogenetic inference. *In: The Origins and Relationships of Lower Invertebrates.* Conway Morris, S., J.D. George, R. Gibson, and H.M. Platt. (eds.). Clarendon Press, Oxford.: 274–296.

Storch, U. 1991. Pripulida. *In: Microscopic Anatomy of Invertebrates.* Volume 4. Harrison, F.W. and E.E. Ruppert, (eds.) Wiley-Liss, New York, NY: 333–350.

Winnepenninckx, B. M. H., T. Backeljau, and R. M. Kristensen. 1998. Relations of the new phylum Cycliophora. *Nature* 398: 636–638.

Winnepenninckx, B., T. Backeljau, L.Y. Mackey, J. M. Brooks, R. De Wachter, S. Kumar, and J.R. Garey. 1995. 18S rRNA data indicate that aschelminthes are polyphyletic in origin and consist of at least three distinct clades. *Mol. Biol. Evol.* 12: 1132–1137.

■

Phylum Sipuncula (Sipunculida)

Sipuncula [sigh-PUN-ku-la; L., *sipunculus,* little siphon] is a small phylum of about 320 species of vase-shaped, wormlike, marine organisms. They are commonly called peanut worms because their contracted bodies resemble a peanut. When extended, the **trunk** is usually vaselike or plump (Fig. 1). The anterior part of the body or the neck region, called the **introvert,** constitutes at least one-half to two-thirds the length of the worm, and is capable of being rapidly everted and retracted. Segmentation and setae are lacking. At the end of the introvert is the mouth, surrounded by modified, lobate, ciliated tentacles. The tentacles are hollow, but do not communicate with the body cavity. Most sipunculans (sipunculids) live a sedentary life in burrows or tubes. Internally, sipunculans have a spacious coelom and an elongated, U-shaped, digestive system (Fig. 1). The mouth is located at the anterior part of the body from which the gut is directed posteriorly only to be recurved, opening at the anus, which is located near the junction of the introvert and trunk.

Classification

Two classes are recognized.

1. **Class Phascolosomatidea.** Sipunculans with tentacles confined to an arc surrounding the nuchal organ. Peripheral, circumoral tentacles are absent. Examples: *Aspidosiphon* and *Phascolosoma.*

2. **Class Sipunculidea.** Sipunculans with peripheral, circumoral tentacles. Examples: *Phascolopsis, Golfingia, Phascolosoma* and *Sipunculus.*

■ Observational Procedure:

Examine the external anatomy of several peanut worms (Fig. 1). Locate the anterior and posterior ends, trunk, introvert, mouth with tentacles, and anus. Note the variations in size and shape of tentacles among species available for study.

From *Invertebrate Zoology,* Sixth Edition, Robert L. Wallace and Walter K. Taylor. Copyright © 2002 by Pearson Education, Inc. Published by Prentice-Hall, Inc. All rights reserved

Phylum Sipuncula

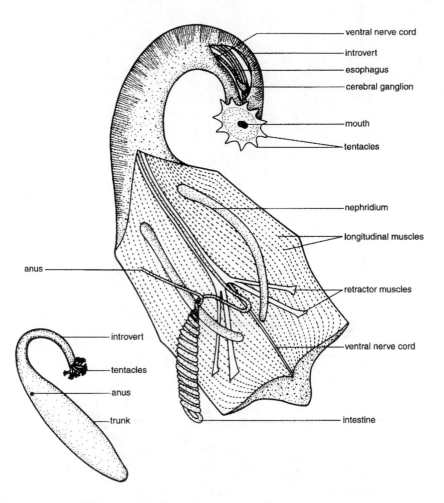

Figure 1. External and internal anatomy of the sipunculan, *Phascolosoma agassizii.*

If specimens are available for dissection, make a shallow, midsagittal, dorsal incision with scissors through the body wall slightly to one side of the anus. Extend the cut forward to the tip of the introvert and backwards as far as possible. Pin the body wall open and locate the internal organs (Fig. 1). Observe the introvert under a dissection microscope to see the many minute spines and sensory papillae. Examine the inner side of the tentacles surrounding the mouth and find the groove that conveys food to the mouth. ∎

THE LOPHOPHORATES

Lophophorates constitute a group of coelomates (Phoronida, Bryozoa, Brachiopoda) each possessing an anterior crown of tentacles called a **lophophore**. This structure is responsible for feeding and gaseous exchange. Traditionally a lophophore is defined as a set of tentacles encircling the mouth, but not the anus, and into which a portion of the coelom (mesocoel) extends (Hyman 1959: 229). Although there are exceptions, typical lophophorates are sessile, vermiform or clamlike organisms with a reduced head, U-shaped digestive tract, and a leathery to hard case.

Based on Hyman's definition of the lophophore, Phylum Entoprocta does not possess a lophophore. Nevertheless some argue for an affinity between Entoprocta and Bryozoa (Nielsen 1977b) and we cover them here (cf. Mackey et al. 1996).

The phylogenetic position of the lophophorates is as controversial as ever, and several competing phylogenies have been proposed over the years. They may be a closely related group (clade) with affinities to the deuterostomes (Zimmer 1973; Farmer 1977; Valentine 1981; Willmer 1990). Valentine (1973) suggests placing them in the Superphylum Lophophorata and Emig (1984) recommends that that group receive the status of phylum. However, an opposing view is offered by Nielsen (1977a, 1985, 1995) who considers lophophorates to be an unnatural assemblage of protostomes (Bryozoa) and deuterostomes (Phoronida and Brachiopoda).

Phylum **Cycliophora**, was proposed to have affinities to the Bryozoa and Entoprocta (Funch and Kristensen 1995) but that view has been challenged by Winnepennickx et al. (1998).

Emig, C. 1984. On the origin of the Lophophorata. *Z. Zool. Syst. Evolut.-Forsch.* 22: 91–94.

Farmer, J.D. 1977. An adaptive model for the evolution of the Ectoproct life cycle. R.M. Woolacott and R.L. Zimmer (eds.), *Biology of Bryozoans*. Academic Press, NY, pp. 487–517.

Funch, P., and R.M. Kristensen. 1995. Cycliophora is a new phylum with affinities to Entoprocta and Ectoprocta. *Nature* 378: 711–714.

Halanych, K.M., J.D. Bacheller, A.M.A. Aguinaldo, S.M. Liva, D.M. Hillis, and J.A. Lake. 1995. Evidence from 18S ribosomal DNA that the lophophorates are protostome animals. *Science* 267: 1641–1643.

Hyman, L.H. 1959. The Invertebrates: *Smaller Coelomate Groups,* Vol. 5. McGraw-Hill NY.

Mackey, L.Y., B. Winnepennickx, R. De Wachter, T. Backeljau, P. Emschermann, and J.R. Garey. 1996. 18S rRNA suggests that the Entoprocta are protostomes, unrelated to Ectoprocta. *J. Mol. Evol.* 42(5): 552-559.

Nielsen, G. 1977a. The relationship of Entoprocta, Ectoprocta and Phoronida. *Am. Zool.* 17: 149–150.

Nielsen, C. 1977b. Phylogenetic considerations: the Protostomian relationships. R.M. Woolacott and R.L. Zimmer (ed.), *Biology of Bryozoans*. Academic Press, NY, pp. 519–534.

Nielsen, C. 1985. Animal phylogeny in the light of the trochaea theory. *Biol. J. Linn.* Soc. 25: 243–299.

Nielsen, C. 1995. *Animal Evolution*. Oxford University Press, NY.

Valentine, J.W. 1973. Coelomate Superphyla. *Syst. Zool.* 22: 97–102.

Valentine, J.W. 1981. The Lophophorate Condition. Lophophorates, Notes for a Short Course. University of Tennessee, Knoxville, TN.

Willmer, P. 1990. *Invertebrate Relationships: Patterns in Animal Evolution*. Cambridge University Press, Cambridge, UK.

Winnepennickx, B.M.H., T. Backeljau, and R.M. Kristensen. 1998, Relations of the new Phylum Cycliophora *Nature,* 393: 636–638.

Zimmer, R.L. 1973. Morphological and developmental affinities of the Lophophorates. G.P. Larwood (ed.), *Living and Fossil Bryozoa*. Academic Press, New York, pp. 593–599.

Phylum Bryozoa

Phylum Bryozoa [BRI-o-ZO-ah; G., *bryo*, moss + G., *zoa*, animals] comprises a group of sessile, predominantly colonial lophophorates, some of which superficially resemble hydroids or macroalgae. Many of the 4,000 living (extant) species of bryozoans are found in the marine shallow subtidal zone, but specimens have been recovered from depths greater than 8,000 m. There are a few common freshwater genera. The common name "moss animal" is fitting, because bryozoans grow in water as colonies, sometimes forming mosslike blankets of growth over the object to which they are attached (Fig. 1). Two alternate names are used for this phylum: Ectoprocta and Polyzoa. Ectoprocta emphasizes that the anus is located outside of the lophophore in contrast to the Phylum Entoprocta or Kamptozoa. Polyzoa emphasizes the colonial aspect of members of the phylum.

Although each individual unit, or **zooid**, is usually less than 1 mm, the colony, or **zoarium**, may attain many centimeters in length and contain thousands of zooids (Fig.1). An individual zooid consists of two basic parts: a protective exoskeleton called the **zoecium** (zooecium) and the softer, internal viscera. Zoecia may be gelatinous, chitinous, or calcareous and are secreted by the epidermis of the body wall. The body wall and zoecium together are referred to as the **cystid**, while the rest of the animal, including the lophophore, digestive apparatus, and associated viscera, constitutes the **polypide**. In forms with calcareous zoecia, an orifice permitting eversion and retraction of the lophophore may be covered by a lid or **operculum**.

Some bryozoans have more than one type of zooid and therefore are polymorphic. **Autozooids** are responsible for feeding (Fig. 2), while **heterozooids** have other diverse functions. For example, the heterozooids called **avicularia** (Fig. 3) resemble bird beaks that open and close rapidly to deter predators or settling larvae. Another type of heterozooid, the **vibraculum** (Fig. 4) sweeps away debris, settling larvae and tube-building invertebrates. In the sand-dwellers, *Discoporella* and *Cupuladria*, the vibraculum is used to move these bryozoans vertically through and over the sand.

All freshwater and most marine bryozoans are hermaphroditic. Some species have internal fertilization and brood-developing embryos until they are competent to settle. An example of this is the **coronate** larvae of *Bugula* (Fig. 5A). These spherical larvae are nonfeeding (lecithotrophic) and have sufficient maternal reserves to survive up to 24 hours. Other nonbrooding bryozoans have external fertilization, releasing huge numbers of gametes into the water column. If fertilized, planktotrophic larvae, such as the flattened, bivalve-like **cyphonautes** larvae of *Membranipora* (Fig. 5B) result. Depending on food availability, these larvae may spend weeks to months in the plankton before settling. After attachment and metamorphosis the resulting zooid, called the **ancestrula**, grows and produces additional zooids by budding.

Much marine research has focused on bryozoans for three reasons: (1) some bryozoans contain, or harbor bacteria that contain, novel chemical compounds that are presently being tested as cancer cell inhibitors.

From *Invertebrate Zoology*, Sixth Edition, Robert L. Wallace and Walter K. Taylor. Copyright © 2002 by Pearson Education, Inc. Published by Prentice-Hall, Inc. All rights reserved

Figure 1. Freshwater bryozoan colony, *Hyalinella*.

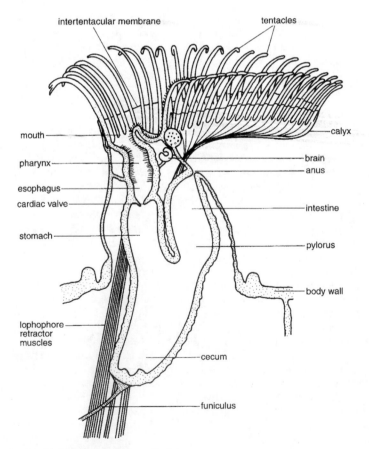

Figure 2. A freshwater bryozoan zooid showing internal morphology.

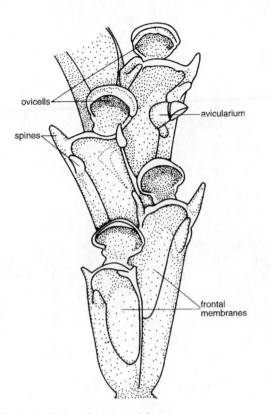

Figure 3. Portion of a colony of *Bugula*.

Figure 4. Vibraculum.

(2) Bryozoans settle in huge numbers on submerged surfaces such as the hulls of ships and industrial intake pipes, thereby creating a major biological fouling problem. (3) It is easy to obtain large numbers of larvae for experiments. Recent research on larvae of *Bugula* shows they preferentially settle in small crevices and survival is greater in these locations (Walters 1992a,b). Additionally, researchers have found that in still water, larvae of *Bugula* repeatedly contact and leave surfaces in search of a suitable settlement spot. However, in moving water, once a larva contacts a surface, the larva explores the surface until it settles, is consumed or destroyed by resident invertebrates, or is dislodged (Walters et al. 1999).

Walters, L.J. 1992a. Field settlement locations on subtidal marine hard substrata: is active larval exploration involved? *Limnol. Oceanogr.* 37:1101–1107.

Walters, L.J. 1992b. Post-settlement success of the arborescent bryozoan *Bugula neritina* (L.): the importance of structural complexity. *J. Exp. Mar. Biol. Ecol.* 164:55–71,

Walters, L.J., G. Miron, and E. Bourget. 1999. Endoscopic observations of invertebrate larval substratum exploration and settlement. *Mar. Ecol. Prog. Ser.* 182: 95–108.

Classification

Three classes of bryozoans are recognized.

1. **Class Phylactolaemata.** Freshwater polymorphic bryozoans comprising about 50 species usually with a horseshoe-shaped lophophore and statoblasts. Calcified zoecium is lacking. Examples: *Fredericella, Pectinatella, Plumatella*, and an unusual form, *Cristatella*, where the entire colony slowly glides on a muscular sole.

2. **Class Stenolaemata.** Marine bryozoans with tubular, calcified zoecia. One extant order (Cyclostomata) and several orders that became extinct during the Paleozoic. Example: *Crisia*.

3. **Class Gymnolaemata.** Mostly marine bryozoans with a circular lophophore and polymorphic zooids.

   a. **Order Ctenostomata.** Mostly marine bryozoans with noncalcified zoecia and a stoloniferous to somewhat flattened growth form. Zooids without an operculum. Examples: *Zoobotryon, Amathia*, and *Paludicella* (freshwater genus).

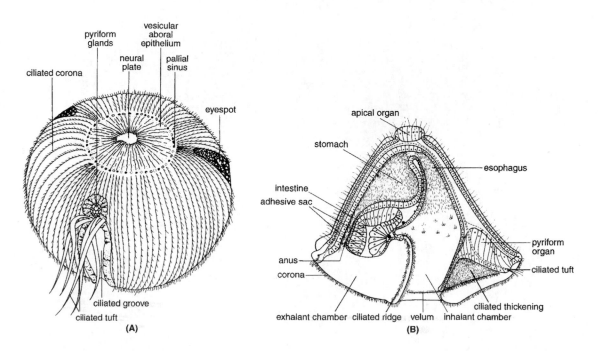

Figure 5. Generalized bryozoan larval types. (A) Coronate. (B) Cyphonautes. (After Woolacott & Zimmer, and Nielsen, respectively.)

b. Order Cheilostomata. A large group of widely-distributed marine bryozoans having a box-like, variably calcified zoecium, with an operculum. Zooids are polymorphic with avicularia and/or vibracula. Examples: *Bugula, Cupuladria, Discoporella, Electra, Membranipora,* and *Schizoporella.*

■ Observational Procedure:

We will begin our observations of bryozoans with a prepared slide of the common marine cheilostome *Bugula* because it is easy to see the general features of the phylum. Specimens from other genera will then be compared to *Bugula.*

Bugula

1. Although the zooids of *Bugula* are small (ca. 500 μm long), colonies may attain heights of a few centimeters (Fig. 3). Examine a prepared slide or preserved specimen under a dissection microscope or low power of a compound microscope. Start by focusing on a zooid at the base of the colony and scan the entire colony, taking note of the branching pattern formed by asexual budding. What type of branching pattern does *Bugula* exhibit? Occasionally one may find a specimen with a developing bud.

2. As you scan the colony you should note the predominance of the autozooid. However, the avicularia may be seen attached to the autozooid by a short **peduncle**. Examine an avicularium in profile under higher magnification and observe the rostrum (beak), mandible, and powerful musculature that closes the mandible. A sharp tooth may be seen on the mandible.

3. Now observe the lophophores of several autozooids (Fig. 2). How many tentacles does an autozooid have? If the bases of the tentacles were connected by a line, what would be the general shape of the figure thus created?

4. Try to locate the mouth which is centrally located at the base of the tentacles. Inside the zooid lies the gut and associated viscera.

5. Scan the colony and find an individual that allows you to trace the entire digestive tract. Beginning with the mouth, locate the esophagus, cardiac valve, stomach with caecum, pyloric valve, rectum, and anus (Fig. 2). Note that the anus empties outside the lophophore. Trace the guts of other zooids. Is food present?

6. If the specimen were part of a fully grown colony it may have **ovicells**. These globular or hemispherical structures will be situated at the distal (upper) end of some of the zoecia. Inside you may see a developing embryo.

7. Not all of the autozooids are still functional. At the

Phylum Bryozoa

base of the colony several almost empty zoecia may be seen. In some of these you may see a small, darkly stained structure. This is the **brown-body**; it consists of the cellular remnants of a degenerated zooid.

8. Compare *Bugula* and a cnidarian hydroid such as *Obelia*. List the similarities and differences you see and organize your findings in tabular form. For example, compare *Bugula* and *Obelia* in size, location of zooids, and overall body shape. Are tentacles grouped the same way about the mouth for both animals? Is polymorphism displayed to the same extent in each phyla? If not, how does it differ? Trace the gut in each specimen and note how it is different. Finally, devise a simple key, table, and/or word description that will permit someone who has never seen these organisms to distinguish them.

Encrusting Marine Bryozoans

Observe a specimen of an encrusting bryozoan (Fig. 6). Details of dried specimens may be improved by adding a drop of bleach to remove the outer coverings. To enhance the contrast of the calcareous skeleton you may wish to add a dab of food coloring, using a fine-tipped camelhair brush, to a few zooids. Note how the growth form differs from that of *Bugula*. The autozooids are found in calcareous, boxlike zoecia so that the entire colony resembles a brick wall. At one end of the zooid an orifice can be seen which may or may not have a lid-like operculum. Ovicells, avicularia, vibracula, and spines may be present depending on the species.

Freshwater Bryozoans

In contrast to the two marine gymnolaemates just studied, now observe a freshwater phylactolaemate such as *Pectinatella* and/or *Plumatella*. Are shapes of their lophophores the same as those of *Bugula*? How would you describe the shapes? Note the numerous tentacles in this species. How many are there? Trace the gut of your specimen. How is it similar to that of *Bugula*? Running from the lophophore to the base of the animal you may see the lophophore retractor muscle; it should not be confused with the **funiculus**. The funiculus, if present, may be seen attached to the base of the stomach and connected to the body wall. Scattered along the length of the funiculus may be several statoblasts in various stages of development (Fig. 7).

Live Specimens

1. Observe the manner of rapid retraction and gradual extension of the lophophore. Describe how the lophophore is retracted and extended. (NB: This is a good example of a muscular/fluid hydraulic mechanism.)

2. Note moving cilia on the tentacles in expanded individuals. One also may observe flicking of the whole tentacles. This process, which varies among species, is a mode of transporting food particles toward the mouth and rejecting unwanted materials.

Figure 6. Encrusting marine cheilostomate bryozoans.

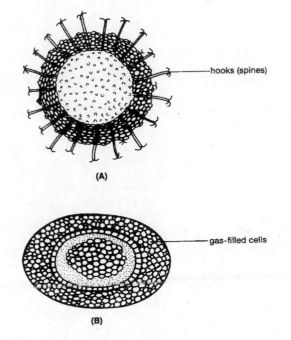

Figure 7. Phylactolaemate statoblasts. (From Barnes, after Allman.)

Phylum Bryozoa

TIME (IN MILLIONS OF YEARS)

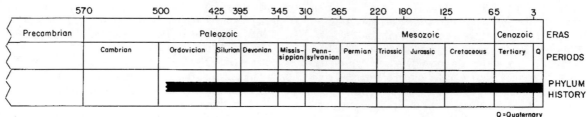

	570	500	425	395	345	310	265	220	180	125	65	3	
Precambrian	Paleozoic							Mesozoic			Cenozoic		ERAS
	Cambrian	Ordovician	Silurian	Devonian	Missis-sippian	Penn-sylvanian	Permian	Triassic	Jurassic	Cretaceous	Tertiary	Q	PERIODS
													PHYLUM HISTORY

Q = Quaternary

Figure 8. Geologic history of the Phylum Bryozoa.

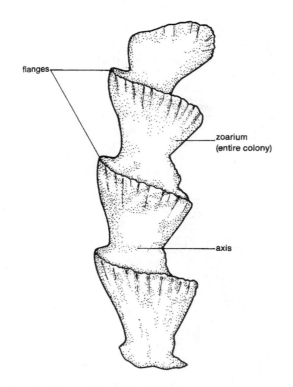

flanges

zoarium (entire colony)

axis

Figure 9. The fossil bryozoan *Archimedes.*

3. Using a Pasteur pipette, gently add a few drops of water containing some yeast, carbon black, or carmine red near the lophophore and observe the feeding currents. Note that the feeding currents run down into the center of the lophophore crown and then out the sides between the tentacles.

4. In active colonies of some encrusting cheilostomates, such as *Membranipora,* the autozooids lean away from a particular area thereby leaving a blank site called a **chimney**. Chimneys represent areas where water, filtered by the lophophores, exits the colony's surface. These transient structures cannot be seen when the lophophores are retracted but appear to be important in preventing interference between neighboring lophophores. Chimneys apparently have a constant location on the surface of the colony. To verify this, observe the pattern of chimneys across the colony's surface before you disturb the zooids and after the lophophores re-emerge. Periodic ingestion of particles by the pharynx and the rotating food cord in the stomach should be observed.

Fossil Forms

First appearing in the early **Ordovician Period** nearly 500 million years ago, bryozoans have a rich geologic history (Fig. 8) with more than 16,000 described species. Unfortunately, a formidable nomenclature exists within the literature on fossil bryozoans. We will not take time to present the details of this discipline. Identification and detailed study are done from longitudinal and tangential thin sections which have been prepared from fossils.

Observe the fossil specimens available for study using a hand lens or dissection microscope. Students should be able to observe the orifice of each individual zooid. One interesting genus, *Archimedes,* which occurred from the **Mississippian** through **Permian Periods**, resembles a water-screw and was named after the inventor of that device (**Fig. 9**). Examine several fossil bryozoans for the presence of numerous small bumps scattered fairly uniformly over the surface. Many fossil stenolaemates have these bumps. They are known as **monticules** and are believed to be the Paleozoic equivalent of the chimneys discussed above. ■

Phylum Brachiopoda

Brachiopoda [brak-e-OP-o-da; G., *brachio*, arm, G., *pod*, foot] contains about 400 species of lophophorates found in marine intertidal areas to depths up to 7,600 m. The animals are less than 10 cm long and are enclosed in two shells. At first glance brachiopods resemble bivalve mollusks. However, they are different in two major ways: (1) brachiopods possess a lophophore and (2) the shell is very different from that of bivalves. Shells of most bivalves are arranged laterally, consisting of right and left valves, the plane of symmetry passing between the valves. Valve orientation in brachiopods is such that the two valves assume a dorsoventral position and are normally bilaterally symmetrical; the plane of symmetry passes through the valves (Fig. 1). Furthermore, brachiopod valves are often dissimilar in size and shape (Fig. 2); in most bivalves the shells are nearly mirror images of one another. In most brachiopods the larger **pedicle valve** is ventral and the smaller **brachial valve** dorsal. In epifaunal inarticulate brachiopods, this size relationship is reversed. Another feature of most modern brachiopod shells is the posterior extension of the ventral valve to form a **beak** that bears a **foramen** for exit of an attachment stalk or **pedicle**. This makes the shell resemble a Roman oil lamp and it is for this reason that brachiopods are called **lamp shells** (Fig. 2D). The two valves may articulate by teeth and sockets at the posterior margin. If teeth and sockets are absent, a complex musculature permits sliding and rotation of the valves.

Classification

The Phylum is divided into two classes.

1. **Class Articulata.** Brachiopods with articulating teeth and sockets at the posterior margin of the shell. In the beak of the ventral valve is a foramen through which the pedicle passes, permitting attachment of the animal to hard substrates. The digestive tract is incomplete, ending as a blind intestine. The shell is composed of $CaCO_3$ (calcite). Examples: *Laqueus*, *Terebratalia*, and *Terebratulina*.

2. **Class Inarticulata.** Brachiopods that lack articulating teeth and sockets. A large pedicle serves as an anchor in sediments or for attachment to hard substrates. In some species the ventral valve is cemented firmly to the substrate. Digestive tract is complete. Most shells are composed of $Ca_3(PO_4)_2$. Examples: *Crania*, *Discinisca*, *Glottidia*, and *Lingula* (a genus in existence since the **Silurian Period**).

■ Observational Procedure:

1. Compare the general shell morphology of an articulate brachiopod (*Terebratalia*, Fig. 1 and *Terebratulina*, Fig. 2), an inarticulate brachiopod (*Lingula* or *Glottidia*, Fig. 3), and a bivalve mollusk (the oyster *Crassostrea* or clam *Mercenaria*). Identify

From *Invertebrate Zoology*, Sixth Edition, Robert L. Wallace and Walter K. Taylor. Copyright © 2002 by Pearson Education, Inc. Published by Prentice-Hall, Inc. All rights reserved

Phylum Brachiopoda

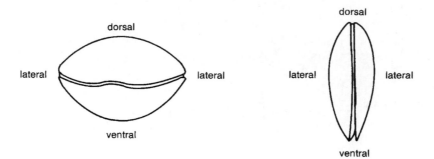

Figure 1. Comparison of the shell morphology of a brachiopod and a bivalve mollusk. Both are shown in an anterior view, thus right- and left-hand sides of the organisms may be determined.

dorsal and ventral valves of each specimen. Contrast the symmetry of the brachiopods with that of the bivalves. How do the shells of the bivalves resemble the two brachiopods? What are the differences?

2. Identify anterior and posterior ends of each brachiopod. Setae will be visible along the lateral shell margins of *Lingula* (Fig. 3). The brachiopods should have at least a portion of the pedicle visible. How might each of these specimens be oriented in its natural habitat? Compare these positions to the two bivalves and/or other specimens provided by your instructor.

3. Examine the internal anatomy of an articulate-brachiopod by separating the two valves (Figs. 2 and 4). To do this gently pry apart the valves at the anterior until the hinge breaks. During this procedure, one or more sets of muscles may be pulled off their attachments. Note where they were attached. Sometimes it may be necessary to cut the adductor and/or diductor muscles using a fine dissection blade to separate the valves completely. Take care not to destroy the lophophore and other internal organs.

4. Observe the looped lateral arms and central coiled portion of the lophophore. How does the lophophore of

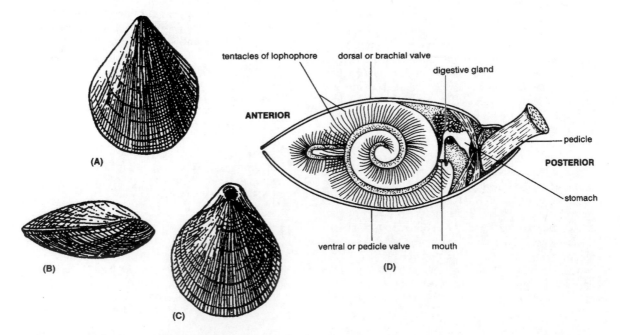

Figure 2. *Terebratulina,* an articulate brachiopod. (A) Ventral view of pedicle valve. (B) Side view. (C) Dorsal view of brachial valve. (D) Sagittal section showing the internal anatomy.

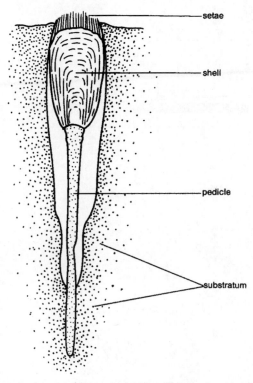

Figure 3. *In situ* view of the inarticulate brachiopod *Lingula.*

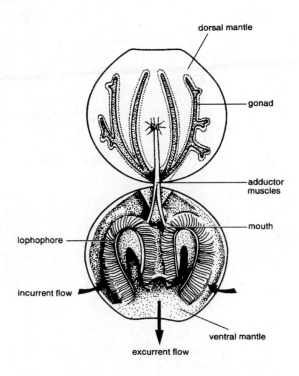

Figure 4. Interior of the articulate brachiopod *Laqueus californianus.* Arrows indicate the course of water currents.

brachiopods compare to that of other lophophores? How are they similar; how do they differ?

5. The digestive glands should be visible at the posterior end of the shell (Fig. 2D). They are composed of many spherical structures called **acini** [L., *acinus,* a berry] and resemble bunches of grapes.

6. The gonads are often best seen in the posterior parts of the branches of the coelom that extend into the mantle as structures called mantle canals.

7. Your instructor will provide additional directions if live brachiopods are to be examined (e.g., a study of feeding currents).

Fossil Forms

In comparative terms, fossils brachiopods (ca. 10,000 species) far outnumber present-day forms. Extinct brachiopods are found in **Cambrian** deposits, but achieved their greatest diversity during the **Ordovician** and **Devonian Periods** and their greatest specialization in the **Permian Period** (Fig. 5). Some fossil specimens were

much larger than species of today, measuring greater than 35 cm wide. As in other animal groups, that possess a rich fossil history, paleontologists have developed a complex nomenclature associated with brachiopods.

Observe specimens of fossil brachiopods comparing their general shell morphology with specimens of living species (Fig. 6). Attempt to find the following structures: dorsal and ventral valves; beak with foramen; presence of any external ornamentation (spines, plication furrows and crests, fold and sulcus); growth lines; commissure line between the valves.

Occasionally, specimens are found with the shell cavity exposed. Such specimens should be examined for the presence of the following features: hinge dentition, lophophore skeletal supports, pallial markings (mantle), platform (muscle attachment), and scars on the inside of the shell indicating muscle attachments. How do fossil specimens compare in their general structure to extant specimens? Are there any significant differences? ■

Phylum Brachiopoda

TIME (IN MILLIONS OF YEARS)

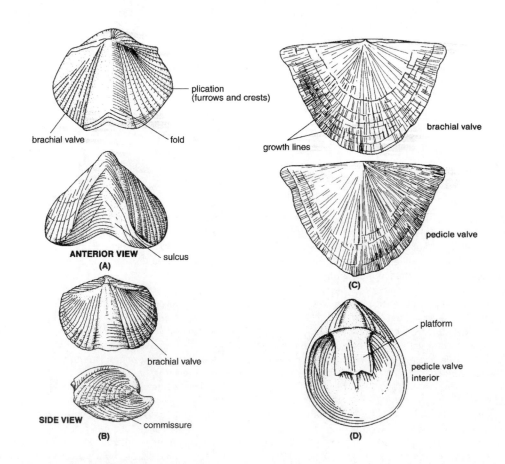

Figure 5. Geologic history of the Phylum Brachiopoda.

plication (furrows and crests)

brachial valve — fold

brachial valve

growth lines

ANTERIOR VIEW — sulcus
(A)

pedicle valve

(C)

brachial valve

SIDE VIEW — commissure
(B)

platform

pedicle valve interior

(D)

Figure 6. Fossil brachiopods. (A) *Paraspirifera* (Devonian, articulate). (B) *Platyrachella* (Devonian, articulate). (C) *Rafinesquina* (Ordovician, articulate). (D) *Trimerella* (Silurian, inarticulate).

264

Lophophorate Phyla		Worksheet 11
Name: _____		Date: _____
Course #: _____ / Section #: _____		Grade: _____

1. The possession of a lophophore in the phyla Phoronida, Brachiopoda, Bryozoa, and Entoprocta has traditionally served to indicate that these phyla are related. Recent research, based on molecular data and other evidence, indicates that the lophophorates may not constitute a natural group. How would you resolve this seemingly conflicting relationship? Are there other features possessed by members of the phyla that could be used to support their close relationship?

2. What other major invertebrate taxa (class or subclass) can you name that resemble the Phylum Brachiopoda where fewer extant species are present today compared to the fossil record? Does this foreshadow extinction in the near future for brachiopods?

3. In the exercise on brachiopods you were asked to compare the shell morphology of an articulate brachiopod, such as *Terebratulina*, with that of the oyster, *Crassostrea*. Write a concise essay on similarities and differences that you observed.

DEUTEROSTOME PHYLA

All deuterostomes are enterocoelomates with radial, indeterminate cleavage. If we ignore for the moment the putative relationship of certain lophophorates (see Nielsen 1977, 1985, 1995), only four phyla make up the deuterostome line: Echinodermata, Hemichordata, Chaetognatha, and Chordata. These four phyla are very heterogeneous in structure, function, and development. Echinodermata is a large phylum exhibiting the greatest diversity among the deuterostomes, including forms familiar to people visiting the seashore (e.g., sea stars, brittle stars, sand dollars, sea urchins, and sea cucumbers). Hemichordata and Chaetognatha are small phyla of marine worms, together containing fewer than 200 species. Placement of the Chaetognaths remains controversial. Placement of the recently discovered group of extinct primitive deuterostomes, the vetulicolians, (Phylum Vetulicolia) is problematic (Shu et al. 2001, see also Gee 2001). They may be primitive deuterostomes, basal to the Echinodermata, or they may occupy a more terminal position, arising just before Phylum Chordata. Most members of the Phylum Chordata are vertebrates and possess a vertebral column.

Alldredge, A.L. 1976. Appendicularians. *Sci. Am.* 235(1): 94–102.

Barrington, E.J.W. 1965. *The Biology of Hemichordata and Protochordate*. W. H. Freeman, San Francisco, CA.

Bone, Q., H. Kapp, and A.C. Pierrot-Bults. (eds.). 1991. *The Biology of Chaetognaths*. Oxford Univ. Press, London.

Gans, C., and R.G. Northcutt. 1983. Neural crest and the origin of vertebrates: a new head. *Science* 220: 268–274.

Gee, H. 2001. On being vetulicolian. *Nature* 414: 407-409.

Ghirardelli, E. 1995. Chaetognaths: two unsolved problems: the coelom and their affinities. *In: Body Cavities: Function and Phylogeny. Lanzavecchia*, G., R.Valvassori and M.D. Candia Carnevali. (eds.). Mucchi, Modena.: 167–185.

Harrison, F.W., and E.E. Ruppert. (eds.). 1996. *Microscopic Anatomy of Invertebrates*. Volume 15. *Hemichordata, Chaetognatha, and The Invertebrate Chordates*. Wiley-Liss, NY.

Nielsen, C. 1977. The relationship of Entoprocta, Ectoprocta and Phoronida. *Amer. Zool.* 17: 149–150.

Nielsen, C. 1985. Animal phylogeny in the light of the trochaea theory. *Biol. Jour. Linn.* Soc. 25: 243–299.

Riisgård, H.U. and I. Svane. 1999. Filter feeding in lancelets (amphioxus), *Brachiostoma lanceolatum. Invertebr. Biol.* 118: 423–432.

Shu, D.-G., S. Conway Morris, J. Ham, L. Chem, X.-L. Zhang, H.-Q.Liu,Y. Li, and J. N. Liu. 2001. Primitive deuterostomes from the Chengjiang Lagerstäte (Lower Cambridge, China). *Nature* 414: 419-424

Stokes, M.D., and N.D. Holland. 1998. The lancelet. *Am. Sci.* 86: 552–560.

Telford, M.J., and P.W.H. Holland. 1993. The phylogenetic affinities of the chaetognaths: a molecular analysis. *Mol. Biol. Evol.* 10: 660–676.

Phylum Echinodermata

Members of the Phylum Echinodermata [ee-KI-no-DER-mah-tah; G., *echinos*, a hedgehog + G., *derma*, skin] are among the most familiar invertebrates observed by people visiting the seashore. Echinoderms get their name from the fact that most have **spines** and **tubercles** that project from the surface of the animal. The endoskeleton is composed of calcareous **ossicles** or **plates** that vary in shape and their connection with each other. The skeleton is covered with a thin ciliated epidermis or is embedded in a rather thick, leathery body wall.

There are about 6,500 living species of echinoderms including sea lilies, sea stars (or starfishes), brittle stars, sand dollars, sea urchins, and sea cucumbers. Approximately 13,000 fossil species are known. Echinoderms are distributed widely, being especially abundant in the Indo-Pacific areas. This strictly marine phylum lacks parasitic and colonial members. None is segmented. The echinoderms are the major invertebrate phylum of **enterocoelous deuterostomes.**

A major characteristic of these largely bottom-dwellers is the basic **pentamerous,** radial symmetry of the adults. This means that an echinoderm's body is arranged typically into five (or multiples thereof) similar and equal parts that radiate from a central axis. The radiating areas, which bear the **tube feet** (or **podia**) of the unique **water-vascular** (or **ambulacral**) **system,** are called **arms** (or **ambulacra, rays,** or **radii**). Between two ambulacra is an **interambulacral** (or **interradial**) area. The oral surface contains the mouth and the aboral surface is away from the mouth.

The water-vascular system is the most distinguishing feature of echinoderms. It is basically an organ system of canals or tubes derived from the spacious, ciliated **enterocoelom.** The water-vascular system serves in locomotion, food gathering, respiration, chemosensation, and excretion.

Unlike most adult echinoderms, the microscopic larvae are bilaterally symmetrical. The first echinoderms were not radially symmetrical either; this results in a primary bilateral symmetry upon which the dominant radial symmetry is superimposed. This is why the echinoderms are placed in the Bilateria and not in the Radiata. The origins of this group including their bilateral beginnings lies deep in the early **Paleozoic Era** (Fig. 1).

Classification

Phylum Echinodermata is divided into six classes. The most recently discovered group of echinoderms, Class Concentricycloidea (composed of a few species), will not be examined here.

1. **Class Asteroidea.** Unattached, flattened, star-shaped echinoderms with a mouth that is centrally located on the underside of the body and with hollow arms that are not demarcated sharply from the central disc. Asteroids are commonly called sea stars or starfishes. An aboral madreporite and numerous pedicellariae are present in many species. Open ambulacral grooves, located on the oral side of the arms, contain tube feet with or without suckers. Examples: *Asterias, Pisaster, Astropecten, Luidia,* and *Solaster.*

From *Invertebrate Zoology*, Sixth Edition, Robert L. Wallace and Walter K. Taylor. Copyright © 2002 by Pearson Education, Inc. Published by Prentice-Hall, Inc. All rights reserved

Phylum Echinodermata

TIME (IN MILLIONS OF YEARS)

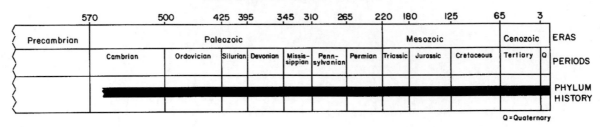

		Paleozoic								Mesozoic			Cenozoic		ERAS
Precambrian	Cambrian	Ordovician	Silurian	Devonian	Missis-sippian	Penn-sylvanian	Permian	Triassic	Jurassic	Cretaceous	Tertiary	Q	PERIODS

570 · 500 · 425 · 395 · 345 · 310 · 265 · 220 · 180 · 125 · 65 · 3

PHYLUM HISTORY

Q = Quaternary

Figure 1. Geologic history of the Phylum Echinodermata.

2. Class Ophiuroidea. Unattached, flattened, star-shaped echinoderms with a mouth that is centrally located on the underside of the body and with elongated and movable solid arms that are demarcated sharply from the central disc. Ophiuroids are commonly called brittle stars or serpent stars and basket stars. The madreporite is located on the oral side. Pedicellariae and hepatic ceca are lacking. Ambulacral grooves are closed. Examples: *Ophioderma, Ophiothrix* (brittle stars) and *Gorgonocephalus* (basket star).

3. Class Echinoidea. Discoid, globoid, or cylindrical echinoderms lacking arms. Echinoids are commonly called sea urchins, heart urchins, and sand dollars. The madreporite is located on the aboral surface. Ambulacral grooves are closed. Most have a masticatory apparatus called Aristotle's lantern. Skeleton (test) is rigid with movable long and short spines. Examples: *Strongylocentrotus, Arbacia* (sea urchin), *Echinocardium, Moira* (heart urchins), and *Mellita* and *Clypeaster* (sand dollars).

4. Class Holothuroidea. Echinoderms with a cylindrical and elongated body stretched on an oral-aboral axis. Holothuroids are commonly called sea cucumbers. Arms are absent and the madreporite is located internally. Tube feet at the anterior end are modified to form oral tentacles. Endoskeleton consisting of microscopic, separate ossicles are embedded in a usually leathery body wall. No spines or pedicellariae present. Ambulacra represented by closed canals. Examples: *Cucumaria, Thyone,* and *Leptosynapta.*

5. Class Crinoidea. Echinoderms with a cup-shaped body (theca) to which are attached 5, 10, or more long, hollow arms used to gather food. Crinoids are commonly called sea lilies and feather stars (comatulids). The oral surface, bearing the mouth and anus, faces upwards, while the crown or calyx contains all the visceral organs. Tube feet lack suckers. No madreporite, spines, or pedicellariae are present. Examples: *Florometra* and *Cenocrinus* (sea lilies), *Neometra,* and *Antedon* (feather stars).

A. Class Asteroidea

Asteroidea [AS-ter-OI-de-ah; G., *aster*, star + G., *eidos*, form] is perhaps the best known group of echinoderms, containing the sea stars or starfishes. The 1,800 species of sea stars are distributed widely throughout coastal waters of the world. Some sea stars are voracious carnivores feeding on oysters, barnacles, clams, and other marine animals; other are detritus feeders, mud swallowers, or opportunists. The digestive system is well developed. The ciliated enterocoelom is filled with a fluid containing free-moving, phagocytic amoebocytes called **coelomocytes**. These cells, as well as the tube feet of the water-vascular system and **dermal branchiae** (**papulae**), aid in the removal of the nitrogenous wastes (ammonium). Gaseous exchange also occurs through the tube feet and dermal branchiae. The skeleton is made up of calcareous ossicles bound together by connective tissue and muscle fibers. Outer circular and inner longitudinal fibers lie beneath the dermis. The tube feet contain well-developed longitudinal muscles.

The common North Atlantic sea star, *Asterias forbesi,* will be studied as our representative asteroid. Other genera such as *Pisaster* may be available for observation, and the following account will apply to either.

■ Observational Procedure:

External Anatomy
Obtain a preserved and/or dried specimen of the sea star. For the dried specimen, one that has been opened and cleaned is preferred.

Phylum Echinodermata

1. The radial symmetry is very apparent with all of the five rays radiating from the **central disc** (Fig. 2). Although adult sea stars and other echinoderms are radial, they retain vestiges of bilateral symmetry. To appreciate this, a brief consideration will be made of Carpenter's method of designating the radii and interradii. The system can be applied to other adult echinoderms; however, we will use the sea star for instructive purposes.

2. Place the dried (or preserved) specimen on a piece of construction paper with the calcareous, button-shaped **madreporite** on the aboral surface facing upwards and closest to you (Fig. 2). Trace the outline of the sea star on the paper and indicate the approximate position of the madreporite. Draw an imaginary line from the madreporite through the opposite **ray**. Continue this line by drawing it on the paper. This ray is designated A and the remaining rays (B, C, D, and E) are lettered counterclockwise from ray A when viewing the sea star from the aboral surface. Add these other lines to the paper.

3. The interradii are designated by the letters of the rays that enclose them (i.e., AB, BC, CD, DE, and EA). Add these labels to the figure. If the animal were cut beginning at the madreporite and extending through the center of ray A, the two halves would be mirror images of one another. Therefore, the animal would conform to a bilateral symmetry. If the animal were cut at right angles to the plane of symmetry, the body consists of three rays (the **trivium**) and the two opposite rays, C and D, comprise the **bivium**. The madreporite lies on the center of the bivium and in the CD interradius. Add these labels to the figure. Save this figure for examination when you study the sea cucumber (Class Holothuroidea).

Aboral Surface

Take a preserved sea star and place it in a dissection pan with the oral surface facing down.

1. Observe the aboral surface (Fig. 3). Note that the aboral surface is spinose with short, calcareous spines covering the area throughout. There is a thin, ciliated epidermis covering the sea star's body including the spines. Observe the structural details of the outer surface with a dissection microscope. Around the bases of the spines are finger-like, fleshy, grayish sacs. These are the **dermal branchiae** (or **dermal papulae**). They are ciliated, hollow projections continuous with the body cavity, serving as respiratory and excretory organs (Fig. 4A).

2. Around the spines and throughout the sea star's surface are the minute, pincer-like **pedicellariae** that keep the body surface free of debris and small organisms. Pedicellariae are modified spines, covered with epidermis, and unique to the echinoderms. The pedicellariae should appear as tiny, whitish specks in your specimen, especially on a dried one. Pedicellariae may be stalked or unstalked. Gently scrape the aboral surface of the preserved sea star with your scalpel. Spread thinly a small amount of the scrapings on the slide. Add a drop of water and cover with a coverslip. Observe under low power and then under high power. Note that the pedicellariae are pincer-like and each is opened and closed by adductor and abductor muscles (Fig. 4B). Examine a prepared slide showing the pedicellariae. Spines and pedicellariae are also found on the oral surface. Examining the pedicellariae for birefringence will highlight the calcium carbonate ossicles.

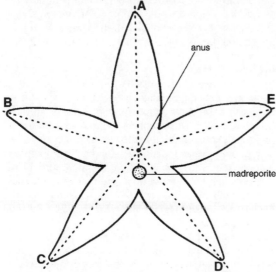

Figure 2. Aboral view of a sea star showing Carpenter's system of designating the radii and interradii. See text for discussion of the system. (After Meglitsch 1972.)

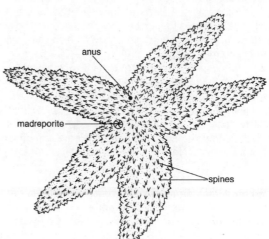

Figure 3. Aboral view of sea star.

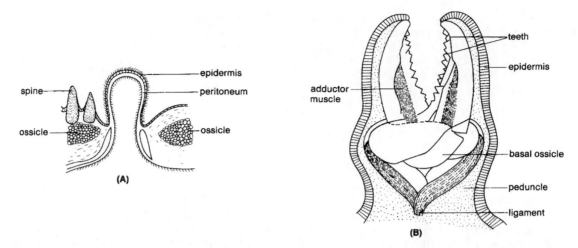

Figure 4. Surface structures on sea stars. (A) Section through the body wall of a sea star showing a papula or dermal branchia. (After Cuenot, *Traite de Zoologie*, Vol. XI, Grasse, Ed.) (B) Pedicellaria of a sea star.

3. Two openings occur on the aboral surface (Fig. 3). The madreporite, mentioned previously, is the hard, button-shaped plate. If viewed under the dissection microscope, the madreporite's grooves can be seen. The madreporite is part of the water-vascular system to be studied later. The second opening, the anus, is located in the BC interradius and opposite to the madreporite. It is very small and difficult to locate, some sea stars lack the anus.

Oral Surface
1. Turn the sea star over so that the oral surface is facing up. Locate the mouth (Fig. 5); this opening is surrounded by a thin, **peristomial membrane.** Note the paired **oral spines** that extend from each interradius and around the mouth; they protect the mouth and help move food into the opening.
2. Running from the mouth to the tip of each ray is an open, **ambulacral groove** with protective **ambulacral spines** covering each groove. In life, these and the oral spines are movable. In each ambulacral groove are the fleshy **tube feet** (or **podia**), elements of the water-vascular system. These highly contractile tubes terminate in sucker-discs. Not all sea stars have suckers on their tube feet.
3. At the distal end and on the oral surface of each arm is an eyespot formed by numerous, pigment-cup ocelli. These are sensitive to light. Near the eyespot is a small modified tube foot (**tentacle**), which lacks a sucker.

Internal Anatomy
To study the internal anatomy of the sea star, you will remove the specimen's aboral body wall.

1. Place the preserved sea star with the oral surface down. With scissors, cut off the tips of each arm. Insert the scissors inside the tip of one arm and cut along the edges (i.e., dorsolateral margins) of each arm. Do not cut too deeply. Make sure the body wall at each interradius is cut fully. Cut around the madreporite to leave it attached to the lower part of the body.
2. Carefully lift the aboral surface off the oral side. As you remove the aboral surface, detach all fleshy material adhering by mesenteries to the inner surface of the aboral covering. If the dissection is done properly, you should have all fleshy materials intact and in the lower half of the sea star's body. None of the organs should be adhering to the aboral part of the body wall. The exposed body cavity is the spacious enterocoelom.

Digestive System
Refer to Figures 6, 7, and 8 as you read these instructions on examining the digestive system.
1. Locate the short **esophagus** which leads internally from the mouth. The esophagus opens into the large, muscular **cardiac** portion of the stomach. When the sea star feeds, it everts the stomach through the mouth and presses the fleshy tissue against the food. After digestive enzymes have acted upon the food, the stomach and partially digested contents are retracted into the body by **retractor muscles** attached to the ambulacral ridge (Figs. 7 and 8).
2. Aborally the cardiac stomach leads into the smaller, thin-walled **pyloric stomach.** This pentagonal stomach receives enzymes from five pairs of **pyloric ceca** (or **digestive glands** or **hepatic ceca**). In each arm locate the paired digestive glands. The pyloric stomach leads

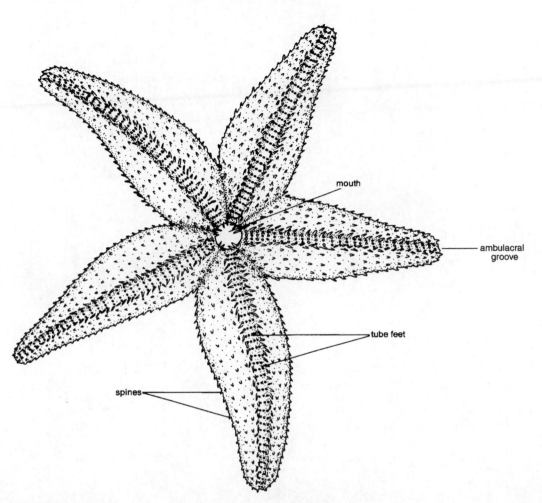

Figure 5. Oral view of a sea star.

into a very short, inconspicuous **intestine.** A branched sac, the **rectal ceca** (or **intestinal ceca**), of unknown function, lies on top of the pyloric stomach, but has a connection with the intestine. Beyond the opening of the rectal ceca, the short **rectum** leads to the **anus.**

Skeletal System

1. To study the skeleton of the sea star's arm, remove the hepatic ceca in one ray. Note the distinct **ambulacral ridge** composed of middle and lateral rows of ambulacral ossicles (Figs. 8 and 9). Examine the ridge on your dried specimen. The large, ovoid ossicle at the end of the ridge in the central disc area is the **odontophore.** *Speculate*: Are sea stars segmented? As you study the other classes of echinoderms, consider this question again.

2. Locate the two whitish, threadlike **retractor muscles** that attach the ambulacral ridge and the cardiac stomach. Note that the lateral ambulacral ossicles form the sides of the ambulacral groove on the oral surface, and the fleshy tube feet of the water-vascular system extend through these ossicles. The lower ends of the lateral ossicles rest on a series of **adambulacral ossicles** (Fig. 9). The latter bear the long, slender, movable **ambulacral spines** observed along the groove on the oral surface. The **inferomarginal ossicles** compose the bottom lateral row of strutlike ossicles. Lateral to these, and forming the upper lateral row along the length of the arm, are the **superomarginal ossicles.**

3. Make a cross section of a piece of the arm and observe it under the dissection microscope to see more clearly the above-mentioned ossicles and their relationship to each other. If you have a cross section of an arm from a dried specimen, or prepared slide, examine these using a microscope. Study the inner face of the aboral covering and note its ossicles.

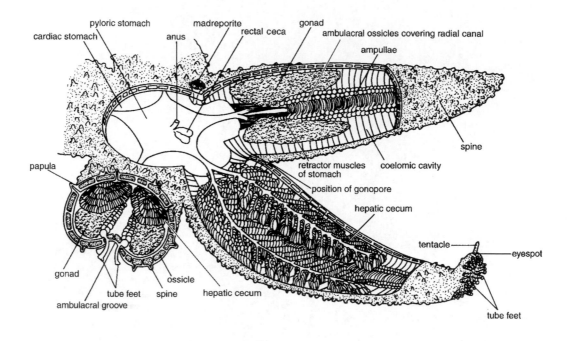

Figure 6. Internal aboral view of a sea star showing the digestive system. (After Sherman and Sherman.)

Figure 7. Diagrammatic vertical section through a ray and the central disc of *Asterias*. (After Chadwick.)

Phylum Echinodermata

Figure 8. Internal aboral view of a sea star after the digestive system has been removed.

Figure 9. A schematic view of the cross section of a sea star's arm.

Phylum Echinodermata

Reproductive System

Asterias is dioecious.

1. Locate the two gonads at the base of each arm (Figs. 6 and 8). These resemble a cluster of grapes. During the reproductive season the gonads nearly fill each arm. At other times, they are small and occupy a small space. Speculate on whether your specimen was taken during its reproductive season or at another time.

2. Two gonads are connected by a single gonoduct that terminates as a single gonopore or gonopore cluster located between the base of the arm in each interradius.

3. Examine a prepared slide of sea star development and locate the large, unfertilized egg showing the nucleus and nucleolus (Fig. 10A). Fertilization occurs after the gametes are shed in the water. The zygote undergoes cleavage and soon it develops into a free-swimming, bilaterally symmetrical larva, the **bipinnaria** (Fig. 10B). Initially the surface is covered with cilia which eventually become confined to definite ciliated bands used in locomotion and feeding.

4. The bipinnaria in many asteroids, including *Asterias*, becomes a **brachiolaria larva** with the appearance of three additional arms near the sucker at the anterior end (Fig. 10C). The brachiolaria later settles down and metamorphoses into a young sea star. Examine whole mount preparations of these microscopic larvae, locating the ciliated bands, mouth, and anus.

Water-vascular System

Remove the overlying organs and locate the following structures of the water-vascular system (Fig. 11): (1) the **madreporite** and (2) the **circumoral canal** (or **ring** or **water canal**) are connected by (3) the calcified **stone canal**; (4) five **radial canals**, one in each arm on the oral side, lead off the **circumoral canal**; (5) short **transverse** (or **lateral**) **canals** arranged in a staggered fashion connect the radial canals and the (6) **tube feet**. This system operates as a hydraulic system. On the inner wall of the circumoral ring and in an interradial position are nine, fleshy **Tiedemann's bodies** in which amoebocytes are formed. An individual tube foot consists of a closed cylinder with a sucker at the distal end and a bulblike **ampulla** at its proximal end. In many sea stars and other echinoderms, but not in *Asterias forbesi,* one to five muscular, saclike **Polian vesicles** connect to the ring canal. Their precise function is unknown.

Nervous System

The nervous system consists of a plexus of fibers and neurons underlying the epidermis and in the gastrodermis. Remove the tube feet from one ambulacral groove. Observe the minute, yellowish or brown cord that runs along the bottom of the groove along the entire length

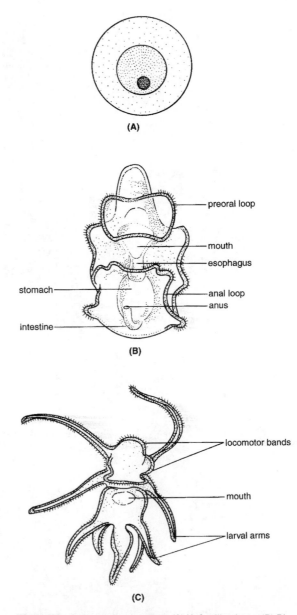

(A)

(B)
- preoral loop
- mouth
- esophagus
- anal loop
- anus
- stomach
- intestine

(C)
- locomotor bands
- mouth
- larval arms

Figure 10. Sea star development. (A) Unfertilized egg. (B) Bipinnaria larva. (C) Brachiolaria larva.

of the arm. This is the **radial nerve cord** (Fig. 9). This constitutes the **ectoneural** portion of the nervous system. The **endoneural** portion may be seen in the oral walls of the cardiac and pyloric portions of the stomach and in the median folds of the hepatic ceca. An apical portion of the nervous system occurs medially on the inner surface of the aboral body wall. This single cord is fused with the other four cords in the center of the disc.

Phylum Echinodermata

Figure 11. Water-vascular system of a sea star. (After Sherman and Sherman.)

The apical portion is difficult to find and should not be confused with the large, very apparent, apical longitudinal muscle bands of the arms (Fig. 9).

Microscopic Examination
Obtain a prepared slide of a cross section of the arm of a sea star. Using Figure 9, locate the following structures: epidermis, dermis, peritoneum, the various ossicles, enterocoelom, dermal branchiae, pyloric ceca, tube feet, transverse canal, radial canal, radial nerve, and ambulacral groove. If your slide were made from a young sea star, you will not see the gonads or spines.

What do the papulae look like in cross section? How are they adapted to be structures of gaseous exchange? Describe the hepatic ceca. Are they thin-walled and hollow like a balloon or not? What other observations can be made about the hepatic ceca? Discuss the significance of the internal structure of the hepatic ceca with regard to their function.

Are ossicles present in the cross section? To answer this question look for birefringence with crossed polarized filters. If ossicles are composed primarily of calcium carbonate, how could they have been removed during the manufacture of the slide? Is there evidence for muscles being present in the body wall? Where are they positioned and of what significance is that location?

Again the use of crossed polarizing filters will allow you to answer these questions. Compare and contrast the structure of the ampulae to the tube feet. Finally, correlate the structures you see in the slide with those of the dissected specimen.

Live Specimens
When studying live sea stars, exercise care so that the animal is given sufficient time to release its hold before it is lifted from the substratum. If removal is done too quickly, the tube feet may be ripped apart. Also while working with the animals, return them to the seawater every few minutes to prevent drying out.

1. Obtain a sea star and place it into a small dish filled with seawater. Observe the aboral surface of a sea star using low power of a dissection microscope. Are the dermal branchiae visible? Identify the pedicellaria. How large are these structures? Are dermal branchiae and pedicellaria distributed evenly over both sides of the animal?

2. The entire surface is ciliated. To visualize the cilia place an amount of a dilute suspension of carmine powder, carbon black, or fine sand grains on the aboral surface and watch what happens.

3. Carefully turn the animal over and observe its tube feet. Inspect the sucker discs at the distal ends of the feet. How do these suckers function?

4. Remove the sea star from the dish and place it, oral surface down, onto a wet Plexiglas plate. Keep the plate level and observe movement from above and below. Do all the tube feet appear to work in unison? Does there appear to be a pattern to the action of a single tube foot? Does one arm seem to lead and the others follow? What happens when the animal comes upon an obstacle? As you watch the sea star move attempt to determine whether the leading arm ever changes. Describe the locomotory activity of a sea star.

5. Adjust the plate so that it is at an angle of 30° or more. How does the sea star react? Experiment by changing the angle of the tilt. Does the sea star change its locomotory behavior? Slowly turn the plate upside down. What does the sea star do now? Does the sea star move when the plate is held upside down, but at an angle? Summarize your observations and answer the following questions. When moving over a surface do sea stars use their tube feet to pull themselves, push themselves, or do they use a combination of both? What method do you use when you walk?

6. To test your conclusions about sea star locomotion, try the following exercise. Using string, secure a sea star onto a wire mesh screen with its oral surface up. (*Do not tie the arms too tightly as this may damage the animal.*) Now place a cover glass on to the ambulacra at the distal end of one arm. What happens to the cover glass? Describe the stepping action of the tube feet. Which of the tube feet in the ambulacra are active: only the ones in contact with the glass or all of them? While the glass is being moved, observe the tube feet of the other arms. Are they moving? In what direction are they moving? Is there an overall pattern of action of tube feet in all five ambulacra? Change the position of the cover glass to a different ambulacra. Does this change the pattern of movement of the tube feet? When do arms act as leading arms and when do they act as trailing arms?

What do these observations indicate about motor control by the central nervous system (CNS) of sea stars? *Speculate*: Based on these observations would you say that the CNS of sea stars is sophisticated or unsophisticated? (More advanced studies on the control of locomotion are offered in steps 10 and 11.)

7. Remove the animal from the wire mesh restraint, place it oral side down on a flat surface, and observe righting behavior. How long does it take and how is this accomplished? How do the arms work in coordinating this activity? How do the tube feet aid in righting? How many of the arms become anchored to the surface before the animal can right itself? Are the same arms always involved in righting behavior?

8. Carefully lift a sea star up and place a small piece of shrimp (1–2 cm long) directly under the mouth and return the animal to a glass holding tank. Over the course of the next 30–60 minutes examine the animal to see if you can observe feeding. Notice how the stomach **everts** during this process. (NB: disturbing the animal while it is feeding may cause feeding to cease.)

9. If a burrowing sea star is available (e.g., *Astropecten*), observe burrowing behavior. (To observe burrowing, you will need to provide a tub or aquarium filled with seawater and with a substratum of sand at least 5 cm deep.) Describe how burrowing is accomplished by *Astropecten*.

10. The next series of observations is **optional** as it requires surgery to be done on the specimen while it is alive. (Although the damage will look severe, sea stars have strong powers of regeneration. If the animal is well cared for after the operation, it should be able to repair itself.)

This procedure may be done with the animal free or restrained as discussed in step 6. At the base of the interradius DE, cut the arm into the ambulacra so that the radial nerve is severed (Fig. 7). Determine how this affects locomotion. Make another cut, this time into the interradius BC. How do the arms act now in locomotion? Is there a change in the pattern in which arm leads and which trails? Cut the remaining interradii one by one, each time determining how this affects locomotion.

11. Obtain another animal and sever one arm entirely so that the arm still contains a portion of the nerve ring. How does this arm move? Does it act as a leading or a trailing arm? Sever another arm, but this time do so to exclude the nerve ring. How does this arm move? Does it act as a leading or a trailing arm? Consider how the presence (or absence) of a connection to the nerve ring coordinates locomotion.

12. Return the animals to their aquarium and over the course of the next several months observe the regeneration abilities of sea stars. ■

B. Class Ophiuroidea

Members of Class Ophiuroidea [O-fee-ur-OID-de-ah; *G., ophis*, a serpent + *G., oura*, tail + *G., eidos*, form] are called brittle stars because of their tendency to fragment when disturbed, or serpent stars because their long slender arms wriggle in a snakelike motion. Included in this class are the largest echinoderms, the basket stars; these forms have highly branched arms whose ends tend to coil. *Gorgonocephalus* is a basket star that is often available for classroom observation (Fig. 12).

Because of the basic star-shaped body and pentamerous condition, ophiuroids resemble the asteroids. As you study these organisms you will see distinct differences between the two groups. Many zoologists consider ophiuroids to be the most successful of echinoderms because they are the largest group, with 2,000 living species. Ophiuroids often occur in dense aggregations on the sea floor. Certainly brittle stars are the most mobile members of the phylum. There are burrowing ophiuroids and a few can swim. The only commensal echinoderms are ophiuroids. For our laboratory study, *Ophioderma* or some similar brittle star, will be used.

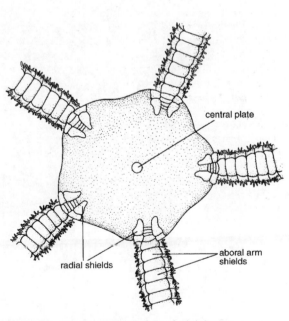

Figure 12. *Gorgonocephalus*, a basket star.

■ Observational Procedure:

External Anatomy

Obtain dried and preserved individuals for your study.

1. Note that the central disc is composed of calcareous plates or shields arranged in a distinct fashion (Fig. 13). Are these plates arranged in some pattern or are they random? The small disc is flattened and rather smooth, lacking the conspicuous and numerous spines observed in the sea star. The disc of some species is spiny, and there is variation in the pattern of the shields. Using a dissection microscope, examine the dorsal side for the madreporite. Is it present there? Is an anus evident?

2. Observe the oral surface containing the mouth (Fig. 14). Use the dissection microscope to observe the plates and other external features better. The plates on the oral surface of the central disc consist of the large, interradial **oral shields** (or **buccal plates**), two **aboral** (or **angular**) **plates** lying on either side of the oral shield, and the inward-pointing jaws that extend toward the mouth (Fig. 14). Note that the jaws bear teeth at their apices and **oral papillae** along their sides.

3. One of the oral shields is modified as the madreporite of the water-vascular system. The madreporite's oral position differs from that observed in the sea stars where it is located aborally. Examine the arms of your specimen and note the lack of

Figure 13. External aboral surface of a brittle star.

central plate

aboral arm shields

radial shields

Phylum Echinodermata

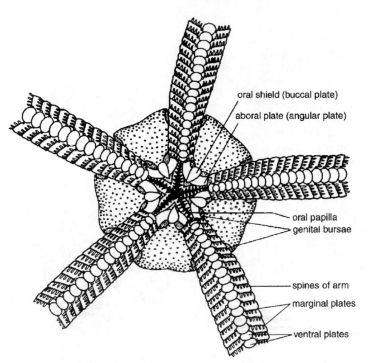

oral shield (buccal plate)

aboral plate (angular plate)

oral papilla
genital bursae

spines of arm

marginal plates

ventral plates

Figure 14. External oral view of *Ophioderma*.

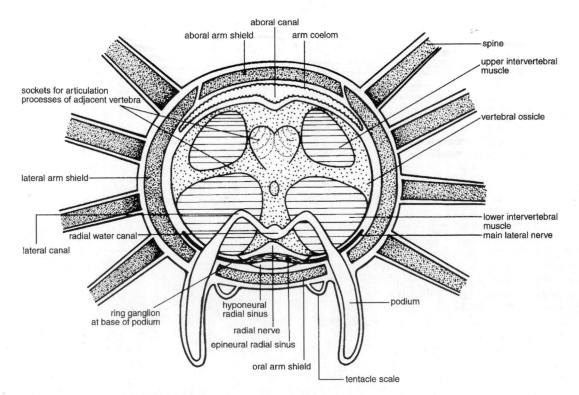

aboral canal

aboral arm shield arm coelom

spine

upper intervertebral muscle

sockets for articulation processes of adjacent vertebra

vertebral ossicle

lateral arm shield

lower intervertebral muscle

main lateral nerve

radial water canal

lateral canal

podium

ring ganglion at base of podium

hyponeural radial sinus

radial nerve

epineural radial sinus

oral arm shield

tentacle scale

Figure 15. Cross section of a generalized ophiuroid arm. (After Barnes.)

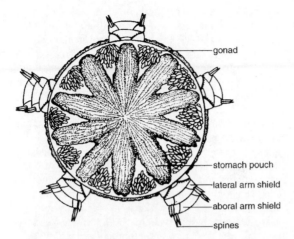

Figure 16. Internal anatomy of an ophiuroid, aboral view.

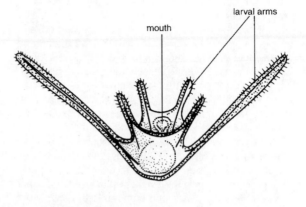

Figure 17. Ophiopluteus of a brittle star.

ambulacral grooves. Are dermal branchiae or pedicellariae present?

4. The arms are very flexible because they are composed internally of a series of disc-shaped, calcareous **vertebrae** connected by large, intervertebral muscles (Fig. 15). Break off a section of an arm from your specimen and using a dissection microscope examine both ends of the arm. (NB: The ossicles may be cleaned with bleach, but rinse the remaining material with tap water before handling.) Locate both sides of a vertebral ossicle. On one side of an ossicle you should observe the **sockets** that articulate with the **processes** of an adjacent socket (Fig. 15). What type of joint is this? Where else in the animal kingdom are these joints found? How do such joints permit the snakelike movement of the arms? If these organisms possess vertebrae, why aren't they considered to be members of Phylum Chordata, Subphylum Vertebrata? The vertebrae represent the ambulacral ossicles that have become located internally.

5. Four longitudinal rows of plates surround the vertebrae externally: one aboral arm plate, two lateral arm plates, and one oral arm plate (Fig. 15). Along the outer margins of the lateral arm plates are holes through which the tube feet extend. Note the vertical row of spines protruding between the lateral arm plates (Fig. 14). How does their position compare to that of the podia? Unlike most asteroids, ophiuroid tube feet lack suckers.

6. Locate the small, external openings on the oral surface within the central disc and alongside the arm margins. These are **bursal slits** (Fig. 14). There are five pairs of them and each slit leads inward to a **bursa**, which is an internal sac formed by an invagination of the disc's oral surface. Gaseous exchange occurs across the bur-

sae as seawater is pulled in and expelled. In *Ophioderma* and other brittle stars, the gametes are stored temporarily in these slits. In some species (not *Ophioderma*) the bursae serve as brood chambers for the developing brittle stars as well as in respiration. In addition to gas exchange and reproduction, the bursae may be the principal sites for nitrogenous waste removal.

Internal Anatomy

1. Using a preserved specimen, cut away the surface of the aboral disc. The ophiuroid's enterocoelom is much reduced from that of the sea star. Locate the large, saclike stomach with 10 **stomach pouches** (Fig. 16). Alternating in position with these pouches are the gonads and bursae. The stomach is connected to the mouth by a short esophagus. An intestine, hepatic ceca, and anus are lacking. Unlike asteroids, the digestive system in ophiuroids is confined to the central disc. Ophiuroids are scavengers, filter feeders, or suspension feeders. The tube feet are used to capture food.

2. The water-vascular and nervous systems are similar to those of asteroids, with some minor differences. These systems will not be studied in your dissections.

3. Although most ophiuroids are dioecious, hermaphroditic species are not uncommon. Ophiuroid reproduction is similar to that of asteroids. The bilaterally symmetrical larva, when present, is an **ophiopluteus,** characterized by eight arms (Fig. 17). Compare this larval form to the brachiolaria larva of the sea star (Fig. 10C). How are they similar? How are they different? The ophiopluteus develops gradually into an adult; there is no sessile stage. Examine slide preparations of the larva. Look for the mouth and anus. Are there ciliated bands similar to those found in asteroids?

Live Specimens

Remember to return the animals to the seawater every few minutes to prevent drying out.

1. Place the brittle star in an aquarium and observe its locomotion. Does one arm always lead the others? Determine whether the animal pulls or pushes itself along. How do the arms react when they make contact with objects? Do brittle stars move differently over smooth and rough surfaces? Why are these animals also called serpent stars? How does locomotion in the sea stars compare to that of brittle stars?

2. Remove the brittle star from the aquarium and place the animal on a Plexiglas plate. How does it move now? What happens when the plate is tilted to an angle of 30° or more? Provide the animal with a surface that has some relief (e.g., holes and bumps). Is the animal better able to keep its purchase on this surface than the smooth one? Examine the ambulacral region of the animal. How do the tube feet of the brittle star differ from that of the sea star? How are brittle stars like freehand rock climbers?

3. Turn the animal over and observe righting behavior. How is it accomplished? Is righting done differently in the sea stars and the brittle stars?

4. If a brittle star that has been starved is available, attempt the following exercise on feeding. Place the animal in a small aquarium of clean (clear) seawater. Add a small amount of very finely-ground clam (or another mollusk) to the water. What is the brittle star's response? After several minutes add a few drops of a dilute solution of toluidine blue to the seawater near to the arms of the animal. What do you see? Illumination from the side may aid you in making these observations. Correlate your observations to what you know about brittle star feeding. ■

C. Class Echinoidea

Sea urchins, sand dollars, heart urchins (spatangoids) belong to the Class Echinoidea [ECH-in-OI-de-ah; G., *echinos*, hedgehog + G., *eidos*, form]. There are approximately 1,000 living species of these free-moving echinoderms found in the littoral and benthic zones of the oceans. The body is globular to disclike in shape with movable spines covering the exterior. The spines function in protection, burrowing, keeping the body surface clean, and helping to right the body should it become upended. The gonads of some regular sea urchins are used for food by some people.

Echinoids have a rigid endoskeleton called the **test**. The test and spines are covered with a ciliated epidermis. The ossicles of the test are flattened and sutured together firmly so that in most echinoids the individual ossicles are immobile, unlike the condition in most echinoderms. A body musculature is lacking on the inner surface of the test. The interlocking ossicles radiate in rows from the aboral apex to the mouth that is located in the center of the oral surface. The ambulacra and interambulacra are formed by ossicles arranged in 10 alternating double columns that converge at the two poles. The ambulacral plates have paired holes or pores through which the tube feet extend; holes are lacking on the interambulacral ossicles. Echinoids lack projecting, free-moving arms similar to those of asteroids and ophiuroids.

Although the dominant symmetry is radial, as observed in sea urchins, some echinoids have a secondary, bilateral symmetry. Because of this difference in symmetry, echinoids are divided into two groups: (1) the **regular** echinoids (sea urchins) with radial symmetry and (2) the **irregular** echinoids (heart urchins and sand dollars) with bilateral symmetry superimposed on the radial one.

■ Observational Procedure: Sea Urchin

External Anatomy

Obtain a cleaned specimen (one with the spines removed) and a preserved, complete specimen of a sea urchin, such as *Arbacia* or *Strongylocentrotus*. The following instructions will use both.

1. Note the globular or ovoid shape with the oral surface being flatter than the aboral one. Locate on the oral surface the five ambulacra composed of rows of double ossicles and the five double rows that constitute the interambulacra (Fig. 18). The ambulacra have pores for the tube feet, whereas the interambulacra lack the holes.

Phylum Echinodermata

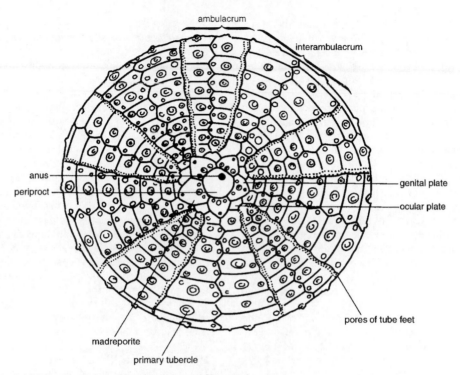

Figure 18. Test of *Arbacia*, aboral view. (After Sherman and Sherman.)

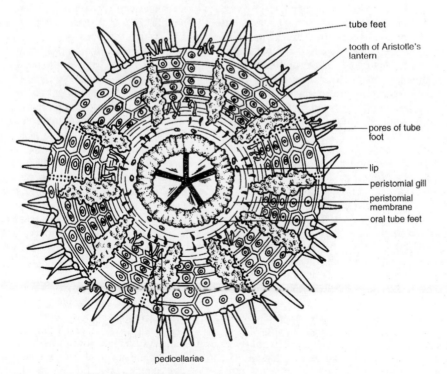

Figure 19. Oral view of a sea urchin. (After Sherman and Sherman.)

2. The anus is at or near the center of the aboral surface; a membrane (the **periproct**) with embedded, minute ossicles bears the anus. In a cleaned specimen the periproct will probably be missing. Five **genital plates** surround the anus; one is modified as the madreporite. How does the madreporite plate differ from the genital plates? On each genital plate locate the **gonopore.** This is where the gametes exit. Does the madreporite possess a gonopore? How many gonopores are present?

3. Alternating with the genital plates locate the five **ocular plates** each of which coincides with an ambulacral region. On each ocular plate find the tiny pore through which passes a light-sensitive tube foot in life.

4. Observe the pattern of the numerous bumps (**tubercles**) to which spines are attached. Do they occur in both the ambulacral and interambulacral regions? Are all the tubercles the same size? Is there a pattern to the distribution of the 1° and 2° tubercles? Using a hand lens observe the smallest of the tubercles. These are the bases to which the pedicellaria attach. How numerous are these structures?

5. The base of each tubercle forms a joint with the concave end of a spine. This attachment permits movement of the spines. Take a disarticulated spine and fit it onto a tubercle and determine for yourself how this joint works. What type of joint is this? Where else in the phylum and in the animal kingdom are ball-and-socket joints found? Do they all work in the same way?

6. Study the structure of the spines and pedicellariae under the dissection microscope. The latter in most echinoids are stalked and three-jawed. A number of sea urchins have poisonous pedicellariae, but not *Arbacia*. Are the spines a uniform length all over the body? Besides the ball-and-socket joint are spines jointed anywhere else? Break a dried spine in half and examine the broken side using a dissection microscope. Are spines solid or hollow?

7. Using a dissection microscope or hand lens examine the surface of the cleaned test closely. What does the zig-zag pattern of interlocking plates represent? These are the ossicles, but they are all fused. Are all of the ossicles the same size? Describe how the ossicles fit together to produce the test. This type of architectural structure has been around since the 1950s. Who invented it and what name was it given? What other animals have you studied that possess this domelike structure? In carbon chemistry there is an unusual arrangement of 60 carbon atoms that gives this same sort of structure? What name is given to that?

8. If you have extra cleaned specimens try the following exercise to determine the weight to strength ratio of the echinoid version of the geodesic dome. Weigh your specimen to the nearest one tenth of a gram. This is the mass (M) of the test. Now arrange a system whereby weights may be added to the specimen in a manner so that they do not fall off. Add weight a few grams at a time to increase the crushing force (F). How much weight did you end up adding before the test failed? How did the test fail; was it crushed completely or did it just crack at one point? From the class data determine the weight-to-strength ratio for these sea urchin tests. To do this plot on an X-Y axis all values of F as a function of M. Is there a strong correlation? Consider how such a light-weight structure can carry so much weight. How is F redistributed by the test?

9. In the preserved specimen locate the mouth on the oral surface (Fig. 19). The opening is surrounded by a peristomial membrane that is thickened along the inner edge to form a lip. Find the five pairs of short, **oral podia** and the five pairs of bushy, **peristomial gills** in the membrane. These gills are evaginations of the body surface. Exchange of respiratory gases occurs in these gills as well as across the tube feet. Do you see pedicellariae and small spines in the peristomial membrane? You should see protruding through the mouth five teeth, the chewing parts of **Aristotle's lantern.** This complex structure, unique to most echinoids, will be studied later.

Internal Anatomy

This dissection requires that you do not cut too deeply into the test.

1. Place the urchin oral side down in the dissection pan. Take a pair of scissors or a fine saw and cut through and around the equator of the test. You may remove spines to help in the cutting process, but keep the two halves together while cutting. Carefully open the two halves, and as you do this, detach or cut the mesenteries holding the gut together.

2. In the oral half locate Aristotle's lantern (Fig. 20). The main components of this complex structure are five radially arranged, calcareous plates called **pyramids,** a large assortment of other plates and muscles, and five oral teeth projecting at the tip of each pyramid. The lantern can be protruded or retracted through the mouth. Sea urchins use their sharp teeth to scrape, tear, and pull food materials. Most sea urchins are herbivores, feeding primarily on algae growing on rocks and similar surfaces.

3. Surrounding the lantern, the **ring canal** with its associated **Polian vesicles** may be seen. The vesicles are opposite each interambulacrum. The **stone canal** and **axial organ** ascend aborally off the ring canal. The former terminates at the madreporite on the aboral surface. The axial organ is part of the hemal system. This system, found also in other echinoderms, is composed of a complex of channels that are difficult to follow in preserved specimens; the system will not be studied. The exact function of the axial organ is unknown. The **radial canals** leave the ring canal. At that juncture you

Phylum Echinodermata

Figure 20. Internal anatomy of a sea urchin. (A) Lateral view. (B) Oral-aboral view. (C) Details of Aristotle's lantern. (After Sherman and Sherman.)

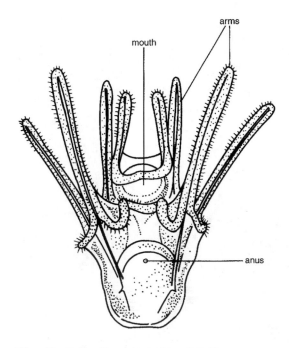

Figure 21. Early echinopluteus of an echinoid.

may have difficulty locating the canals, but they, along with ampullae of the tube feet, may be observed along the inner surface of the test. Note the lack of body muscles attached to the inner test wall. What would account for the lack of this musculature?

4. The digestive system consists of the mouth, a buccal cavity, and a pharynx (the interior of Aristotle's lantern) that leads to a long **esophagus** (Fig. 20). Trace the esophagus to the **small intestine** that curves around the inside of the test in a counterclockwise direction as viewed from the aboral surface. The small intestine leads to a **large intestine** that makes an almost complete circuit in the opposite direction. Some workers call the two circuits of the intestine the **stomach.** The large intestine leads to the short **rectum** that opens at the **anus.**

5. Running along the inner surface of the oral part of the intestine locate the ciliated **siphon.** This tube connects the esophagus at one end and the intestine at the other end. The precise function of the siphon is unknown. It may remove water from the intestinal contents, thus concentrating enzymes and food during the initial stages of digestion.

6. Examine the inner surface of the aboral half of the test and locate the five **gonads.** Are these located in the ambulacral or in the interambulacral areas? Each gonad opens to the outside by a genital pore, observed when the external anatomy was studied.

7. All echinoids are dioecious. Fertilization is external in the sea water and a bilateral larva, the **echinopluteus,** forms. The larva metamorphoses into a juvenile urchin without settling down. Study slides of the echinopluteus (Fig. 21). Note that the echinopluteus larva of echinoids superficially resembles the ophiopluteus (Fig. 17). Compare the larval forms of the echinoderms examined so far. How are they similar? How are they different?

Live Specimens

When studying sea urchins, exercise care so that the animal is given sufficient time to release its hold before it is lifted from the substratum. If removal is done too quickly, the tube feet may be ripped apart. Also while working with the animals, return them to the seawater every few minutes to prevent drying out.

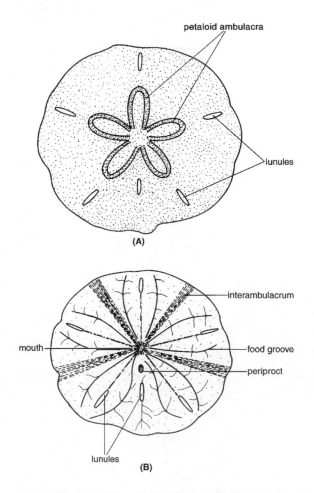

Figure 22. Sand dollar. (A) Aboral view. (B) Oral view of a sand dollar.

1. Place a live sea urchin such as *Arbacia, Lytechinus,* or *Strongylocentrotus* in a small dish of seawater that will restrict its movements. Observe the animal under low power of a dissection microscope. Are dermal branchiae present? Determine whether the epidermis is ciliated. Turn the animal over and observe the oral side, locating the peristome, buccal tube feet, gills, and **sphaeridia.** The latter are short, bean-shaped spines that function as organs of equilibrium.

2. Observe the action of the tube feet on both sides of the animal. Examine the function of the tube feet closely. Do all possess suckers? Do those on the aboral side have different behaviors than those on the oral surface? How do the tube feet of the sea urchin differ from those of sea stars and brittle stars? Find the five light-sensitive tube feet that exit the test from the genital plates. Are they any different in form or behavior from the other tube feet?

3. Identify the pedicellaria and compare them to those of the sea star. Are they the same size? Take a probe and gently prod the animal. How do the spines and pedicellaria respond to the disturbance? What direction do the surrounding spines and pedicellaria point when one spine is handled? Slowly push on a spine. What happens? Does the spine seem to lock into place? This phenomenon is accomplished by **catch** or **cog muscles** that are located at the base of the spine. These muscles may be anesthetized by blowing carbon dioxide over the animal. What happens to the spines when this is done?

4. Attempt to observe the action of the jaws of Aristotle's lantern. How does it function in obtaining food?

5. Place the sea urchin in an aquarium and observe its movements. How do these animals use their spines in locomotion? Turn the urchin upside down and observe righting behavior. Is it different from what you observed in the sea star or brittle star? At the discretion of your instructor, you will remove tube feet and sphaeridae from the region of the peristome. How do these ablations influence righting behavior?

■ Observational Procedure: Irregular Urchins

Sand Dollar and Sea Biscuit

Obtain preserved and cleaned sand dollar such as *Mellita* and cleaned tests of the sea biscuit *Clypeaster* and a sea urchin.

1. Compare the tests of the sand dollar and sea biscuit to that of the sea urchin. Are the tests of the sand dollar and sea biscuit similar to that of the sea urchin? How do they differ? Are fused ossicles evident on the external surface? In answering this question you may find that using a hand lens or dissection microscope will

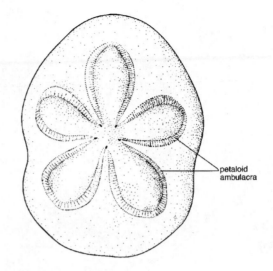

Figure 23. Sea biscuit (*Clypeaster*).

bring too much magnification. To see the ossicles, try rotating the test to observe the surface from different angles. Fusion of the ossicles in the test reaches an extreme degree in these forms.

2. Examine the preserved specimen of the sand dollar, noting the covering of small, numerous spines. How do these spines differ in size and distribution from that of the sea urchin? Determine whether they function as a ball-and-socket joint. Using a dissection microscope find the minute tubercles that cover the outer surface of the cleaned tests. How many of these ball-and-socket joints are present on the tests of these organisms? Are they located on both sides? If tube feet are not used in locomotion by these forms, how do they move? (Compare your answer to the observations that you will make later using live sand dollars.)

3. Locate the mouth on the oral surfaces of these animals. Both sand dollars and sea biscuits possess a modified Aristotle's lantern that cannot be protracted through the mouth. (NB: These structures are often sold as novelties, called "doves," or "angels," in sea-side gift shops.) Unlike regular sea urchins, the anus of irregular echinoids has moved from the aboral center to the posterior edge of the body or into the posterior **lunule** (Fig. 22).

4. Lunules are the elongated notches or holes on the sand dollar and their numbers vary among different species. At least in some forms, the lunules aid the sand dollar in burrowing in the sand, although spines are the principal structures for that purpose. Lunules are absent in the sea biscuit (*Clypeaster rosaceus*) of Florida and the West Indies (Fig. 23).

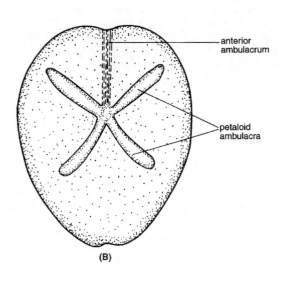

Figure 24. Heart urchin. (A) Oral view. (B) Aboral view.

5. On the clean specimens, examine the aboral surface under the dissection microscope and observe the five **petaloids** (the ambulacra) that resemble a flower. Find the holes that contained the tube feet. These aboral podia function in gas exchange, but not movement. Peristomial gills like those of sea urchins do not occur in the irregular echinoids.

6. At each interradius and near the base of the petaloids are the **gonopores,** each surrounded by a **genital plate.** Can you determine which of the genital plates functions as the madreporite? To do this you may need to examine several different specimens and/or species to see the pattern. At the base of each petaloid locate the **ocular plate** and the hole that bore a light-sensitive tube foot in life.

7. The internal anatomy of both the sand dollar and sea biscuit is similar to that of sea urchins. Because of the difficulty in dissection, their internal anatomy will not be studied. However, their internal architecture is interesting and should be examined. Obtain a cleaned dried specimen of a sand dollar that has been broken open and examine the inside. How does the inside of the sand dollar compare to that of the sea urchin? Suggest a function for these structures in the living animal. Now examine the internal anatomy of a sea biscuit test that has been cut in half. Does this organism have internal supports as in the sand dollar? Is the test wall thick or thin? What other features are present in the test wall of

the sea biscuit? Speculate on the function of the perforations and cavities.

8. If sufficient specimens are available, you may wish to analyze the weight-to-strength ratio of sand dollars (and/or sea biscuits) as was done for the sea urchin. Replot the data from the sea urchin study along with that of the sand dollar. What does this information indicate about the strength of the tests of these organisms?

9. If a live sand dollar is available for study, place the animal in a small dish of seawater and examine it using a dissection microscope. Is the epidermis ciliated? Are dermal branchiae, pedicellaria, spines, or tube feet visible on either the oral or aboral surface? How large are the spines and tube feet? What are they doing? Sprinkle a small amount of sand on the aboral surface and watch what happens. Observe burrowing behavior. How do these animals bury themselves? How is the sand dollar like an arthropodian milliped?

Heart Urchins (Spatangoids)

Heart urchins are similar to the sand dollars and sea biscuits just examined. Obtain a cleaned test of an irregular echinoid for study.

1. Note that the body of the heart urchin is egg- or heart-shaped and on the aboral surface there are petaloid ambulacra containing tube feet for gaseous exchange (Fig. 24).

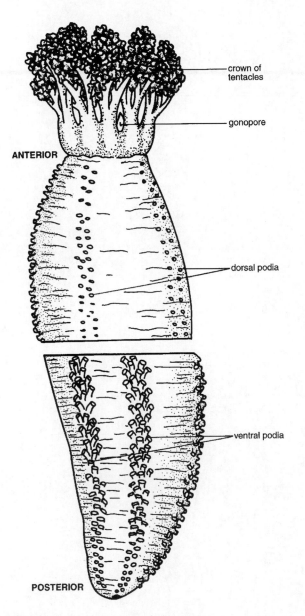

crown of tentacles

gonopore

ANTERIOR

dorsal podia

ventral podia

POSTERIOR

Figure 25. External view of a sea cucumber.

2. The mouth and peristome are located toward the anterior end of the flat, aboral surface, and the anus is at the posterior or more pointed end. There are three anterior ambulacra and two posterior ambulacra on the aboral surface. These ambulacra contain pores through which the tube feet protrude.

3. Small, dense spines cover the body surface; the spines are similar to those of sea urchins and sand dollars. Heart urchins lack the complex Aristotle's lantern. Both sand dollars and heart urchins feed on minute organic materials.

4. How do irregular echinoids compare to the other members of their class? Is the construction of the test more similar to that of the sea urchin or of the sand dollar? ■

D. Class Holothuroidea

Sea cucumbers are rather bizarre-looking echinoderms. Indeed they are unlike other members of the Echinodermata in a number of features. There are approximately 1,000 living species of the Class Holothuroidea [HOL-o-thur-OI-de-ah; G., *holothourion*, a kind of zoophyte + G., *eidos*, form]. They are common in the littoral areas of the sea and also constitute an important fauna of the marine abyss.

The body of a sea cucumber is elongated on an oral-aboral (anteroposterior) axis (Fig. 25). The oral end

Phylum Echinodermata

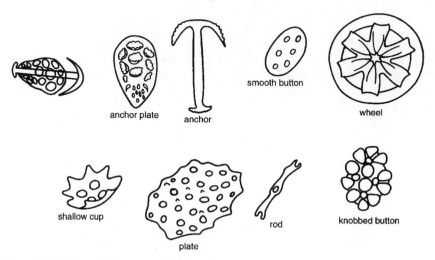

Figure 26. Ossicles of several types of sea cucumbers.

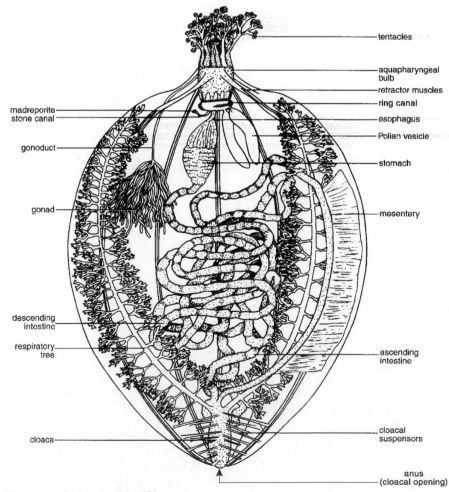

Figure 27. Internal anatomy of a sea cucumber (*Thyone*).

contains the mouth that is surrounded by a number of food-gathering **tentacles.** These mucus-covered structures are modified tube feet and usually can be retracted within the sea cucumber's body. The opposite end bears the anus. The spineless body wall of most sea cucumbers is leathery and contains an embedded endoskeleton of microscopic, calcareous ossicles that are not fused with each other. Tube feet are scattered over the body surface (*Thyone*), grouped in five ambulacral areas (*Cucumaria*), or totally lacking (*Leptosynapta*). Sea cucumbers move about by muscular contraction of their body, aided by the tube feet when present.

Sea cucumbers are typically dioecious and fertilization occurs in the water. During development many species pass through two larval stages: first, an **auricularia** and second, a **doliolaria.** These microscopic larvae resemble those found in other members of the Echinodermata.

Sea cucumbers are noted for their great powers of regeneration. When disturbed or under stress, the animal is unusual in being able to **eviscerate** the internal organs. This is perhaps a means of distracting predators; *Holothuria* and a few others, can eject a sticky mass of **Cuvierian tubules,** that entangle the predator. Regeneration of the lost organs then occurs after the sea cucumber crawls to safety.

■ Observational Procedure:

External Anatomy

Obtain a specimen of *Cucumaria* and/or *Thyone*, or a similar species suitable for dissection.

1. How is the body surface of the sea cucumber obviously different from the other echinoderms examined? Determine the oral-aboral axis of the specimen. Feel the body surface. How does it compare to the other echinoderms examined so far? Is there any evidence of ossicles?

2. In *Cucumaria* the tube feet are present in five distinct ambulacral areas, three on the ventral surface and two on the dorsal surface. Retrieve your sketch of the symmetry of the sea star and relate it to *Cucumaria*. Ray A is on the midventral line according to Carpenter's designation of the radii, discussed in the exercise on asteroids. The tube feet on the somewhat flattened, ventral surface (the **sole**) are better developed than are those on the dorsal surface. Do all the sea cucumbers available for study have the same arrangement of tube feet?

3. Isolate the endoskeletal ossicles for examination by removing a section of the body wall and boiling it in a small quantity of bleach (sodium hypochlorite). (NB: Be sure to do this under safe conditions: e.g., in a fume hood with the window guard down.) During this process the body wall will be dissolved. When the bleach cools, decant it, rinse the ossicles in tap water, and examine them using a compound microscope (Fig. 26). Do these ossicles resemble in any way those of other echinoderms?

Internal Anatomy

1. Beginning at the posterior end, make a ventral incision through the body wall and extend this incision through the anterior end. Open the body wall laterally and pin it to the dissection pan. Cover the specimen with water. As you study the internal anatomy, refer to (Fig. 27).

2. The enterocoelom in sea cucumbers is spacious. In life the body cavity is filled with coelomic fluid containing various types of amoebocytes. The peritoneal cilia produce a current that moves the coelomic fluid throughout the enterocoelom.

Digestive System

1. This system consists of the mouth, expanded pharynx, short esophagus, muscular stomach, and long intestine that leads to the muscular rectum (Fig. 27). In *Cucumaria*, but not in *Thyone*, the esophagus is absent and the stomach is poorly developed. Note the muscles that attached the rectum to the inner surface of the body wall.

2. Find the pair of highly branched **respiratory trees** that extend off the rectum (Fig. 27). The muscular rectum pumps water into the trees and expels it back to the sea. Exchange of respiratory gases occurs within the trees, which are unique to seawater cucumbers. However, the burrowing forms, such as *Leptosynapta*, lack them and exchange of respiratory gases occurs across the body surface.

Water-vascular System

1. Surrounding the pharynx is a hard structure called the **calcareous ring** to which **retractor muscles** are attached posteriorly. These muscles retract the entire oral region inside the body. The calcareous-ring complex may be homologous with the Aristotle's lantern of echinoids.

2. At the base of the pharynx just behind the calcareous ring is the **ring canal.** The dorsal madreporite is connected to the ring canal by the stone canal. The internal position of the madreporite is unlike that of other echinoderms. One to several (often two) saclike, **Polian vesicles** arise from the ring canal. Follow these where they join the canal (Fig. 27). Some specimens may have small vesicles, whereas others may have greatly expanded vesicles. The Polian vesicles may maintain pressure within the water-vascular system.

3. Locate the five **radial canals** off the ring canal that run anteriorly to the oral tentacles and then descend to the aboral end of the body. The canals follow the large, **longitudinal muscles** that are attached to the inner surface of the body wall. These lie under the five am-bulacral areas. The canals lead into numerous side canals that connect with the tube feet in the ambulacra. The longitudinal muscles also join the retractor muscles at the anterior end. In addition to these muscles, note that the inner body wall is lined with **circular muscles.** The circular and longitudinal muscles allow the sea cucumber to expand and contract its body.

Reproductive System

The reproductive system is simple in these dioecious animals (Fig. 27). Find the moplike **gonad** that consists of a tuft of fine filaments. The gonad increases in size with the approach of sexual maturity. Do you think that your specimen was sexually mature when it was taken? Holothurians are the only echinoderms with a single gonad. A gonoduct carries eggs or sperm anteriorly to a genital papilla located between two dorsal tentacles. Microscopic examination of crushed gonadal filaments will reveal the sex of your specimen. The round head and long tail of the sperm can be seen when stained with methylene blue and examined under oil immersion. Eggs of the female are large and ovoid.

Live Specimens

1. Focus your attention on the cloacal opening of a live animal. Is it slowly opening and closing? Using a Pasteur pipette, place a small amount of seawater that was colored with methylene blue stain near the opening of the cloaca. What happens to the stain? What does this indicate is going on?

2. Try rotating the animal onto a different side. Does it turn back around (right itself)?

3. Observe burrowing behavior in a sea cucumber by placing the animal in a large glass bowl filled with sea-water and a sufficient quantity of sand to permit bur-rowing. How does the sea cucumber bury itself? Is this behavior anything like the burrowing observed in other echinoderms you studied?

4. How do sea cucumbers react to stimuli? Take care in these investigations; some sea cucumbers will evis-cerate if abused. If it is appropriate to do so, your instructor will demonstrate this phenomenon. Examine the ejected organs to determine which ones were expelled. What possible advantage can this behavior provide the sea cucumber? What other animals ablate body parts when attacked? ■

E. Class Crinoidea

The Class Crinoidea [cri-NOI-de-ah; G., *krion,* a lily + G., *eidos,* form] contains about 100 species of sea lilies and an additional 600 species of feather stars or co-matulids [KO-mat-u-lids; L., *comatus,* hairy] (about 600 living species). Crinoids have a worldwide distribution in warm and frigid waters and live at depths ranging from a few meters to over 5,000 m. Some species are gregarious, often forming huge local populations.

The living species represent a mere remnant of a once-thriving group in the geologic past. The crinoid fossil record dates back to the **Cambrian Period** and over 5,000 fossil species have been described from the **Paleozoic Era** (Fig. 1).

Most crinoids living today are the stemless comat-ulids, whereas in the past the majority of species were attached permanently to the sea floor by a **stem** (or **stalk**). Comatulids are attached to a substrate by a stem in their early development, but break away and move about on their jointed **cirri,** somewhat in a walking fash-ion, or swim by lashing their arms (Fig. 28). Sea lilies are similar in structure to the comatulids, but have a stalk for attachment (Fig. 29).

■ Observational Procedure:

1. Obtain a specimen of a stemmed crinoid and a stemless comatulid such as *Antedon.* Observe that the body consists of the cup-shaped **calyx** (**theca**) housing the internal organs, the arms constituting a food-gath-ering apparatus, and the attachment device (**stem** and/or **cirri**) for clinging to the substratum (Fig. 28 and 29). The combination of the calyx and arms is called **crown.** Feather stars lack the stalk, but have cirri for grasping the substratum.

2. The cup-shaped calyx is composed of external cal-careous plates and is attached by its aboral surface. The membranous covering of the calyx is the **tegmen;** it is the oral surface of the organism (Fig. 30). Embedded in the tegmen are minute, calcareous plates. Also in the tegmen are tiny, ciliated canals that open into the ente-rocoelom. These openings may function as a madreporite. Note that the tegmen is divided radially into five ambu-lacral and five interambulacral areas (Fig. 30). The mouth is situated at or near the center of the tegmen and the anus occurs in one of the interambulacral areas. The

arm

pinnules

calyx

cirri

Figure 28. External view of a feather star (comatulid).

anus is on an elevated **anal cone** that directs feces away from the mouth. Unlike other echinoderms, crinoids have the oral surface directed upwards.

3. Extending from the periphery of the crown are the five arms. Each arm, along with its ambulacral groove, may branch once or several times, forming 10 or more arms. How many branches does your specimen have? What advantage might a large number of branches offer a sedentary, suspension feeder?

4. Note the rows of spherical, yellow-brown dots along the sides of each ambulacral groove (Fig. 31B). These bodies are **saccules** and may serve as waste deposit areas. To see the saccules, observe them with a dissection microscope. The margins of the ambulacral grooves bear movable plates called **lappets.** These can close over the ambulacral groove. Within the grooves are the tentacle-shaped tube feet bearing mucous-secreting papillae used for food capture. Ampullae are lacking on the tube feet. Cilia within the ambulacral groove propel the food to the mouth. Crinoids are suspension feeders.

5. Extending laterally off each arm find the numerous jointed **pinnules** (Fig. 30). The ambulacral grooves of the pinnules are continuous with the main arm grooves; both podia and lappets occur in the pinnules. Gametes develop from the germinal epithelium in those pinnules located along the proximal half of the arm length. Both the arms and pinnules are composed of ossicles of the endoskeleton.

6. The stem is composed of a series of stacked, disc-shaped ossicles, each perforated by a central, axial canal for passage of components to certain organs. The discs are known as **columnals.** Because of the internal skeletal ossicles, the stalk has a jointed appearance. View these structures on a fossil crinoid (Fig. 29).

7. Crinoids are dioecious. The gametes rupture through the pinnule walls. The fertilized eggs remain attached to the pinnules as in *Antedon* or they are shed in the seawater. The free-swimming larva is a nonfeeding **vitellaria,** similar to that of sea cucumbers (Fig. 32). The larva settles to the bottom of the sea floor and develops eventually into an adult.

Due to the difficulty involved in the dissection, the internal anatomy of the crinoid will not be studied. ■

Figure 29. External view of a sea lily.

Fossil Echinoderms

Because of their hard, calcareous endoskeleton, echinoderms fossilize well and their fossil record is rich. According to many zoologists, this ancient group dates to the lower **Cambrian Period** (Fig. 1). Despite a rich fossil record, the exact relationship of the echinoderms to the other invertebrates and to the chordates is unknown.

Most of the fossil species were stalked, sessile, and had the oral surface along with the ambulacral groove directed upwards. Many possessed extensions of the groove in a pinnule-like projection called **a brachiole** (Fig. 33A). These fossils were similar to modern-day sea lilies. More than likely the ambulacral system of tube feet was first used for feeding, rather than for locomotion. Later the podia served for locomotion and several independent lines toward bilateral symmetry ensued.

Three of the oldest groups (**Cambrian Period**) recognized currently are Helicoplacoidea, Carpoidea, and Blastozoa (Fig. 33).

Phylum Echinodermata

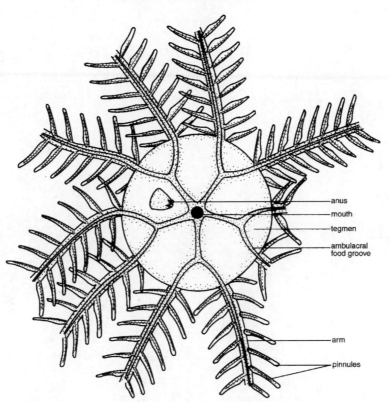

anus
mouth
tegmen
ambulacral
food groove

arm

pinnules

Figure 30. Oral surface of a crinoid.

lappets

pinnulars

(A)

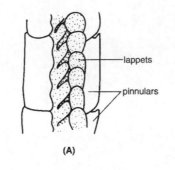

podia

water-vascular
system canal

saccule

spiny terminal
pinnulars

(B)

Figure 31. Crinoid arms structure. (A) Part of a crinoid pinnule showing lappets and ambulacral groove. (B) Section through the tip of a crinoid pinnule showing the podia and saccules.

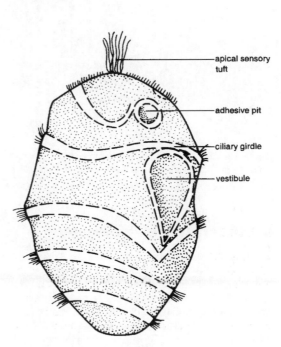

apical sensory
tuft

adhesive pit

ciliary girdle

vestibule

Figure 32. Crinoid vitellaria larva.

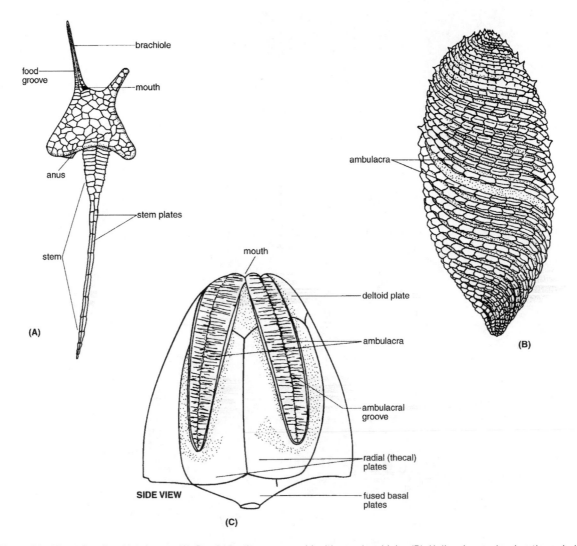

Figure 33. Three fossil echinoderms. (A) *Dendrocystites,* a carpoid with one brachiole. (B) *Helicoplacus* showing the spiral ambulacrum. (C) *Pentremites,* a blastoid showing ambulacra. (After various sources.)

■ Observational Procedure:

1. Observe the fossil echinoderms available for your study. Whenever possible determine the oral-aboral axis and recognize the radial symmetry. Do the specimens all exhibit a pentamerous body plan? Locate ambulacra and the interambulacra. Do they resemble the ambulacra and the interambulacra of the extant specimens?

2. If possible relate each specimen to a present-day form. Do any of these specimens resemble modern echinoderms sufficiently for you to assign them to a subphylum or to a class? What evidence did you focus on to do this simple classification?

3. If whole fossil crinoids are available for study compare their form to Figure 29. Examine the columnals. Are they hollow? What sorts of patterns, grooves, or embossments are present?

4. If the calyx of a blastoid is on display, locate the following features: ambulacra, interambulacra, mouth, anus, and various plates (deltoid, radial, basal). How does this specimen qualify as an echinoderm? ■

Phylum Echinodermata

Phylum Echinodermata	Worksheet 12
Name: _____	Date: _____
Course #: _____ / Section #: _____	Grade: _____

1. Compare the characters in the chart below for each class of Echinodermata.

Character	Asteroidea	Ophiuroidea	Echinoidea	Holothuroidea	Crinoidea
Madreporite					
Pedicellaria					
Tube feet					
Means of respiration					
Spines					
Aristotle's lantern					
Polian vesicle					
Larva type					

295

Phylum Echinodermata

2. Give a possible explanation why the madreporite of sea cucumbers is located internally instead of externally.

3. Sea lilies, as implied by their names, were formerly classified as plants. Explain how this might have happened. What features are possessed by these echinoderms that caused early invertebrate zoologists to think they were plants?

4. Why is the intestine of many species of sea cucumbers and sea urchins greatly elongated compared to the short intestine of sea stars?

5. What features possessed by echinoderms might indicate they are related to chordates?

■

Phylum Hemichordata

Hemichordata [hem-ee-KOR-dah-tah; G., *hemi*, half + G., *chorda*, string] contains about 85 species of burrowing or sessile, enterocoelous, marine animals. Their bodies are divisible into an anterior **proboscis,** middle **collar,** and a long posterior **trunk** (Fig. 1). **Pharyngeal gill slits** for gas exchange occur in most hemichordates. Other features include a complete digestive system, open circulatory system, nervous system combining invertebrate and vertebrate features, and separate sexes. Two classes of this widely distributed phylum are represented by acorn worms and pterobranchs.

Pterobranchia [ter-o-BRAN-chi-ah; G., *pteron*, wing + G., *branchia*, gills] consists of fewer than 15 small (1–5 mm) species. Most of these uncommon, deep-water invertebrates live in secreted tubes forming colonies or aggregations. Extending dorsally from the collar region are one or more arms bearing several food-gathering, hollow, ciliated tentacles. Pterobranchs may be more closely related to phoronids (Phoronida) and brachiopods (Brachiopoda) than to enteropneusts. Graptolites, an enigmatic group of fossils, may be pterobranchs. Because of the rarity, unavailability, and small size of pterobranchs, they will not be studied in this exercise.

There are approximately 70 species of acorn worms in the Class Enteropneusta [en-TER-o-NEUS-tah; G., *enteron*, gut + G., *pnein*, to breathe]. These slow-moving worms range from a few millimeters to greater than 1 m in length. They are found in shallow waters of intertidal and littoral zones beneath shells and rocks, in seaweed, or burrows dug in mud or sand. The burrows are generally **U**-shaped and mucus-lined. Enteropneusts are either suspension feeders or deposit feeders. Those of the former type trap minute food particles in mucus on the proboscis moving that material to the mouth by ciliary action. Deposit feeders extract organic materials from the vast amount of sand and mud that they consume. Undigested remains are deposited on the surface of the sediment as coiled **fecal casts.**

Acorn worms are dioecious. Gametes from the gonads in the trunk region escape via a pore into the water. Fertilization is external and development is either direct or indirect. Many species produce a free-swimming, ciliated **tornaria larva** that is similar to the bipinnaria larva of sea stars (Echinodermata: Asteroidea). Asexual reproduction after fragmentation has been reported from some enteropneusts.

Classification

1. **Class Pterobranchia.** Hemichordates possessing one or more pairs of tentacular arms arising from the dorsal area of the collar. One pair of gills present or gills absent. Examples: *Rhabdopleura* and *Cephalodiscus.*

2. **Class Enteropneusta.** Hemichordates with numerous gill slits. Examples: *Saccoglossus* and *Balanoglossus.*

From *Invertebrate Zoology,* Sixth Edition, Robert L. Wallace and Walter K. Taylor. Copyright © 2002 by Pearson Education, Inc. Published by Prentice-Hall, Inc. All rights reserved

Phylum Hemichordata

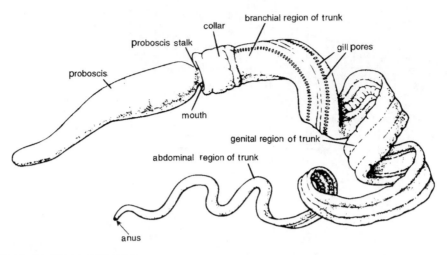

Figure 1. External view of the hemichordate.

■ Observational Procedure:

Whole Acorn Worm

1. Obtain an acorn worm such as *Saccoglossus (Dolichoglossus) kowalevskii* which lives along the North American and European Atlantic coasts. Place in a small dish containing water and examine it using the dissection microscope. Locate the three body regions: proboscis, collar, and trunk (Fig. 1). Each region corresponds to the body divisions of a typical deuterostome (e.g., **protosome, mesosome,** and **metasome**). Internally, each region has its own coelomic cavity: a single protocoel of the proboscis, paired metacoels of the collar, and paired metacoels of the trunk. These and other internal structures will be examined later when you study a longitudinal section of the worm.

2. Locate the proboscis of your worm and the others available in the lab. What shape is it? What sorts of characteristics would you predict it possesses for this activity? A narrow isthmus, the **proboscis stalk,** connects the proboscis to the collar region (Fig. 1). Be very careful should you attempt to find this shaft of tissue, for in doing so you may damage the specimen.

3. Focus your attention on the collar. Describe the shape of this structure. Is the collar a uniform shape? Attempt to locate the mouth on the anterior margin of the ventral side of the collar. (Be careful here.) It should be found just below the proboscis stalk (Fig. 1). The mouth marks the ventral side of the animal. Using a dissection microscope, examine the dorsal side of the proboscis and attempt to locate the small **proboscis pore** on the stalk. This pore allows water to enter and leave the protocoel during burrowing. Why might this be important to the functioning of the proboscis? If you can-

not find this structure, you may be able to see it when you examine a longitudinal section of the worm.

4. Most of the animal's body consists of the trunk which has a midventral and middorsal **longitudinal ridge** (Fig. 1). The trunk can be divided into three regions; locate each region on your specimen as it is discussed. (1) The anterior **branchial** region contains numerous U-shaped gill slits. Locate the **gill pores** in paired rows along the dorsolateral area of the branchial trunk region. Each pore leads to an internal branchial sac that communicates with the slit. (2) The middle **genital** region contains the gonads. (3) The posterior **abdominal** region contains intestine with the paired **intestinal diverticula.** After passing through the gut, undigested materials are eliminated by the terminal anus.

5. If you are to dissect the specimen, your instructor will provide you with the appropriate instructions. Otherwise, set the specimen aside but do not return it to the museum jar just yet. You may need to refer back to the specimen while you study some of the internal structures of the animal.

Slides—*Balanoglossus*

Longitudinal and Sagittal Sections

1. Obtain longitudinal and sagittal sections of an acorn worm such as *Balanoglossus*. Examine each section under low power of a compound microscope to become familiar with the orientation of the specimens on the slides. Locate the proboscis, collar, mouth, and pharyngeal region with gill slits. As you proceed through this portion of the exercise, it will be best if you are able to examine more than one slide. Although you will be examining longitudinal sections each may show a slightly

Phylum Hemichordata

different aspect of the animal, and thus provide a different view of important anatomical features.

2. Locate the proboscis and describe how it is constructed. The outermost layer is the epidermis, a region rich in glandular cells bearing both cilia microvilli. Switch to medium magnification and examine the entire edge of the proboscis. Are the glandular cells evenly distributed in the epidermis? If not, where are they concentrated? What function does it serve to have gland cells concentrated in one region or another? Using some advanced lighting conditions (i.e., high power and phase contrast) you may be able to see the cilia, which otherwise show up as a thin fuzzy region.

3. Beneath the epidermis locate the **basal lamina** and a layer of connective tissue **dermis.** Below those two layers find the regions of circular and longitudinal muscles. How can you tell the circular and longitudinal muscles apart? What is their function in the proboscis? Locate the protocoel (Fig. 2). This body cavity is not extensive and may seem to be subdivided into channels due to the presence of intervening tissue. On the dorsal side of the animal, attempt to find the proboscis pore on the proboscis stalk (Fig. 2). This channel connects the protocoel to the outside. How do the circular and longitudinal muscles, protocol, and proboscis pore function in the burrowing action of the proboscis?

4. Using low power scan the basal region of the proboscis where it connects to the stalk. In this area locate the narrow **buccal diverticulum** or **stomochord.** In the past, this feature was thought to be a **notochord** (Fig. 2), and because of that, hemichordates were placed in Phylum Chordata. Locate the **proboscis skeleton** (Fig. 2). Switch to high power and examine this structure for cells; are any present? The proboscis skeleton is cartilaginous and wishbone in shape with the wings extending into the collar. What function(s) might this structure serve?

5. At the base of the proboscis, just anterior to the proboscis skeleton, locate a network of vessels. This is the **glomerulus,** a structure believed to have excretory functions. Behind the glomerulus and dorsal to the stomochord is the heart. Where is the protocoel in relation to these other structures? Given this spatial relationship, how might excretion be accomplished? Locate the anterior nerve ring; it should be found above the heart almost in the wall of the proboscis.

6. Focus your attention to the region of the collar, noting the presence of folds. Is the epidermal layer of the

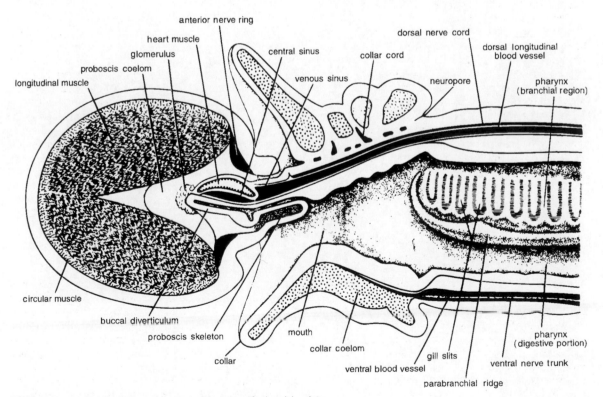

Figure 2. Internal sagittal view of the anterior region of a hemichordate.

collar as richly supplied with glands as was the proboscis? The largest anatomical features to be seen in the collar region are the mouth and buccal cavity. Locate cavities of the mesocoel in the dorsal and ventral sides of the collar. Also try to find the dorsal and ventral nerve cords. Extensions of the collar nerve cord may appear as a series of cavities (Fig. 2). When these cavities open to the outside they are referred to as **neuropores.** Are any neuropores present in the sections available for your study? The dorsal and ventral blood vessels also may be found. Are any structures resembling the proboscis skeleton present in the collar region? What distinguishes the proboscis skeleton from the other structures in this region?

7. Finally, examine the pharyngeal or branchial portion of the upper trunk. The most obvious feature present here is the large empty space of the pharynx. Locate the cavities of the metacoel in the dorsal and ventral sides of the collar. Locate the gills and their support structures, the gill arches. Note that the gill tissue is very thin and, of course, cellular. Observe that their skeletal supports (the **gill arches**) are thicker and acellular. You should be able to trace the blood vascular system as a series of winding tubes that lead to the gills. Other structures that you may see at this level include mucous glands and ovaries or testes.

Cross Section (trunk, through level of the intestine)

1. Obtain a cross section of an acorn worm such as *Balanoglossus.* Examine the section under low power of a compound microscope to become familiar with the orientation of the specimen. As noted in the previous section, when you proceed through this exercise, it will be best if you examine more than one slide.

2. Locate the large open space in the center of the section; this is the pharynx. Determine the dorsal and ventral side of the animal. The structures that will aid you the most in making this determination are the **skeletal supports** of the gills. They originate on the dorsal side and pass ventrally around the pharynx. Locate the gill skeletal support and examine them under high power. How are they similar to the proboscis skeleton?

3. Switch back to a lower power and find the dorsal nerve cord and beneath it the dorsal blood vessel. On the opposite side of the animal, locate the ventral nerve cord and beneath it the ventral blood vessel.

4. Locate the metacoel; it is the space between the pharynx and the longitudinal muscle. Now focus your attention to the gill slits; these are openings in the pharynx that communicate to the outside via the external gill pores. Find the following structures: (1) gill slits; (2) the space between the gill slits and the external gill pores; (3) gill pores; (4) gill bars. ∎

Phylum Hemichordata

Name: _____   Date: _____

Course #: _____ / Section #: _____   Grade: _____

1. Why were the hemichordates once placed with the phylum Chordata?

2. How does the dart-shape form of chaetognaths aid in their locomotion?

3. Here are two more phyla with common names that include the word worm. What is a worm and why are there so many wormy organisms? Discuss.

PHYLUM CHORDATA

Nearly 50,000 extant species comprise the Phylum Chordata, but most of them are members of the Subphylum Vertebrata [VER-ta-BRA-tah; L., *vertebratus*, jointed or articulated]. The two other Subphyla, Urochordata [U-ro-kor-DA-tah; G., *uro*, tail + G., *chordata*, string] and Cephalochordata [SEF-a-lo-kor-DA-tah; *cephala*, head], are of some interest to both invertebrate and vertebrate zoologists as members may be similar to the ancestral vertebrates. All chordates possess paired pharyngeal gill slits, a dorsal tubular nerve cord, and a supportive notochord during some portion of their lives.

Alexander, R.McN. 1975. *The Chordates.* Cambridge Univ. Press. Cambridge.

Alldredge, A.L. 1976. Appendicularians. *Sci. Am.* 235(1): 94-102.

Barrington, E.J.W., 1965. The Biology of Hemichordata and Protochordata. W.H. Freeman and Co., San Francisco, CA.

Barrington, E.J.W., and R.P.S. Jefferies. (eds.). 1975. Protochordates. *Symp. Zool. Soc. Lond.* 35.

Berrill, N.J. 1950. *The Tunicata.* Ray Society, London.

Berrill, N.J. 1955. *The Origin of Vertebrates.* Oxford University Press, Oxford.

Berrill, N.J. 1961. Salpa. *Sci. Amer.* 204: 150-160.

Bone, Q. 1972. *The Origins of Chordates.* Oxford University Biology Readers. Number 18. Oxford University Press, London.

Gans, C., and R.G. Northcutt. 1983. Neural crest and the origin of vertebrates: a new head. *Science* 220: 268-274.

Goodbody, I. 1974. The physiology of ascidians. *Adv. Mar. Biol.* 12: 1-149.

Gutmann, W.F. 1981. Relationships between invertebrate phyla based on functional-mechanical analysis of the hydrostatic skeleton. *Am. Zool.* 21: 63-81.

Holland, L.Z., and N.D. Holland. 1998. Developmental gene expression in Amphioxus: new insights into the evolutionary origin of vertebrate brain regions, neural crest, and rostrocaudal segmentation. *Am. Zool.* 38: 647-658.

Jefferies, R.P.S. 1986. *The Ancestry of Vertebrates.* Cambridge University Press, Melbourne.

Løvtrup, S. 1977. *The Phylogeny of Vertebrates.* Wiley, London.

Maisey, J.G. 1986. Heads and tails: a chordate phylogeny. *Cladistics* 2: 201-256.

Millar, R.H. 1971. The biology of ascidians. *Adv. Mar. Biol.* 9: 1-100.

Riisgård, H.U., and I. Svane. 1999. Filter feeding in lancelets (amphioxus), *Brachiostoma lanceolatum. Invertebrate Biology* 118: 423-432.

Romer, A.S. 1967. Major steps in vertebrate evolution. *Science* 158: 1629-1637.

Stokes, M.D., and N.D. Holland. 1998. The lancelet. *Am. Scientist* 86: 552-560.

Wickstead, J.H. 1967. Chordata sub-phylum Acrania (= Cephalochordata) family Branchiostomidae. *Fiches d'Identification du Zooplankton* 11.

Phylum Chordata

Most of the nearly 50,000 species comprising the Phylum Chordata (kor-DAH-tah; G., *chorda*, string) are vertebrates (Subphylum Vertebrata) because they possess a vertebral column. However, this phylum contains two nonvertebrate subphyla, Urochordata (sea squirts, or ascidians) and Cephalochordata (lancelets), containing about 1,400 species. Both subphyla comprise the Acrania (ah-CRAY-ne-ah; G., *a*, without + G., *crania*, skull) whose members are commonly called **protochordates** or **prochordates**. Protochordates are benthic, marine, small in size, and lack a cranium that houses the brain. In contrast, the vertebrates comprise the Craniata (Cray-ne-AH-ta; G., *crania*, skull). Formerly, the hemichordates

or tongue worms (Phylum Hemichordata) were also considered to be protochordates, but recent work indicates that the animals lack features common to chordates. Chordates have four unifying structures at some time in their life: **paired pharyngeal gill slits, dorsal notochord, dorsal tubular nerve cord**, and a **postanal tail**. Although some instructors prefer to omit part or all of the Phylum Chordata leaving them to courses in vertebrate zoology, the nonvertebrate chordates are valid subjects for study by students of invertebrate zoology. Members of the Subphylum Cephalochordata have a fossil record beginning in the mid-**Cambrian Period** (Fig. 1).

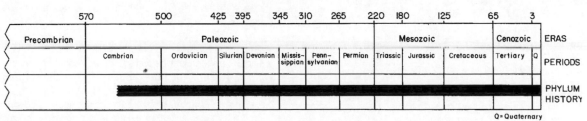

TIME (IN MILLIONS OF YEARS)

	570	500	425	395	345	310	265	220	180	125	65	3	
Precambrian		Paleozoic							Mesozoic			Cenozoic	ERAS
	Cambrian	Ordovician	Silurian	Devonian	Missis-sippian	Penn-sylvanian	Permian	Triassic	Jurassic	Cretaceous	Tertiary	Q	PERIODS
													PHYLUM HISTORY

Q= Quaternary

Figure 1. Geological history of the Cephalochordata.

From *Invertebrate Zoology*, Sixth Edition, Robert L. Wallace and Walter K. Taylor. Copyright © 2002 by Pearson Education, Inc. Published by Prentice-Hall, Inc. All rights reserved

A. Subphylum Urochordata (Tunicata)

Subphylum Urochordata [URO-chor-DA-tah; G., *uro*, tail, + G., *chorda*, string] is comprised of small to medium-sized individuals that scarcely resemble the chordate description. The three chordate characteristics are present only during the larval stage. In the adult the gut is U-shaped, with a spacious pharynx perforated by numerous gill slits. Because the body is covered with a tough test or **tunic**, urochordates are commonly called **tunicates.**

Classification

These exclusively marine, free-living, filter-feeding chordates lack segmentation and hard parts. Of the three commonly recognized classes, only members of Ascidiacea and Thaliacea will be studied in this exercise.

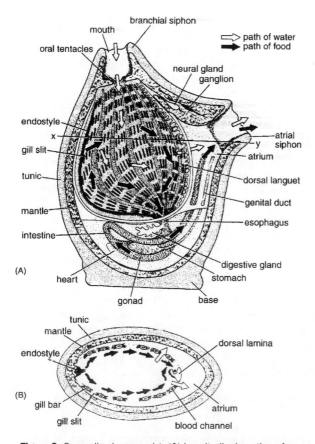

Figure 2. Generalized sea squirt. (**A**) Longitudinal section of a sea squirt depicting movement of water and food particles. (**B**) Cross section of sea squirt at the level of line X-Y. (After Sherman and Sherman and other sources.)

1. Class Ascidiacea. Shallow to deep-sea, sessile or sedentary, barrel- or bag-shaped urochordates, commonly called sea squirts. Adults are either solitary or colonial in jelly masses containing a few to many minute individuals. Ascidians are often constituents of the marine- fouling community. The tunic, which may be massive, is a composite of protein and a polysaccharide resembling cellulose, a rare item found in animals. Most species are monoecious. The larval stage resembles a tadpole. Examples: *Aplidium (=Amaroucium), Botryllus, Ciona, Corella, Ecteinascidia, Molgula, Perophora,* and *Styela (= Cynthia).*

2. Class Larvacea (Appendicularia). Small, solitary, planktonic urochordates in which the adult appears to have conserved the organization of the ascidian larval stage (**neoteny**); that is, the adults resemble the tadpole larva of an ascidian. The larvacean body is ovoid in shape with a long thin tail. These urochordates live within gelatinous cases or houses that they secrete. Example: *Oikopleura.*

3. Class Thaliacea. Planktonic, colonial urochordates (or with a life cycle where colonial and solitary forms alternate). Members of the class are often called pelagic tunicates or salps. Individuals are somewhat barrel-shaped with a large open pharynx. Colonies range in size from a few centimeters to several meters. Locomotion is accomplished by a rhythmic contraction and expansion of the tunic that results in a jet propulsion. Examples: *Pyrosoma* and *Salpa.*

■ Observational Procedure: Class Ascidiacea

Whenever possible, observe living animals. Place the specimens to be examined in a small bowl filled with water enough to cover the animals. Use sea water if live animals are used, allowing them sufficient time to relax and extend their siphons. Try not to disturb the animals once they have relaxed. If your specimens are small and transparent, you may wish to make your observations with the aid of a dissection microscope. Lighting from the side or beneath the animals may facilitate your observations.

Solitary Ascidians

Begin your observations with a solitary ascidian such as *Corella, Ciona, Molgula* and/or *Styela (= Cynthia)* (Fig. 2).

1. What features do these animals possess that would permit you to recognize them in the field? Are your live specimens producing inhalant and exhalant currents of water?

Which siphon is inhalant and which is exhalant? How strong are the currents and how are they produced? The following directions will aid you in answering these questions.

Using a Pasteur pipette, gently deposit a few drops of a dilute suspension of carmine power or carbon black near each siphon. How do the particles move? If the particles are taken into the animal, where do they enter? One aperture, the inhalant, oral, or **branchial** (G., *brachium,* gill) siphon takes water into the animal, while the other, the exhalant or **atrial** (L., *atrium,* vestibule) siphon directs water out of the animal (Fig. 2).

If your specimen is sufficiently transparent, it may be possible to track the movement of particles into the digestive tract. Do the particles accumulate within the gut? Over time you may be able to see the entire gut fill with this colored food. Are any of the particles rejected immediately, or do they all go into the animal? Do any particles exit the animal via the atrial siphon before passing through the gut?

2. Feel the covering or tunic that encases the animals. What descriptive terms would you use to describe the tunic (hard, soft, firm, flexible)? If you felt the tunic of a live animal, what happened when you touched the animal? Why are these ascidian commonly called **sea squirts**? Do they squirt from only one siphon? How is expulsion of water accomplished?

3. The branchial siphon is located at the anterior end and is directed parallel to the long axis of the body. The atrial siphon indicates the dorsal side of the animal (Fig. 2). Determine the anterioposterior axis of your specimen. How are these animals bilaterally symmetrical? Which side is left and which is right? Tunicates are usually attached to a substratum. To what sorts of substrata are your specimens attached?

4. Examine the body of *Ciona* or *Molgula* more closely. Two regions compose the body: thorax or **branchial** and abdomen or **visceral.** To differentiate these regions you must be able to observe the internal structures of your specimen (Fig. 2). This may not be possible unless the tunic is transparent enough to permit light to pass through. If your specimens do not permit internal observations, obtain one or more whole mount slides of a specimen, such as the colonial ascidian *Ecteinascidia,* and make the following observations. [NB: *Ecteinascidia* is a colonial ascidian (see below), but may be examined here to get a good idea of ascidian morphology. The study of more than one slide may be necessary for you to complete these observations.]

5. Identify the branchial and atrial siphons. Next, locate the pharynx that marks the branchial portion of the animal. How large is the branchial portion of the body with respect to the entire animal? The pharynx is perforated with many gill slits (stigmata) and longitudinal gill bars, the tissues that surround and support the gill slits. How numerous are the gill slits? Just inside the pharynx locate the oral tentacles: between the branchial and atrial siphons, is the **subneural gland** (or neural gland). The function of the gland is not known. A ciliated groove, the **endostyle**, runs midventrally down the pharynx. The groove secretes a mucus that picks up food particles and carries them to the short esophagus. The **dorsal lamina**, a ciliated fold, is located on the side opposite of the endostyle.

6. At the base of the pharynx is the esophagus. This marks the beginning of the visceral portion of the animal. Trace the esophagus from the pharynx to the stomach and then to the intestine. The intestine travels up the dorsal side of the animal, becoming the rectum before terminating at the anus. On which side of the body does the anus empty? Locate the genital duct and the genital openings. Where are they located? Why might the atrium be considered to be a kind of a **cloaca**?

7. The following directions are to be used if you are to dissect a specimen. The purpose of the dissection is to open the pharynx so that gill slits may be examined and so that both the endostyle and dorsal lamina will be exposed. To do this, begin cutting from the branchial siphon down the left side of the body. This cut should be near, but not on, the ventral margin (Fig. 2).

Insert the point of a pair of scissors into the branchial siphon and carefully cut through the tunic and beneath it, the mantle. Continue the cut down to the base of the animal and then around the base and up through the atrial siphon. Complete the cut by inserting the scissors into the atrial siphon and cutting up to the branchial siphon.

Carefully trim any extra tissue holding the left and right halves of the animal together and remove the left side of the animal exposing the pharynx. Pin the sea squirt to the base of a dissection pan and cover it with water. Identify the structures previously examined in steps 5 and 6. Remove a piece of the pharyngeal wall, cover it with water, and examine it using a microscope. Locate the gill slits and gill bars. If a live specimen were used, note the activity of the cilia.

Colonial Ascidians

There are two kinds of colonial ascidians: social and compound. The former are connected by a **stolon,** while the latter are embedded in a common tunic.

1. *Social Ascidians*—If available, observe the colony organization of a social ascidian such as *Ecteinascidia* or *Perophora* (Fig. 3). How are the individuals arranged on the stolon? Is there a pattern to the arrangement? Are all individuals of the colony the same size? Identify the internal structures in the individuals. The directions given above (steps 3 through 5) may be

Figure 3. A colony of *Perophora*. (After Sherman and Sherman.)

followed for *Ecteinascidia*. In addition, note the presence of stalks at the posterior (aboral) end of the animal. What do they represent?

2. *Compound Ascidians*—Observe a compound ascidian such as *Aplidium* (= *Amaroucium*) or *Botryllus* (Figs. 4 and 5). These specimens tend to resemble a slab of hardened jelly, and may contain hundreds of in-

dividuals (**zooids**) within the colony. What features do these animals possess that would permit you to recognize them in the field? How does the tunic of a colonial tunicate feel? Is it the same as that of the solitary ones you examined? Determine whether a live colonial ascidian will squirt when disturbed?

3. Observe your specimen using either a hand lens or a dissection microscope and locate the clusters of **zooids** with their individual buccal siphons and their single, common atrial siphon. Note how groups of zooids form a collective unit with a common atrial siphon. This functional unit is called a **rosette** (Fig. 4). Which of these openings is larger, those of the branchial siphons or the common atrial siphon? In relaxed specimens, attempt to measure the siphon diameters and determine whether the cross-sectional area of the branchial siphons of a rosette equals or exceeds that of the common atrial siphon. (To do this you will need to use a dissection microscope equipped with an ocular

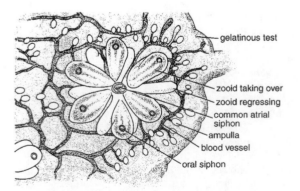

Figure 4. Portion of a colony of *Botryllus*. (After Sherman and Sherman.)

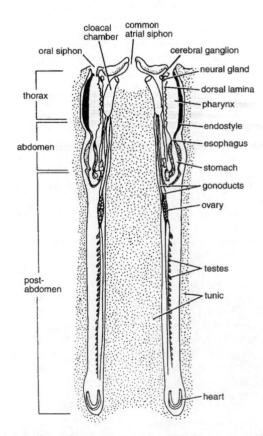

Figure 5. *Aplidium* (= *Amaroucium*). Longitudinal section of a portion of two zooids in a colony. (After Sherman and Sherman.)

Figure 6. Ascidian tadpole larvae. (A) Head. (B) Cross section through the tail. (Sherman and Sherman and other sources.)

micrometer). Consider the significance of the relationship of total cross-sectional area to the hydrodynamics of water movement through the rosette.

4. Using a sharp, single-edged razor blade, carefully dissect out one or more zooids from the common tunic. Be careful to get an entire animal for study. Place the zooids in a depression slide, add some water, and cover the preparation with a coverslip. Examine the zooids with the aid of a dissection microscope. Note that the body form is more elongate than in the solitary tunicates. The branchial (thorax) and visceral (abdomen) regions are again present, but colonial forms also possess a **postabdomen.** This region contains the gonads and heart (Fig. 5). Locate these organs in your specimens.

Tadpole Larva

1. Examine a whole-mount slide of ascidian tadpole larva (Fig. 6). More than one slide may be needed to complete these observations. Identify the head and tail regions. Describe the body shape. Why is this larval stage given the name tadpole? Differentiate the tunic from the rest of the body tissues.

2. At the anterior end locate the **adhesive papillae.** What do these structures resemble? Also locate the epidermis, branchial and atrial siphons, endostyle, branchial basket (pharynx with gill slits), and digestive system (esophagus, stomach, intestine, and anus). Just posterior to the branchial siphon locate the **cerebral vesicle** (sensory vesicle) with **cerebral ganglion, statolith,** and **ocellus** (eyespot). Locate the dorsal nerve cord that runs toward the posterior end of the animal just above the notochord. Find the longitudinal muscle bands (dorsal and ventral) that surround both the nerve cord and notochord. Dorsal and ventral fins extend the length of the tail (Fig. 6). Is the notochord birefringent? What does this tell you about its composition? What component of the tadpole larva is birefringent? What is the biochemical composition of the tunic that would make it birefringent?

3. Compare the general organization of the siphons, branchial basket, and internal organs of the larval stage to that of the adult (Fig. 6). How are they similar? What portion of the tadpole larva will become the oral siphon? Where will the aboral region develop?

4. Compare the structures found in adults with those of the larvae. To do this, make a list of those structures that are present in both stages. Although differing in size, how are these structures similar? Also inventory the structures unique to the tadpole stage and note their specific function. ■

■ Observational Procedure: Class Thaliacea, Salps

Live thaliaceans, such as *Salpa* and *Pyrosoma,* are not readily available from commercial supply houses and, unfortunately, these delicate animals do not preserve well. Nevertheless, a general understanding of salp morphology is possible even with preserved materials. Place a salp in a small bowl filled with water and examine it using a dissection microscope.

1. The anterioposterior axis may be determined by locating the bulbous gut near the atrial siphon (Fig. 7). This lies in the posterior region of the body. At the other end is the buccal or oral siphon. Locate each end and the openings of each siphon.

2. Note the transparent gelatinous tunic. Gently nudge the tunic with a blunt probe. How does it differ from the tunic of the sea squirts you have just studied? Beneath the tunic, located in the body wall, are the muscle bands. How would these bands be used in creating a jet propulsion of the animal through the water?

3. Most of the body is taken up with the spacious atrium, but you should also find the endostyle and the comblike **gill bar.**

4. Given the overall body plan of salps, contemplate how they are adapted for a planktonic existence. ■

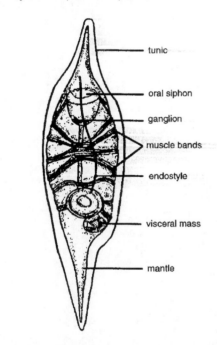

Figure 7. Generalized thaliacean.

B. Subphylum Cephalochordata

Members of Cephalochordata [CEPH-a-lo-chor-DA-tah; G., *cephala*, head, + G., *chorda*, string], are a very small group of benthic, marine, fish-like chordates. The animals lie buried in shallow sands, usually near the shore, where they filter out suspended food particles. Because of their blade-like appearance, cephalochordates are commonly known as lancelets. In the past, individuals often were referred to by the old genus name *Amphioxus.* Although adults only range in size from 4 to 8 cm, lancelets can be very significant in the benthic ecology of certain regions as their populations can reach enormous numbers. Up to 5,000 individuals per square meter have been reported in shallow Caribbean waters. In Asia billions of lancelets are harvested for food.

Classification

About 25 species in two genera are known. Example: *Branchiostoma* (= *Amphioxus*).

■ Observational Procedure:

Whole Mount. Obtain a prepared whole mount of *Branchiostoma*. Most of the internal organs can be seen through the translucent skin. A tunic is absent.

1. Using a dissection microscope, identify the anterioposterior axis and the dorsal and ventral sides (Fig. 8). The animal is compressed laterally and pointed at both ends, the posterior end being thinner and more pointed. How do the etymons of amphioxus and lancet fit the shape of this animal? Note the absence of a distinctive head region; the blunt anterior end encloses a cavity, the **vestibule,** by a **buccal** or **oral hood.** Is your specimen lying on its right or left side? What other features can you make out at this level (Fig. 8)?

2. Switch to a compound microscope to continue your study. At the anterior end locate the rostrum and below that the oral hood (Fig. 9). Lining the edges of the oral hood are the tentacles or **buccal cirri** that project outside. How do they resemble a cage? What function might the cirri serve? Inside of the buccal cavity, locate the **wheel organ.** In the living animal this ciliated structure creates a current that brings food to the ventral mouth, surrounded by the buccal or oral cirri. Just in front of the wheel organ on the roof of the buccal cavity, locate **Hatschek's pit.** How is this structure well positioned for the production of mucus which aids in feeding? Posterior to the wheel organ is the **velum** with **velar** or **oral tentacles.**

3. Behind the velar tentacles, locate the large pharynx composed of gill bars alternating with gill slits (Fig. 9). These structures slope at an angle of about 45° to the long axis of the body. Identify the **endostyle** on the ventral margin of the pharynx. Food and water separate in the pharynx, with the water passing through the gill slits, into the **atrium,** and out the **atriopore.** The atriopore corresponds to the atrial siphon of tunicates.

4. Posterior to the pharynx the gut narrows into an esophagus that widens into the stomach. Anteriorly a blind diverticulum, the **digestive** or **hepatic cecum,** extends into the atrium along the right side of the pharynx. The hepatic cecum produces enzymes into the intestine. From the stomach the gut again narrows into the intestine. At the junction of the stomach and intestine is the **iliocolonic ring.** This structure usually stains darker than the rest of the gut. Near the caudal fin, the intestine opens to the outside through an anus. Note that the anus does not empty into the atrium as in the ascidians (Fig. 8).

5. Above the gut locate the notochord, dorsal nerve cord, and dorsal fin ray (Fig. 8). Note that the fin ray appears to be constructed as a series of boxes. These are the **fin-ray boxes.** Compare the structure of the fin ray with that of the notochord; how can they be distinguished? The ventral fin located between the atriopore and tail (caudal fin), also contains fin-ray boxes. In both dorsal and ventral fins, these compartments taper off before the tail begins. Fin-ray boxes are believed to be food storage chambers.

6. Note how the notochord is composed of a series of compacted disc-shaped structures; each of these is a modified muscle cell, specialized for skeletal support. Amphioxus swims using a sinusoidal motion. Speculate on how a notochord, consisting of a stack of discs, might be better able to handle the shear forces generated during sinusoidal swimming than a solid flexible bar.

7. Examine the **myotomes** (Fig. 8). What is their shape and how are they arranged along the body? What is the

Figure 8. Lateral view of *Branchiostoma*. (After Sherman and Sherman.)

Phylum Chordata

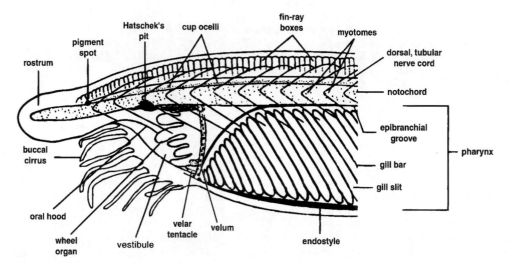

Figure 9. Enlargement of the anterior end of *Branchiostoma*. (After several sources.)

functional significance of this arrangement? Is amphioxus segmented? Of what significance is this to amphioxus? How many times has true segmentation evolved in the invertebrates?

8. Examine the nerve cord from its anterior extreme to the posterior end. Is it the same thickness the entire length? On the dorsal side of the anterior extremity, attempt to locate the **neuropore** (Kölliker's pit), a ciliated opening to the outside. Just posterior to the pit the nerve cord enlarges slightly as a brain or cerebral vesicle. What other features are evident within the nerve cord? At the anteriormost end is a small, dark **pigment spot** and scattered down its length along the ventral margin are the **cup ocelli** (Figs. 8 and 9). Examine the cup ocelli using high power magnification. Why were they given their name? Cup ocelli tend to be concentrated at the anterior end of the nerve cord. They are more numerous in the region of the buccal cavity and the end of the pharynx (Fig. 8).

Cross Section. Obtain a prepared slide with cross sections of an amphioxus through several levels, at least one should be through the pharynx. As you find the structures described below, note their location in the whole organism.

1. Begin your observations with a section through the level of the pharynx (Fig. 10). At the dorsal surface find the dorsal fin and fin-ray box. (At this level the ventral fin will not be present.) Below the dorsal fin locate the nerve cord. What evidence indicates that it is tubular? Can you see any nerves exiting the nerve cord in your section? (You may have to examine all the sections on the slide to find a ventral root nerve.) Directly below the nerve cord is the notochord. Is there anything dis-

tinctive about the notochord in this or any of the other sections?

2. Just below the notochord attempt to find the paired dorsal aortae. To either side of the nerve cord and notochord, locate a stack of muscle masses, the myotomes. How many myotomes do you see on either side of the body? Are these muscle masses paired? Do all pairs have the same cross-sectional area? Why not? Re-examine a whole mount of amphioxus and determine why the myotomes look like this in cross section (Fig. 8). Note how these muscle units appear to be stacked one upon the other up the side of the body.

3. Locate the sheets of connective tissues (**myocommas** or **myosepta**) that separate the myotomes. Examine the sheath which surrounds the notochord. This is the **notochord sheath;** its fibrous nature is seen best using phase contrast lighting. Note how it connects to the myosepta. What function might this network of sheaths serve in locomotion (i.e., the myocommas interconnecting with the notochord sheath)? Scan the body wall of the entire organism. Are other muscles evident? In cross sections at the level of the pharynx, locate the transverse muscle layer. What function might it serve?

4. Examine the pharyngeal region (Figs. 8 and 10). At the most dorsal part of the pharynx, locate the **epibranchial groove** (hyperpharyngeal groove) and at the most ventral part, locate the endostyle (hypobranchial groove). What is the shape of these structures? Are they ciliated? In some preparations the pharynx will still contain food. Examine your sections to determine what food amphioxus eats. How is food gathering in amphioxus similar to that in ascidians?

5. The gill slits, and gill bars that support them, slope downward from the anterior to the posterior at an angle of about 45°. However, each gill slit is really two slits separated by a **secondary gill bar,** extending between the **primary gill bars.** The two may be distinguished by the presence of fine cross bars or **synapticula.** The synapticula run perpendicular to the gill bars, connecting primary bars, but by-passing the secondary bars (Fig. 10).

6. Protonephridia (tubular flagellated solenocytes) are present dorsally, just below the notochord. They connect the small coelom to the artium. Locate the ventral aorta just below the endostyle. These structures are usually difficult to find, so you may need to examine several slides to locate them.

7. To either side of the pharynx find the atrial cavity. Inside the artium locate the hollow digestive or hepatic cecum (liver). (Remember that the digestive cecum is found only on the right side of the body. What does it mean if you were to find this structure on the left side of the body in your slide?) Examine the cells that line the lumen of the digestive cecum. What features does the cecum possess that indicate a digestive function?

8. Amphioxus is dioecious. Small, dense cells comprise the testes, while cells of the ovaries are larger and fewer in number. Is your specimen male or female? Be sure to examine specimens of both sexes so that you can tell them apart.

9. Examine the body wall and locate the epidermis and dermis layers. Two metapleural folds may be seen in the body wall in sections of amphioxus through the pharynx. If your cross section is a composite of several sections from different levels, locate the pharynx (or gut), notochord, nerve cord, atrium, and myotomes in each. As you locate these structures attempt to determine the approximate level from which the section was cut in the organism. ■

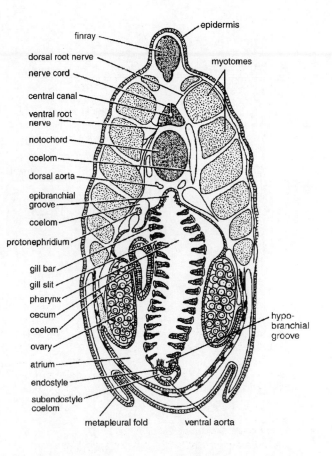

Figure 10. Cross section of *Branchiostoma* at the level of the pharynx. (After Sherman and Sherman.)

Phylum Chordata

Chordata	Worksheet 14
Name: _____	Date: _____
Course #: _____ / Section #: _____	Grade: _____

1. Using the following chart, make a brief list of those structures that are present in both adult and larval ascidians. Also inventory the structures unique to the tadpole stage and note their specific function.

Common Structures	Tadpole Structures	Function
1.		
2.		
3.		
4.		
5.		

2. In compound ascidians such as *Aplidium* and *Botryllus* the total cross sectional area of the branchial siphons of a rosette is less than that of the common atrial siphon. Discuss the significance of this relationship to the hydrodynamics of water movement through the rosette.

Phylum Chordata

3. Is amphioxus segmented? How many times has segmentation evolved in the invertebrates? Discuss.

4. In amphioxus, the myocommas interconnect with the notochord sheath. What function might this network of sheaths serve in locomotion?

5. Assume that you are studying a slide of the cross section amphioxus. If the digestive cecum is found only on the right side of the body in this animal, what simple explanation would account for finding this structure on the left side of the body as it appears on the slide?

Zoology 250
Survey of the Invertebrates

Laboratory Manual

2014/2015

Biological Sciences Department
Arts and Science Faculty
MacEwan University

Student Name: _____   **Student I.D.** _____

Lab Section: Wednesday

    Time:

    Room: 6-143

Lab Instructor: Christina Elliott

    Office: 6-117F

    Phone number: 780-633-3281

    Email: elliottc24@macewan.ca

    Office hours:

Acknowledgement: This manual is an adaptation of the Department of Biological Sciences, University of Alberta, Zoology 250 lab. We thank Dr. R. Palmer, R. Koss and the Department of Biology, University of Alberta for permission to use their lab documents and for their assistance and co-operation.

Table of Contents

ZOOLOGY 250
LABORATORY SCHEDULE
WINTER 2015

LAB		**DATE**
Lab 1	Microscopy, Diversity of Invertebrates & the Protists	January 14
Lab 2	Phyla Porifera, Cnidaria & Ctenophora	January 21
Lab 3	Phyla Platyhelminthes & Nemertea	January 28
Lab 4	Phyla Nematoda, Nematomorpha, Rotifera & Acanthocephala	February 4
Lab 5	**Mid-term Laboratory Exam (15%)**	February 11
	Reading week – no labs (trip to Bamfield)	February 18
Lab 6	Phylum Mollusca - Part I	February 25
Lab 7	Phylum Mollusca - Part II	March 4
Lab 8	Phylum Annelida & Sipuncula	March 11
Lab 9	Phyla Onycophora, Tardigrada & Arthropoda: Crustaceans	March 18
Lab 10	Phylum Arthropoda: Other Arthropods	March 25
Lab 11	Deuterostomes - Phylum Echinodermata, the Lophophores, Phylum Hemichordata & the lower Chordates	April 1
Lab 12	**Final Laboratory Exam (20%) (Not cumulative)**	**April 8**

General Information

I. Introduction

The laboratory in Zoology 250 will be used to demonstrate the evolutionary relationships among living representatives of selected invertebrate organisms. These relationships have been determined based on **cladistic analysis** of **homologous characters** and are presented in the form of a **cladogram** or **phylogenetic tree**. Cladistic analysis is a quantitative method for determining relatedness among organisms based on the study of shared characters that were inherited from a common ancestor. The analysis yields a detailed pattern of branching relations called a cladogram (see the example Metazoa cladogram at the end of this section).

In the lab, we will observe representatives of most major invertebrate groups. Our objective will be to:
1. Look at key morphological and anatomical characteristics that are used for defining invertebrate groups and in understanding their relationships and classification.
2. See how the forms of these features are related to the way that they are used by invertebrates to move, feed, respire and reproduce. Whenever possible, we will observe live specimens to demonstrate this.

II. Student Responsibilities

As students, you are expected to attend all laboratory sessions and to participate in all lab exercises. You must be prepared beforehand by previewing the lab exercise and reading all relevant information in your lab manuals and textbook. You must handle all specimens (both live and preserved) with care and respect. Follow all safety precautions as advised below in this manual and from instructions given to you by your laboratory instructor.

III. Equipment and Supplies

You will need a standard dissection kit, including a scalpel handle and blades, fine-pointed scissors, forceps, needle probes and a blunt probe (available in the bookstore). We have some equipment in lab, but it is beneficial to have your own complete set. A notebook, pencil and ruler will be useful for recording your observations.

You are required to bring to all labs a copy of the MacEwan University Custom Edition *Zoology 250 Lab Manual* with *Invertebrate Zoology: A Laboratory Manual* by R.L. Wallace and W.K Taylor (sold in the bookstore). Your textbook, *Biology of the Invertebrates*. 7th edition 2014 by Jan Pechenik, and *A Photographic Atlas for the Zoology Laboratory*. 6th Edition, 2010 by K.M. Van De Graaff and J.L. Crawley are two useful references you may also consider bringing to the lab (both available in the bookstore). (Your copy of *A Photographic Atlas for the Biology Laboratory* you may have purchased for Biology 108 would be useful if you do not wish to purchase the Zoology edition.) The U. of A. Zoology 250 website (www.biology.ualberta.ca/courses.hp/zool250/Z250.html) is also a useful resource.

IV. Safety

In some of your labs you will be working with living and preserved biological materials, some of which are potentially dangerous. In addition you will be using reagents, some of which are toxic, caustic, flammable, etc. The Department has provided safeguards wherever possible, as well as competent supervision, but ultimately it is your responsibility to be careful. Carelessness on your part can result in serious injury and/or illness in yourself as well as in others. In the interest of safety and of making the laboratory exercises a valuable part of your education, please adhere to the following basic rules of operation:

Eating and drinking are not allowed in the laboratory. You should wear a lab coat (available in the bookstore) in the lab and keep hair, loose clothes, etc. under control. **Do not wear contact lenses in the lab**, especially in the labs involving work with preserved specimens, solvents and chemicals. It is recommended that you wear safety glasses when you are undertaking your dissections. Safety glasses may be purchased in the bookstore and will also be available in the lab when dissections are to be undertaken. Report any injury, no matter how slight, to the lab instructor so that proper care can be administered immediately. Cover cuts on hands with band aids or latex gloves if necessary. Wash your hands with soap and water when you have completed your lab work. For safety reasons, jackets and coats should be hung on the coat racks provided in the lab, and backpacks, handbags, etc. placed under the benches away from aisles. **Cellular phones** must be put away while you are in the lab.

Specimens (both living and preserved), equipment, glassware, and chemicals should be used and handled with care. Notify your lab instructor if any of the specimens, equipment or supplies are damaged, not working properly or are broken. Report all spills and accidents, no matter how small, immediately to your lab instructor. Do not handle any living specimen without the express permission of your instructor.

It is your responsibility to return all slides and specimens to their respective areas and to properly dispose of all wastes. You must clean your work area at the end of the lab and clean and return any microscopes to their storage areas.

Each student is responsible for knowing the proper evacuation procedure in the event of a fire. Therefore, become familiar with the evacuation route from the lab room you are in. If the fire alarm sounds, leave the building immediately using the assigned route. Do not return to the building until directed to do so by your lab instructor.

V. Evaluation

The laboratory is worth 40% of your final grade in Zoology 250. The lab grade will be determined on the basis of two lab exams and two marked dissections:

Midterm Exam - 15%

Dissection I – 2%

Dissection II – 3%

Final Lab Exam - 20% (Non-cumulative)

The exams are practical exams, with questions involving live and preserved specimens. The final lab exam is non-cumulative. The format of the marked dissections will be discussed at the beginning of the term. Forty percent (40%) of the overall course grade is from the laboratory component. Therefore, it is very important that all labs be attended and that the material is covered thoroughly. Each lab runs just twice during the week, so there are not many opportunities to make up a missed lab session. **Remember, even if you do not attend the lab, you are still responsible for the material. Lab attendance will be recorded and five percent (5%) will be deducted from your final lab grade (out of 40%) for each missed lab, unless an acceptable, verified excuse is provided to your Zoology 250 lab instructor.** *Because of the importance of attending all the labs and adequately covering the material presented in them, if two or more labs are missed without valid, documented reasons, you will not receive credit for the laboratory component of the course.*

At the start of each week's lab, there will be a pre-lab talk given by your laboratory instructor which will outline what is to be covered during the lab, provide additional background information, inform you of changes to the lab exercise, go over safety procedures, and demonstrate techniques and use of equipment. **Because of the importance of the pre-lab talk it is imperative that you are in the lab at the start of each week's lab. If you are more than 10 minutes late for the lab you will be penalized two percent (2%) from your final lab grade (40%) for each time you are late and depending on the day's lab exercise and how late you are for the lab, your lab instructor will assess whether it is possible for you to attend the remainder of the session.**

Clade for Kingdom Animalia (Metazoa)

Revised clade from <u>Tree of Life</u> for <u>Kingdom Animalia</u> (after Ruppert and Barnes 1994, p 1052)

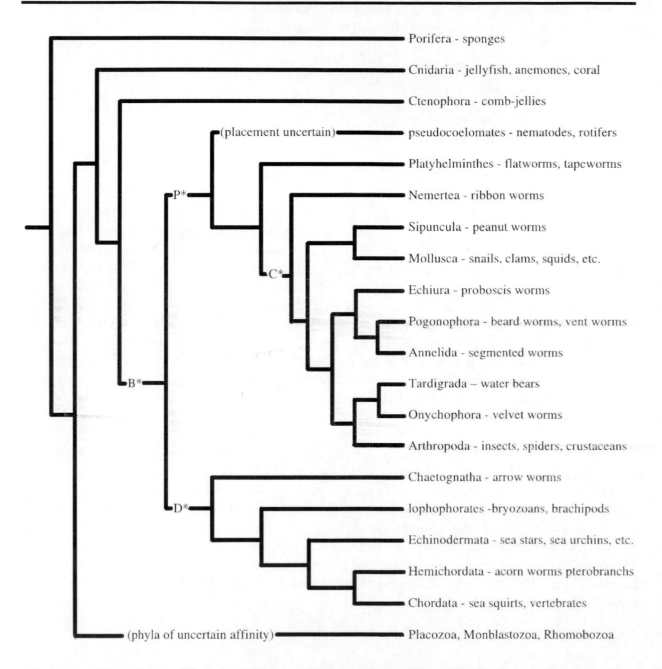

* Trait supporting each clade (** plesiomorphic - a primitive state, not unique to clade):

  B = Bilatera: a) bilateral symmetry, b) cephalization, c) triploblastic organization (extensive mesoderm),
  d) organ-system level of organization, e) protonephridia.

  P = Protostomia: a) spiral, determinate cleavage, b) mesoderm from mesenchyme cells,
  c) mouth (and sometimes anus) from blastopore, d) multiciliated cells.

  C = Coelomate Protostomes: a) coelom via schizocoely

  D = Deuterostomia: a) radial, indeterminate cleavage**, b) coelom via enterocoely,
  c) blastopore yields anus, d) tripartite coelom & body plan, e) monociliated cells

Lab 1
Diversity of Invertebrates, Microscopy and the Protists

I. Objectives

1. To observe representatives of all major invertebrate taxa.

2. To note differences in sizes, body plans and life styles of major invertebrate taxa.

3. To begin to learn relationships among invertebrate phyla.

II. Introduction

In this lab you are presented with examples of all of the major invertebrate phyla that we will be looking at in more detail throughout the term. Observe and make notes of all of the organisms but DO NOT ATTEMPT TO MEMORIZE THE CLASSIFICATION or other details of the specimens. Rather, complete the table in the handout, paying particular attention to the following features:

1. Type of skeleton (none, exoskeleton, endoskeleton, hydrostatic skeleton).

2. Type of symmetry (none or asymmetrical, radial, bilateral).

3. Size [microscopic, small –(< 1 cm), medium – (1-10 cm), large –(>10 cm)].

4. Body form (segmented, non-segmented).

5. Life style (predator, herbivore, parasitic, filter-feeder).

6. Habitat (marine, fresh-water, terrestrial).

7. Cool stuff: what is neat about the specimen.

III. Partial Classification of the Invertebrates

Note: Classification schemes are hypotheses that reflect our best guesses about the relationships of various taxa. As a result, the schemes are in a state of constant revision; the designations and placement of particular taxa may vary.

PROTISTS (unicellular eukaryotes; approx. 35 phyla)
    Diplomonads
        Giardia intestinalis (cause of beaver fever) one of the 'animal' flagellates; most primitive living eukaryote

    Ciliophorans (ciliates) includes the most complex single-celled organisms
        Paramecium sp.

    Apicomplexa (sporozoans) all parasitic
        Plasmodium sp.

    Amoebozoans (Amoebas)
        Chaos sp., Amoeba sp., Entamoeba histolytica

KINGDOM ANIMALIA (the Metazoa)

    Phylum Porifera (sponges; 3 classes)

        Class Calcarea (marine; calcium carbonate spicules)
            Grantia sp.

        Class Demospongiae (95% of living sponge species)
            Euspongia sp. (marine; commercial bath sponge)
            Spongilla sp. (freshwater; common species in Alberta ponds)

        Class Hexactinellida
            Euplectella sp. (Venus's flower basket, a glass sponge)

    Phylum Cnidaria (hydroids, jellyfish = medusae, anemones= polyps; 4 classes)

        Class Hydrozoa (hydroids & relatives)
            Hydra sp. (freshwater solitary polyp)
            Obelia sp. (marine; colonial polyp stage)
            Gonionemus sp. (marine; medusa stage)
            Physalia sp. (marine; of interest because of its painful stings; colonial hydrozoan not a medusa)

        Class Scyphozoa (medusae & relatives)
            Aurelia sp. (marine; medusa stage)

        Class Anthozoa (anemones & all solitary or colonial polyp forms)
            Metridium sp. (a common, large plankton-feeding anemone)
            Corals

Phylum Platyhelminthes (flatworms & relatives; 4 classes)

    Class Turbellaria (flatworms)
        Dugesia sp.

    Class Trematoda (flukes)
        Clonorchis sp. (Chinese liver fluke)
        Fasciola sp. (sheep liver fluke)

    Class Cestoidea (tapeworms)
        Taenia sp.

    Class Monogenea
        Neopolystoma sp.

PSEUDOCOELOMATES
Phylum Nematoda (round worms; 2 classes)
    Ascaris suum
    Turbatrix aceti (vinegar eel)
    Necator sp. (human hookworm)
    Enterobius sp. (human pinworm)

Phylum Rotifera (rotifers; 3 classes)
    various rotifers

Phylum Acanthocephala (spiny-headed worms; 4 classes)
    Macracanthorhyncus sp.

Phylum Nematomorpha (horsehair worms; 2 classes)

COELOMATE PROTOSTOMES
Phylum Mollusca (snails, clams, squid & relatives; 7 classes)

    Class Polyplacophora (chitons)
        Cryptochiton stelleri

    Class Gastropoda (snails, slugs, etc.)
        Prosobranchs
            Limpets
            Abalonc shcll
            Nucella sp. (dog whelk; rocky shore predators of barnacles &
                mussels)
            Conus sp. (tropical snail that eats worms, other snails & fish)

        Pulmonates
            Helix sp. (herbivorous landsnail)

    Class Scaphopoda (tusk and tooth shells)

Class Bivalvia (clams, mussels & relatives)
> **Subclass Heterodonta** (clams)
>> freshwater 'mussel'
>> goeduck (marine clam)

> **Subclass Pteriomorpha** (mussels, oysters, scallops)
>> *Mytilus* sp. (marine mussel)
>> *Ostrea* sp. (marine oyster)
>> *Chlamys* sp. (marine scallop)

Class Cephalopoda (squids, octopus & relatives)
> **Subclass Nautiloidea**
>> *Nautilus* sp. (chambered shells)

> **Subclass Coleoidea**
>> cuttlefish
>> squid
>> *Octopus* sp.

Phylum Annelida (segemented worm; 3 classes)

> **Class Polychaeta**
>> Errantia (free-living)
>>> *Aphrodite* sp. (sea mouse)
>>> *Nereis* sp. (segmented worm)
>> Sedentaria (tube dwellers)
>>> *Chaetopterus* sp. (parchment-tube worm)
>>> *Eudistylia* sp. (feather-duster worm)

> **Class Clitellata**
>> **Subclass Oligochaeta** (earthworms)
>> *Lumbriculus* sp. (freshwater oligochaetes)
>> *Lumbricus* sp. (terrestrial earthworm)

>> **Subclass Hirudinea** (leeches)
>> *Hirudo medicinalis* (medicinal leech)

Phylum Onychophora (velvet worms)

Phylum Arthropoda (arthropods; 6 extant classes)

 Subphylum Chelicerata

> **Class Merostomata** (horseshoe crab)
>> *Limulus* sp. (ancient marine horseshoe crab)

> **Class Arachnida** (spiders)
>> various spiders

Subphylum Mandibulata

Class Crustacea
        Subclass Branchiopoda (fairy shrimp, clam shrimp, water fleas)
                Order Cladocera
                        Daphnia sp. (water flea)

        Subclass Copepoda (copepods)
                various copepods

        Subclass Ostracoda (seed shrimp)

        Subclass Branchiura (fish lice)

        Subclass Cirripedia (barnacles)
                Balanus sp.(acorn barnacle)
                Pollicipes sp. (gooseneck barnacle)

        Subclass Malacostraca (most of the familiar & commercial crustaceans)
                Superorder Peracarida (amphipods, isopods & relatives)
                        freshwater amphipods

                Superorder Eucarida
                        Order Decapoda
                            lobsters
                            crayfish
                            Pagurus sp. (hermit crab)
                            Hemigrapsus sp. (true crabs)

Class Insecta
        Subclass Pterygota (winged insects)
                    cockroach (Order Blattodea)
                    grasshopper (Order Orthoptera)
                    beetles (Order Coleoptera)
                    butterflies & moths (Order Lepidoptera)
                    ants, bees, wasps (Order Hymenoptera)

        Subclass Apterygota (wingless insects)

Class Myriapoda (Centipedes and Millipeds)

COELOMATE DEUTEROSTOMES

Phylum Echinodermata (sea stars, sea urchins, sea cucumbers & relatives; 6 classes)

Class Stelleroidea (sea stars, brittle stars)
Subclass Asteroidea (sea stars)
Pisaster ochraceus (common rocky shore West Coast sea star)
various species

Subclass Oiphuroidea (brittle stars)

Class Echinoidea (sea urchins)
Strongylocentrotus sp.
various species

Class Holothuroidea (sea cucumbers)
Cucumaria sp.

Class Crinoidea (feather stars)

Phylum Brachiopoda (lamp shells)

Phylum Bryozoa (moss animals)

Phylum Hemichordata (acorn worms & relatives; 2 classes)

Class Enteropneusta (acorn worms)
Dolichoglossus sp.

Phylum Chordata (invertebrate chordates (5 classes) & vertebrates)

Subphylum Urochordata (sea squirts, larvaceans & relatives)

Class Ascidiacea (sea squirts)
Ciona sp.
Molgula sp.

Subphylum Cephalochordata (lancelets)
Branchiostoma sp.(closest living relative of vertebrates)

Subphylum Vertebrata (the vertebrates)

IV. The Protozoa

These are unicellular eukaryotes, which, as the primitive condition, are non-photosynthetic. The Protozoa, or protists, is not a formal taxonomic category as the classification is very much in flux.

> **The Excavata**
> > **Phylum Euglenozoa**
> > > - euglenids (phytoflagellates; most are photosynthetic)
> > > - kinetoplastids (zooflagellates; free living, symbiotic or parasitic)
> > **Phylum Choanomonada**
> > > - choanoflagellates
> > **The diplomonads**
> > > - flagellates without mitochondria, including *Giardia* sp.
>
> **The Amoebozoa**
> > **The Gymnamoebae**
> > > - naked amoebas, *Entamoeba*   Amoeba proteus, chaos chaos
>
> **The Rhizaria**
> > **Phylum Radiolaria**
> > > - radiating axopodia
> > **Phylum Foraminifera**
> > > - most with calcium carbonate tests
>
> **The Alveolates**
> > **Phylum Ciliophora**
> > > -ciliates
> > **Phylum Dinozoa** (Dinophyta)
> > > - dinoflagellates
> > **Phylum Apicomplexa** (sporozoans)
> > > - parasites: gregarines, coccideans including *Plasmodium* spp.

The purpose of this exercise is: 1) to give you a general introduction to the diversity of Protozoa; 2) to practice manipulating small organisms and 3) give you practice using the compound microscope.

1. With the micropipet, practice isolating single protozoans from the pure cultures that have been provided (*Paramecium* sp.). Transfer a dozen or so protozoans to one dish, then three or four to a second dish, and finally one protozoan to a third dish. Practice using methyl cellulose to "slow-down" the protozoans you are trying to observe.

2. Your lab instructor will have a list of various living protozoans to observe. How many of the major groups can you identify? How many organelles can you identify? Refer to figures in the lab manual and your lecture notes.

3. Demonstrations:

a) Various Excavates. *Trypanosoma* sp. (Kinetoplastids). Using Figure 7b (p. 10) identify: the undulating membrane, kinetoplast, nucleus, and flagellum. Recall lecture notes regarding African sleeping sickness. Compare to the live *Euglena* you observed. What kind of differences do you note? Also, compare to *Giardia* sp., a diplomonad.

b) Various Ameboids (p. 12-16). *Chaos chaos* and *Amoeba* sp., (Figure 9) *Entamoeba histolytica* (Figure 10); *Arcella or Difflugia* (Testacea) (Figure 11)

c) Various Ciliates. You have already seen *Paramecium* sp. (Figure 23c, p. 26). Many of the living protozoans from the mixed cultures are also ciliates. On demonstration is *Stentor* sp., a large trumpet-shaped ciliate (Figure 26a, p. 30).

d) *Plasmodim vivax* (Apicomplexa); this is one of four malarial parasites of humans. Note the enlarged, stippled, host erythrocytes. An illustrated account of *Plasmodium's* life cycle is given on p. 23 (Figure 20).

e) *Monocystis* sp. is a parasitic protozoan (Apicomplexa) that lives in the seminal vesicles of Oligochaetes. It should be possible to isolate this protozoan from the worms provided in lab. Follow the procedure outlined by your instructor. You should be able to observe cysts and perhaps even the larger trophozoites (see Figure 18 on p. 20).

f) Various Rhizaria. Examine the Radiolarians (p. 17-18) and Foraminiferans (p. 16). What are some similarities that you can see, or some similarities that you know from looking at the labelled diagrams of live specimens?

4. The following manipulations should also be attempted:

a) Using yeast stained with Congo red, trace the formation and change in pH of food vacuoles in *Paramecium* sp. (Blue -pH 3 or less, orange -pH 5 or more), as it feeds.

b) Observe the *Paramecium* sp. starting with the procedure on p. 27. By dropping 2% iodine on the slide you should cause discharge of trichocysts in *Paramecium* sp. (p. 28). What are trichocysts used for?

c) Compare the rate of contractile vacuole formation and breakdown after 0.25% sodium chloride or distilled water is added to the slide. Any of the ciliates may be used.

Slides

- Euglena
- Trypansoma
- Amoeba
- Entamoeba
- Pelomyxa
- Arcella

- Radiolaria strew
- Foraminifera
- Paramecium trichocysts
- Paramecium in fission
- Stentor
- Vorticella

- Dinoflagellates
- Plasmodium vivax

Lab 2
Phyla Porifera, Cnidaria and Ctenophora

I. Introduction: Phylum Porifera

Sponges are one of the **most primitive** (but successful) forms of living, multicellular organisms. They are **sessile** and **feed by filtering** particulates from water with specialized filtering/pumping cells called **choanocytes** (note similarity to choanoflagellates).

The skeletal support system in sponges includes rod-like structures called **spicules**, which are made of either calcium carbonate or silicate. These are often enmeshed within a matrix of the protein **spongin** (a form of collagen).

Sponges exhibit three body plans (**asconoid, syconoid, leuconoid**) that differ mainly in the complexity of the water transport system. This system has many small **incurrent openings**, one or a few large **excurrent openings**, and flagellated cells (**choanocytes**) along the incurrent canals that can simultaneously pump and filter. There are two main types of sponge larvae: a solid **parenchymula** larva, and a hollow **amphiblastula** larva.

Most sponges are marine, but species are found in freshwater as well. *Spongilla* sp. is a local freshwater type that will be available for observation.

↳ amoebocytes / archaeocytes

II. Phylum Porifera (sponges)
Phylum Porifera
     Class Calcarea
     Class Hexactinellida
     Class Demospongiae

1. Class Calcarea:
Do the exercise on *Sycon* (p. 41) using *Grantia* sp., a sponge of similar body construction. See the syconoid body plan in Figure 4 (p. 38).

2. Class Hexactinellida:
Demonstration: Venus's flower basket. (Please handle with extreme caution!). See Figure 9 (p. 43) for the finer structure of *Euplectella* sp.

3. Class Demospongiae:
Do the exercise on *Spongilla* sp. (p. 41). Note: We have no prepared c.s. or l.s. slides of *Spongilla* sp., and no living or preserved gemmules (see Figure 6 on p. 39). Note the demonstrations of the Commercial sponge (*Euspongia* sp.) and Freshwater sponge (*Spongilla* sp.). See also Figure 8 (p. 42).

4. Spicules:
Do some spicule magic on the side bench – siliceous spicules will remain and calcareous spicules disappear when exposed to HCl. Which type(s) are present?

III. Introduction: Phylum Cnidaria and Ctenophora

Cnidarians and ctenophorans are **diploblastic** (**ectoderm** and **endoderm**). Their body wall consists of an outer epithelium, the **epidermis**, and an inner epithelium, the **gastrodermis**, with an extracellular layer, the **mesoglea,** between these two layers. They are typically **radially symmetrical** with 4-, 6-, 8-, or 12-part symmetry. Two general life forms occur, the **polyp** (benthic) and **medusa** (pelagic). The mesoglea layer is most extensive in swimming forms (medusae) because it is used as a skeletal support and as an antagonist to muscle action. All cnidarians have a **hydrostatic skeleton** but many also secrete a calcareous or horny exoskeleton, allowing them to be quite large in size.

Cells called **cnidocytes** have **nematocyst** organelles that are used for stinging and entangling prey. The cnidocytes are often concentrated in the epidermis of **tentacles** but can also be found in the living tissues lining the gut of Scyphozoans and Anthozoans.

Many Hydrozoans and Scyphozoans exhibit **metagenesis** ("**alternation of generations**"), existing for a time as a polyp and for a time as a medusa. Anthozoans have lost the medusa stage completely. Medusae are produced by simple **budding** in Hydrozoans and by **strobilization** in Scyphozoa. Medusae of Hydrozoa are usually small, with a **velum**, simple **bell** margin, and a simple **manubrium** without cnidocytes. Medusae of Scyphozoans are often large, have no velum, have a notched bell margin, and have a large, elaborate manubrium that has cnidocytes. Polyps also differ among the classes. In Hydrozoans, the polyp mouth is a simple opening and the **gastrovscular cavity** is simple and lacks cnidocytes. In Anthozoans, the polyp mouth opens into a sleeve-like pharynx, the gastrovascular cavity is divided by septa and it has cnidoyctes. Complex colonial forms in which a "division of labour" occurs, exist in some Hydrozoan and Anthozoan species. Anthozoans include hexacorals, the solitary anemones and the colonial true (stony) corals, and the colonial octocorals. The epidermis of colonial stony corals secrete an **exoskeleton**, whereas the mesoglea of octocorals secrete an **endoskeleton**. Most cnidarians have a simple **planula larva** (Figure 8E, p. 55).

Ctenophorans (comb jellies) are exclusively marine organisms. They are generally free-swimming animals. Most have tentacles with adhesive **colloblast** cells used to capture prey. Their diploblastic bodies have eight radially arranged ciliated bands (**comb rows** or **costae**). Ctenophores move by beating the cilia of the costae.

IV. Phylum Cnidaria and Phylum Ctenophora: the diploblastic phyla
Phylum Cnidaria
> Class Scyphozoa - jelly fishes
> Class Cubozoa - sea wasps
> Class Hydrozoa - *Hydra* sp., *Obelia* sp. and *Aurelia* sp.
> *Subphylum* Class Anthozoa
>> Subclass Zoantharia (Hexacorallia)   - sea anemones
>> Subclass Alcyonaria (Octocorallia)   - sea fans, corals

Phylum Ctenophora
> Class Tentaculata – tentaculate species
> Class Nuda - no tentacles present

Phylum Cnidaria

1. **Class Hydrozoa:**

   a) Transfer living *Hydra* sp. (an atypical freshwater hydrozoan) in a few drops of distilled water to a small Petri dish and examine under a dissecting scope or low power of a compound microscope. Identify the **mouth, hypostome, tentacles, body column, basal disk**, and, if present, ovaries, testes, and buds (see Figure 4, p. 51). Note movement; touch with a needle and observe contraction and change in shape. Introduce some small zooplankters, e.g. *Artemia* sp. to culture medium and observe, hopefully, capture. How is this accomplished?

   b) Discharge of *Hydra* nematocysts: use procedure on p. 51 (#4). Examine the structure of a nematocyst (Figure 2, p. 48). Can you see them firing?

   c) Observe prepared longitudinal and cross section slides of *Hydra* (see p. 51, #5, and Figure 5). Note the **epidermis, mesoglea,** and **gastrodermis**.

   d) *Obelia* sp., (a colonial, marine hydrozoan.) Using a prepared slide, note the feeding polyps (**gastrozooids, with hydranth**) and the reproductive polyps (**gonozooids or gonangia**) (see p. 54-56, omit cs/ls). Observe the prepared slide of the *Obelia* medusa.

   e) Demonstration of hydrozoan medusoid forms: *Gonionemus* sp. (see p. 57-58).

   f) Demonstration of colonial hydrozoan Portuguese man-of-war *(Physalia* sp.) (p. 60-61).

2. **Class Scyphozoa:**

   a) *Aurelia* sp., do exercise, p. 62. Note anatomy of medusa, including the **gastric pouch, gonad, oral arms of manubrium, mouth, tentacles, statocyst** (in **rhopalium**), and radial canals that may be visible, Figure 15 on p. 63. Note the differences between the Scyphozoan, *Aurelia* sp., and the Hydrozoan, *Gonionemus* sp.

   b) Examine slides of various life cycle stages (**planula, scyphistoma, strobila** and **ephyra**) of *Aurelia* sp., Figure 15 on p. 63.

3. **Class Anthozoa:** SubPhylum Anthozoa.

   a) Observation of sea anemone, *Metridium* sp. You may have an anemone that has already been cut longitudinally, or you may need to cut your own. Be careful not to cut too deep (scissors may be a good choice here). Follow the procedure on p. 67-69. (Note: There is no c.s. of Metridium p. 69 #15). Be sure to identify the 3 outer regions: **pedal disc, scapus** and **capitulum,** as well as the interior **septal filament, septum, retractor muscle, acontia, siphonoglyph, wall of pharynx, oral disc, peristome** and **fosse.**

   b) Demonstration of various corals (p. 71). Note Hexacorals and Octocorals.

   c) Living anemones may be on demonstration.

Phylum Ctenophora

Ctenophores (comb jellies) are exclusively marine predators. Most are weak swimming and planktonic. Like cnidarians, comb jellies are diploblastic and exhibit radial symmetry. See the preserved specimen on display (p. 76). Note the location of the **statocyst**. Make sure you note the differences between this phylum and the Cnidaria.

Statolith in text?

most
hermaphroditic
Cydippid larva.

<u>Slides</u>

- spongilla - gemmules.

- grantia

- hydra C.S./l.S.

- hydra W.M.

- hydra amoeboid ovum
     early or any
     engorged
     Sm
     nematocysts.

- metridium C.S./l.S.

- obelia young medusa.

- obelia hydroid.

- aurelia planula larva.

- aurelia ephyra

- aurelia scyphistoma

- aurelia strobila

Lab 3
Acoelomates
Phyla Platyhelminthes and Nemertea

I. Introduction

Platyhelminthes (flatworms) are **triploblastic, dorso-ventrally flattened** worms with well-defined organ systems (muscular, excretory and reproductive). All are **cephalized**. Flatworms, although **triploblastic** (embryos with well-defined ectoderm, endoderm and mesoderm) and **acoelomate** (absence of pseudocoelom or coelom), possess no blood-vascular system. Their small size and flattened shape allows them to exchange gases by diffusion through the body wall across a living **tegument**. Platyhelminths have layers of circular and longitudinal muscles and an internal skeleton of cellular **mesenchyme**.

Turbellarian flatworms (Acoels, Polyclads, Triclads, and Rhabdocoels) are **free-living predators and scavengers.** Their digestive system consists of a **mouth** (mid-ventral or anterior), a **gut** (simple or branched) and a muscular **pharynx**. There is no **anus**. These flatworms often move via **pedal waves** that begin at the anterior and move to the posterior, and many aquatic forms live in benthic zones.

Trematodes, Monogeneans and Cestodes are **parasitic** flatworms closely related to Rhabdocoels. Parasitic platyhelminths have a well-developed reproductive system but have reduced or lost many other organ systems.

Parasitic flatworms often have **elaborate life cycles** that involve one (most monogeneans), two (typical **digenean** trematodes), or multiple (≥ 2, many cestodes) hosts. Some are important human parasites.

Nemerteans (ribbon worms) have many features in common with platyhelminths but are distinguished by a protrusible **proboscis** that lies in a fluid-filled cavity above the gut. They also have a complete digestive system that ends in an anus.

The excretory system of platyhelminths and nemerteans includes **protonephridia (flame cells)** that pump water and some metabolites into excretory canals using cilia.

<u>Slides</u>

Planaria double mount
Planaria 3 regions c.s.
Clonorchis wm.
Fasciola wm
 - miracidia
 - metacercaria
 - Cercaria. diff. types.

 - Schistosoma mansoni in liver sec
 - Schistosoma ♂ & ♀ wm
 - Taenia composite
 - Taenia cysticercus
 - Taenia wm mature proglottid.

II. Phylum Platyhelminthes

Phylum Platyhelminthes
      Class Turbellaria - free-living flatworms
            Order Acoela
            Order Tricladida
            Order Polycladida
            Order Neorhabdocoela (considered a superorder elsewhere)
      Class Trematoda - digenetic flukes
      Class Monogenea
      Class Cestoidea (Cestoda)
         Subclass Cestodaria
         Subclass Eucestoda - tapeworms

A. Class Turbellaria

1. Order Acoela:
Living specimens should be available as a demonstration. Note the differences in shape from the other turbellarian groups, and keep in mind the differences in gut structure.

2. Order Tricladida:
Living specimens of *Dugesia tigrina*, a triclad found in Alberta, are available for observation. Note the 3-branched digestive system (Figures 1 and 2, p. 83).

a) Place two *Dugesia* into a petri dish containing distilled water. Do the exercises and identify the structures described on pages 82-85. Examine *Bdelloura*.

- Note and sketch the colour patterns. Do all specimens have the same colour patterns?

- Is there a difference between the dorsal and ventral surfaces? Why?

- Observe the eyes, auricles, and note general shape of the head.

- Add some carmine particles and observe ciliary action under the microscope.

- To detect **rhabdoids** (and **rhabdites**), observe the ventral surface of *Dugesia* sp. under a coverslip. Use high power of the microscope.

3. Order Polycladida:
Polyclads are entirely marine.
See the demonstration of *Leptoplana* sp. Can you distinquish the digestive tract? How does the digestive tract of polyclads differ from that of a microturbellarian or a triclad?

4. Order Neorhabdocoela:
Microturbellarians are found in both freshwater and the oceans. They are common, although inconspicuous, in standing waters in the Edmonton vicinity.
See the demonstration of *Mesostoma* sp. (Order Neorhabdocoela).

b) Locomotion:

- Observe the gliding type of motion, and pedal waves.

- Touch an animal with a blunt instrument. Do you observe a different type of movement?

- What combination of structures aid in locomotion? Remember these worms have both longitudinal and circular muscles.

- These animals can clamp lightly to the sides of the dish. This is accomplished by adhesive glands located on the ventral side. Other glands secrete mucus, aiding the cilia in locomotion. Can you see mucus trailing behind a moving specimen? By placing carmine particles into the dish, the mucus trails may be more apparent.

c) Orientation to light:

Place three or four *Dugesia* into a petri dish containing dechlorinated water and cover with a foil for 10 minutes. Then partially uncover the dish by moving the foil to a part of the dish not containing *Dugesia*. Shine a strong light directly into the dish. Observe the response. Did *Dugesia* move towards the dark area or did the specimen avoid this area? Explain.

d) Response to contact:

With the same animals, touch the ventral and then dorsal surface with a blunt instrument. Try placing a planarian on its back (dorsal surface). Explain the response. Is the animal thigmotactic? Is the dorsal surface response the same as that of the ventral surface? With this information explain the righting action of *Dugesia*.

e) Feeding observations: (Depending on availability of white worms)

Place one starved *Dugesia* with one white worm, (an oligochaete), into a petri dish containing dechlorinated water. Using a dissection scope observe the feeding response. Note the protruding pharynx of *Dugesia* as it feeds on the worm. Cut off the pharynx, and under low power of the microscope, observe peristalsis of excised pharynx. What is the function of this activity? Note how *Dugesia* wraps itself around the prey. Can you detect mucus being secreted by *Dugesia*?

f) Observe cross section slides of *Dugesia* at various levels, and note the visible structures (Figure 4, p. 85).

337

B. Class Trematoda - parasitic flukes

Trematodes are common endoparasites found in all classes of vertebrates. There are more than 11,000 species. The life cycle always includes at least two infective stages and at least two hosts. The first host (intermediate) is typically a snail, and the final host (definitive) is a vertebrate. In some species there may be more than one intermediate host.

1. Observe and sketch prepared slides of:

   a) Whole mounts of *Fasciola hepatica* (p. 85-87).
   b) Whole mounts of adult *Clonorchis* sp., the Chinese liver fluke (p. 87-88).
   Label the major structures. Become familiar with the full lifecycle.

2. Observe and sketch the following larval stages of *Fasciola hepatica* (Figure 9, p. 90): Become familiar with the full lifecycle.

   a) **miracidium** (can you see the cilia?)
   b) **redia** (note mouth, intestine, and cercariae within the body of the redia)
   c) **cercaria** (note oral sucker and tail)
   d) **metacercaria** (note the thickened cyst wall)

3. Demonstration of adult *Schistosoma* sp., the blood fluke. This is a slide of a copulating pair; the female is carried within a groove of the male (Figure 8, p. 89). Become familiar with the full lifecycle.

Pay particular attention to the life cycles of these trematodes. What are the similarities and differences between the life cycles of liver flukes and the blood flukes?

C. Class Monogenea:

Most monogeneans are ectoparasites and live on the scales or gills of fish. Since their hosts are fast moving organisms they possess a large attachment organ called a **haptor,** or opisthaptor (Figure 10, p. 93).

Note the demonstration of the adult monogenean, *Neopolystoma* sp.
Neopolystoma sp. lives in the urinary bladder of toads. Examine the diagram of the life cycle of this organism and note how it is synchronized with that of the toad.

D. Class Cestoidea (Tapeworms)

Cestoda

Cestodes are endoparasites commonly called tapeworms. Their life cycles require one, two, or on occasion more than 2, intermediate hosts. The intermediate hosts are usually arthropods and vertebrates.

The body of a cestode is composed of 3 regions, an anterior region called the **scolex**; a **neck;** and a **strobila**. The scolex is adapted for adhering to the host. The neck gives rise to a series of **proglottids**, collectively called the strobili.

Two common tapeworms of the intestine in humans are *Taenia solium*, the pork tapeworm, and *Taeniarhynchus saginatus*, the beef tapeworm. *Taenia solium* is sometimes called the "armed" tapeworm, because the **rostellum**, at the anterior end of the scolex, bears a double row of hooks. There is neither a rostellum nor hooks in *T. saginatus* (see Figure 12, p. 95).

1. Demonstration of adult specimen of *Taenia* sp. Note the **scolex** and its **suckers**. Immediately posterior to the scolex is the **neck**, where new proglottids are formed. About 1/3 of the way along the strobila from the scolex one finds **mature proglottids** (containing the functional reproductive organs), and further posterior are **gravid proglottids**, consisting essentially of a uterus distended with fertilized eggs.

2. Examine the whole mount of a mature proglottid. Identify the reproductive structures as indicated on Figure 14 (p. 97) and also illustrated on the appended figure. With respect to reproduction, each proglottid is essentially a true hermaphroditic animal. Although inter-proglottid fertilization is the norm it is suspected that occasionally intra-proglottid self-fertilization takes place. With this in mind, can you track the route of sperm and eggs and locate the site of fertilization? The fertilized eggs are stored in the uterus.

3. Examine the demonstration of the **hexacanth** larva (**onchosphere**) (Figure 11, p. 94). Note the 3 pairs of hooklets. The larvae are distributed to the tissues, via the blood, where each develops into a bladder worm or **cysticercus** (Figure 11, p. 94).

4. Examine a slide of a cysticercus. The cysticercus is essentially a bladder-shaped structure, the walls of which invaginate to produce an inverted scolex. When improperly cooked pork (or beef) is eaten, the cysticercus is digested out, evaginates the scolex, attaches to the intestinal wall, and develops into the adult.

5. Become familiar with the life cycle of a pork tapeworm.

6. Note the demonstration of an adult *Echinococcus granulosus*. These tiny tapeworms consist of 4 sections; a scolex and 3 proglottids. The larval stage forms **hydatid cysts** (Figure 15, p. 98), a fluid filled cyst that can contain as much as 2 litres of fluid and many daughter cysts containing larvae. This is an example of asexual reproduction in the larval stage.

III. Phylum Nemertea

The nemerteans are elongated, flattened worms referred to as ribbon worms. Most are rather small, usually less than 20 cm, but there are species that are upwards of 30 m long! The characteristic feature shared by all nemerteans is the proboscis apparatus.

Examine the preserved ribbon worm. Find the anterior end and proboscis (Figure 1, p. 102).

Lab 4
Aschelminthes
Phyla Rotifera, Nematoda, Nematomorpha, Acanthocephala
The Pseudocoelomates.

I. Introduction

The Aschelminthes is a supra-phyletic grouping of convenience. The evolutionary relationships among these phyla are very controversial. However, there are some common features among these groups, notably:

- All phyla are **triploblastic** with well-developed organ systems.
- All (except the phylum Acanthocephala) have a complete gut with a specialized **pharynx** used for pumping fluids.
- Most are round in cross-section. Small forms are **acoelomate** (lack fluid-filled internal spaces); most others have a fluid-filled internal space called a **pseudocoelom**, which functions as a hydrostatic skeleton.
- Most phyla have a retractable or eversible head end (often armed with spines - e.g., Acanthocephala).
- Smaller forms exhibit **eutely** (fixed number of cells in adults).
- Most are enclosed in a tough, non-living **cuticle** that limits growth and thus, must be molted.

Nematodes may be the most numerous of all metazoans and occur in most environments (marine, freshwater, moist terrestrial). Many are parasitic, some causing human infections.

Nematodes possess only longitudinal muscles (no circular) and the fluid filled pseudocoelom acts as an antagonist against which the muscles work.

Besides nematodes, other aschelminthes include nematomorphs (horse-hair worms), acanthocephalans (spiny-headed worms) and rotifers.

Nematomorph adults are long and cylindrical, superficially resembling Nematodes. They are short lived and it is the parasitic larva that is the dominant stage in the life cycle.

Parasitic forms (nematodes, acanthocephalans) may have simple or complex life cycles. Acanthocephalans are all **endoparasitic** worm-like animals that possess a short anterior spiny proboscis.

Rotifers are common in freshwater and have a three-part body (**head**, **trunk**, and **bifurcate foot**) with a ciliated **corona** or **wheel organ**. Some are so small they may be confused with protozoans. Rotifers reproduce by **parthenogenesis** during most of their lifecycle.

II. Phylum Rotifera

Observe the living specimens and prepared slides of various Rotifers. Do the exercises on pages 109-113 (if yeast suspension is available, try feeding the rotifers; step 7, p. 110).

III. Phylum Nematoda

A. To better understand the anatomy of the Nematoda you will be doing dissections of the male and female roundworm, *Ascaris suum*, a common parasite found in the intestine of pigs (p.182-185). Try to do the dissections with the specimen under water. There are also prepared slides of cross sections of male and female *Ascaris* available to observe while you dissect. For both sexes, recognize the **mouth, intestine, cuticle,** and **lateral lines**. In females, recognize the **vagina, uteri, oviducts** and **ovary**. In males, look for the **seminal vesicle, vas deferens**, and **testis**. Become familiar with the *Ascaris* life cycle.

CAUTION! When handling and dissecting *Ascaris* you must wear latex gloves. Although these specimens have been preserved, eggs from females have a very resistant outer covering and may not have been killed. Be careful not to put your fingers in your mouth and wash your hands thoroughly when the dissection has been completed.

B. Observe the living culture of *Turbatrix aceti* (the "vinegar eel"). These free-living nematodes occur abundantly in unpasteurized vinegar. They can tolerate extreme acidic chemical conditions and feed on bacteria and yeast in the vinegar. Observe the thrashing, swimming motion of the worms. The worms are often in entangled groups around yeast particles.

Using a pipette, remove several specimens to a glass slide and cover with a cover slip. You may have to slow the worms using methyl cellulose. Observe both male (about 1.5 mm in length) and female (somewhat larger, ca. 2.0 mm in length) worms under the compound scope. You should be able to recognize some of the following structures: clear fluid of pseudocoel (in which are suspended many fat droplets), pharynx, nerve ring, intestine, and female or male reproductive system (Figure 2, p.177).

C. Observe the following nematode demonstrations:

   1. Tri-radiate pharynx of a nematode (p. 185).

   2. *Necator americanus* (human hookworm) (p. 179).

   3. *Trichinella spiralis* encysted in muscle and adults (p. 180).

   4. *Ascaris lumbricoides* eggs (p. 182).

   5. *Enterobius vermicularis* (human pinworm) (p. 178).

   6. Filarial worms: *Loa loa* (eye worm)

      Onchocera volvulus (human filarial worm, causes river blindness)

      Wuchereria (filarial worm of humans, causes elephantiasis) (p. 179).

   7. *Caenorhabditis elegans* (model organism in genetics research).

IV. Phylum Nematomorpha:

Note the demonstration of an adult horsehair worm. The adult form of these organisms has a pseudocoelom but lacks a functional gut. It is the parasitic larva that is the dominant part of the life cycle (Figure 1, p. 187-188).

V. Phylum Acanthocephala:

Acanthocephalans are endoparasitic pseudocoelomates that possess a protrusible proboscis armed with spines. This structure aids the organism in attaching to its host's intestine.

A. Demonstration of a spiny-headed worm of pig (*Macracanthorhynchus* sp.)(p. 117).

B. Prepared slide of an Acanthocephalan, external anatomy (p. 116).

C. Demonstration of larvae (cystacanths) within freshwater amphipods (scuds) that cause the scuds to alter their normal behaviour (see the article provided).

VI. Water Samples

Water samples may be available for you to examine. Use this exercise as a review of the first four labs. Sample this material and view it under the microscope. Using your lab manual and any other references available, identify as many organisms as possible. Use an eyedropper to take material from the water-air interface, mud-water interface, the middle of the jars, etc. You may find protozoans, *Hydra*, microturbellarians, rotifers, gastrotrichs, nematodes and perhaps other organisms. Many of these organisms move rapidly, but they can be slowed by introducing a little methyl cellulose to the sample.

-Ascaris cs.
Ascaris pharynx.

Lab 6
Phylum Mollusca: Part I

I. Introduction: Phylum Mollusca

Molluscs are the second most diverse phylum of invertebrates (in terms of number of named species). They are **triploblastic, coelomates**. Their bodies include a **head**, a muscular **foot** and the internal organs or **visceral mass**. Characteristically, parts of molluscs are enclosed by a secretory epithelium (called the **mantle**) which defines a space called the **mantle cavity**. The mantle secretes a calcareous shell that often has an outer organic layer (the **periostracum**). Most molluscs have a **radula** (flexible ribbon of chitinous teeth) and a distinct gill type (**ctenidium**) that may be used for filter-feeding as well as respiration. Gills may be numerous (chitons); paired (most molluscs); single or absent (some gastropods); or large (some bivalves). Bivalve gills may take one of three forms: **protobranch**, **lamellibranch**, or **septibranch**. The coelom of molluscs arises by **schizocoely** and has become quite reduced in adults.

Chitons are sedentary, grazing animals with multiple shell plates and ctenidia that suggest an early divergence from other molluscs. Gastropods have one shell (sometimes lost) and feed by rasping, drilling or harpooning prey. Bivalves have two shells and burrow. Most are filter feeders and hence have lost the radula. Scaphopods have tubular-shells and burrow. Cephalopods have reduced or absent shells (except for Nautilus) and are fast, intelligent predators.

Phylum Mollusca
    Class Monoplacophora
    Class Polyplacophora – chitons
    Class Aplacophora - solenogasters
    Class Gastropoda - snails and slugs
        Prosobranchia – *conches, limpets, periwinkles + whelks*
        Opisthobranchia – *nudibranchs.*
        Pulmonata – *air breathing land snails*
    Class Bivalvia (=Pelecypoda) - clams, mussels, oysters, and shipworms
        Subclass Protobranchia – *small, primitive, deep water*
        Subclass Pteriomorphia (Lamellibranchs) – *mussels, scallops, oysters.*
        Subclass Heterodonta (Lamellibranchs) – *clams, cockles.*
        Subclass Anomalodesmata (Septibranchs)
    Class Scaphopoda - tusk and tooth shells
    Class Cephalopoda
        Subclass Ammonoidea - fossil ammonites
        Subclass Nautiloidea - chambered nautilus
        Subclass Coleoidea
            Order Sepioidea - cuttlefish
            Order Teuthoidea - squid
            Order Octopoda – octopus

II. Mollusc Anatomy

A. Class Gastropoda.

You will be working with *Helix* sp., a terrestrial pulmonate snail (see p. 129). The preserved specimens are usually not satisfactory for a detailed dissection, but you should be able to recognize the various parts of the shell (compare to Figure 6, p. 127). Remove the shell and identify the **head**, **foot**, and **visceral mass**. Can you distinguish the coiled **digestive gland**? Locate the **radula**, remove it, and observe it under the dissecting microscope. Attempt to find other internal structures in your snail, such as the **dart sac**, the **crop** and the **flagellum**.

B. Class Bivalvia.

Study the shell structures and internal anatomy of *Mercenaria* sp. (Venus clams) (p. 132-136, omitting "other-specimens" exercise on p. 136). This is a marine lamellibranch that burrows into soft substrate. Pay special attention to the muscle scars on the shell. Note the **umbo** and **cardinal teeth**, **pallial line** and **sinus**. Internally, find the **demibranch gill, foot, visceral mass, labial palps, posterior** and **anterior adductor muscles, incurrent** and **excurrent siphons, digestive gland, gonad, stomach, ventricle** and **pericardium**.

If *Anodonta* sp. is on demonstration, examine it as well. Compare the anatomy of the two bivalves. Especially note the **byssal threads** and differences in the foot.

C. Larval Molluscans

Examine the various larval stages of molluscs described on p. 136: **trochophore**, **veliger** and **glochidium** larvae.

III. Demonstrations

Examine the examples of living freshwater, marine and terrestrial molluscans in the various terraria, and the freshwater and marine aquaria. The lab instructor will help you determine what is in each aquarium.

Study the demonstration specimens of the various molluscan groups. The demonstration specimens will be on display this week and next week, but attempt to see these demonstrations this week because the entire lab period next week will probably be required for the squid dissection. The demonstrations were selected to correlate with lecture material.

You should try to determine how each group has modified the basic molluscan body plan to suit its way of life. How has the shell/head/foot/mantle been modified? How do these modifications relate to locomotion, acquisition of food, etc.?

1. Class Polyplacophora: (chitons) note eight shell plates, the foot, and symmetry (Figure 2, p. 125).

2. Class Gastropoda; Subclass Prosobranchia: most of the world's species of snails belong to this large subclass. On demonstration are keyhole limpets and abalone (*Haliotis kamtschatkana*).

3. Class Gastropoda; Opisthobranchs:

   a) nudibranchs (sea slugs).
   b) pteropods (sea butterflies) - no examples in lab

4. Class Gastropoda; Pulmonates:

   a) Recall *Helix* sp. from your dissection
   b) Compare dextral and sinistral shells of freshwater pond snails.
   c) land slugs –shell-less molluscs. How do they respire?

5. Class Bivalvia; Subclass Protobranchia: "nut shells" - no examples in lab

6. Class Bivalvia; Subclass Anomalodesmata: (septibranchs)

7. Class Bivalvia;
   Subclass Pteriomorphia
   a) *Mytilus* sp. (attached to hard substrate via byssal threads).
   b) oyster (cemented to hard substrate).
   c) scallop (*Pecten*) (an unattached pteriomorph).

   Subclass Heterodonta
   d) shipworm (a wood-boring heterodont).
   e) freshwater clam (a shallow-burrower in soft substrate).
   f) razor clam (a deep-burrower in soft substrate).

8. Class Scaphopoda: (tusk shells). Note the shape of the shell. How are they oriented when alive?

9. Class Cephalopoda; Subclass Nautiloidea: *Nautilus* sp., the chambered nautilus, is the only extant genus of Nautiloid (Figure 26, p. 148).

10. Class Cephalopoda; Subclass Ammonoidea: These are all fossils. All had external shells. They are commonly called ammonites. Note the external shell. (Figure 27, p. 149).

11. Class Cephalopoda; Subclass Coleoidea: internal shells or no shell at all.
    a) Order Scpioidea: *Sepia*, the common cuttlefish (also note cuttlebone and sepia ink) and *Spirula*, the deep-sea cuttlefish.
    b) Order Teuthoidea: squids, (also note their egg clusters).
    c) Order Octopoda: the octopus.

Lab 7
Phylum Mollusca : Part II

I. Phylum Mollusca: Class Cephalopoda, Subclass Coleoidea

The squid dissection is probably the most detailed dissection done in this course, and to do a thorough job it will take almost the entire 3 hours. Follow the procedures starting on page 141. Be sure to spend some time on the external anatomy. Most students want to rush right in to the dissection and fail to spend any time on the external features! Make sure you see the reproductive structures of **both** sexes (p. 137 – 147) by trading specimens with another group. Try to examine one organ system at a time so you are not taking the "scatter gun" approach. This way, you will not destroy some organs in your attempt to find others lying beneath. The only way to relate functions to organs is to study them in a **systematic** way.

Try to organize your examination into the following categories. You should be able to identify, and know the function of, at least the following organs:

A. Exterior examination: spend some time on the outside of the squid. Identify the **fins, arms, tentacles, collar, inhalent and exhalent siphons, siphon valves, eye,** and **articulating ridge.** retractor muscles

B. Reproductive system: some of these features will be the first thing you see when you open the mantle, especially if you have a female. In females, you will want to identify **nidamental glands, ovary, oviduct, oviducal opening** and **oviducal gland**. If you have a male, look for the **testis, vas deferens, spermatophoric sac, s**permatophoric gland, **spermatophores,** and **penis**.

C. Digestive system: this system and the circulatory system overlap a bit – you may need to look at them interchangeably as you seed out other structures. Try not to remove anything until you are certain you have identified it. Look for the **pharynx, buccal bulb, jaws, radula, caecum, stomach, intestine, rectum,** and **ink sac**.

D. Circulatory system: look for the **gills, kidney region, median mantle artery, the lateral mantle artery, anterior mantle vein, efferent branchial vein, branchial artery, systemic heart, branchial hearts, anterior and posterior vena cava, anterior and posterior aorta.**

E. Nervous system: look for the **cerebral and pedal ganglia, stellate ganglia, optic ganglion, parts of the eye.** Underneath most of these organs, look for the **pen.**

II. Display of molluscan shells.

Please make sure to examine the display of various molluscan shells if you didn't have time last week. These shells show remarkable diversity of shapes, sizes and colours. Can you suggest some functions for this diversity?

Lab 8
Phyla Annelida and Sipuncula

I. Introduction

Annelids are elongated, **segmented** worms with a sub-terminal mouth and terminal anus. Segmentation (**metamerism**) is conspicuous in the coelom, body-wall muscles, excretory, reproductive and nervous systems. Segmentation is thought to be an adaptation for a burrowing way of life. Segmentation allows for precise control of the shape of body compartments which allows annelids to walk, swim, or burrow, sometimes with the aid of fleshy projections called **parapodia** and bristles (**setae**). Internal transport involves a blood vascular system (with hearts and capillary beds), coelomic fluid or both. Excretion is by a segmentally arranged **metanephridial system** consisting of paired nephridia in each segment.

Polychaetes are marine worms with conspicuous parapodia and a **pharynx** that can be either **eversible** (errantia) or **fixed** (sedentaria). Polychaete parapodia are often bilobed (**notopodium** and **neuropodium**), paddle-like structures with many setae. In many of these worms they are used for respiration as well as locomotion. The majority of polychaetes are dioecious.

Oligochaetes are mainly terrestrial and freshwater species that lack parapodia but have retained setae. Oligochaetes are all monoecious.

Hirudineans are found in marine, freshwater and terrestrial habitats. The coelom is not compartmentalized and is largely filled with connective tissue. Leeches have no parapodia or setae. Like oligochaetes, leeches are monoecious. They also have a fixed number of segments, generally thought to be 34.

Sipunculid worms are unsegmented, surface-deposit feeding marine worms with two coeloms; a large one filling the trunk and a small one in the tentacles. The whole anterior end of the worm (the **introvert**) can be extended by high coelomic pressure and retracted by large, paired retractor muscles.

Annelids and sipunculids share some similar developmental characteristics, namely the typical protostome features of spiral cleavage and a **trochophore larva** (Figure 9, p. 161). This larval form is <u>not</u> found in the Clitellata. These groups also have similar nervous systems, similar body wall musculature, and similar excretory systems comprised of metanephridia.

II. Phylum Annelida

Phylum Annelida
        Class Polychaeta
                Errantians
                Sedentarians

        Class Clitellata
                Subclass Oligochaeta

                Subclass Hirudinea

A. Class Polychaeta

1. Proceed with the external and internal anatomy of *Nereis* sp., an unmodified errantian (p. 156-159). You should be able to identify the head and its parts (Figure 3), the **prostomium, peristomium**, and associated sensory structures (**palp, peristomial cirri, and antennae**); the **pharynx, gametes** (maybe), **septa, dorsal blood vessel, esophagus, stomach-intestine, esophageal caecum, nephridia, ventral nerve cord, circumpharyngeal connectives**, and **dorsal brain**.

   [handwritten note in margin: to Oligochaeta]

2. Examine a **parapodium** and its parts - you will want to disconnect it to examine under the dissecting scope. Make sure you see the **notopodium** and **neuropodium** and the two **acicula** (Figure 4, p. 158)

3. Examine the cross section of *Nereis* sp. Identify the muscles (**dorsal** and **ventral longitudinal,** as well as **oblique**), **ventral blood vessel** and **nerve cord, coelom** and **intestine** Figure 6, p. 160.

4. There is a wide variety of demonstrations of polychaetes. Study these specimens and note their modifications from the general polychaete body plan. Based on these modifications make educated guesses about how and where each species lives. Use your text and lab book to supplement your observations.

   a) Unmodified errantian: *Nereis* sp. (sand or rag worm) – Figure 5, p. 159.

   b) Modified errantian: *Aphrodita* sp. (sea mouse).

   c) Sedentarian in soft substrate (no tube): *Arenicola* sp. (lugworm)

   d) Sedentarian in soft substrate (sandy tube): Sabellid (Peacock worm).

   e) Sedentarian in soft substrate (mucous tube): *Chaetopterus* sp. - see p. 160-161.

   f) Other polychaete specimens may be on display, such as feather duster worms.

   g) If available, observe living polychaetes in the marine aquarium.

B. Class Clitellata
Subclass Oligochaeta
1. *Lumbricus* sp.

Be sure to study the behavioural responses before proceeding to the external & internal anatomy of the earthworm *Lumbricus*.

a) Obtain a live specimen. Place the worm onto dry filter paper; observe its movements. Can you feel the setae? Can you hear the setae scraping against the paper? Is the movement on wet paper different from that on dry paper? From that on smooth glass?

b) Anatomy. You are probably already familiar with the general anatomy of the earthworm from first-year biology courses and even high school biology courses. Today's exercise (p. 162-168) treats the anatomy in more detail, and you should become familiar with all the anatomical structures and their functions. Again, try to follow the guide when dissecting so you examine one system at a time and don't destroy structures before you have had a chance to see them. Your goal should not be to try to find structures as quickly as possible but to find out where and how each structure fits within the system it belongs to. This is a very delicate dissection so proceed slowly!

Externally, try to identify the **prostomium, mouth, periostomium** and **anus**, as well as the **clitellum** and pairs of **setae**. See if you can make out the female and/or male **genital pores**.

Internally, you will need to examine the worm from the head to the clitellum. See if you can make out the **buccal cavity**, and examine the **pharynx, esophagus, calciferous glands, crop, gizzard**, and **intestine**. For the reproductive system, you will easily be able to see the large **seminal vesicles**, and the round **seminal receptacles**. The female organs are present, but will not be visible to you. Look for the **cerebral ganglion** at the anterior end, and the **ventral nerve cord** underneath the digestive system. Note the numerous **septa**, the result of segmentation in the annelids, and the **nephridia** that are separately present in each of those segments.

add in cross section. (eg c̄ typhlosole)

c) *Monocystis* sp. is a parasitic protozoan (Sporozoa) that lives in the seminal vesicles of earthworms. It should be possible to find this protozoan in your anaesthetized worm using the following procedure. Using forceps, pinch off small pieces of the seminal vesicle and remove to a depression slide containing 0.75% NaCl solution. Gently tease apart the seminal vesicle material and examine it under the microscope. You should be able to find **cysts** and perhaps the larger **trophozoites** (see Figure 18 on p. 20).

2. Examine the live enchytraeids (the "white" worms that you fed to *Dugesia*) if they are available. These are small oligochaetes often found in rich organic matter. Other species are aquatic. Examine their external anatomy with the aid of a microscope. How are they similar to *Lumbricus*? How are they different?

353

Subclass Hirudinea

1. Examine the demonstrations of the various groups of leeches. These demonstrations are set to correlate with lecture material. You will **not** be asked to distinguish **between** the various taxa of leeches on the lab examination, but you should be able to recognize a leech! Note the **anterior** and **posterior suckers**.

> a) Order Rhynchobdellida -- the proboscis leeches (blood meal from invertebrates and fish).
>
>> - Family Glossiphoniidea (feed on invertebrates).
>> - Family Piscicolidae (fish leeches).
>
> b) Order Gnathobdellida -- the jawed leeches (blood meal from warm-blooded animals).
>
>> - Family Hirudidae (aquatic when not on hosts).
>> - Family Haemadipsidae (land leeches)(not available).
>
> c) Order Pharyngobdellida -- the worm leeches (these are predacious leeches; they **do not** take a blood meal).

III. Phylum Sipuncula (peanut worms)

Examine the specimens of *Sipunculus* sp. on display. These are non-segmented, coelomate worms. Most sipunculans are sedentary, extending the introvert from the safety of a burrow or tube. Note the **introvert** on the demonstration specimen. Can you see the tentacles? What is its function? (see Figure 1, p. 252).

Lab 9
Phyla Onycophora, Tardigrada and Arthropoda - Class Crustacea

I. Introduction

Onycophorans (velvet worms) have been called an evolutionary "missing link" because they share some characteristics with both annelids and arthropods. They are terrestrial, but live in moist habitats because their cuticle is thin and not waxy. They are active nocturnally – possibly also due to water retention reasons. They are like arthropods because they have, among other common characteristics: chitin in their cuticle, a hemocoel instead of a true coelom, and gas exchange via spiracles. Like annelids, they have, among others: no jointed appendages, longitudinal, circular and oblique muscles, segmented nephridia, and a hydrostatic skeleton for locomotion.

Tardigrades (water bears) have 4 pairs of non-jointed appendages, each of which has two or more claws. Water bears can go into a state of metabolic torpor and can survive freezing and drying for long periods of time. This is called cryptobiosis.

Arthropods are the largest and most diverse phylum of animals. They are segmented animals with **jointed exoskeletons** composed of **chitin**, a light-weight, flexible protein. In many arthropods the body segments have become fused into distinct body regions called **tagmata**. The arthropod exoskeleton must be molted to allow for growth. This usually includes parts of the fore- and hindguts! An individual body segment is composed of four skeletal plates, a dorsal **tergum**, 2 lateral **pleura**, and a ventral **sternum**, although these plates may be fused and difficult to discern. Arthropod movement is accomplished by the action of discrete muscles attached to the inside of the exoskeleton. The exoskeleton provides protection and mechanical support as well as a surface for muscle attachment.

Various arthropod groups can be distinguished by:
   a) the number of tagmata (2 or 3),
   b) the location of the mouth in the embryo and adult, and
   c) the number of segments bearing **antennae** in the adult (0, 1, or 2).

The limbs of trilobites and crustaceans are usually **biramous** (2-branched) consisting of an **exopodite** as one branch and the endopodite as the second branch. The basal portion (protopodite) may have various projections as well, often modified as gills. Limbs of chelicerates and uniramians have a single branch (**uniramous**).

The coelom in arthropods is greatly reduced (limited to the space around the gonads) but is replaced by another space, the large **hemocoel**. The dorsal, contractile heart is perforated with pores (**ostia**) to circulate **hemolymph**.

Respiration is accomplished through a variety of means:
   a) **book gills** in aquatic forms or **book lungs** in terrestrial forms;
   b) flattened or filamentous **gills** derived from limb branches in crustaceans and trilobites; and

c) **spiracle/tracheal** systems in uniramians and some arachnids.

Excretion is by **Malpighian tubules** that empty into the gut (terrestrial uniramians and arachnids) or by **saccules** that open outside the body via ducts adjacent to a few appendages (crustaceans).

The brain consists of three regions. A **protocerebrum** innervates the mouthparts and head appendages, a **deuterocerebrum** innervates the first segment, and a **tritocerebrum** innervates the second segment. Most arthropods possess **compound eyes** composed of many units (**ommatidia**), each with its own lens and photosensitive cells.

Most arthropods are dioecious.

II. Phylum Onycophora

Examine the preserved specimen of an onycophoran. List the features that are shared with annelids and those shared with Arthropods. (See p. 191-193).

III. Phylum Tardigrada

Examine a prepared slide of a water bear. Tardigrades are pseudocoelomates with some arthropod characteristics. Large numbers of live tardigrades are often found living among bog mosses, so if available, try to observe water bears from a hydrated moss sample.

IV. Phylum Arthropoda: Class Crustacea

Phylum Arthropoda (in part)
    Subphylum Mandibulata (in part)
      Class Crustacea
        Subclass Branchiopoda
            Order Anostraca - brine shrimp
            Order Notostraca - tadpole shrimp
            Order Conchostraca (clam shrimp)
            Order Cladocera - *Daphnia* sp. (water fleas)

Know to
Subclass.

        Subclass Ostracoda - seed shrimp

        Subclass Copepoda

        Subclass Cirripedia - barnacles

        Subclass Branchiura - fish lice

Subclass Malacostraca
    Superorder Hoplocarida - stomatopods
    Superorder Peracarida
        Order Amphipoda
        Order Isopoda
    Superorder Eucarida
        Order Euphausiacea - krill
        Order Decapoda
           Suborder Natantia - "true", edible shrimp
           Suborder Reptantia
               Infraorder Macrura - lobsters & crayfish
               Infraorder Anomura - hermit crabs
               Infraorder Brachyura - "true" crabs

1. Observe living *Daphnia* sp. (Subclass Branchiopoda, Order Cladocera) and living copepods (Subclass Copepoda). Slides of *Daphnia* sp. will also be available. What crustacean characteristics can you see in *Daphnia*? Note the **carapace** (covering the entire body except the head), the single **compound eye**, the large **second antennae**, and the thoracic appendages. Be able to identify the structures shown on Figure 22 (p. 215).

2. External anatomy of the crayfish (Subclass Malacostraca, Eucarida, Macrura). Identify the following structures (p. 220-226): **carapace, rostrum, cervical groove, eyes, abdomen, telson, anus**, male and female **genital openings, opening of green gland, branchiostegites**. Identify all of the appendages (a good idea is to mount one set on an index card). Include: **antennule, antenna, mandible, 1st maxilla, 2nd maxilla, 1st maxilliped, 2nd maxilliped, 3rd maxilliped, periopod, male gonopid, pleopod,** and **uropod.** You need not be concerned with the branches (i.e., ischiopodite, meropodite, etc.) of the various appendages, but you should be able to recognize each appendage.

3. Proceed with the dissection and study the internal anatomy of the doubly injected crayfish (pages 226-228). Note the **stomach and associated muscles**; the **gastric mill**; the **green gland**; **digestive gland** (liver); **testis** or **ovaries**; **supraesophageal ganglia**; the **intestine**; **heart**; **gills**. Also note the **mandibular adductor**, which you may see when you remove the upper exoskeleton, or it may be removed when you take out the mandible.

4. Demonstrations: You should study the demonstrations closely. You should be able to recognize each of these subclasses and the orders listed within each.

    1. Slide of **nauplius larva**, the basic type of crustacean larva. Note also **zoea** and **megalops** larvae of crabs (Figure 35, p. 230).

    2. Subclass Branchiopoda:
        a) Anostraca (Fairy shrimp). This particular species is the largest fairy shrimp. It is found in Alberta. Living cultured brine shrimp (*Artemia* sp.) may also be available.
        b) Notostraca (Tadpole shrimp). These are also found in Alberta. (Note large carapace and phyllopodia.)
        c) Cladocera. You have already observed living *Daphnia* sp

3. Subclass Cirripedia: (Barnacles) (p. 218-219)
   a) Free-living Cirripedia. Note the examples of both stalked and non-stalked barnacles.
   b) Parasitic Cirripedia. *Sacculina* sp. is a parasitic barnacle found in crabs (re. lecture notes).

4. Subclass Branchiura: (Fish "lice"). These are ectoparasites on the skin and gill cavity of freshwater and marine fish. See the demo of *Argulus* sp.

5. Subclass Copepoda: Living specimens and prepared slides. (Figure 24, p. 217)

6. Subclass Ostracoda: These are commonly called seed shrimp. They can be seasonally abundant in Alberta waters (Figure 23, p. 216)

7. Subclass Malacostraca: The largest group of crustaceans, including many edible types (Figure 20, p. 213).

   a) Superorder Hoplocarida (Mantis shrimp).
   b) Superorder Peracarida
      i) Order Isopoda. (Living isopods may be available.) Isopods are found in marine, freshwater and terrestrial habitats. They are the largest group of terrestrial crustaceans.
      ii) Order Amphipoda. These are the common "shrimp" you may have observed in lakes and ponds in Alberta. (Remember back to the acanthocephalan parasites in the adult amphipods.)
   c) Superorder Eucarida
      i) Order Euphausiacea. (Krill). The great blue whale feeds on these small crustaceans.
      ii) Order Decapoda. Note the various examples of decapod crustaceans from the following groups.
         Natantia (Swimming forms: eg. Shrimps).

         Reptantia (crawling forms)
            Macrura: lobsters and crayfish (See above).
            Anomura: hermit crabs.
            Brachyura: "true" crabs, (Various species).

Lab 10
Phylum Arthropoda: Other Arthropods

I. Phylum Arthropoda: Other Arthropods (in part)

Phylum Arthropoda (in part)
> Subphylum Trilobitomorpha
>> Class Trilobita - trilobites
>
> Subphylum Chelicerata
>> Class Merostomata - horseshoe crabs
>> Class Arachnida - spiders, mites, ticks, scorpions
>
> Subphylum Mandibulata
>> Class Myriapoda –centipedes, millipedes
>> Class Insecta - insects

A. Do the short exercise on the external anatomy of the grasshopper (pages 232-235). Compare this insect's mouthparts (Figure 37, p.234) and other appendages with those of the crayfish and also with those of the mosquito and the lepidopteran (p. 238), both of which are on demonstration. Recall the various adaptations to mouth parts in the Class Insecta. Also note the shape of the antennae, and compare to common insect antenna types (Figure 47, p. 240). Work your way through the internal dissection starting on p. 236 and identify the **hemocoel, reproductive organs, gastric caeca, malphighian tubules, nerve cord** and **ganglia**.

B. Compare the external features of the "daddy longlegs" (Class Arachnida, Order Opiliones) with those of true spiders (Class Arachnida, Order Araneae). Refer to Figure 13, p. 209 for the opilione and to Figure 12 for the spider. For both the "daddy longlegs" and the spider locate the following structures and determine how these structures differ for each: **prosoma, opisthosoma, carapace, eyes, pedipalps, chelicerae, walking legs,** and position of **genital opening**. In addition, on the spider identify the following: **pedicel,** opening of **book lungs, spinnerets,** and **modified terminal end of male pedipalp, chelicera,** and **fang**. For the opilione, identify the following: **spiracular openings, openings of odoriferous glands**. Recall behavioral differences (from lecture notes). ~~repugnatorial~~ gland

C. Demonstrations. You should be able to recognize, and give the indicated classification for, the following groups:

> 1. Class Merostomata: (the horseshoe "crab"; *Limulus* sp.). The horseshoe "crab" is not a true crab, but a primitive marine arthropod related to spiders and scorpions. It is found in shallow water along the east coast (Figure 6, p. 203).

> 2. Class Arachnida: (spiders, including black widow spiders; scorpions (Figure 9, p. 206); mites (p. 211); daddy-long legs (p. 209). These animals (and also Merostomata) lack antennae and have the first pair of appendages bearing pincer-like chelicerae (Figure 12).

> 3. Class Myriapoda: Millipedes and Centipedes

a) Order Chilopoda: (centipedes, p. 243). The first trunk appendage is called a maxilliped and it ends in a hollow poisonous fang. Most of the other trunk segments bear one pair of appendages.

b) Order Diplopoda: (millipedes, p. 242). Most of the observable trunk "segments" are actually a **fused pair of segments**. Therefore they each have two pairs of appendages.

4. Class Insecta: Spend some time learning the various orders of insects on demonstration.

a) Order Ephemeroptera (mayflies). These are the most primitive of the winged (pterygote) insects. The nymphs are aquatic.

b) Order Odonata (dragonflies and damselflies). Both the adult and the nymphs (which are aquatic) are predators.

c) Order Orthoptera (grasshoppers and crickets).

d) Order Mantodea (praying mantis). The mantids are carnivorous. They wait for their prey with the fore legs lifted, hence praying mantis.

e) Order Blattaria (or Blattodea) (cockroaches) Cockroaches have an enlarged shield-like pronotum that protects the head.

f) Order Isoptera (termites) (sometimes considered a subgroup of Blattaria) Wingless infertile males and females comprise the worker and soldier casts. Only the reproductive cast (kings and queens) is winged.

g) Order Hemiptera ("true" bugs). This is a large group. Those on demonstration are called water boatmen (Corixidae). They are abundant in Alberta water, especially in autumn. All hemipterans have sucking mouthparts. In addition to water boatmen, note whole-mount slide of *Rhodnius* sp. (recall lecture notes).

h) Order Coleoptera (beetles). This is the largest order of insects. Note both adults and larvae. The first pair of wings is modified as a protective device.

i) Order Lepidoptera (moths and butterflies). There are many more moths than there are butterflies. Moths are fast-flying insects; butterflies are generally slow-flying. Moths hide by day; butterflies fly in bright sunlight. Moths are readily eaten by insect-feeding birds whereas many butterflies have acquired flavours that are unpleasant to most birds. The larvae of both groups are caterpillars, having five or fewer pairs of abdominal prolegs.

j) Order Diptera (two-winged flies). Economically, this is the most important order. The hind wings are reduced to two small drumstick-like structures called halteres. There are many groups. Tsetse flies and mosquitoes are on demonstration. The common names of some other important dipterans are black flies, crane flies, midges, houseflies, horse flies, fruit flies, etc.

k) Order Siphonaptera (fleas). The wings are suppressed. Bodies are laterally flattened.

l) Order Hymenoptera (bees, wasps, ants and other important groups). There are two pairs of wings. The hind wings are linked via hooks to the front wings. The ovipositor of the female is modified into a stinger.

Lab 11
The Deuterostomes
Phylum Echinodermata; the Lophophorates;
Phylum Hemichordata; and the lower Chordates

I. Introduction

The deuterostomes are a diverse assemblage of organisms. The embryological development of a deuterostome differs from that of a protostome in three significant ways. The **blastopore is posterior** and typically becomes the anus. The mouth then forms as a new opening at the anterior end. Cell cleavage is radial, not spiral as in protostomes, and the cells are said to be indeterminant.

Echinoderms are all marine and exhibit **pentamerous radial symmetry**. Huge numbers of calcareous **ossicles** and **spines** make up the mesodermally derived, endoskeleton. Echinoderms have adapted a portion of their coelom into a unique, fluid-filled, complex **water vascular system** connected to many **tube feet**. This system functions in locomotion, feeding, attachment, respiration, and circulation. The tube feet are extended by hydrostatic pressure. A sieve plate (**madreporite**) connects the water vascular system to the external seawater. In addition to the water vascular system, three other coelomic systems are present: a **perivisceral**, a **hyponeural** and a **genital**. A **nerve ring** surrounds the mouth and gives rise to five branches (**radial nerves**).

Different forms of larvae occur among the echinoderm classes. The larvae are active feeders and exhibit bilateral symmetry, a clue to the bilateral ancestry of the echinoderms. Sea stars commonly have **bipinnaria larvae** (Figure 10, p. 274), and sea urchins have **echinopluteus larvae** (Figure 21, p. 284).

Lophophorates are all sessile or sedentary as adults. They are characterized by a crown of ciliated feeding tentacles, the **lophophore**. This structure resembles the feeding structure found in pterobranch hemichordates.

Worm-like hemichordates in the Class Enteropneusta have a well-developed **pharyngeal basket** with **ciliated slits** that resembles those of some chordates (lancets), suggesting a phylogenetic affinity with the chordaes.

Urochordates, (phylum Chordata), also have a **pharyngeal basket** with slits, and their **tadpole larva** possess other chordate characteristics, notably a **muscular post-anal tail**, a **dorsal hollow nerve cord** and a **notochord**.

Cephalochordates, (phylum Chordata), also possess a dorsal, tubular nerve cord, a notochord, pharyngeal gill slits, and a post-anal tail.

II. Phylum Echinodermata

Phylum Echinodermata (in part)
    Class Stelleroidea
        Subclass Asteroidea - sea stars
        Subclass Ophiuroidea - brittle and basket stars

    Class Echinoidea - sea urchins, heart urchins, sand dollars

    Class Holothuroidea - sea cucumbers

    Class Crinoidea - sea lilies and feather stars

A. Subclass Asteroidea

1. Examine the external and internal anatomy of *Asterias* sp. or *Pisaster* sp. a common sea star (p. 268-276). You should be able to identify: **oral** and **aboral** surfaces, **mouth, dermal branchiae, spines, pedicellariae, ambulacral grooves, tube feet**, "**eyes**", **cardiac stomach, pyloric stomach, retractor muscles of stomach, digestive glands** (hepatic caeca), **rectal caecum**, components of **water vascular system** (including the **madreporite, stone canal, ring canal, radial canal, lateral canal, ampullae** and **tube feet), radial nerve cord** (this is really fun when you find it), and the **gonads**.

2. Observe the living asteroids in the marine aquarium. Note the activity of the tube feet (may be best seen on the urchin). Depending on the availability of live specimens, the lab instructor may demonstrate the following: (1) righting reaction, by placing a starfish onto its aboral side. How is this reaction accomplished? (2) Tube foot locomotion, by placing the starfish into a pan of very cold sea water.

3. Slide demonstration: Cross-section of sea star arm (see Figure 9, p. 273). Note as many structures as are visible from the list above.

4. Slide demonstration: Whole mount of pedicellaria. What is the function of these structures?

5. Observe the wide variety of other sea stars on demo.

B. Subclass Ophiuroidea

1. Demonstration of brittle stars (p. 277).

2. Demonstration of basket stars (p. 277).

C. Class Echinoidea

1. If available, observe living sea urchins in marine aquarium. Note tube feet.

2. Observe the labelled demonstration of **Aristotle's lantern**. This structure is used in feeding (Figure 20, p. 283). You do not have to learn the parts, just recognize this structure.

3. See the demonstrations of sea urchins and sand dollars (see p. 284).

D. Class Holothuroidea

1. Do the external and internal anatomy of *Cucumaria* sp. (p. 287-290). Identify: **oral** and **aboral** regions, **mouth**, **tentacles**, **tube feet**, **anus**, **pharynx**, **stomach**, **intestine**, **cloaca**, **respiratory tree**, **gonads**, components of **water vascular system** (including the **madreporite, stone canal, ring canal,** and **polian vesicle** – note that these are much longer than they look in the diagram – how do these components differ from those of *Asterias* sp.?), and **calcareous plates** (i.e. endoskeleton) after dissolving with bleach.

2. Observe living holothuroids in marine aquarium.

3. Demonstration of preserved holothuroids.

E. Class Crinoidea

Demonstration of feather stars (p. 291).

III. The Lophophorates

Phylum Bryozoa (moss animals)
Phylum Brachiopoda (lamp shells)

A. Phylum Bryozoa

Examine demonstrations of bryozoans. Bryozoans are the largest group of lophophorates. They are mainly colonial. Bryozoans are primarily marine, however there are a few species found in Alberta. Note the colonial nature and the prominent lophophore on the demonstration specimens. (Figure 2, p. 256).

B. Phylum Brachiopoda

Brachiopods have an extensive fossil record. Of the 30,000+ species identified only about 350 are present today. Examine the brachiopods on demonstration. How does the shell compare to that of a bivalve (p. 262)? Which side is dorsal? Note the flexible pedicle that attaches the animal to the substrate.

IV. Phylum Hemichordata

Class Enteropneusta (acorn worms)

Examine the preserved specimen (*Dolichoglossus* sp. or *Balanoglossus* sp.). Note the distinctive proboscis and collar (Figure 1, p. 298). Where is the mouth? Can you see any pharyngeal slits? What chordate characters do these specimens possess?

V. Phylum Chordata

Subphylum Urochordata (sea squirts)
Subphylum Cephalochordata (lancets)
Subphylum Vertebrata (covered in Zoology 224)

A. Subphylum Urochordata

1. Examine a preserved sea squirt (*Ciona* sp. or *Molgula* sp.) and observe the pharyngeal basket (Figure 2, p. 304) Does this specimen seem chordate-like? Now examine the prepared slide of the ascidian tadpole larvae. What chordate characteristics can you identify on it?

B. Subphylum Cephalochordata

Examine the whole mounts, preserved specimens and model of a lancet (*Branchiostoma* sp.). How does it feed? What Chordate characteristics are evident in *Branchiostoma*? (Figure 8, p. 309)

Index

DNA, 2, 11, 34, 154, 174, 253
  chloroplast, 2
  circular, 154
  extranuclear, 2
  linear, 154
  naked, 2, 11
  structure, 253
  variations in, 154
DNA sequences, 34, 174
Dog tick, 209-210
dogs, 13, 184
Dracunculus medinensis (guinea worm), 176
Dry weight, 41
Dysentery, 13
  amebic, 13

E

Ears, 113, 168
Earth, 1, 249
Earthworms, 21, 155, 161-162, 180
Ecdysis, 106, 174
Echinococcus granulosus, 95-98, 105
Echinoidea, 268, 280, 295
Ecology, 308
Ectoparasites, 81, 93
Egg, 9, 86, 89, 116, 131, 147-148, 184, 209, 218,
    225, 230, 236-237, 274, 286
  development, 9, 116, 274
Eggs, 39, 86, 89, 92, 95-97, 112, 116, 131, 147,
    165, 175, 177-178, 180-182, 184-185,
    195, 205, 211, 215, 225, 230, 235-236,
    290-291
  fertilization and, 39
Eimeria, 3
Ejaculatory duct, 185, 236
Electron micrograph, 28
Electron microscope, 19
Elements, 19, 35, 39, 43, 72, 270
Elephantiasis, 178
Elevation, 50, 133
Elimination, 112
Embryo, 109, 161, 206, 258
embryonated eggs, 177, 184
Embryonic, 9, 91, 106, 119, 162
Embryonic development, 9, 162
  animal, 162
Encystment, 91
Endoderm, 47
Endoparasites, 19, 81
Energy, 217
  forms of, 217
  free, 217
Entamoeba, 3, 12-13
  E. histolytica, 13
Entamoeba histolytica, 3, 12-13
Enterobius vermicularis, 176-178
Enterobius vermicularis (pinworm), 176
Envelope, 98
Environment, 161
Enzyme, 62, 65, 69, 144
Enzymes, 50, 53, 69, 136, 270, 284, 309
  extracellular, 136
  small intestine, 284
Epidermis, 46, 47, 49, 51, 53-54, 56, 69, 72,
    81-83, 85, 91, 101-102, 115, 159-160,
    162, 164, 192, 211, 255, 267, 269,
    274-275, 280, 285-286, 299, 308, 311
Epithelial cells, 34, 164, 185
epithelium, 47, 59, 133, 167, 291
Equilibrium, 62, 285
Erythrocytes, 14, 22-23
Esophagus, 65, 86, 130, 136, 142, 144, 146, 159,
    164-165, 167, 175, 185, 195, 227, 230,
    236-238, 258, 270, 279, 284, 289, 305,
    308-309
Euglena, 2, 4, 6-7
Euglena gracilis, 7
Euglenid, 2
Euglenoid movement, 7
Euglenoids, 7
Euglenophyta, 2, 5
Eukaryotic cell, 1
Euplotes, 4, 25, 30-31
Europe, 168, 206
Eurypterids, 204
Evidence, 2, 24, 34, 43, 69-70, 74, 89, 91,
    106-107, 115, 119, 133, 148, 150,
    153-154, 157, 174, 176, 178, 180, 189,
    193, 204-205, 232, 250, 253, 265, 275,

289, 294, 310
Evolution, 34, 40, 80, 107, 119, 154, 174, 199,
    250, 253, 302
  chordate, 302
  definition of, 253
  evidence of, 119
  of arthropods, 199
  phylogeny and, 154
  rRNA, 34, 80, 107, 174, 250, 253
Evolutionary biology, 34
evolutionary relationships, 106
Excretion, 1, 267, 299
Exercise, 14, 20, 33, 41, 43, 91, 99, 126-127, 153,
    157, 162, 165, 173, 177, 180, 231, 236,
    265, 275-276, 280, 282, 284, 289,
    297-298, 300, 304
Exhalation, 137
Exocytosis, 11
Experiments, 257
Expiration, 235
Extension, 37, 139, 147, 204, 213, 222, 259, 261
External fertilization, 255
Extracellular digestion, 65, 136
Eye, 1, 12, 41, 83, 129, 140, 147, 201, 204,
    214-217, 219, 222, 234
  structure, 147, 201, 204, 219, 222, 234
Eyes, 40, 121, 123, 133-134, 139, 142, 147-148,
    150, 155, 157, 201, 203-204, 206-209,
    212, 220, 222, 229-234, 241, 244
  compound, 147, 201, 203-204, 220, 222,
    230-231, 234, 241, 244
  evolution of, 40
  iris, 147
  structure of, 40, 133, 147-148, 231, 234
eyespot, 7-9, 32, 62, 64, 91, 270, 308
Eyespots, 2, 10, 82-83, 105, 129, 170-171, 195

F

Families, 107, 191
Family, 39, 92, 209-210, 232, 302
  of humans, 92
Fangs, 207
Fascicles, 41
Fasciola, 81, 85-87, 89, 91-92, 105
Fasciola hepatica, 81, 85-87, 89, 91, 105
Fasciolopsis buski, 86, 105
Feather stars, 268, 290
Feathers, 72
Fecal contamination, 13, 180
Feces, 10, 21, 27, 134, 177, 184, 291
Female reproductive system, 184
Females, 22, 89, 109, 177-179, 184, 191, 195,
    204-205, 211, 218, 228, 236, 239
Femur, 232, 235, 239
Fertilization, 23, 39, 62, 75, 131, 184, 255, 274,
    284, 289, 297
Fever, 199, 209-210
Fiber, 28, 195
Fibers, 35, 39-41, 53, 68-69, 84, 97, 136, 138-139,
    165, 167-168, 171, 185, 187, 195, 268,
    274
Fiddler crabs, 246
Filament, 3, 32, 66, 68-69, 72, 225
Filter feeders, 49, 156, 279
filters, 16, 37, 41, 214, 275
  membrane, 37
Fire, 49, 239
FISH, 3-4, 11, 23-24, 61, 82, 91-93, 115, 168, 213,
    220, 308
Fission, 1, 3-4, 7, 11-12, 14, 19-25, 28, 49, 62
Fixation, 182-183
Flagella, 2-5, 7-11, 19-20, 53, 216, 222
  movement, 2-3, 7, 9, 11
  of dinoflagellates, 5
  structure, 5, 9, 19, 222
Flagellate, 3, 7, 226
Flagellates, 1-2, 4-5, 7, 11, 25
  Giardia, 2
  Leishmania, 2, 11
Flagellum, 1-2, 4, 7, 9, 11, 37, 131, 212-213, 222,
    225, 234
Fleas, 50, 200, 214, 232
Flies, 200, 232, 238, 241
Flight, 231, 234
Florida, 4, 62, 70, 72, 206, 285
Flowers, 232, 237, 239
Flukes, 81, 85, 87-89, 92-93, 97
Follicle, 211-212
Follicles, 211-212

hair follicles, 212
Food, 1, 7, 12-14, 19, 24, 27, 29, 31, 47, 50, 53,
    62, 64, 67, 72, 101, 109-110, 112-113,
    121, 126, 132, 135-136, 146, 151, 156,
    160, 165, 185, 204, 214-215, 217-218,
    220, 222, 225, 227, 229, 233, 236-238,
    252, 255, 258-260, 267-268, 270,
    279-280, 282, 284-285, 289-291, 297,
    304-305, 308-310
  contamination, 13, 185
  dried, 72, 259, 268, 282
  handling, 279
  pH, 165
  regulation of, 165
  safety, 289
  storage, 7, 165, 309
Food chains, 217
Food processing, 214
Food vacuole, 1, 12, 19, 27
Food vacuoles, 1, 12-13, 24, 27, 53
  of Paramecium, 27
Food web, 214
foods, 87
Foramen magnum, 233
Fossil, 16, 34, 43-44, 73-74, 121-122, 136,
    149-150, 156, 201, 204, 206, 253, 260,
    263-265, 267, 290-292, 294, 303
Fossil record, 16, 74, 265, 290, 292, 303
Fossils, 1, 46, 74, 121, 156, 174, 201, 260, 263,
    292, 297
  arthropod, 174
  dating, 74
Fovea, 121
Frogs, 3
Frustules, 57

G

Gamete, 8, 20
Gametes, 21, 23, 25, 56-57, 65, 86, 134, 158, 161,
    255, 274, 279, 282, 291, 297
  algae, 282
Gametocyte, 22
Gametogenesis, 8, 17, 22, 183
Ganglia, 83, 95, 101, 121, 142, 159, 167-168, 230,
    237
Gas, 50, 59-61, 106, 121, 126, 148, 150, 207, 279,
    286, 297
Gas exchange, 106, 207, 279, 286, 297
  spider, 207
Gases, 282, 289
Gastrodermis, 46, 47, 49-51, 53-54, 56, 62, 65, 69,
    84-85, 167, 274
Gastropods, 121-122, 126-129, 148
Gastrovascular cavity, 46, 47, 50-51, 53-54, 56,
    59, 61-62, 65, 67-70, 72-73, 77
Gene, 93, 107, 302
Gene expression, 302
  analysis of, 302
Generation, 89, 91
Genus, 9, 11, 14, 16, 21, 29, 31, 33, 43, 72, 76,
    109, 122, 131, 136-137, 156, 196, 206,
    211, 231, 257, 260, 261, 308
Germ layers, 1
Giardia, 2, 9-10, 14, 33
Giardia intestinalis, 9-10
Giardiasis, 32
Gill filaments, 225
Gill slits, 297-298, 300, 302, 303-305, 308-310
Gills, 23-24, 81-83, 122-124, 128, 134, 141,
    144-145, 160, 199, 204, 220, 226,
    229-230, 248, 282, 285-286, 297, 300
  arthropod, 199
  fish, 23-24, 82, 220
  sea star, 285
Glands, 22-23, 81-82, 86, 91, 95, 110, 118, 124,
    130-131, 141, 144, 147, 160, 165,
    192-193, 195, 207-208, 211, 213, 219,
    230, 236-237, 244, 263, 270, 300
  function, 86, 124, 131, 141, 165, 207, 211, 230,
    244
Globigerina, 3, 16
Glomerulus, 299
Gonads, 49-50, 56-57, 62, 65, 69, 102, 109, 119,
    136, 161, 191, 230, 263, 274-275,
    279-280, 284, 297-298, 307
Gonyaulax, 2, 4
grains, 27, 275
granules, 22-23, 34, 126, 164, 202
Grapes, 263, 274

Vorticella, 4, 25, 28-29

W

Walking, 191, 202, 204-207, 209, 213, 222, 225,
   229-230, 239, 290
Wasps, 232
Water, 1, 4, 9-10, 12, 21, 24, 27-28, 37, 39-41, 47,
   50-51, 53, 56-58, 60-62, 64, 67-69,
   72-73, 76-77, 82, 91, 109, 113, 116, 124,
   126, 128-129, 132, 134-135, 137, 141,
   147-148, 150, 157-158, 160, 164-165,
   169, 171, 176, 180, 184-185, 187, 195,
   200, 214-215, 217-219, 222, 225,
   227-229, 239, 255, 257, 260, 263,
   267-271, 274-275, 277, 279-280, 284,
   289, 297-298, 304-305, 307-309, 312
   diffusion, 1
   forms of, 217, 284
   structure, 9, 27, 37, 40, 47, 61, 67-68, 73, 82,
      124, 126, 141, 147-148, 150, 160,
      165, 171, 184, 218-219, 222, 225,
      263, 275, 289, 298, 309
Wind, 61, 184, 212
Wings, 200, 231-232, 234, 236-237, 240-241, 299
   insect, 200, 231-232, 234, 237, 240-241
Wolves, 99
Wood, 10, 82, 132, 136, 200, 209, 241
Wood tick, 209
Work, 10, 81, 86, 157, 162, 164, 168, 185, 195,
   214, 247, 276, 282, 303
Worms, 81, 99, 101, 115, 154, 155-157, 159-162,
   164, 170, 175-180, 184, 187, 189,
   191-192, 251, 266, 297, 303
Wuchereria bancrofti, 176-177, 179

X

Xenopsylla cheopis, 199

Y

Yeast, 110, 260
Yellow fever, 199
Yolk, 86

Z

Zoonosis, 95, 175
zygospore, 8-9
Zygote, 9, 20-23, 56-57, 274
   protozoa, 57
Zygotes, 20-21